WHAT PEOPLE ARE SA

IDENTITY AND THE QUARTERED CIRCLE

From the basics of "Harm None" to the intricacies of working with spirits, elementals, divination, sacred geometry and so much more with a strong moral code of ethics, this is a "must have" book for the library of any witch! I wish I had this book 40 years ago!

Marie Snow Taber, aka the Ditch Witch

Herbalist, owner of Earthcraftyr Handcrafted Gifts From Nature's Bounty

Identity and The Quartered Circle is a watershed book for advanced students (and a challenging one for some new seekers). It leads us from the ordinary manner of being into a world of glorious possibilities using all our faculties, not just our spiritual aspects.

Elspeth Odbert, co-founder of The Haven Way in West Virginia, teacher and storyteller, author of *Gylantra's Journey, "The Challenge,"* and related audio CDs: *Out of the Forest and Gylantra's Legacy.*

To all seekers of their authentic Selves and lovers of Earth's magic and mystery, there is no better way-shower than Dorothy Abrams. In *Identity and the Quartered Circle* she has distilled years of metaphysical and spiritual teaching into a comprehensive and accessible guide to the deep re-membering of who we are. No matter if one is new or seasoned on this path, what awaits the reader is a treasure trove of information, engaging stories, compelling practices...

Carol Ohmart-Behan, is a writer and teacher of Earth-wisdom through Labyrinth and Sacred Pilgrimage with resonant connections to Glastonbury, UK...the ancient Isle of Avalon. Her website is http://goldenspiraljourney.com

Dorothy Abrams brings all the wisdom and insight of a shamanic practitioner and Wiccan priestess into the modern world with computers and

the internet. This form of paganism is all-inclusive, humanistic and traditional, as well as very modern; focused on spiritual evolution of the soul and enlightenment of the self. Is it honest, is it helpful, is it kind? Yes, *Identity and the Quartered Circle* is all that and so very much more!
Virginia R. Waldron, director and founder of the RoseHeart Center, Fayetteville NY, certified consulting hypnotist and accredited instructor in past life regression through IBRT. Virginia is also certified in Life Between Lives and Spiritual Regression, through The Michael Newton Institute. She teaches classes in Angelology, Reincarnation and Past Lives, Self-Hypnosis, Meditation, and Working with Your Spirit Guides and Angels.

In Identity and the Quartered Circle: Studies in Applied Wicca, Dorothy L. Abrams brings her extensive experience in teaching to the written page in a way that systematically introduces us to the world of Wicca. The book encourages us to go deeper into a relationship with ourselves, Gods and Goddesses, eventually completing the circle. Through multicultural examples, stories and ritual she walks us through the spiral of Wicca Life.
David Bennett, author of *Voyage of Purpose: Spiritual Wisdom from Near-Death back to Life*. www.DharmaTalks.com

Speaking to the reader in terms which explain, reassure and entice, Dorothy Abrams' plentiful academic and historical references illuminate the ground rules of this mysterious and complex subject.
Mano Mannaz, Avalon EarthKeeper in Glastonbury, visionary artist and author of *The Truth Sings in Circles*

Identity and the Quartered Circle

Studies in Applied Wicca

Identity and the Quartered Circle

Studies in Applied Wicca

Dorothy L. Abrams

MOON BOOKS

Winchester, UK
Washington, USA

First published by Moon Books, 2013
Moon Books is an imprint of John Hunt Publishing Ltd., Laurel House, Station Approach,
Alresford, Hants, SO24 9JH, UK
office1@jhpbooks.net
www.johnhuntpublishing.com
www.moon-books.net

For distributor details and how to order please visit the 'Ordering' section on our website.

ISBN: 978 1 78099 279 2

A CIP catalogue record for this book is available from the British Library.

Design: Stuart Davies

Printed and bound by CPI Group (UK) Ltd, Croydon, CR0 4YY

CONTENTS

Preface

Identity and the Quartered Circle is a book I wrote for people interested in deepening their self-knowledge within a spiritual context. Although I developed this path in a Wiccan neo-Pagan context, these ideas have a wider application. Anyone who examines their personal identity will find interesting questions here. *Who am I? Why am I here? Where did I come from? Where am I going?* I ask these questions over and over to help the reader come up with the answers. The answers rarely come easy.

To make the journey clearer, I incorporate the arts: journaling, sketching, collage, crafts, chanting, drumming, dance and storytelling. The arts bring us closer to ecstasy in a familiar and safe way. We do not have to excel in any artistic endeavor. Our work need not be published nor performed outside our homes. We only need to give the effort necessary to craft our truth so we can see or hear it. We can have fun with the projects. Or we can keep them simple and move on to the text.

Why include the arts? Most of the material in this book comes from nearly 20 years of teaching Pagan spirituality. Teaching adults requires creativity. No one wants to hear the 'sage on the stage' droning on and on as if the subject is more important than the students. It never is. People come to classes with years of experience in being human. They have even more experience being spirits, though they may not know it. The arts give us each a chance to express our truth, examine our assumptions and create different visions of who we are. The arts mirror us as creators.

Furthermore, good teachers come to class prepared to discuss ideas. They tell stories. They challenge students to explore new material with personal meditation and journaling and then find their own stories. All of us dream up songs, dances or rituals to celebrate our learning. We recreate myths and make magic in ritual. We paint, draw, sculpt, sew or whittle. We do what we can, and step out farther to try something new. The result may not be great art, but we remember what we learned when we work new ideas into our own creative projects.

Consequently, this book asks you to stop reading and do something with your ideas. Get out of your head. Use your body and heart to understand your soul. I ask you to play along with the artistic process even if you are certain you aren't creative. Enjoy it. Have fun. Try new things. Then go back and read some more. This is a book to chew on, not to race through. When you finish, you may well know more about yourself than you expected. You certainly will know more about the circle and its quarters in modern Paganism.

No one needs years of study to start reading this book. The first chapters introduce you to the most basic ideas as if you never heard of them. The rest builds on the beginning. You should be able to figure it out as you go along, even though I keep deepening the study and broadening the cultural connections about circles and quarters and identity.

On the other hand, people who have been practicing various Pagan faiths for years will find the book moves from familiar subjects into some deeply healing and esoteric studies. This book is a challenging course by the time you get half way through it. Yet the book is only the beginning. It is about you, the infinite circle and its divisions.

There is much more to the Pagan path, but *Identity and the Quartered Circle* limits itself to subjects related to moving energy in a circle or a spiral, understanding the divisions of the circle into halves and quarters, and then meeting the spirit beings associated with those notions, all in our search for identity. To begin with the simple ideas about circles and self, then to move all the way to the deep complexities of sacred circles and spiritual personifications is enough for one text.

This is a journey that I have taken myself. I still learn more about circles and quarters of circles every time I work on this book or teach a class. Sometimes I read a passage with a jolt of surprise. I forgot I knew that.

So perhaps I will write other books that embrace the Gods and Goddesses, investigate spell work and magic, or design rituals for the wheel of the year and phases of the moon. For now it is sufficient to see how the circle we cast on the earth echoes in the sky and resonates with the seasons. For now it is enough to feel the ebb and flow of these energies move through us and harmonize with our lives as we grow, mature and die along with the seasons and the moon. When we understand that is who we are and why we are here, then it is clear we arose from All Being and mean to go back there. Our return is possible once we understand we disappear with winter and the dark moon but return with spring and rise with the new moon. When we embrace that truth, then that will be the time to think about 'What's next?'

DLA October 2012

Acknowledgments

No book is written in a vacuum. No writer does this by herself. In my quest for identity, my education and support team comes mostly from the Web PATH Center, the spiritual community I founded in 1994 with my partner Merlin and some other brave souls who shared in the dream. Some people involved in the Web PATH Center have left, returned, joined in as newbies, started their own groups, and broken away to do other things. Each one of them has a piece of this book. We started this community as a teaching circle, and that is what it still is. A teaching circle in the Pagan world is a church in the Christian world. We come together to celebrate sacred events; we love and support each other; we teach our children and each other; we explore what it means to be human and spirit; and we embrace the Divine. None of us are finished learning yet. I am grateful for every single soul who came through the Web. Every one of you brought a blessing. Every one of you taught me something. There are hundreds of you. By these words I honor every single one.

I told Sapphire, our Web Council Chair, in 2012 that I did not dare mention any one by name in the acknowledgments because as soon as I did, others would be left out. Still, a few names need special mention because they have helped in the specific construction of this book.

Let me start with Sapphire, Diane VanNorman, who helps me keep hearth and home together so I can be free to write. There would be no book without her. She is also one of the individuals who stepped up to assume leadership duties in the Web PATH Center because it needed to be done. Amber and eh'Lorhylii are two other Council officers, but only two of many who have taken on the Webwork while I write.

Teachers for Web classes also played an important role in making this a book. Ditchy, Ravija, Pegqua, Satira, Elise, Leviathon, Shadow Dancer, Stonelight Weaver, Galadrial, SoftMoonRising, Silver

Lightning, and many more brought their own insights to classes taught in our sun room while I wrote this book in the office. Before that, Soft MoonRising, Avian, Snowfire, Equinox, Lilith, Akosua and others helped design parts of the original teaching modules. Some of your ideas are in this book. I appreciate that contribution and recognize this was a common dream.

I also thank Katrina Schell who read my manuscript and gave me praise and advice on how to improve it. I respect her academics and know it is a better book with far fewer capital letters because of her.

I want to recognize Lydia Rosell from Auburn NY. She was our first teacher when Merlin and I asked the first questions about Witches and celebrating the moon. She took Merlin and I into her sacred circle and encouraged us to trust our instincts. She pointed us to books and answered our questions. She modeled magical living. She taught us how to conduct a ritual. She lives openly as a Witch and never blinks. She is a friend, a mentor and a teacher. This book would not have been a glimmer in my imagination if it were not for Lydia.

That is also true of my partner Merlin aka Eric Anthony Reynolds. He has been my priest in ritual, my man-in-black, my co-teacher, a healer and ethicist from the beginning of our path. I thank and praise him for his wisdom in our work. He has supported me in the hard times, evaluated my writing, proof-read and given me feedback. He offers brutal honesty when a turn of phrase rings false or flowery. He puts big question marks in the margin if my writing is too obscure. He insists on shared power, polarity and the balance of male and female energy, and he fixes things. He fixes cars. He repairs plumbing. He maintains equipment, welds, woodworks, and makes the computer printer talk to the computer. He dreams big. He discusses ideas in the hot tub and pushes them farther when they need to grow. He slows my rushing thoughts down when I am ready to take off on a tangent. He asks questions and answers them. He trusts me and he loves me. I am a lucky Witch and I know it. Now you do too.

I also need to thank Moon Books for taking me on as a writer, Pagan Writers Community on Facebook for introducing me to Moon Books, and my friends at the Rochester Writers Association, particularly Sue Motes Fenn, who heard me out and insisted this was the time and place to get the book done. Writing a book is a solitary task but publishing one is a community effort. Thank you.

Chapter 1

In the Beginning

In any spiritual journey we begin with ourselves where we are, who we understand ourselves to be, and how we believe we connect to the beings around us. In truth, we cannot begin anywhere else. The journey studied in this book through Web Wiccan Consciousness is no different. To learn to relate to the Elementals, Gods, Goddesses and Powers we must know who we are. The journey I offer here is an examination of self through the lens of the arts, ritual, and magic. Art, ritual and magic are intimately connected to us. Their path takes us through the circle and its division into four equal parts. Those parts or quarters are identified with the four directions, the Elementals, and Guardians of the Watchtowers. At the end of the journey, we find ourselves changed. We have become more aware of who we are through the sigil of Web Consciousness.

What is Web Wiccan Consciousness?

It is the Pagan awareness which has grown out of our own spiritual quest over half a lifetime. Together with my partner and friends, I began studying Paganism in the 1980s. Around 1994 we established the Web PATH Center, a Pagan teaching and healing circle which offered a spiritual community to people in Central New York and others through the mail and later the internet. We offered classes, first in Wicca I: To Know the Magic, an introductory course that takes about 40 hours of class time to complete. This was followed by Wicca II: To Will the Magic, a class in ritual, healing, ESP and ethical magical interventions. Wicca II has grown to include 50-60 hours of instruction and class projects. Wicca III: To Dare the Magic came next. Wicca III is a daring venture in emotional healing, psychic skills and personal transformation through storytelling, performance and ritual. Class instruction and performances run between

80-100 hours. Finally Wicca IV: To Keep Silent was born. Having only had enough students to teach it twice, Wicca IV takes five or six onsite weekends over a year and a day with homework projects, independent study and online discussion. The focus is internal, meditative and contemplative.

Having finished teaching these cycles, I have taken a leave of absence from the classroom to write about these seminars. The workbook materials we used are all original works. I thought to distill them into a book so more people could experience their power. Instead I have expanded them, using a different approach than most other authors. This book, *Identity and the Quartered Circle* addresses the student's personal quest for identity, creation of sacred space and the exploration of the four directions: north, east, south and west. In this book, we begin from the introductory lessons of the apprentice and challenge ourselves all the way through to the advanced experiences of the adept. In essence, the reader sees the ordinary ritual of circle casting evolve into our use of circle casting as a door to transcendent mystic experience.

As I began to consider this project I remarked to the Ditch Witch, a highly trained adept herself, that Web Wicca had morphed to an eclectic spiritual tradition barely recognizable as Wicca if one were to evaluate it by the standards of Gardnerians, Alexandrians or the Faerie Craft. She laughed in full agreement. Perhaps it is misleading to insist I still practice Wicca and am a Witch, but that is part of my identity and I will not relinquish that. Nevertheless, within the Web PATH I call on shamanic practices, yoga, Buddhism, the human potential movement, light workers, channelers, Reiki, the Tao, the Orishas, and even Christianity to expand my awareness of who we are and where we are going. Web Wiccan Consciousness is wide indeed. I hope you will enjoy the journey as much as I have.

Three Axioms to Live By

Our first axiom in Web Wiccan Consciousness is: *All Being is interconnected.* All Being: those we think are good and those we think are evil; those we believe are animate and others imagine are inanimate; those who appear human and those in spirit; those that are divine and those that are animal; those who live now and those who lived at some other time—ancestors and descendants, historical greats and the common folk. I perceive the connections among all these beings as a Web, thus the name Web PATH Center. That Web is an important sigil or symbol in my thinking. We build on that structure as we explore the self and other.

For most people, the separation between and among self and other seems real in this dimension, so real that transcendence beyond the duality of 'them and us' boggles the mind. Such thoughts draw us into a dream world of science fiction, fantasy and theoretical physics. Great truth resides in those dreams. We are ourselves and each other. We are woven into the energy and power of All Being. We are encompassed in the circle of life, not outside of it. Nothing, not one thing, is excluded from All That Is. If we can catch hold of this truth, we will stop feeling isolated. We will be *us* not *me*. The connection with All Being is a great healing gift for the heart. Understanding this idea requires us to release our illusion of separateness. We live on the edge of both unity and separation. Embracing this truth is difficult for the ego, but healthy for the soul.

The second axiom connected to the first is: *All time is now; all space is here.* When we first hear that phrase, our rational minds recoil. We experience the chronology of time every day as the sun moves across the sky. We know we are older this year than we were last. We know life ends in death after time passes for us. We know we complete a school year and move to the next grade, that we celebrate the seasons one after another. We know history. We see the change from an agricultural society through the industrial age to the electronic revolution. How could all time be concurrent?

The past, present and future are artificial constructs we as a planet have embraced to make our three dimensional reality, known as the earth plane, work. These truisms of time are bendable. We can psychically travel across their boundaries. We can step outside them, and do so whenever we participate in ritual or magic. We come back to them because they define the earth plane. Time provides comfortable boundaries. The boundaries are not essential. They do not apply in other dimensions. At this point in our discussion, openness to the possibility that all time is now is all that is required. We do not have to understand it, and perhaps we cannot comprehend it. We do, however, experience the oneness of time when we become our Selves.

Our rational minds react to the suggestion that all space is here in an equally disbelieving way. We know we can only be in one place at a time. Geography is defined. Nations may redraw their boundaries after wars, treaties and cataclysms. Nevertheless we know the Alps are in Europe. The Mediterranean Sea sits north of Africa. The Atlantic Ocean divides the eastern and western hemispheres. How can all space be concurrent?

Our perception of geography is a convenience for the cognitive brain which works at a slower vibration than the sacred mind. In ordinary reality we live as if we cannot be in two or more places at once. Our brains would be very confused if we found ourselves in Paris and New York at the same time. As our spiritual awareness grows, we learn that the constraints of ordinary reality can be bent by moving between the worlds.

People do appear here and there at the same time by separating the physical and astral bodies. The possibilities of dream travel and journey work taken to their deepest levels offer us abilities which the uninitiated term paranormal. Many people do not explore these possibilities because they fear other realms and paranormal experiences. That is a choice. It is not the only choice. Again we do not have to understand how this works, nor choose to experience the dislocation of time or space. All that we need is a willingness to consider the possibility without concluding people involved in these practices are nuts. We are perfectly sane, seeing both sides of the mirror at the same time.

The third axiom is that *all work, magical and mundane, should be done after the soul is grounded.* Grounding is a meditation available to everyone of every spirituality and religion. It includes centering, focus and connection with the heavens and the earth. People ground when they practice yoga, Tai Chi, and meditation. Soloists and actors ground before they step on stage. Surgeons ground before they make the first cut. Yet we are infrequently taught how to ground or even told that we should. I recommend grounding before starting the car and turning onto the highway. As a student, I ground before taking a test; as a teacher, before entering the classroom. Certainly one needs to ground before ritual, before magic, and before writing poetry. There are many methods, but here is a beginning.

Grounding Meditation

Sit quietly and be still in your body. Straighten your spine as if a thread were attached to your crown which draws your head upward. Breathe deeply from the bottom of your belly through your chest and shoulders. Count the breath in for four beats and out for six. Empty your lungs of all that stale air stored in the bottom by pushing your belly in on the exhale.

After half a dozen of these deep and cleansing breaths, focus your breath into your center (heart or belly as you wish). Breathe the fresh air into your body and then breathe out as if the air was expelled by that center. Take half a dozen centering breaths, enough to feel as if all of you emanates from your center outward.

When you feel balanced and centered imagine that you are a tree. Your torso is the trunk. Your arms are the branches, your fingers and hair the twigs and leaves. Visualize this as clearly as you can. Then, with purpose, breathe down your spine as if it is a channel in your tree trunk. Send roots out of your tail bone into the earth. Your roots move easily through your chair, the house, the basement, and strike into the earth with no impediment. Imagine that.

As you continue breathing, the breath sends the roots deeper and deeper into the earth. Feel the roots pass through the soil, from loose top soil through the subsoil, around rocks, mole tunnels, through sand and gravel, aquifers all the way to the bed rock. Feel the bed rock. Acknowledge its density, temperature and strength. Then send out root hairs across the rock to attach the tree to the crevices and cracks that are there.

Breathe this connection down to the rock with appreciation and gratitude. Then with the inhaled breath, consciously draw the strength of the rock up through the roots as a tree would draw nutrients and water through its roots. With each inhale, the strength and stability rises higher until it reaches the spine. Pause and appreciate that connection.

Then systematically draw the strength of the earth from the bedrock into the body, sending it down the legs to the toes, up the torso to the heart. Let the heart pump the strength of the earth through the body with the blood. It infuses every limb, every organ, every cell all the way to the tips of your leaves. Oh, I mean your hair and fingers. When your tree is completely saturated with the earth energy, let its power spout out of your fingers and crown like a fountain.

The energy shoots up into the air and then falls back down around you like a gentle shower, re-entering the earth. This energy soaks down into the earth and rejoins the roots. It connects with the energy drawn up from the bedrock and re-enters your body at the spine. You become part of a cycle of energy coming up through your spine, through your body, out of your head, back to the roots and up through your body, again and again and again. You are filled with earth energy, stabilized, strong and well.

Now focus your attention on the crown of your head. Imagine this is the crown of the tree or the top of its canopy. Open your crown to the sunlight and energy of the sky. As a tree draws in sunlight for photosynthesis, so you draw in celestial energies to feed and nourish you. The celestial energy sinks down through your spine, is pumped about your body by your heart, and then enters the earth through your roots to feed and nourish the earth. This energy works with the earth energy. Together they awaken your wisdom, make your thoughts clearer and more creative. You see yourself as more than you did before.

Feel these two energies rising and falling through your body in two streams. You have always been connected to the earth, the sun, the moon and the stars. You have not always been aware of that connection. Remember this when you remember who you are.

Grounding with the earth and the celestials can remain within you all day. This centering and empowerment can travel with you, keeping you balanced and safe. Or, when the work is completed, a class ended or a test taken, you can release the grounding before going on about your business. In that case, consciously retain whatever earth and celestial energy you need to be energetic and release the rest back to its source. At any time when the energy within is too strong, too buzzy or disorienting, place your hands on the ground and send the excess out and back to the earth. You may send excess celestial energy out of your hands arcing across the sky to cleanse the air and return to its origins. Remembering to keep what you need is important. It maintains both health and security. It fosters wisdom and connection.

Your grounding release does not need to be as detailed as your connection to the earth, though you might reverse the process step by step if your energy is running very high. A simple release, however, is usually sufficient. Note I DO NOT call this ungrounding. At no time do I wish to encourage anyone to disconnect entirely from the earth powers. We are always connected, though sometimes we lose the sense of that. Instead, release the extra energy you called in from the earth and sky in order to accomplish your day's tasks. Keep your own energy always, and add to it as needed. Releasing the energy accumulated during the day—energy from the earth, the sky and other people—is an excellent way to fall into a restful sleep. That is of value to many powerfully psychic people who find a full night's rest hard to come by.

Grounding Release Meditation

Again be still in your body. Breathe deeply as before, first as a cleansing breath and then as a centering breath. Be aware of the celestial energies moving in from your crown, down your spine and out of your roots. Slow the speed of that energy and draw it up from your roots with your inhaled breath. Feel it rise within you, leaving what you need in your legs, torso and heart. When you reach your heart, exhale with a powerful breath and send the excess celestial energy coursing up through your head, arms and out of your crown and fingers. Breathe deeply and give it another push with your breath, sending with it your appreciation and gratitude to the source of these energies. A spirit of thankfulness is appreciated by everyone.

Sit quietly again and assess your physical being. See where the energy seems unbalanced. What is too still? What hurts? What is too lively? With the breath move the energy around your body until you feel the same, back to front, top to bottom, right to left. Then deliberately slow the fountain spouting out of your head. Let the energy fall back down inside your body, seeing its level fall through the head, shoulders and arms, chest, torso, all the way down to the base of the spine. Pull the excess energy up from your legs and feet to the base of the spine. Before releasing the energy down your roots to the earth, check your body and its balance one more time. What do you need? Move some energy from the pool at the base of the spine to the places in need. When you are convinced you are well-balanced, release the excess energy from the base of the spine down the roots. Feel it descend in the same track the roots took when you struck them down through the earth. It may filter out through lateral roots and root hairs. That is okay. At the bedrock, send the remaining excess energy into the bedrock with deep gratitude. You are nourishing the earth with love and magic. She can use this to heal herself and others in the same way you were energized and healed by this experience.

Then with great gentleness, detach your roots from the rock. Draw them upwards with the inhaled breath, through the layers of soil, gravel and water. Return them through the house, back to your body. Stop and consider the gift you have given yourself, the change you have created in your energy. Know you can do this whenever you need to because you are part of the earth, part of the celestials, a body a soul and a spirit. Blessed Be.

The Book of Shadows

In class, I ask students to keep a journal of their work, a private record for the individual. Gardnerian Witches in England in the 1950s and forward called that a Book of Shadows. Gerald Gardner is credited as being the father of modern Wicca because he published information in the United Kingdom about the religious practices of covens in England. Whether or not the neo-Pagan or neo-Wiccan paths stemmed from his instruction or had an older antecedent is a matter of debate among well-meaning people who think they know. For our purposes, we need only know there is credible information on both sides of the argument. I like the name Book of Shadows (BOS). Using those words reminds us our thoughts and practices are personal and private. They are not always clear and reside in the mists of consciousness. Shadows are friendly things, attached to us by the light. There is nothing sinister in them. Even when we delve into the shadows of Jungian psychology, our shadows become allies. They are us. If you prefer to call your Book of Shadows by the name diary, journal or grimoire, you would certainly be the judge of what is best. Whatever you call it, you need one. In fact you may need two. A Book of Shadows may record rituals, meditations, research and essays about your spiritual path. A journal may catch the overflow of sketches, poems and musings which are not quite ready to be entered in the official record.

A Book of Shadows can be a loose leaf notebook. Create a graphic cover design and dress it up, because this is indeed a special document. The advantage of a loose leaf binder is in the flexible nature of it. Pages, subject dividers, artwork, all manner of things can be added and subtracted as we move along the journey. To a biographer and historian, however, that is exactly the problem with it. What is the true chronology? How did a person discover a new insight, and when? In the four-dimensional world of time and space those things can matter.

A BOS can be a chronological journal in a bound blank book. Some find the handwritten nature of the account to have magical significance. Dedicated crafters make their own books, paper and ink. Natural inks can fade badly, so some thought to preservation is necessary. A handwritten book preserves the chronology of the journey, but finding an entry and organizing topics is more difficult. Placing the contents on a computer file at the same time leaves the 'search' command as a vital option. Of course some contemporary Witches create an e-BOS on their computers and leave it at that. To them I say BACK UP! Keep hard copies and flash drives up to date. I suppose one could retrieve lost e-data in a meditation back through time, but why do it the hard way?

The folklore of the BOS includes the claim that a coven or circle of Witches had one book among them. When a new coven was hived off to become independent, the priestess or priest copied the original book to take to the new group. Some also claim the account was written in mirror reverse letters, runes or code. I suppose some were. Nowadays everyone keeps their own BOS in most circles. It is in the writer's native language, often on the computer, and very personal. This is the 21st century. Life does not need to be that difficult, but if the mystery of secrecy appeals, 'an that ye harm none, do what ye will.'

In your BOS, you may include answers to questions posed here, diagrams of altars, accounts of how you found your magical tools, how you cleansed them and if you consecrated them to your hand alone. People include descriptions of their ritual dedications, initiations and vows taken or refused. They may write about their state of mind, their visions and meditations surrounding those mile markers. They may record Goddess and God stories they have heard, or write versions of their own for future telling. They record the details of spells, magic and healing work they do, preserving anonymity where it should be maintained. A BOS, like any diary, can be hacked or read by prying eyes. Writing about someone's illness requires sensitivity and a commitment to confidentiality.

I encourage people to include original artwork, collage, design, pressed flowers, herbs, songs and poetry—any and all things that give meaning to the student's quest for wisdom and self. Chance encounters with strangers, odd coincidences, card readings and divinations, books that seem significant, an annotated bibliography of magical writing, websites and films have a place in the BOS.

A Witch's BOS records rituals, psychic events, manifestations and ceremonies. Group rituals usually have a program or outline for the priest and priestess to use, if not for the entire gathering. Those belong in the Book of Shadows. Leading meditations and trances is an art. The induction for trance work and resulting visions are valuable additions to the BOS. Similarly, creating beautiful altars is another artistic endeavor. Pictures, sketches and descriptions help record the events. Ritualists build a file of ideas. They record meditations and invocations that were effective. These are valuable resources for future rituals. Even people practicing the craft in solitude benefit by keeping records of their work. We remember what worked, what is replicated and what is a one-time anomaly.

Do all Witches keep this kind of record? In all its completeness? No. I don't even have all that pulled together in one place. I wish I did. I wish I had started at the very beginning and made my BOS as a handwritten record in a bound book to preserve how my ideas developed. I wish I had a loose leaf notebook carefully divided into subjects. I wish I had my computer files organized in one place and backed up that way. I do not. All of it is there in one way or another, but it is messy, incomplete and sometimes illegible. Alas. There is still time to get organized!

Each person's BOS is individually kept and confidential. We share them only with a select few if at all. So buy a book, make a book, create a file on your computer, but begin with your first questions about identity and dedicate a BOS as a discovery journal which notes your progress from fledgling to soaring eagle spirit.

Identity

Being part of the universal web of consciousness gives us a doorway into the alternatives of time and space. To travel that web safely we begin with ourselves. In your Book of Shadows write down the answers to the questions below. Use your stream of consciousness, recording the first things which come to mind. Our answers to these questions change over time. The point is to begin.

Who am I?
Where did I come from?
Why am I here?
Where am I going?

When I taught high school English, I started the students out each year with those questions in the hope that at the end of the year after reading great literature, engaging in reports and deep discussions and writing about their thoughts and reading, the students would have an inkling of what the answers were for them. There are, of course, no right or wrong answers. These are deeply personal questions that reflect wisdom about our place within the Web of Life. That wisdom may change as we mature and evolve from year to year. Each place on the Web, however, is right and perfect for us right where we are. The challenge I ask the student to accept is that our wisdom will change and grow. How we describe ourselves today must not be the same as it was or will be. Else why bother with spiritual studies and Goddess-based ritual?

I often say at the close of ritual or ceremony *'Remember who you are.'* It is to these questions I refer (in part.) *Who am I? Where did I come from? Why am I here? Where am I going?* As a ritual facilitator (i.e. priestess) I want the celebrants to enter into a deeper relationship with themselves, the Gods and Goddesses, the other people in the circle and with the ancestors and spirits who also attended. Remembering who we are involves all those questions and creates a great variety of answers.

These answers reflect our experiences, studies, beliefs and values. We will look at that in later lessons, but for right now, understand as deeply as you can: *Who are you? Where did you come from? Why are you here? Where are you going?* Be sure to put the date on your listing. Be as complete as possible, thinking of every role you play, every duty you have, every aspiration you carry, every dream you conceive, every past inkling you have uncovered. We will use them in a yantra which appears at the end of this book as a sigil of Web Consciousness.

Identity and Naming

In the civil rights movements of the 20th century, a great deal of attention was paid to the right to name oneself. I remember sitting in a workshop at a national convention of the National Organization for Women (NOW) with a group of women who agonized and argued over the appropriate naming of women of color. The conference organizers and other white women unwisely referred to them as nonwhite, as if white were the standard. We were quickly made aware that white women are a minority of women in the world. The rest of the women did not wish to be named as 'other than white.' The consensus in the meeting and one which has won out over time was 'women of color.' Yes, arguments were made that white is a color too and that the phrase sounded too much like the unacceptable 'colored people,' but the important wisdom of the meeting was that the women named themselves. It was part of their standing in their power. For the same reason, adult women of all ethnicities were challenged not to call themselves girls because it gave away their power as adults. That wisdom has not found wide acceptance even yet, but the ideas are still relevant. A female over 18 is a woman; an adult legally responsible for herself.

What we were discovering in the 1970s and that others had discovered before us is that the right to name one's self is a deep and magical act. The names we accept or create are words of power. In the Genesis story of creation our archetypal mother and father, Eve and Adam, were told to name all the creatures of the earth and to have power and dominion over them. What and who we name becomes, in some esoteric fashion, ours.

So how do we name ourselves? Which of those names speaks to roles we fill and which speaks to who we really are? Which speaks to our core identity and which to the games we play? Those are important questions. Do not slough them off.

Here is an example. A woman named Sylvia who has three children names herself as a working mother, but then adds she is mother to Jason, Sam and Sally. Okay, that is more specific, but telling me that Jason is an 18-year-old football player headed to college on scholarship, that Sam is married and expecting his first child this winter and Sally is only four and will start preschool in January makes Sylvia's statement much clearer. Add that she and her husband of 25 years both work in their own business running a pharmacy and that both of them are licensed pharmacists further defines how she is a mother working outside of the home, a professional woman and parenting her children in a two-parent household. None of the roles work independently of the others.

Sylvia then explains she is named for her grandmother Sylvia, her mother's mother, and that the name means forest; she loves to wander the woods and identify medicinal plants in the woodlands. She makes potions and salves and provides these to her family to keep them well and in balance with the natural world though she does not attempt to sell them through her pharmacy.

Sylvia is much more than a working mother. She needs to find words that summarize what she does and who she is. The ones she chooses will be very informative for her and for the rest of us. Our identity is revealed in *how* we name ourselves as much as it is revealed by *what* we name ourselves.

Once you have written your answers to the questions: *Who am I? Where did I come from? Why am I here? Where am I going?*, review your descriptions and see what details are needed to make those descriptions uniquely yours. Include your given name, surname(s) and sacred names. Cite their meanings and how they came to be yours. Look at them carefully and note new insights into your identity that your names give you. Then sit with that insight, meditate on it and see where it leads. When you think you understand who you really are, open yourself to the next chapter.

Chapter 2

What the Experts Say

Think of the work completed in Chapter 1 as a pre-test in identity. This chapter examines what some scholars and psychologists have written in description of our identities and how they change as we grow. We do not often credit the differences in us, vainly trying to 'always be the same.' We are not. Certainly our personalities change and develop with brain and body maturation. Sometimes our character gets stuck in worries at a stage of development which we might otherwise have passed through had it not been for grief, violence or trauma. Taking a look at how various people have described human psychology can reveal some of the difficulties we can choose to address through therapy and spirituality. Nothing about us is set in stone. We can heal at all levels. Healing is one of the purposes of this life journey. In other words, healing my mind and emotions is one of the reasons I am here—both healing myself and learning how to heal others. Most of us find the same purposes in our quest to understand why we are here.

When we get through with the examination of expert opinion, we will again consider our big four questions. *Who am I? Why am I here? Where did I come from? Where am I going?* These are deeply spiritual questions. The answers to them are wild and magical. As they find their initial answers to those questions, many people seek a naming ceremony which declares their power to the community, family, clan or spirits because they have found new levels of self in this journey. The point in taking a magical name is personal. The name comes from the Goddess. Our search for it is a significant part of our awakening. In the Web tradition we are sent to seek it out ourselves. No other person names us.

Erik Erikson (1902-1994)

Erik Erikson is known for his work in identity formation and the eight stages of identity which we travel from birth through adulthood.[1] He was born in Germany. Ahead of World War II he immigrated first to Denmark and then the United States. Interestingly enough, he combined the work of his original teacher Sigmund Freud together with his studies in the U.S. where he observed and considered the ideas of the Oglala Lakota about human growth and development. His eight stages are: infancy (trust issues), toddler (autonomy), early childhood (initiative), middle childhood (achievement), adolescence (trying on roles), young adult (intimacy), middle adult (mentoring), older adult (synthesizing /evaluation).

Erikson provides a good jumping off point for discussion, though we need not accept his ideas or anyone else's as the final word in human development. Erikson described eight stages from the cradle to the grave. An individual might need healing in any of these stages even though their chronological age is that of an adult. Unresolved soul lessons might require therapy or spiritual intervention to repair lack of trust, self-image or confidence. This interpretation given below of Erikson's work reflects how I use the information.

Infancy: Trust: Does the home environment create security? Is the universe a safe place? An adult who feels at risk more often than not may benefit from discovering where that insecurity started. A parent may wish to focus on reassurance for their infants. All of us benefit by understanding our life cycles and place in the universe well enough to know that we are safe and secure. To the degree that sounds impossible, we find our need for a deeper spiritual grounding. The journey inward can open up our fears and place them in a healing context.

Toddlers: Independence: Did the child learn how to make decisions and how to conform? Finding a balance between what one wants and what society requires is important in soul growth. An adult who finds themselves at odds with authority all the time or is unable to cooperate under ordinary circumstances might wish to return to their terrible twos to find out why their soul still screams 'No!' even when the logical answer is 'Yes!' A spiritual practice that balances free will with convention can open up our oppositional behavior so we can see inside of it. Having both freedom to create one's path and training in how to play well with others balances the soul.

Early Childhood: Initiative: Could the child initiate play, make friends, follow personal preferences or were those connections made for her/him? An adult's self-esteem starts with early efforts to reach out toward others. Adults who suffer from shyness and a lack of confidence may benefit from a retrospective about their early childhood. Working with friends in a Wiccan spirituality that allows them to launch a ritual or class squarely on their own can help build both experience and confidence.

Elementary Grades: Achievement: Was the child encouraged for work well done? Was the child encouraged to progress in a nurturing and positive home and school? Adults who underestimate their talents may need to rethink their standards and self-assessment. Negative messages about their intelligence, creativity or accomplishments received in grade school stick with the soul. New messages can replace the old ones. Meditation and affirmations about our abilities begin the spiritual healing of old wounds.

Adolescence: Peer Groups and Mentors: Was the teen mentored to develop ethics, to make independent decisions and to form positive peer relationships? Adults who find it difficult to be different may still be peer driven. Adults who rebel against all conformity fight self-defeating battles at home and work. Adults who are willing to cross social norms into criminal mischief, lying cheating, and manipulation benefit from examining what the rules were when they were teens. We tend to copy what we learned then, but we do not have to repeat the mistakes of our peers and parents.

Young Adults: Intimacy: Does the 20-30-something adult know how to be nurturing, caring and loving with family, spouse and children? Can the individual be a reliable friend and coworker? Fear of commitment and neglectful parenting indicate weaknesses in forming intimate relationships. These soul lessons may connect with earlier ones in the area of independence, self-esteem and initiative. Parents who struggle with the difficulties of child rearing and adults who break commitments to friends and organizations may benefit from reviewing their history with promises—those kept and those broken. Are they repeating old patterns? Are they grieving earlier betrayals? Rebuilding personal boundaries may be both a psychological and spiritual journey.

Middle Age: Creativity: Does the 40-60-year-old know how to bring creative energies to the work place, to build positive traditions within family and community and to exert leadership? Adults who duck responsibility, who keep themselves too busy to build connections with people at work and lack friends have soul lessons in their 'pending' file about intimacy and the importance of peer groups. People who cultivate their identity as 'loners' and claim they are not in any way creative tend to feel dissatisfied with life. They may benefit from re-examining their adolescent peer groups and young adult relationships. If they felt disconnected from their peers then, the pattern may have followed them through middle age. Participation with friends and family in a spiritual community may open the heart to both love and creativity. Isolation is frequently a reflection of shyness and fear.

Older Adults: Assessment: Does the elder see value in the life well-lived? Does he or she have more hopes for the future? In the absence of a positive self-assessment, does the elder experience depression or despair? Older adults are among those often over-prescribed with antidepressants. Their bodies are more sensitive to medications and yet their age group is not well studied for drug side effects. Older adults may benefit by reframing their past to include accomplishments they discredit. Children who leave the nest and succeed even though they live far away are to be celebrated, not criticized. Financial need at the end of life may not be the result of poor planning. In this economic market, anticipating what might happen requires prophecy and clairvoyance. Self-forgiveness and forgiveness of others is a great leap in soul growth.

Journaling on Your Past

In your BOS or personal journal, tell your story of how you experienced one of Erikson's stages of development. Who were the important people in your life? Where were you? What stands out in your memory? What did you need? What did you learn? What do you wish had happened? What sense do you make of it now? Remember to date your entry. Your assessment may change over time.

People who disagreed with Erikson's theories from the perspective of women's studies, African American studies, Native American Studies, and Asian Studies set out to describe other specific educational analyses popular in the 1970s and 1980s. Those alternative educational paths grew out of people's efforts to understand their identity as a different culture within the culture Erikson described. So how does this work in Wiccan/Pagan Studies? Are we sufficiently communal to have meaningful differences with the mainstream which Erikson represents? I think not—not yet. But what do you think?

Discussion Questions

Is there sufficient difference in the neo-Pagan culture to set us apart from the mainstream values represented in our schools? How do you see those differences?

Is there a significant difference between our medical institutions and health care compared to our alternative therapies of herbals, Reiki and hands-on healing?

How can we combine them? Can we find medical doctors who respect them?

Do we participate in the economic institutions of our civilization including banking, investments and retirement systems? Why or why not, or in what ways?

You may want to gather friends or family members together to talk about some of these ideas. Perhaps you will help advance our Pagan culture in the 21st century as you consider the possibilities.

Carl Gustav Jung (1875-1961)

An Erikson contemporary, Carl Jung from Switzerland saw identity differently.[2] He proposed that each personality has four key archetypes as components: shadow, anima, animus and self. In Pagan thought, this description takes on added importance because of the writings of Starhawk and others who are themselves psychologists and counselors working within a Jungian framework. Simply stated, the shadow self is the unknown, repressed, or latent part of our consciousness which is not readily accepted or accessible. Much of our magical working and healing targets the shadow self as needing exploration or resolution. The anima and animus are our male and females selves, aka our soul and true nature. The self includes All Being or God and reunites the fragmentation which both the soul and its human host experience on the way to self-knowledge. Indeed Jung identified multitudes of other archetypes dealing with personality, but that is material for another day. We will explore the shadow in Chapter 12 and the anima-animus with meditation in Chapter 6. Meanwhile, here are two questions for your BOS.

Journaling on the Archetypes

Do you think recognition of Jung's four archetypes—the shadow self, the male/female dynamic in one's personality, and the Divine presence in the soul—similar to what Starhawk presents in *The Spiral Dance*—is helpful in neo-Pagan practice? Why or why not, or in what ways?

Which if any of those archetypes do you find in your own identity at this point?

Date your thoughts about you and archetypes. They may change as you learn more.

Jean Piaget (1896-1980)

Piaget, the Swiss scientist, described early human developmental stages in four parts which can give Pagan children difficulty in school and adults difficulty in therapy because of its placement of 'magical thinking' (the opposite of cause and effect) as a preschool characteristic. Educators and counselors can fail to make any distinction between a child's expectation of having their needs met automatically by loving parents or faery godmothers and a Pagan's belief in spirit beings and faeries or a Christian's belief in God and angels. Criticism of spirituality as a childish notion is a misreading of Piaget, but it dogs us nonetheless. My use of 'magical thinking' in what follows is descriptive and not critical of using magic or spell work to alter our lives.

Piaget's four stages are these:

(1) *Infancy Through Age 2:* Sensory-motor development in which the baby takes in information through the five senses. The baby is most concerned about physical skills and makes little difference between self and other.

(2) *Preschool Ages 2-7:* Pre-operational development in which the egocentric stage peaks and falls off (No! Mine!). The child reacts, engages in 'magical thinking' as opposed to logic or cause and effect.

(3) *Childhood Ages 7-11:* Concrete operational development in which motor skills continue to develop. Logical thinking emerges but requires good mentoring, thought remains literal and concrete.

(4) *Adolescence Ages 12 and Up:* Formal operational development in which abstract thinking, cause and effect, symbolism, and abstract logic make sense to the individual and become available for daily use.

Piaget indicated these stages represent platforms in the individual's education. The person may struggle with the transition to the next level before suddenly he or she 'gets it.' Once the mind grasps the new way of being it freely generalizes it to other areas of life. Thus, a person might spend the requisite years in a single stage of development practicing the skills which were learned rapidly when the mind was ready and prepared.

In other words, the child 'gets it' around age seven that the necessities of life are provided by Mom and Dad and the work they get paid for, but between ages seven to 11 they may not credit the need for one or both parents to leave and go to work and earn that money. They may need repeated mentoring until they understand 'money does not grow on trees.' In fact they may pressure one parent to be at home when doing so is difficult or impossible based on the responsibilities of their jobs. Parents wonder why the child tries emotional blackmail to keep them home, but the tactic makes sense from the child's point of view.

With their first paper route or babysitting jobs around age 12 and continuing after that, the demands for work and the connection to their paycheck becomes clearer. Then the child may understand the connection between work and money, but still thinks Mom and Dad will come through with the latest and greatest electronic gizmos despite the economic crisis created by a layoff or rise in fuel costs.

When the teen is confronted with the realities of insuring her/his first car and paying for the gas, the penny drops! Depending on the maturity level and amount of mentoring they have experienced, they may or may not generalize their own economic struggles to comprehend the fact money indeed does not grow on trees in their parents' world either. At each stage the youth practices skills to comprehend roles and expectations, but mentoring and consistency are key to understanding.

Think about your own history and Piaget's stages of growth and write about yourself in your BOS.

Journaling about Symbolic Thinking

Assess yourself according to Piaget's stages of development.

At what point did you develop the ability to think symbolically (abstractly)?

What is your first memory of that? How easy is it for you now? What do you think that means?

In your Pagan experience, is the ability to work symbolically or the ability to be specific and concrete more important to you?

Abraham Maslow (1907-1970)

Add to these ideas about personality development Abraham Maslow's hierarchy of needs[3] and we have a full tool box of terms and concepts to explore human identity. Maslow's theories can be understood, and most often are, as a broad-based pyramid in five sections:

The Needs of the Body. Our need for air, water, food, shelter, sleep, sex and excretion make the base of the pyramid.

Our Need For Safety: Our need for physical safety, personal protection and security for our property; adequate money and resources; predictable behavior from our comfort zone of friends, family, community; good health make up the second layer of the pyramid laying across the base.

Our Need for Nurture and Belonging: Our need for friendships, family, sexual intimacy, group connection or membership make up the middle layer of the pyramid sitting atop the bottom two.

Our Need for Esteem: Our need for self-esteem, confidence, achievement, and respect—both given and received—make up the fourth layer of the pyramid just below the apex.

Our Need for Self-Actualization: Our need for ethics, creativity, problem-solving, and freedom from prejudice, from bias, from manipulation, and the appreciation of facts/education /analysis sits on top of the pyramid.

As the soul grows, we achieve mastery over each area and provision for these needs becomes part of our lives. Maslow has us move from one stage as a priority to the next, realizing that although we never outgrow our need for the lower layers, they never take primacy over all else once we have transcended them. A health crisis, for example, may focus attention on the second layer even though the soul may be operating on the fourth or fifth layer, but a full regression to a need only for safety and nothing more does not occur, according to Maslow. I am not so certain of that, but he was.

For an adult to reach self-actualization (top of the pyramid) she or he must have resolved difficulties in acquiring physical safety, a sense of belonging, and esteem, according to Maslow. A person who is thirsty and hungry cannot provide for shelter needs ahead of food and water. A person who lacks adequate housing and security cannot seek depth in love relationships. A person who is unloved and an outsider cannot exude confidence and develop self-esteem. A person who has low self-esteem even though the other needs are met will not behave ethically or live free of external controls and will pass on a culture of fear and prejudice to the next generation.

This has interesting applications in understanding the Pagan community's difficulty in creating alliances, working cooperatively and promoting common interests in a collective manner. Witch wars make much more sense if we understand they express the unmet needs of the people engaged in them. In her book *Truth or Dare*[4]

Starhawk discusses the nature of group development and process. She makes the observation that it is a natural part of group process for groups to break up. Certainly anyone who has started a Pagan group to celebrate ritual and build a community experiences this growth and ultimate disintegration from at least some of their friends.

Group dynamics can be an experience in frustration and disappointment. If instead we can ground and center ourselves sufficiently to offer love with an open hand which allows people to come and go, even if they leave in a huff, then we may survive and be able to reform the group so continuity is not lost. Understanding that people come into a spiritual community with their baggage helps us not be offended or hurt by their departure, even if leave-taking is done in anger. Leaving is not betrayal. Leaving is not rejection. Leaving is growth. When an individual or a group within a community no longer feels at home, it is time to grow. Leaving home is one way to do that.

From the language of family and sisterhood used in many spiritual communities, I suspect that folks want to jump right up to the third level of Maslow's pyramid when they have not yet addressed their needs for physical provisions and safety. Frequently I am called 'sister' or 'mother' by people I barely know. Since I believe familial relationships need time to evolve along with trust and disclosure, the nicknames ring false to my ears. Trying to forge a family connection before its time can become detrimental if an adult is seeking rescue from past pain and loneliness instead of resolution. If we love each other and ourselves without expectations we can allow for variations within the community. If not, we fight.

A Pagan community can weather the departure of key leaders and teachers. Groups can successfully re-form themselves and continue on their mission. One of the values which assists in keeping continuity is that of encouraging people to develop self-esteem and confidence (Maslow's level 4) and challenging them to continue toward self-actualization within a strong ethical framework. A large portion of this book focuses on the tools and concepts for ethical growth.

Not everyone who seeks to join a circle or coven shares a commitment to the Wiccan Rede or the Rule of Three. Disunity comes from people having different ethical values or from the individual being challenged on issues of safety or belonging from Maslow's work. The combination of these differences vary with the individual. However, the spiritual teacher or ritual facilitator does well to remember someone busy in their life path in creating financial security or experiencing great financial distress may have difficulty seeing the larger picture of ethical spiritual growth. The emergence of identity from the morass of crises experienced in everyday life is a gradual process.

Journaling on Maslow's Pyramid

Draw a triangle divided in to five layers and in your own words place the stages of development according to Maslow in the appropriate layers. Annotate them to fit you. Give yourself credit for your growth from where you started to where you are now.

The pyramid of needs helps answer two of our four questions: *Where did I come from? Where am I going?*

How then do we understand our soul development? Where do we get stuck? As an exercise in application, list your summary of Maslow's layers in your journal and describe how you meet the needs represented in each layer. Be as detailed as possible so that you can ascertain your stage of development and challenge according to Maslow. Remember this is his theory. A theory, any theory, has its blind spots and flaws, as will our understanding of it. Use his ideas as a tool to further explore who you are. The layers beyond your current comfort zone give you clues about where you are going!

A second exercise in applying these ideas uses Erikson's chart. In your journal, list his six stages of development. Describe what you experienced in each stage of development that supports or challenges the generalizations in the chart. Work with a broad stroke here or you will be writing your autobiography, which is not my intent in the exercise. Instead create questions to help you apply the patterns to your experience. Leave the later stages of life blank if you have not reached your middle or later years yet.

For example, *what did you learn about trust and mistrust as a baby?* Talk to people who were there, if you can. Let them help you remember. Or use regression in a meditation to recall how it felt to be a babe in arms. Look at old pictures. *How have those lessons shaped your identity?* This gives you a clue to where you came from. Do the same with all the stages you have passed through.

Understanding Power

One of the constants we all share is our interaction with power. Many people who have experienced oppression in their family settings, in education or religious institutions, on the job or in society resist the call to stand in their power. They believe power is evil. We all were raised on the old saw, 'Power corrupts, absolute power corrupts absolutely.' Surely power is a bad thing and being powerful will turns us into monsters! Students resist self-actualization because it makes them powerful. (It also makes them responsible but that is another discussion.)

Starhawk offers insight into the issue of power in her book *The Spiral Dance.*[5] She cites three kinds of power: *Power over, power with and power within.* In the Pagan community at large, we are exploring these concepts of power in an effort to find another way to be. *Power over* is the model we see reflected in our institutions where authority is organized in a hierarchical manner. Everyone has a boss. The lines of power trickle down from the top. The people at the bottom have very little power. Because this is the dominant model of power, our places of employment, schools, families, nearly every group imaginable lines itself up after this model. It is orderly and familiar. *Roberts Rules of Order* depends on it. Conducting a class without a head teacher often results in chaos. Leading a committee meeting of the whole without a chair and agenda leaves us wandering around in the wilderness. Does it have to? No. But our concept of power, order and achievement leave us little vision for anything else. Still, *power over* can tend to encourage dominance by powerful individuals. The minority voice can be lost and with it their wisdom.

Power with is seen when people work in consensus. If we are all paddling along in a canoe, the people fore and aft steer and power the journey, but each paddler contributes to the common goal. If one of them starts to work against the synchronized effort, everyone soon sees a loss of momentum. Yet any one of the paddlers might choose to slow the process. The same thing happens when a committee works by consensus. Everyone needs to participate and chip in their energy or the goals are not reached. A consensus may not be reached readily, but if the commitment to working with everyone's *power with* is genuine, the process is more important than the goal.

That is a soul lesson of its own. For example, if we cannot agree to hold a SummerFest or set up a concert series, then in consensus workings the issue must be tabled until we can agree on a course of action. Sharing power in that way does not integrate with our society. The demands of our political and financial institutions work on an up or down vote. Majority rules. Because that is the default mode for groups, any organization founded on consensus models must constantly make adjustments. What do we agree on? How can we build the required fiscal reports and planning from that? How can we fulfill the need for fundraising in ways we all accept? If someone agrees to the concept but not to the work and responsibility, where does that leave us? How long can we table this until everyone agrees? Is someone abusing the group process by stonewalling to get their own way?

The Web PATH Center attempts to work by consensus, but that has meant that the committee structure lacks efficiency and participation. There is in the rank and file a ready willingness to 'let George do it.' There are lots of good reasons for reasonable people to do that. They are, after all, busy providing security and nurture for their families at home. Many have not stepped into the challenge of self-esteem and confidence. Still, the value at hand is that we share power.

My partner Merlin worked for the New York State Department of Health in a program (WIC) devoted to the nutritional needs of women. Management attempted to be inclusive and gave lip service to the concept of working by consensus but, as they all discovered, if one person truly was not in agreement, efforts to browbeat the black sheep into agreement quickly disintegrated the consensus model, which had no deep roots and was under pressure to perform by state standards. Pretense prevailed when management claimed that consensus was reached with one in dissent. Well, that is not consensus is it? Consensus truly forces us to give up goals and agree that the people are more important than the program and the process is more important than the outcome. That is a struggle for people committed to sharing power.

I hasten to add we can share power with each other without being committed to consensus-based decision making. We can work hard to be sure that even the softest voice is heard and considered before a democratic decision is made. The U.S. Supreme Court models a piece of that value when they issue minority opinions. The Justices who agree and are in the majority sign on to the majority opinion. Individually they can add their own majority opinions to clarify their personal views. The Justices who disagree can write individual minority opinions or sign on to a collective dissenting view. I am sure feelings run high in these heady waters, but the voices are heard and on record for the future. Power is shared among the Justices even though there is a chief. Power is defended, argued, championed, wielded, and brought to bear on each other. But it is also a collective or community of equals. Shared power requires intelligence, strength and some political savvy. It is not necessarily all sweetness and light. The individual is asked to stand in her or his own power. If we are sincere in that, then the views of the dissenter are valued and publicized so they are not lost.

The third type of power Starhawk identifies is *power within, or empowerment*. The Web classes, shamanic journey circles and rituals all focus on empowering the individuals in this community to stand in their own power.

Think of the Magician card of the Tarot. If we look closely at the card we see the Magician has all the tools of the Witch at hand: the wand pointing to the heavens, the athame, chalice and pentacle on the table with a staff (large sized wand) on the table. He draws down power from above with his right hand and directs it to earth with his left. The power passes through him and empowers him as it creates transformation (magic) in the natural realm.

The truth of grounding, standing in our power, spell casting, the cone of power, psychic and shamanic workings, channeling, and automatic writing is found in empowerment by the crystal grids, ley lines and/or spirits. This is the stuff Pagan spirituality is created from. If we remain caught up in power struggles or in care-taking (the first two levels of power) we will never reach the transformative levels of empowerment. Reaching those levels is crucial to our soul development and the re-creation of the earth.

There are two understandings I hold as most important in all this psychological and educational theory. *The first is that identity is multi-layered*. Understanding this complex layering will become more pertinent and more challenging as we proceed through the chapters in this book. The reminder to look beyond the surface is important at every level of Wiccan study.

The second understanding is that identity is mutable. A great deal of psychological work insists that personality does not change, that it is genetically linked to our DNA. This view supports the triumph of Nature over Nurture. I disagree. Fortunately for the scientific Pagan, so do some current researchers. Sharon Begley wrote in the On Science column of *Newsweek* that DNA is not destiny.[6] She cited two current researchers: Carol Dweck of Stanford University and David Clayton of the University of Illinois. Dweck bases her conclusion that personality is mutable and shaped by life experiences on observations and measurements of students. Those who have relevant course work and mentoring grew in their capacity to reach outside themselves, be self-reliant and cope constructively with challenges as opposed to students who did not take the courses or have the mentors. In other words, classes like those given at the Web in Wicca and Shamanism really do make a difference in people's maturity and development.

Similarly, David Clayton studied zebra finches and found that unfamiliar birdsong stimulated brain responses resulting in new behavior. In rats, loving tactile mothers who groomed their babies had offspring whose brains showed inactive DNA related to fear and neuroticism. What we as humans experience as love and nurturing, hugs and genuine interest in each other decreases our mental reactions of defense, flight or fight. Can we then extrapolate that we in the Web PATH Center may free ourselves to create new ways of being by building community and repairing self-esteem and abusive personal histories? Is that not the essence of magic?

David Keirsey (1921-)

We have one last reference to consider before we reassess our journaling on identity. David Keirsey wrote two books with the titles *Please Understand Me* and *Please Understand Me II.*[7] His work in the area of personality or temperament profiling provides a questionnaire to assist the reader in ascertaining their key tendencies. There is a 16-question test and a 70-question test. Keirsey was a faculty member at the University of California Fullerton and worked 20 years in public schools with troubled students. He trained other teachers to do the same. His organization extends this training to faith-based communities, corporations and others interested in better comprehending human behavior. He builds on many of the educational theorists including Carl Jung and the Myers-Briggs Type Indicator. Keirsey identifies four general types: Artisan, Idealist, Guardian and Rational with 16 combination roles from those.

Reading his work was helpful to me. I fit in as an intuitive thinker and rationalist with a strong emphasis on leadership, planning and development. When I first did those assessments, they resulted in a spontaneous soul retrieval of my Amazon Warrior Woman of the radical 1960s and 70s who had fragmented off under pressure from political struggles lost in the 80s. Her return was a deep healing. We will discuss soul fragmentation in greater depth later, but in making our initial personal claims of identity, it does us good service to remember we may be missing important components of our souls because of the traumas and challenges of everyday life. Those fragments change who we see in the mirror of our meditative reflections because of their loss and in their return. Soul retrievals can be assisted by a trained shamanic worker as a healing practice.

Journaling: A Reassessment of You

Now who are you? Give yourself a day or two to chew on these concepts. Talk about them with your friends or family. Then go back to the original questions and ask yourself again:

Who am I?
Why am I here?
Where did I come from?
Where am I going?

Add these insights to your journal.

Chapter 3

The Circle and the Snake

Everything tries to be round. So said Black Elk, the Lakota shaman.[8] The sacred is expressed in the infinite pattern of a circle that continues around the path without end. The image of the snake holding its own tail—Ouroboros—has expressed the concept of infinity for people in cultures around the world. The word itself comes from the Greek. Plato used Ouroboros to describe the initial animal being that existed before creation as one without appendages or senses, swallowing its own tail. This divine animal was complete unto itself, providing its own nourishment, needing nothing. The origin of Ouroboros finds roots in Asia and in Egypt before the Greeks. The coiled serpent and dragon motifs are found in the oldest art.

Reclaiming Snake Images

What is this about? In part it is about veneration of the serpent for healing, merger with the Divine, and personal transformation. People in the Euro-American cultural traditions may struggle with serpent imagery. They find a reflexive shudder against snakes rather than enlightenment or healing. The positive aspects of the snake's symbolism is important in Pagan traditions, enough so that we will spend time seeing how the wisdom circles around and spirals in on itself like Ouroboros. We begin that wisdom with familiar images of the snake in the electronic age and their origins which may not be so familiar.

In medicine we find the caduceus, a healing staff entwined with snakes. The model adopted by the U.S. Army prior to World War I included both snakes. Later the imagery was changed to a single snake. The caduceus staves were symbols connected to Roman Gods Mercury and Asclepius. Their story also reveals ascension to divinity and the power of transformation. A short history/mythology lesson might make that clearer.

Mercury is the messenger of the Roman Gods depicted with wings on his feet because of his swiftness. FTD florists have an image of him in their advertising. Rather than a bouquet of flowers, he carried the caduceus with two snakes in his messenger service for the Gods. In Greece Mercury is equated with Hermes who transported souls to the underworld at death and who served as trickster. In Egypt he was similar to Thoth. Their chthonic (underworld) qualities can also be connected to the energy of the snake which tunnels into rocks, caves and interior places. As trickster, the serpent appears in the Garden of Eden to con Eve into disobedience or enlightenment depending on your interpretation of the creation story. This aspect of Mercury as Sacred Clown who fools people into seeing the truth is as important as his work as healer and messenger. One trickster is not all tricksters. One healer is not all healers. There are links between these deities, but they retain their cultural identities. Nevertheless, the snake winds through all their stories.

Other Gods share this snaky theme. Asclepius is a demigod, the half human son of Apollo. Apollo is identified with the Oracle of Delphi, Pythios the Snake, whose wisdom is passed to the son Asclepius. Apollo is also the God of Health. Asclepius is born as a human infant on his mother's funeral pyre, delivered by the God Hermes. Following the example of his divine father Apollo and of Hermes, Asclepius becomes such a great healer he revives the dead. Eventually, because his work withholds the dead from Hades, God of the Underworld, Hades has him killed. He was bad for business. However, Asclepius' father Apollo, his divine champion Hermes and his revered teacher Chiron appealed to Zeus to elevate him to Godhood as the God of Medicine with his own cult and temples. He is given the symbol of the caduceus to hold in the heavenly constellations. Surviving statues of Asclepius in museums show him standing with a sturdy staff entwined with a snake. Later Ascelpius' daughter Hygeia becomes the Goddess of Health. Like her father she appears accompanied by a snake.

In addition to physical healing, the snakes on the caduceus are the marks of sexual healing (rise of the kundalini) implied in the merger with the Gods which Asclepius experienced in his ascension. More about that later, but remember the connection between the history of the snake and healing. Hippocrates, the man most often cited as the source of western medicine, belonged to the cult of Asclepius. As an influence in western civilization, this story has wide application, including a place in the magical healing arts.

Where else does the snake appear in our cultural references? In the Old Testament, Moses led the Israelites through the desert only to be assailed by their complaints about the food and camping conditions. Jehovah listened to their complaints and apparently thought if they didn't like the manna sent from Heaven then they surely wouldn't like what he did next. He 'sent fiery serpents among the people, and they bit the people' (Numbers 21:6). Fatally so, it says. We don't know what the fiery serpents were, but there is a poisonous red snake indigenous to the region. At any rate, once the people repented of their crankiness, Jehovah told Moses to make a brass serpent replica on a tall pole, raise it up and if the people would look up to the serpent they would be cured of snake bite.

That is indeed reverence for the serpent. The Israelites were all supposed to understand that Jehovah was the healing force. However Jehovah, as any competent God of Light and Dark, brought the snakes and the snakebite serum. I used to be bothered by the symbolism. Was it not inconsistent that in Genesis the old serpent is the villain who seduces Eve away from obedience to God but four books later, the serpent is sent to afflict the people of God until they repent, and then its form is the vehicle of healing? If we consider the circle as Ouroboros then the snake or serpent is the beginning and end of affliction and healing, of crankiness and gratitude, of the Mother Goddess and the Patriarch. Within the context of the circle, the contradictions make sense. '*One thing becomes and another, in the Mother, in the Mother*' is a familiar chant loosely based on a song by

Starhawk. The phrase helps us embrace opposites into the one.

In the Americas, the feathered serpent is intrinsically depicted in the design of the Feathered Serpent Pyramid in Teotihuacan, Mexico. Magnificent sculpted heads adorn the sides of the pyramid in bas relief. This pyramid honors one of the wisest of Gods, Quetzalcoatl. God of the Morning Star, Quetzalcoatl brought maize, calendars and books to the Toltec. He is one of the Shining Ones revered in many cultures. As the creator of humankind, he is also honored as the God of Death and Resurrection. His myths describe his self-sacrifice in the flames chosen in remorse for having seduced a celibate priestess. He carried the expectation of his return from the land of the dead. Again the serpent holds both ends of the circle, the beginning and the end.

The Cosmic Serpent: DNA and the Origins of Knowledge by Jeremy Narby connects the science of healing with its shamanic nature. Narby traveled the jungles of South America with shamans from the indigenous people. He observed their healing trances, art created from those trances and the related healings for their people. In the artwork were rather clear depictions of DNA double helix spirals. The people producing the art had no obvious means of knowing what our electron microscopes had revealed about human DNA. In fact many of the drawings pre-dated the electron microscope. Narby draws the interesting conclusion that the shamanic journeys taken by these healers took them to the essence of life hidden in our bodies. He also suggests this cosmic serpent we call DNA reveals the source of life outside this planet, be that divine or alien.[9] In either case the essence is serpent shaped. As the web of connections reveals itself, the serpent form becomes intrinsic to us as human beings. To reject the snake is to reject the self.

In the writings of Andrew Collins,[10] the Watchers are presented as feather-cloaked beings with elongated serpentine heads. Ken Carey calls them the Bird Tribes.[11] The Book of Enoch referred to them as angels. In fact anthropologically speaking, birds and serpents are closely related. All of these symbols were Pagan venerations of the serpent form which is all but lost on our western culture. Because the circle of the snake symbol is the beginning and the end, there are stories that the Bird Tribes will return. I find that entirely possible. In searching out our identity as humans through Wiccan practice, we may discover history moves in the circle of Ouroboros.

In Paganism many Goddesses carry the snake as a symbol or familiar. We frequently see reproductions of the Minoan Snake Goddess, arms outstretched with a serpent in each hand, on altars. Her less well known companion Goddess housed in the Herakleion Archeological Museum in Crete has her arms stretched forward with serpents twining up her arms to her headdress. Judy Chicago, an American artist, included the Snake Goddess in one of *The Dinner Party* settings (1974-1979)[12] now housed at the Brooklyn Museum, New York. The table scarf stitched in cream, gold and earth tones complements the ivory plate with a brown, black, yellow and tan snakeskin colored vulva image which continues the sensual woman-centered theme of all the plates. The correlation between the Goddess snake imagery and sacred sexuality is key to understanding why the church and state of later western culture attempted to excise the serpent image or denigrate it with associations of sin and evil. The Cretan Goddesses hold the power of the snake in their arms and rejoice in it.

Similar snake imagery appears with the Maenads, members of an ecstatic women's cult and devotees of Dionysus in Greece and Bacchus in Rome. Dionysus and Bacchus were Gods of Wine who celebrated intoxication, feasting, passion and orgies conducted as an adoration of the Gods. The Maenads wore wreaths of ivy or snakes on their heads in their celebrations. They carried a phallic wand topped with a pine cone and wound about with vines or snakes. Fear of women's power has cast the Maenads into the role of murderous women who tore living creatures apart with their bare hands. They became a symbol of evil for the same reasons snakes have been denigrated. In fact the Maenads and snakes are symbols of dynamic female power. This power is the essence of magic denied to all of us by the institutions of our culture. It is the power of ecstasy. Magic and power are still available to both men and women, if we overcome our fear of the misrepresentations fostered by history. We must dare the transformation into beings of power, unbound by convention and excited by love.[13]

In Libya, Lamia is a Snake Goddess having the head and breasts of a woman and the body of a snake. She represents the grief and horror of the mother guilty of killing her children. Her transformation into a monster is attributed to the vengeance of Hera for Lamia's seduction of Zeus and for bearing his children. Lamia receives the gift of prophecy bestowed as a boon to assuage her sorrow. Later she is returned to a human form which she uses as a succubus to seduce innocent men, sapping their strength and sucking their blood.

The Libyan Goddess Medusa of the writhing snaky hair represents women's power, knowledge and wisdom. She is cursed by Athena for desecrating her temple, though it was Poseidon who raped Medusa there. Medusa is beheaded by the hero Perseus who takes her head as a weapon which he eventually returns to Athena.

The stories of these beautiful but tragically wronged Goddesses have been turned into dire folk tales useful for threatening naughty children. I include them here because their fate mirrors the fate of women and Witches in history. Lamia's name was used as a synonym for Witch in medieval times. Medusa was one of the Gorgons who turned men to stone if they looked on her face. Although both Goddesses were betrayed or attacked by certain male Gods, neither of the Gods were held accountable for their actions and neither defended Lamia and Medusa. The cultural bias seems obvious to me, as is often the case in the myths told about our ancient deities. I encourage students to meet any of the Gods and Goddess in meditation to re-tell their stories in contemporary terms, terms which uncover their origins and transform the bloody slanders tossed about by Greek heroes and Old Testament patriarchs to besmirch the reputations of the Old Ones. Lamia and Medusa are two who merit our creative attention.

I began a conversation with Lamia when I saw the Pre-Raphaelite paintings of her by John William Waterhouse.[14] That led me to Waterhouse's source material, John Keats' poem *Lamia* (1819). Interestingly through the course of the poem Keats dropped the snake imagery entirely, not wishing the connection of his beautiful Lamia to the evil of the snake. Both men perceived Lamia as an English rose. She has a peaches and cream complexion, luxurious red hair and white skin. What a Celt! My first insight is based on the obvious. Lamia is a Libyan Goddess with Egyptian origins. Although the Celts spread around Europe, the Middle East and North Africa, she likely had dark brown or black skin, black hair and brown eyes in keeping with her people. She is beautiful, sensual and desirable. She is intelligent. That shows in her features and her measuring gaze when she regards us as hers. She has a surprising gentleness, given the pejorative nature of her stories carried to us through the Greeks. I have learned her touch and spoken with her in dreams since I began this working. She became the Patron of *Identity and the Quartered Circle* from that point. Telling her story from her point of view is then important as we begin our healing and transformation.

Lamia, Her Story

Lamia was the daughter of Belus, King of Egypt and Sidon and ruler of the Mediterranean before the great human civilizations that rose up afterward: the Egyptian pharaohs, the Phoenicians, the Libyans, the Greeks, Romans and Moors. After being trained in the Temples of Egypt and Babylon where Lamia learned transformative magic and grew into her power, she inherited the land of Libya and ruled as Divine Queen. The magical training included that of shapeshifting, also called therianthropy, wherein a God assumes animal shapes either at will or by the magic of another. One of her forms was a snake. Birds and large cats were others. Although her training included the ecstasy of the kundalini she had no children, and was still considered a virgin queen.

As a Goddess Lamia was a maiden of the new moon. The crescent was then her symbol which hung on a silver chain about her neck, glowing on the dark skin of her breasts which were softly rounded, firm, and uncovered. Her bodice held them fashionably high. Her diaphanous skirts of red and gold flowed out from beneath the bodice to her feet, falling in gentle folds around her legs whose shadows teased the eye as she walked. Her midnight hair was thick and reflective of the flickering tapers in her hall. She wore her hair in thick braids, 13 of them caught together at her nape by a jeweled clasp. Her braids lay against her back, reaching near her waist. Beads and gemstones had been woven in them to catch the light and sparkle. Her arms were long and graceful, adorned with silver bracelets and gold charms. A single gold circlet inlaid with green malachite clasped her upper arm on the left. A similar one beset with lapis was on the right. Small stones of the same gems were suspended on fine gold chains from her ear lobes. The lowest lapis brushed her bare shoulders when she turned her head.

Such beauty and power was not to be ignored. Zeus, who ruled the Gods on the north side of the Mediterranean, came to visit unannounced. Lamia kept him waiting in the Great Hall while she perfumed her body and dusted it with powder flecked with gold. She knew little of him, save that he was commanding and handsome with broad shoulders, narrow waist and powerful thighs. He paced impatiently, which Lamia watched in secret. Imperiously, he beckoned servants to bring in the gifts he had carried from the north: olives, wine, bear skins, ermine furs, ice, song birds in gilded cages, banded boxes made of oak. She appraised these treasures from her hiding place and thought him wise. He brought her beauty. She had enough of wealth without his gifts, but beauty—there is never enough of that.

Lamia entered her hall unexpectedly, from a door set cleverly within an arch so it appeared no door at all. Suddenly she stood there in the shadows and sang out his name. 'Lord Zeus!'

Her voice sent shivers down his spine as he whirled around to greet her. All who remember that first meeting recall the air snapped and crackled like lightning as the two held each other's gaze. There was no question of where this would end. He wooed her with all the intensity of an experienced lover. She drew him in with all the seduction of an experienced priestess who had had many lovers worship at her gates in Babylon. Neither mentioned his wife Hera, not at any time. Lamia opened herself to him and fell deeply in love. Not quite meaning to, but seduced by her arts of ardor, so did Zeus. Where he had intended passion he found enchantment. Where he had intended a conquest he found devotion.

Still, there was never anything monogamous about Zeus. He stayed months at a time in the glorious villa of Lamia, situated by the sea. They talked and sang, appreciated the beauty laid before them and made love. Together their children included daughters Scylla and Herophile and a son Akheilos. Zeus was an indifferent father though the children amused him playing at his feet. Lamia doted on them, loving every curve and curl that reminded her of him. When he was gone, called off by duties on Olympus, Lamia taught her children magic and schooled them in the ways of power they should know. Surely they would have their own lands, granted by their father when they came of age.

But Hera grew tired of her husband's dishonesty with his mistress. Living sometimes with Hera and sometimes with Lamia, he pretended neither knew the other. Hera understood her husband much too well, had no illusions about who he was nor what one might expect from him. One day in dark winter, though winter on the north of Africa is never harsh nor very dark, Hera arrived unannounced at Lamia's villa. Escorted by four armed men, she demanded an audience with this upstart Goddess of the Libyans. She paced around the room looking down her aristocratic nose at this much smaller dark-skinned Goddess and stretched her own much lighter arms before her, as if reminding Lamia of her place. Lamia was insulted, and clapped her hands for her own guards to remove the intruders from her home. The doors slammed shut and would not open. Lamia faced Hera with just one female servant at her side.

Then in front of the maid and military men, Hera cruelly informed Lamia, who was now a mature Full Moon Mother, that she had been duped by her lover. Zeus was not only married, he had no intention of leaving Hera if for no other reason than she would never allow it. Hera described her husband's philandering ways in detail, naming names, each one driven like a stake through Lamia's heart. First Hera recalled Leto who hid on the island of Delos to avoid the scorn of the Gods when Zeus left her pregnant so he could marry Hera. Leto bore the twins Apollo and Artemis soon after Zeus's marriage to Hera, but Zeus had little to do with them. Hera didn't like them.

Then there was Europa the Phoenician Princess whom Zeus ravished as a bull. She was kidnapped, taken to Crete and left there as Queen when Zeus was finished with her. Zeus tried to deed her the lands of Europe, named for her, but Hera sniffed in distain. They were all her lands of Asia and could not be divided. Europe belonged to Hera.

Then Hera named Io whom Zeus transformed into a white heifer to hide her from Hera and then left her that way. Io wandered much of the known world once she escaped the confinement Hera had arranged, but Io found nothing but trouble since that meddling Hermes rescued her. As far as Hera knew Io was still a cow. Hera's sneer was palpable.

Lamia distrusted Hera, but there was the sound of truth in her words. Shock wound around her belly and sickened her. This husband Hera described was nothing like Lamia's lover. Zeus could not be so cruel! Hera laughed, pressing on with her tale of Zeus's unfaithfulness. She told of Semele from Thebes, mother of

Dionysius. She died in childbirth for which Hera was wrongly blamed. Callisto was the lover Zeus turned into a bear to hide her from Hera, thereby sealing her fate when she was later killed by her friend Artemis the Hunter. At least that silly child Artemis had an aim with bow and arrow worth something, Hera laughed. Zeus placed Callisto in the Heavens as the constellation Ursa Major, but that seemed small comfort. Finally Hera told Lamia about Ganymede who had been a prince of Troy before being made cupbearer to Zeus, hoping that would shock Lamia into ending the affair before Hera had to take further steps herself.

It worked. Lamia was devastated. This list of Zeus's conquests did not sit with anything Lamia thought she knew about him. She had believed him honorable. He was deceitful, arbitrary, thinking only of his own difficulties in keeping Hera happy. He had no thought for these lovers seduced, beguiled or raped by his lust. Lamia had no desire to roam the world lost in some animal form, cast out of her own lands at the whim of the other Gods. She bowed in tears before the Great Mother Hera promising to deal with Zeus as he deserved. With a secret smile of her own, Hera left Lamia to the task, content she had made ruin of their affair.

Weeks later Lamia stood with Zeus on her palace terrace over the Mediterranean, pointing across the sea toward Greece. Her back straight and stiff, her beauty turned cold, she was unforgiving. Her eyes judged him, sentenced him to banishment from her lands. She was daughter to the Gods of Egypt, Queen of Libya, a Goddess of great powers and magic. Her word would stand against the great Zeus. He tried trickery. He tried threats. He tried tears of regret. He made rash promises he could never keep. She did not yield.

Enraged, he tried to change her into a songbird he might cage and own. Failing that he turned himself into raging bull. Lamia was not afraid. His curses did not work. His magic was not as strong as Lamia's, not when she was angry. His powers met hers and were bent back on him with strength equal to Hera's. How could that happen? When he felt her hot rage beat against his shields he knew she was lost to him. He yielded to her rage and left, turned and sailed back across the sea, humiliated. How dare Lamia send him off? He fumed at his impotence. Returning home he would need to seek forgiveness yet again from his lovely Hera. He was angry at the fairer sex, but not remorseful. Lamia had been a lovely interlude. Hera was an interfering wife.

Lamia watched Zeus go, waiting to see if he would look back, if he would give one sign of his professed love for her or one bit of thought about their children. He did not. He shouted orders to his sailors and then turned his back. Her heart was broken, cold as a stone inside her chest. Her shoulders slumped, unable to hold her head up. Fighting his will, standing against his power had taken all her resolve, all her anger and all her hatred. If she had any left, she would ball it up and throw it at him, sink the damned ship and fling him to Poseidon's mercies. She watched long after the ship sailed out of sight, all day and half the night, wondering if he would turn around. How could love end in anger? How could a God have no care for his children? If he came back what would she do? Embrace him for the children's sake? Believe him if he could explain? Was Hera right, he could not leave Greece? Was her own intuition true; he loved the Mother Hera most? Before the dawn, Lamia went inside and called for wine to ease the pain which started in her gut and wound throughout her body like a snake.

'Give me wine enough so I will forget. Never speak his name in front of me. Never!' She ordered everyone at her palace, including the children who could not claim their father: Scylla, Akheilos, Herophile among the others. It is not a good thing to deny children their father, but that is what she did, and they were the worse for it.

Lamia lay in bitter drunkenness for days, for weeks, for years. She found herself bound by her grief and unable to redeem herself. Her children wandered off and found teachers from the sea. They gave their mother no comfort. Each one reminded her of Zeus. She could not bear to look on them. She hated every mother who was loved by man or children. The darkness of her ire covered Libya like a cloud. It sank into corners where hurt feelings lay and magnified them into terrors. It wound around suspicious women's hearts and tore them from their husbands; for it was clear to Lamia no man could be trusted. Her darkness punished naughty children whom parents beat with cruelty beyond their nature. Her bitterness infected every living thing that saw her, for she was beautiful and she was hard.

She drew lovers to her bed and cast them off by morning so she did not have to look at them. She was indifferent to their pain, ignorant of their fear. She expunged their seed from her womb and let no child take root in her. She troubled pregnancies among her people to save the women all around from pain that was like hers. They needed no children to grieve them more nor men to betray them once they were done with these women of Libya. And still her curses were not enough to stop the lamentations of the woman seduced and scorned and left alone by Zeus. She coiled within herself and mourned.

Eventually Lamia wandered naked out into the desert underneath the stars. She called upon her teachers, but so deeply had pain changed her form they did not hear her. Crying and in complete despair she flung herself upon the sand, and crawled across the dune on her belly like a snake. The sand felt good. She remembered writhing in the sand, burrowing in caves beneath the sand when she was an untried girl in Babylon. Her teacher taught her how to burrow as a snake. She remembered shifting shapes, one organ at a time. She fused her legs, made her torso longer, flexed her back bone, drew her arms around her head and then tasted the air with her tongue. This form found some relief from the unrelenting agony of loss that gripped her soul. How different life was now! Her unfaithful lover's curses could have been no worse than this.

Lamia slid across the sand until she found the caves and entered them. The floors were damp and chill. She descended to the underworld beneath the rocky mouths. She moved silently, smoothly below the earth to seek wisdom at the Gates of Death among the ancestors. Because she was Lamia, the Gates swung open and admitted her, the Immortal Lamia, Goddess of Grief.

And there she faced a hooded guardian who regarded her in silence. She found her voice and begged for help. Trapped in an unending life of pain, she sought out death to end her lamentations. The figure only beckoned her to follow deeper in the earth where she was brought to a pool of tears.

'These are those you have shed my Lady,' said her guide. 'We have saved them for you.'

Lamia drew back. So deep a pool, so dark, reflecting only her grief-stained face. She saw she was a woman still, with arms and breasts and visage changed by her sadness atop the body of a great black snake. She wept for all the joy turned into tears. Her weeping added to the pool which lapped on rocks around her coiled body. They were cold and salty waves of torment.

A day might have passed, or another week of weeping until the guide beckoned her on to follow. She was empty of tears and drained of her sorrows. She felt dry and insubstantial as a shed snakeskin. She followed without thought to a second pond, this one as red as blood. Lamia tasted the air with her tongue: iron and salt. Blood! A pool of blood!

'Where did this come from?' She demanded, half afraid of what she might hear.

'The children,' was the answer. 'Yours and those you caused to die. The men who loved you but could not survive your scorn. The women who despaired and took their lives.'

Her children? The men and women of her lands? Impossible! She turned her head. It could not be! And yet it was. Her children, lost and wandering alone, had sucked her anger inside them. In fury her Scylla harvested sailors on rocks hidden by the waves. Akhilios devoured sailors as a shark. Only Herophile served the greater good as seer in Delphi. Lamia was striken again. Her children, lost. She had failed them. She had failed herself. She had failed her people. Her lovers died. The mothers of her lands lost their babes and killed themselves. Sometimes they killed their children, and their children's children.

She beat her hands upon the rocks around the pool and wailed for all the people, those who lived and those who died. Unbidden, the thought she was no better than the selfish Zeus came on her with a wisdom not her own. It made her sick. She heaved and vomited the bile that fed her anger all these years. She didn't like the truth. She desired to be greater than the great Zeus; more gifted, more powerful. But she was not. Gifts and power are nothing without love. She could lament. She could mourn. She could shift shapes, but unless she loved...well there was no point in pain for lost love's sake. She was a fool with a wasted life. Her guide beckoned her again, and brought her to a reflecting pool of silver.

She gazed at herself, ravaged by her tears and evil deeds, a hag. Her beauty gone, she measured the empty blackness of her eyes and wondered what was left? What atonement could there ever be in such evil? She was lost and left alone.

'Enter, Lamia. Be healed and transformed.' Her guide's hood fell back and then she saw him, Thoth of Egypt, God of Arts and Sciences, of Knowledge and of Wisdom, Judge and Teacher. She bowed her head and did as she was told. As her body entered the pool, the surface shimmered and bore her up. The liquid was denser than her form. She slid across the pool, rolled on its slippery surface for the joy of it. The ecstasy felt foreign but dimly she remembered joy. She remembered! One organ at a time, she took back her female form, her legs, her hips, her narrow waist. Her skin shone almond brown against the shiny silver pond. She stood and walked across the radiant surface. The light caressed her skin, lit up her face and rested in her eyes. She was restored.

She bowed to Thoth for this great gift. Her heart no longer ached. Her beauty was restored. Thoth smiled and sent Lamia home, pointing back the way she came.

'Now make amends,' was all he said.

How Lamia rebuilt her life and addressed the wrongs that she had done is material for another tale. I learned this story from my dreams and meditations with her. The important thing for us to understand is the redemption of the monster, her transformation from good to evil and back again. This cycle is the chthonic nature of the underworld, the ebb and flow of the cycle of seasons, the changing phases of the moon. The snake swallows it tail to bring the circle all the way around to the beginning with some new wisdom added. This circling around experience and truth is essential to the Pagan experience. Our thealogy is based on the turning of the Maiden, Mother and Crone. When we demonize the snake, we miss the point of transformative redemption.

Transformative redemption is soul growth. For the Pagan, there is no need of redemption from a sinful nature. We find the potential for good within the human soul, not evil. In fact good and evil appear as opposite sides of the same coin and we strive to understand a world based on the unified field of All Being. Our personal cruelties on the earth plane arise from grief, fear or anger. We lose our way, resort to violence and abuse, foster wars or court death. We find our way again and repudiate our blind vengeance. We make things right and pay the price. The energy of violence we send out comes home to rest and must be healed both in ourselves and in the injured. The cycle may take place within one lifetime or many. Pagans likely are no better set to understand that cycle between the light and the dark and back than the others of this world, yet the cycle spirals on and on until we see it traced in history. This wisdom belongs to the Snake Goddesses who coil around and grasp their own tails. They lay it out for us to witness.

Thus, in addition to the eternal alpha and omega imagery of

Ouroboros, the snake carries a lesson in growth and change. As the Snake Goddess expands, she sheds her skin and grows another, fresh and more beautiful than the one before. Like her we are evolving, changing, outgrowing ourselves and our past, and becoming new. There is power in her snake form and because of our conditioning from Christian theology, there is fear. Commonly when over-challenged by new ways of thinking, the human psyche retreats to the familiar prejudices, only to return to the new idea in desire for the Divine. This ebb and flow of soul growth is healthy.

Paganism is an entirely different way to think about the self and the world around the soul. Approaching the transformation of the rugged individual who is separate from the Gods into a divine soul who merges with the Gods is a gradual growth. The God Consciousness evolves in the soul as we remember who we are. When our consciousness expands to the point that our old beliefs no longer fit, we shed our old skins and start again in a new one. The new skin allows more growth. We can stretch to fit it as we evolve in deeper and more intimate relationship to the Divine. When the new skin becomes old, too tight for comfort, we shed again. We emerge from that old dried up shell with a tender new version of ourselves so we can begin once more to stretch and grow.

This process repeats for as long as we live. We grow and expand our souls. At death, we shed our human skin entirely and move to the next world, still learning, still evolving. The progress seems incremental but every step is significant. The Kore chant written by Starhawk and the Reclaiming Community in 1978 helps settle that experience in our body, mind and spirit. It deepens the experience of soul evolution when it is spoken without the music or when sung:

> *She changes everything She touches, and everything She touches changes.*[15]

The chant is one that finds more verses as it unwinds, but returns to that chorus to bring us back to our source. One verse I think fits this discussion and reminds us our experiences are like Ouroboros:

> *Everything lost is found again*
> *in a new form, in a new way*
> *Everything hurt is healed again*
> *in a new time, in a new day.*[16]

Experiencing the serpent as a healing, divine ecstatic guide requires growth and courage.

I have on my altar a serpent made from a stick of curly hazelnut. A student made it for me to use as a wand and talking stick. It fascinates people. They sit and stare, mesmerized until I tell them to pick it up. Others seem slightly horrified, and would do anything to avoid accepting it as it is passed around the circle during introductions or commentary. Both the attraction and rejection of the snake form runs deep in us.

Looking Our Fears in the Eye

The degradation of the Pagan serpent symbol by Christian theology begins in the Christian story of Creation. An archangel Lucifer (Bird Tribe/Watcher-type being) in the guise of a beautiful serpent tempts the naïve woman Eve to eat of the Tree of Good and Evil which Yahweh has forbidden. She does so. The Gods take counsel amongst themselves and decide the human pair must be evicted from Eden:

> And the LORD God said, Behold, the man is become as one of us, to know good and evil: and now, lest he put forth his hand, and take also of the tree of life, and eat, and live forever. Therefore the LORD God sent him forth from the garden of Eden, to till the ground from whence he was taken. So he drove out the man; and he placed at the east of the garden of Eden Cherubims, and a flaming sword which turned every way, to keep the way of the tree of life.[17]

Both the tree of life and the tree of knowledge (of good and evil) were located in that paradise. A human with access to both would be a divine human (avatar) like the anthropomorphic Gods. Apparently that was not in the plan at the beginning, or so says the Old Testament.

For that reason the serpent used by the archangel to empower humans was cursed by Yahweh and whoever else he was talking to, confined to crawl on its belly for the rest of time. The implication is that the serpent originally had legs. Vestiges of legs exist in python bodies. As a result of the Creation story and curse on humans in the Judeo-Christian writings, snakes and Satan, evil, temptation and their notion of sin are intricately entwined about each other, forever judged and condemned, along with the naïve woman Eve who thought to become all she was, and the foolish Adam who followed her out of love. Or at least that is the way I take it.

Our abhorrence of the snake then is ingrained culturally. Of course it helps not one bit that some snakes are poisonous. The lot of them are condemned by the ones who could do harm, kind of like the Christian view of humans who are condemned with original sin regardless of their own behavior.

Untangling ourselves from our fears can be a long process. I remember my high school biology teacher Mr. Blankenhorn brought a small garter snake to school in his breast pocket. The little snake curled up warm and cozy until encouraged to peek out at the class. We were invited to hold him gently and learn he was neither slimy nor slippery. He tasted the air around us, but did not bite. A friendly little fellow, he did much to allay my fear of snakes. Years later in one of these auto junk yards where mechanics can go search for used parts, I saw a whole nest of writhing little snakes, not much more than hatchlings, roiling in the sun near the front tire of an old car. I watched them in fascination as they rubbed and coiled around each other in perpetual motion. My cats bring in live snakes as gifts for me to rescue and return outside if I act quickly enough. Twice they brought in discarded skins, one of which I have on my shamanic altar. It reminds me of our growth and cycles in the Web. Finding snakes to befriend is a reasonable lesson in behavior modification for the fearful. Snake phobias only have power over our imaginations when we allow fear to rule us.

Whatever one thinks of these Pagan and Christian cultural myths and stories, the snake is symbolically tied to the circle, wholeness and healing. There is more. To medieval Christians, Ouroboros signified the material world defined by its own boundaries (the snake) and the spiritual world which exists without limits. Since they believed the snake was a symbol of evil, the material world within its boundaries was also evil, controlled by the Great Serpent who was the prince of the air, aka Satan. In the medieval world of dragons and monsters, the evil satanic nature of serpents was obvious. The Great Serpent wound itself around the world in a defining circle, keeping Spirit out of its lands so it could torment human kind with disease, pain and degradation. Only the church could rescue a sinful world from the power of the Great Serpent.

This was an intentional shift away from the Pagan rites and temples where the python was an oracle. The power of the oracle and the temple were replaced by the Christian Mass and cathedrals. Motives for this shift range from deep spiritual conviction to greed and political control of kings and nations. The passion continues today in the evangelical world that condemns any positive image of the snake as thoughts created by Satan to deceive the world. Not only do they condemn neo-Pagans, but also Freemasons, Knights Templar and Spiritualists who no longer fear the snake.

The Christian bias against snakes is not universal, even within Christendom. In some interpretations Ouroboros is a protective figure encircling the world keeping those within safe from the negativity or danger existing outside. Masons' aprons remind the Freemason of a guardian snake who holds the secrets of inner strength. Although the snake image has been removed from the apron I inherited, I understand the image of a snake originally was included on the apron itself. The ties around the waist represent

Ouroboros as an encouragement to the wearer to go deeper into the search for truth or enlightenment; not to stop with the superficial meanings offered up by our culture, but to delve into the secrets of our stories and find what is behind them. The Masonic brotherhood is reminded of that every time they wear the apron.

In western mysticism, alchemists used Ouroboros as a symbol for purification, quite the opposite of their Christian counterparts. One of the most well-known sigils of Ouroboros comes from the second century text *The Chrysopoeia of Cleopatra*. In the center of the snake's circle is the phrase *hen to pan*, 'one is the all.' The snake is colored in, half black/half white, to illustrate the combination of light and dark, good and evil, wisdom and ignorance. Theosophist[18] and Gnostic[19] Christians as well as Pagans can relate to its black and white halves as representations of the duality of the earth plane which faith, study and enlightenment bring into focus as the One.

The snake itself is the beginning and the end, the *alpha* and *omega*, the infinite circle, Ouroboros. The Wiccan Ouroboros is the form of the circle in which we as Witches worship and celebrate the seasons. We descend and ascend, revel in the light and the dark without harm. We create magic in the circle. I once had an apprentice who swore she desired to learn Wicca but wanted nothing to do with the dark cycle of the moon. Had I known she would refuse to walk in balance between the light and the dark, I would not have taken her oaths. She had studied with another Witch and was sent on missions to Hecate. I was lulled into a comfortable delusion that we all understood the Craft takes us into the unraveling of life as well into its affirmation and creativity. She bolted at the first opportunity, leaving us with responsibility to unravel the work done to that point. Ouroboros requires the apprentice and the adept to walk the right-hand path and the left-hand path without harm to self or others. We celebrate the birth into this world and the birth into the next, which we quaintly call death. That is the cycle of one life, full circle.

Enso: The Japanese Word for Circle

The *enso* is a circle of enlightenment, the state of being we aspire to as apprentices and enter as adepts. That enlightenment of merger with the Gods and of our wise detachment is enhanced by meditation. When understood, the *silence* of the adept is seen as *stillness*. There is no love/hate, desire/lack, courage/fear. There is only the circle of life, the be-ing is us and Goddess. When we meditate on the enso, we peal back our illusions, even those about time and space. The *Shin Jin Mei*, written in the 6th century, refers to the Great Way of Zen as 'a circle like vast space, lacking nothing, and nothing in excess.'[20] This statement is often used as an inscription on enso paintings. Apparently writing or drawing the enso is not the way of true Zen. If the student enters the enso, then the meaning of it is the experience and needs no clarification. According to multiple sources, in the 8th century *Keitokudento-roku*:

A monk asked Master Isan for a gatha[21] expressing enlightenment. Isan refused saying, 'It is right in front of your face, why should I express it in brush and ink?'

The monk then asked Kyozan, another master, for something concrete. Kyozan drew a circle on a piece of paper, and said, 'Thinking about this and then understanding it is second best; not thinking about it and understanding it is third best.' (He did not say what is first best.)

Zen circles became a central theme of Zen art. Some are as perfectly symmetrical as the artist can draw them freehand. Lopsided potato shapes speak to another level of being, and are loved and embraced as visions. The key in creating an enso is to make the circle in one or two brush strokes. An enso can be any one of the following:

1. *Mirror enso:* A simple circle, free of any accompanying inscription, leaving everything to the insight of the viewer.
2. *Universe enso:* A circle that represents the cosmos as enclosed

curved space.

3. *Moon enso:* The full moon illuminates all beings equally as does Enlightenment.
4. *Zero enso:* Curved time and space are 'empty,' yet they give birth to All Being.
5. *Wheel enso:* Everything changes, all life revolves in circles as in the Tarot's Wheel of Fortune.
6. *Sweet cake enso:* Zen circles are profound and concrete so common images illustrate Enlightenment as do the simple acts of eating round cakes and finding Truth.
7. *'What is this?' enso:* The most frequently used inscription on Zen circle paintings, this is a pithy way of saying, 'Don't let others fill your head with theories about Zen; discover the meaning for yourself!'

I say the same for the sacred circle. Each one finds the meaning alone.

Create Your Enso

Use art paper and paint, watercolor, or markers. Make the circle in one or two strokes. A brush allows the media to offer more unexpected wisdom, but a marker may bring its own surprises. Hang it on your wall and leave it as a mirror enso at first, until and unless you are given more to add as you have meditated on the form. Seek deep wisdom about the nature of the circle, yourself and sacred space. Then add the drawing and your meditations to your Book of Shadows.

Make a Collage of Circles

Collect images of round things from magazines and catalogs. Include squares or rectangular sections of color, grass, sky, water, trees to use as a background. Gather a glue stick, some cardboard to use as a backing, scissors and your BOS. Then breathe deeply and enter a meditative state. Begin to fit your images together by instinct. Lay your background. Trim the pictures to fit each other. When the collage has taken shape, glue the pieces in place. Meditate on the circles and find the hidden wisdom. Write about it. Add your collage to your BOS.

Chapter 4

The Circle and the Stones

As we have seen, a circle is a symbol or sigil of growth and change. That is the wisdom of Ouroboros. A circle is also an expression of completeness by itself and of beginnings which turn into endings and start over again. The enso may have brought these truths to mind. The circle is also the entrance to sacred geometry and our ancestors' spiritual celebrations of the heavens. Although Paganism has no holy scrolls or grimoires hidden in the Neolithic cave dwellings of the Old World, it has examples of its sacred power inscribed on the land in lines and stone circles. We can appreciate these places on several levels: as artifacts, as art, as places to worship, and guides to the stars, sun and moon alignments in the old calendar. Stone circles are also places of power which connect the energy grid of the planet. This grid or web is still in place and under repair by humans, the deities and perhaps extraterrestrials, unless of course those entities are all the same.

Geometric Definition

A *circle* is defined as a figure with all points on its perimeter set at the same distance from its center. A circle is set by its center. The size of the circle is determined by the length of its radius, the arm that reaches from the center to the edge (perimeter) of the circle. The line that cuts straight across the circle through the center, like the hands of a clock at 6 o'clock and 12 o'clock, is called the diameter, *dia* meaning two. Given this definition, a geometric circle must be absolutely round like a wheel or a dinner plate.

In sacred geometry, forms and figures take on esoteric meaning and power which spring from their nature. They are used to create places of worship, meditation and ritual. The forms of sacred geometry are found in nature, from round floral heads as in the sunflower, to spirals seen in the chambered nautilus or Milky Way galaxy. Bees create hexagonal honeycombs. In sixes flower petals form soft hexagrams (six-pointed stars which combine two triangles). Various crystalline shapes form triangles, hexagons and octagons. The platonic solids include basic shapes we know, like pyramids and cubes, and others not so familiar.

The geometry of a circle includes two concepts we shall study later with the unspoken ritual of circle casting: *pi* and *phi*. That these are spiritual concepts comes as a surprise to many people who were certain the concrete nature of math and science has nothing to do with spiritual practice. In fact they are of the same continuum which circles around and attaches to itself like the snake swallowing its tail. That will become clearer as we educate ourselves and experience the enlightenment of deep spiritual practice. I raise the possibility here to open the mind. When casting a circle in a ritual or drawing one on paper we engage in an act with deep implications to our souls. All is not as simple as it seems. A magical education offers this journey into physical forms used for spiritual exploration. Surprising insight can pop up in ways more meaningful than math class.

The sacred circle, then, is a universal symbol for completeness and eternity. It represents both the unity of all things and the dualism of light and dark, of within and without. The circle is perfect in the usual sense of perfection. A circle is. A thing is not becoming a circle, since any lack of roundness means the form is something else, something not a circle. A circle is sacred space; that protected place of wholeness where we are freed from fear, ego, and strife. No wonder everything tries to be round!

The Sacred Space of Stone Circles

Ancient humans created circles in the landscape, though like our sacred circles cast for ritual and magic, they are not perfect geometric circles. The mathematical discipline of geometry comes from the Greek root words meaning *to measure land*. The sacred places of the earth are measured in the study of geomancy. Geomancy can be a method of divination, i.e. divining truth. Dowsers access the earth wisdom with divining or dowsing rods. One can also use a pendulum. The same techniques are useful in identifying linear connections between stone circles and nodes of power. These linear connections are often called ley lines, which are part of the universal sacred grid that wraps itself around the earth. It is this grid which is being repaired and reconstructed by souls who understand the power of the quartered circle and other sacred forms.

Experiencing the wisdom of the stones is an interactive meditation with the earth spirits. I call her Gaia. The Earth Mother has many names: Anu or Danu in the Celtic past, Demeter or Ceres as Terras Mater in Greece and Rome. Alternatively, from the same classic cultures, she is named Rhea or Hera/Juno. Before that she appeared as Isis and Hathor in Egypt, Pachamama in MesoAmerica, and Shakti in India. I could write a very long list. The Great Mother Goddess identified by the cultural archeologist Marija Gimbutas[22] is found in images throughout the world as a common creator of humankind which pre-dates the monotheistic creators of the Abrahamic traditions by millennia.

Gimbutas' conclusions, based on a lifetime of investigation, are unpopular and widely criticized but cogent none the less. It is still the female of the species that births the next generation. I find it entirely believable that the ancients sought a Mother Goddess as birth mother to humankind, the earth and even the cosmos as they told their stories of how we all began. We shall not now open the question of who are the Gods and where did they come from. An examination of the nature of their sacred space is enough to tackle for the moment.

Stonehenge

Stonehenge on Salisbury Plain, England, is usually the first example of a sacred stone circle that comes to mind. There are many others, up to 900 identified in the United Kingdom alone. Frankly no one has adequately explained who constructed Stonehenge, when and for what purpose. The ancient Druids were once credited with it, but for no verifiable historical reason. Still, as a recognized religion in Great Britain, modern Druids lead the celebrations of the solstices at Stonehenge, which is the prime example of sacred architecture.

Here is what is known about Stonehenge in terms of facts. It was constructed in at least three phases over a period of centuries.

Phase One is believed to have been built before the Celts (Indo Europeans) settled the British Isles, perhaps around 2900 BCE. Those inhabitants were the mound builders who constructed the communal tombs underground which are found across England. They lived as farmer-tradesmen using stone implements. Phase One included the circular bank and ditch 320 feet in diameter which circles 56 Aubrey holes filled with chalk. These holes are six foot circles, four feet deep and similar to holes found in the long barrows located elsewhere in England as burial mounds. Thirty-five of the Stonehenge Aubrey holes were used as burial sites for cremated remains and grave goods. The banks of the ditch around the Aubrey holes were around six feet high, but stand now at only a couple of feet. A 35 foot wide causeway bridges the ditch and enters the circle within the ditch. In the causeway outside the circle is the heel stone, a single outlier facing the entrance. Moving toward the circle from the heel stone are wood post holes, which lead some to conclude there was a gated entrance. Outside the henge are the Greater and Lesser Cursus, also built during Phase One. These are long straight earthworks bound by a bank and ditch. They appear most like a long flat race track, the longer one stretching out for 3,000 yards. Their presence near the site encourages us to view the larger Salisbury Plain complex rather than isolate Stonehenge from its surroundings.

Phase Two was built by early Celts with a more varied social order including priests and warriors as well as farmers and traders. This phase is set some 700 years after Phase One around 2200 BCE and included the 60 bluestones in double rings, which were later removed. Since these stones weighed four ton or more each, this was a significant feat both in the construction and dismantling of the twin circles. The bluestones circles were 86 and 74 feet in diameter, though they were not completed. Two more bluestones marked the Avenue, which was also constructed during this period.

Phase Three is connected to the Wessex warrior/chiefdom society and includes the most elaborate but unfinished work. Phase Three extended from 2100-1500 BCE during which time the builders removed the 60 bluestones and reset them further in toward the center where they are enclosed by the sarsen stone ring. The Wessex society built the five trilithons, the large sarsen stone ring and other major portions of the monument. The last phase remained unfinished so the sarsen ring was left open with more than 20 lintels (cross pieces) never transported or cut. One of the major stones, commonly referred to as the slaughter stone, was in fact an erect pillar which has fallen. One of an intended pair, it was not used for blood sacrifice.

We can also identify with some certainty the use of Stonehenge as an astronomical observatory. The equinox and solstices are identified by the movement of the dawning sun on the stones. However, the 19-year lunar cycle, which is more complicated, is framed by the four station stones erected in Phase Three. That this is intentional is somewhat controversial given what scholars believe is the limited level of mathematic comprehension by a tribal culture. Mainstream archeology and anthropology argue against a conscious charting of the lunar cycle. However, other stone circles reflect similar chartings, thereby reducing the role of chance alignments.

Most such arguments against intentional celestial alignments lack an appreciation of the connection of a Pagan culture with the land it inhabits. That modern analysis overlooks earlier human interaction with the sentient earth, moon and stars is understandable. We think with the logic of our training. Unaware of the ancestors' reasoning and training we miss the depth of observation they were willing to perform, sitting for generations, charting the stars and marking the seasons. If such work is part of a holy office, then time is irrelevant.

The years of a priest's life are well spent contemplating the heavens in stillness. Rather than wonder how the ancients could possibly watch and wait to record the rising and setting of heavenly bodies, we do better to wonder how we have become so disconnected from the earth and celestials. Without a sacred or shamanic world view we are in danger of extinction yet live completely unaware of what may come. The ancients would wonder how we failed to observe that.

The cursus at Stonehenge appears to be a sacred way like those in other parts of the world that are used for moving meditations. Spiritual seekers in Buddhism, for example, walk in a set path, carefully placing their feet until the pace is automatic. The mind moves to stillness as the body moves around the cursus. The pacing may be linear back and forth. It may follow a circle or oval so there is no beginning nor end. We will use a similar experience in our elemental meditations in Chapter 7. This technique, called *kinhin,* is ancient and grounding. In the 21st century we find the cursus path mysterious because we do not know how the sacred mind is opened.

Space used repeatedly for ritual purposes takes on a spiritual energy people can feel centuries afterward, even if they cannot identify it. How much more affecting might it have been to the people who lived there and used the site for cyclical celebrations! The time involved in the planning of such a monument in a world not run by clocks, the effort and physical power of erecting the stones means something different in a pre-historic world than in contemporary society. All of this leaves open the possibility of a lunar and celestial calendar that was no coincidence but part of the plan.

Our personal experience at Stonehenge was entirely spontaneous. Because so many knowledgeable people in the Pagan world had criticized this monument for its commercialism I had thought to skip it in my visits to England. They said the stones were roped off too far away from visitors, the site was too crowded and it had lost its charm. My partner Merlin had grown up in Wiltshire where he had frequently cycled to the pasture that held Stonehenge. He had been able to throw his bike in the bushes and walk freely among the stones. Surely a cleaned up, roped off monument would be a disappointment. We planned to drive by the monument as a simple roadside observation and keep on going. We could not.

Driving east on the A303, Stonehenge appeared suddenly as we mounted a hill; it sprang out of the ground and took my breath away. I imagine the pilgrims walking up the hill had much the same experience as they approached. We turned on the side road and stopped in a farm gate for a better look. The power of place gripped us both and drew us in. We parked in the lot, crossed under the road in the tunnel and came out the other side with hundreds of other people. There were eight large tour buses parked with scores of cars in the lot behind us. We had radio phones in our hands that described the points of interest. The pathway came within feet of the sarsens which were separated from us by a low ring of bungee cords. A woman sat on the ground about a quarter way around the circle and meditated. Everyone respected her space and walked quietly around her.

About halfway around the circle, the rain started. I appealed to the rain spirits but they laughed. Apparently we were to be 'baptized' at Stonehenge. When the downpour let loose in earnest, the crowd ran for cover in the tunnel, every man, woman and child. Since going ahead and turning back were the same distance for us, we shrugged and kept on walking the circle. We came to meet Stonehenge. Sometimes it rains.

The narrator on our recordings told the story of Merlin flying the stones to Salisbury Plain from Ireland. I laughed and looked up at my partner Merlin. Maybe he did in another life. We learned there had been four large outliers around the circle at each of the cardinal points. No official explanation for their function was offered but every Witch knows they marked the places where the Elementals were called. Perhaps guard fires were set there to keep celebrants warm on cold nights, as they were in the 1990s at the Starwood

Festival in New York. I have stood singing songs and sharing wine at guard fires like that. Lines drawn between the outliers at Stonehenge cross at the altar stone. The lintels which lie across the tops of the 13-25 foot sarsen pillars have a mortise and tenon joint. That is, the uprights have a carved opening and the crosspieces have a protruding pin carved from the body of the rock that exactly fit each other to hold them in place and tie the structure together. The cross pieces are curved to continue the lines of the circle. Their ends are carved into tongue and groove connections to further stabilize the lintels and uprights. Each one is estimated to weigh 30-50 tons. I found the ancestors' precision engineering humbling.

When we rounded the northeast side to the circle's entrance to stand on a raised walkway, we looked across the monument and saw we had it to ourselves. No one was there in the rain, save one or two couples on the far side of the ring. The rain had let a bit of sunshine peek through the clouds, but we were as wet as we ever will be. Our raincoats dripped, having absorbed as much rain as they could hold. Our shoes squished. Our hair was plastered to our heads under our hoods. None of that mattered. The Great Stones had spoken to us in their mighty circle. My partner Merlin felt a kinship there, perhaps from other lives or his boyhood. I was a visitor, welcomed but not fully embraced. Nevertheless we both felt initiated by the stones and the storm.

Three of my other favorite stone circles are: Avebury in Wiltshire, UK; Castlerigg near Keswick, Cumbria, UK; and Long Meg and Her Daughters, near Little Salked, Cumbria, UK. Visiting them turned out to be magical, each in a different way.

Avebury Stone Circle

The stone circles at Avebury are part of a complex of sites including Silbury Hill, West Kennet Long Barrow, the Avenues, the Sanctuary and the earthworks and ditches, the outer stone circle and two smaller inner stone circles. They are located in Wiltshire, in south west England. It may also include Windmill Hill and the mound in

Marlboro. The village of Avebury is situated in the midst of it all. When we looked closely, we saw rocks in the stone buildings that likely are pieces of the old megaliths. The church ordered these stone circles destroyed in a fever of zealotry in the 17th century. Some were dropped into holes excavated to hide them. Others were broken up. In 1930 Alexander Keiller dug up and reset many of those buried stones, though there are more underground still. Concrete markers hold the places of some of the missing rocks. Where there were originally 600 or more megaliths, 70 remain. The site is now managed and protected by the National Trust.

The outer stone circle has a diameter of more than 1,400 feet and covers about 28 acres. There are two kinds of monoliths in Avebury Stone Circle. The male phallic stones are cylindrical uprights. The female diamond stones are cut parallelograms set up with one point buried in the ground. The male and female balance is echoed by Silbury Hill, the phallic male energy located across several fields on the main road (A4) about a mile south of the village, and West Kennet Long Barrow, the recumbent female energy located a mile and a half south of the village.

Although there is erosion and pitting in the stones, cup and ring marks, faces, heads and other figures are clearly evident in the stone works. One stone reminded me of a rock in a Hawaiian village I had seen years before which had held a map carved in stone. Knowing what the builders' intentions were 4,000 years ago is nearly impossible. Still, a map looks like a map in any age.

On the day of our first visit to Avebury in 2007, rain threatened though the day was hot and humid. I paused to rest, feeling grumpy and uncomfortable. Our camera film had tangled, so Merlin returned to the car to see if he could salvage any of it in the dark under a blanket. That succeeded, he returned with a new roll of film loaded in the cranky camera. We later replaced the camera first with a better 35mm and then with a digital. Lessons learned.

While I was waiting, grousing about the pictures, the smelly animal dung from the resident sheep and goats all around me, the biting flies and the weather, I thought perhaps I should address my concern to the wind spirits who could reasonably do something about it. No sooner than the idea had come to mind, the sun went under a cloud and a stiff breeze sprang up. The humidity was whisked away with the biting flies and dung odors. The air felt cool and refreshing. I was left gaping around in surprise. There had been no breeze all day long. I recognize magic when I see it. I sang a chant in thanksgiving.

Later I stood before the Swindon Stone, a giant rock that towered above me waiting for Merlin to get our picture in two frames, since I wanted a close up and the rock was too large to fit. We were preparing to leave for the day, so I mentally asked the rock for words of wisdom. What she said was this: 'Remember, all rocks are one rock, all continents one continent, all people one people.' When the pictures were developed, I found a small lamb was laying in the shade beneath her corner, looking up at me wondering whatever was I doing talking to her rock. I smile whenever I remember the encounter.

On another visit to Avebury I was sitting in the picnic area waiting for other people to arrive. I spent my time focusing on the stones. I held my heart open to the past, trying to understand. Two couples and their small children sat at the next table eating lunch. One of them asked me whether it would rain on their lunch since the sky was as cloudy as the forecast had been. I shrugged, thinking it would be anybody's guess. She looked disappointed, saying, 'Oh, I thought you knew.' She then stared meaningfully at the stones.

I smiled at that and shrugged again. 'I think you will stay dry for lunch,' I offered based on absolutely no evidence at all. She nodded and thanked me. Again, I thanked the spirits should they heed my words. My friends were very late. I stayed while the little group of visitors finished eating, dry save three or four large rain drops which fell only to remind us all the rain spirits are whimsical creatures. They cooperate only when they want to.

Avebury is that special kind of place where thought manifests more quickly. But if all rocks are one rock, then that power extends itself around the world. The Avebury Stone Circle our ancestors created in the landscape is replicated when we draw one on paper, set one up on an altar, or cast one in the air for ritual.

Castlerigg

Castlerigg, outside Keswick, in Cumbria, north west England, is situated in a high field surrounded by spectacular peaks in the Fells with names like Skiddaw, Blencathra and Lonscale. Of the circles I have visited, this one reminds me most strongly that the topography ringing the circle is part of the sacred space marked by the stones. I suspect the average tourist is blind to the significance of the natural setting when visiting Stonehenge or Avebury. They cannot miss it at Castlerigg. Some of the stones seem to echo the shape of the hills behind them. At Castlerigg, the Fells draw your attention outward toward them in a reminder of how all stones connect as one. The site is breathtaking. About 38 stones remain with fewer than a handful missing. My partner Merlin sat in place of one of the gaps, hunkered down like a rock. That clearly was his place.

Castlerigg is about 100 feet across. The entrance is on the north side, marked by two larger rocks, though none of the Castlerigg stones are taller than I am at five feet four inches. There is a single outlier stone on the southwest nearly 300 feet away. Attached to the east side of the circle it has a collection of 10 stones forming a rough rectangle called The Cove. Speculation about its purpose is unverified by efforts of archeologists. Three stones in the east and the gap where Merlin sat mark the variations in the moonrise over its 19-year cycle. Six others on the east side mark the sabbat sunrises through the full wheel of the year: Samhain/October 31, Yule/ December 22, Imbolc/ February 1, Lady Day/ March 21, Beltane/April 30, Litha/June 21, Lughnasagh/ August 1, and Mabon/September 21.

Maintained by English Heritage, Castlerigg has no off-street parking, no visitors' center nor commercial gift shop. It sits in its natural state. The walk up the field to the circle is not even a warm up for fell walkers, but sedentary old ladies like me need to remember to wear appropriate shoes and bring a walking stick.

Long Meg and Her Daughters

Like Castlerigg, Long Meg and her Daughters is one of the more complete remaining stone circles, with around 60 stones still in place. Many have toppled and probably another 20 have been removed or buried. It stands alone in a privately owned cow pasture in the north west of England, not as easily located as other stone circles. There is adjacent parking and easy walking access around and through the circle. The crowds are absent. The circle is about 360 feet at its widest, describing an oval shape on a gentle slope. Outside the southwest entrance between a double stone gateway stands the tallest stone, referred to as Long Meg. The feminine name is something of a misnomer since the rock is a red sandstone phallus of impressive proportions. It stands about 12 feet high. The legend is that the Witch Meg and her children were turned to stone by a crusty Scottish wizard, or maybe he was a Christian saint, when they were celebrating their Sabbat. Since the winter solstice sun sets over Long Meg, it likely happened at Yule.

Directly across from the sandstone outlier called Meg is a recumbent granite or limestone rock, one which likely stood erect at some other time. This stone has the naked breasts and hips of a woman turning sideways. To my eyes, the two were a pair joining the male and female energies of the circle in proper Ouroboros fashion, half light/half dark, half male/half female. There are large boulders at the east and west points of the circle as well. My partner Merlin and I only spent part of an afternoon with them, but the stones spoke eloquently to us of the balancing rituals we are so familiar with, those which join the male and female, light and dark.

Oddly, though sources discuss the ancient cup and ring and spiral markings on Long Meg, they fail to mention the split mound at the top looking like nothing other than the glans of a penis. That the outlier is a phallic stone is consistent with many heel stones at the gates of circles. Their shadows stretch through the gates and into the circles at the appointed day and hour of sunrise or sunset, as a lover entering his beloved. The analogies are purposeful for reasons which will become clear as we are prepared for them. Sacred sexuality was and is part of humanity's reconnection with the earth powers.

When we visited Long Meg in 2007, we were moved to leave offerings to the spirits of that sacred space. Other pilgrims had placed flowers and gifts at the feet of Long Meg. We took silver coins, pulled back the grass around the base and tried to slide them close to the place where the stone strikes deeply into the ground. Most of these monoliths have as much as a third of their length buried in the soil to hold them upright. On the first try the coins bounced back out onto the ground as if someone threw them back. Not easily deterred, Merlin tried again. Then it was as if the ground opened up and swallowed the coins. We could not see where they went, but they had been accepted.

In addition, Merlin decided to leave his pentacle with an inset crystal atop Long Meg. Again the spirits of the place gave us opportunity to be sure of our intention. The first throw was short and bounced back at him. The second throw went long and sailed over the top to land near me on the other side. The third try landed the pentacle squarely in the center of the pinnacle of the rock. If it has not been liberated by the local ravens, I assume it is there yet. This of course meant I had to purchase a new pentacle for Merlin when we went further south to Glastonbury in our adventures.

We walked the entire perimeter of the stone circle. I sat and sang several chants to the spirits of the place in gratitude for their longevity. One of them, written by Morning Feather and Will Shepardson of Circle Sanctuary in Wisconsin (1981) celebrated our return to the stones:

We are an old people, we are a new people
We are the same people stronger than before.

Cauldron of changes, feather on the bone.
Arc of Eternity, hole in the stone.

The Sacred Space of Medicine Wheels

A second and similar type of stone circle is the Native American medicine wheel. Although this is a familiar image, our understanding from the perspective of the European Pagan culture is incomplete. Frequently people construct a circle formed of large rocks at the perimeter and believe they are constructing a medicine wheel. This is inaccurate if one is relying on physical labor alone. The construction of a medicine wheel includes communion with the stones, alignment with the stars or with the movements of the sun or moon, and connection with the land on which the stones will rest. The wheel in Wyoming aligns with dawn at summer solstice. Others in Alberta, Canada also seem to align with key stars.

It is no surprise that the scientific community questions the ability of the Native Americans as well as the early Europeans to discover and predict the movements of the stars and planets in the heavens. Radio carbon dating has set the earliest sections of these archeological sites at 10,000 years old. Scientific skepticism need not interfere with our understanding of sacred space and sacred time, nor our confidence in the wisdom of the ancestors.

The actual design of a medicine wheel can vary from a stone circle organized around the center spirit stone, to a stone circle with an avenue moving energy in or out of the circle. There may be radial arms representing the seasons of the year within the circle connecting the center to the perimeter, or the arms may extend out of the circle as if leading beyond space and time. A medicine wheel is a place of power. The line of energy should be palpable. Dowsers should be able to trace them. Keep in mind, there are thousands of stone circles in the western part of the US and Canada that were cobble stones placed to hold down the edges of tipis, now incorrectly identified as ritual circles. That they represented the home/hearth /heart of the family allows that these were sacred spaces, but they were not formal places of ritual medicine or power.

The circles with radials extending outward have been identified by native people to anthropologists as memorials set for people of great influence or impact on the tribe, which they state is not properly a medicine wheel. Perhaps. On the other hand, such a place might also be used for sacred ritual to contact a sage or crone who has crossed over. In using the skills of a spirit walker, conversation and teaching continues beyond death. Certainly such a memorial might be a place of great medicine, but not one identified to outside cultures.

One of the most famous medicine wheels is that located in the Medicine Bow Mountains within the Bighorn National Forest, Wyoming, near the Big Horn River. We identify this wheel with the Ojibwa Lakota traditions, but it may pre-date them.

By now you have likely discerned that the use of the term *medicine* means something more than an elixir of healing. Understood in the tribal context, medicine is a word for power gained by walking in balance with the spirits, the sacred land and the celestials. That state of connection with the Great Spirit or All Being is, of course, healing. It is also much more in that it heals body, soul and spirit.

Beginning a Circle of Stones

Gather up a basket of fist sized rocks from your favorite natural places. You will need at least nine, but perhaps more will volunteer. Ask them if they are willing to work with you on a project and carry the willing ones home. Sit with your rocks and introduce yourself. Talk to them about your identity and listen to what they say about their own. Rock energy is very much slower than human energy, so sit in silence. Be patient. They will have deep solemn insights to share with you. Keep them in a secure place where they will not be tossed aside or thrown out. They are not playthings for children nor curiosities for visitors. Respect them and build a relationship slowly at rock speed.

The rocks may need or want to be cleansed with spring water, moonlight or sunlight. They may wish to be bathed in sage and sweet grass. At this point you do not need a great deal of skill or training in preparing your rocks. Trust them to speak to your heart. Hold them one at a time close to you. When you have met your rocks, discuss with them what sort of circle you should make together. Seek their names, if they are willing to share them. Return those to the wild who wish to depart. Bless the rocks and let them bless you. We will create the circle altar much later in our studies when we have developed a deeper understanding of things. Take the time to prepare for that now, with the intention of completing the project at an appropriate moon, solstice or equinox. Note the images, visions or names gleaned from the rocks in your BOS. Be thankful and offer your rocks any blessing that seems appropriate.

Chapter 5

Casting the Circle

Wiccans work in a circle which is a container of energy: theirs, the earth's and the synergy from those present—humans, Elementals, Gods and Goddess and ancestors. For that reason, when we circle together it helps to have all the humans intending to do the same thing in concert with the spirits. We build the group mind among the humans when we ground using the tree visualization. In addition to sending the tap root deep into the ground, we add lateral roots 360º around the tap root just below the topsoil level. We sense them intertwining with the lateral roots sent out by others in the circle. Lateral roots add stability to a tree and offer humans the same gift when we are engaged in ritual. Because the lateral roots connect us with others in the circle, we feel their energy and are able to merge consciousness with them, co-creating the ritual circle together. The group mind connects with the Elementals when we call the quarters and with the ancestors, Gods and Goddesses when we evoke or invoke their presence later in the ritual.

The Circle as an Energy Sphere

As a container, the circle defines the sacred space we create for ritual. It holds our energy in, concentrates it and allows us to direct it toward a group focus. It also sets up a barrier to extraneous energy from outside. That outside energy is not 'evil' or 'negative' energy, but rather distracting energy. Wiccans vary on whether or not there is 'evil' in the world. If we see the earth as a circle or sphere of energy, then all we call good and all we call evil are joined in the same field of energy. Accepting the illusion of duality (good guys on one side and bad guys on the other) in a ritual setting sets a weaker foundation for our magic and soul evolution. Whether or not we understand how the light and dark combine into one, our leaving open the possibility of such a combination without confusing it by banishing evil with our magical practices will help later. At this point we only need to understand that the circle is an energy construct, one which we erect for ritual purposes and then dismantle when we have finished. The cast circle becomes a real object. It has boundaries, dimension, and duration.

The boundaries of the circle are created by a magical casting created through movement in a clockwise direction under the guidance of the facilitating priest or priestess. When we are finished the boundaries are removed by counterclockwise action. In the northern hemisphere, Wiccans work deosil (clockwise) to enclose a circle and widdershins (counterclockwise) to open one. This follows the path of the sun. Obviously in the southern hemisphere, the direction is reversed. There are other Pagan approaches, but they are not the usual beginning in the Wiccan format. Once it is cast, the circle then reaches over, around and under the sacred space in a sphere.

When a strong circle is cast, the boundaries around it are tangible. The energy is different inside the circle than it is outside the circle. People perceive the difference individually as temperature, texture, vibration, tingling, color, or sound. From the inside, I can reach behind me and feel a vibrant cushion of power sealing us securely inside. The circle appears to me as blue-silver energy, cooler than the air, a rapid humming which is easier to feel than hear. If no one can perceive the circle, it may not have been cast skillfully.

We have to be present in our own center of body/mind/soul before we can create a perceptible sphere of magic. When a circle casting is weak, look to the groundedness of the individual(s) holding the energy of the space. Ideally, the priestess or priest casting the circle has centered and grounded before working for the celebrants. If not, the celebrants are able to hold the sphere of energy we call a circle because of the grounding. That is why in most of our Web circles grounding comes before circle casting. We use the energy of the earth and sun channeled through our bodies to create the sacred space of the circle. Attempting to cast a circle on our own drains our bodies and makes the work more difficult. Casting the circle without earth and sun energy is part of the routine but not one with transformative power. People are more likely to be tired and headachy after ritual if the working is done with human energy drawn from the leaders or from the group. Using the generous energy offered by Gaia and Sol is a much wiser and more powerful choice.

Once the circle is cast, we remain within its boundaries. If someone needs to leave or enter once the circle is complete, we cut a doorway, step through and seal it behind us. Often one person is charged with the responsibility to handle this gateway in and out. The summoner, if the circle has one, is a good candidate. A trained man-in-black is another. People who carelessly crash through the boundaries of the circle on their way in or out tear the fabric of energy and let the sacred space go flat like a leaky balloon. The circle can be repaired and recast of course, but I prefer to prevent these accidents with education. The common wisdom is that small children and animals move freely in and out of sacred space without deflating the magic. That seems to be true from my experience. My cats are particularly attracted by the sacred energy but some of them show up late and leave early. They seem to sense when the magic is finished and have little interest in the closing sequences.

For large group ceremonies and outdoor rituals, either of which may include the general public and people from different traditions, casting a permeable circle is a better choice than a closed circle. Permeable circles mark out sacred space on the ground, but make no effort to seal it. People can come and go at will without disrupting the energy field. Priests and priestesses leading such circles have additional duties in setting up wards around the space and maintaining the magical focus in order to create a ritual worthy of its name. I find it important even in large group celebrations to have a magical focus that provides a truly spiritual experience beyond waving my arms around and blowing sage smoke into the wind. The additional preparation by the facilitators pays off.

From the outside of the circle, if we walk widdershins around the boundaries we may sense the unwinding energy used in releasing the focused sacred space. We can also touch the energy field from the outside to be sure it is there. Some people sense a difference in the circle boundaries between the inside and outside. They feel the same to me. Once you learn to cast a solitary circle, experiment with the walls and note your observations in your BOS. Look for these telltales whenever you work with a magical group. Witches can create or strengthen a circle on their own with their minds if the group working falls short. Performed as a silent service in support of the facilitators, our mental reinforcements help the magic happen for everyone.

The dimensions of a circle vary with the group and purpose. A traditional coven of 13 Witches might find the circle radius of 13 feet effective. Others might like double that space to give room to dance and move around. A solitary Witch practicing in her meditation spot may find a round rug slightly wider than her height sufficient because it allows her to lie down for trance work. I used a four foot wide round rug that my mother made. I remained seated, using it as a cozy meditation circle. Witches who have completed Wicca I at the Web PATH Center receive their Wiccan measure which is three times their height. At the Web each person holds his or her own measure which is typically 15 feet to 20 feet long. When one wishes a truly round circle of substantial proportions the priest or priestess's measure is used as a radius from the center to set the boundaries marked out with chalk, powder or flour. One person holds the end of the measure at the center. Another holds the end out taut at the perimeter, spilling flour or cornmeal on the ground as they walk the circle. Indoors one might use salt, which of course is not good for the plants of the earth. Be aware in some Pagan traditions salt banishes spirits instead of purifying sacred space.

The duration of a circle varies with the casting and intent. In Web rituals, the circle endures for the time of the ritual service. We then disperse the energy intentionally, usually by clapping and singing. I have left a permeable circle in place for the duration of a weekend class or extended festival. That sort of casting is dispersed at the end of the event. The energy of a sacred space used repeatedly for ritual will linger in the room or stone circle. It remains palpable even though the circle casting is dispersed. The same residual power is felt in the great stone circles discussed in Chapter 4. Because the ritual room in our house is only used for meditation, healing and magic, the energy accumulates there in a similar manner, even though the specific circle is released after each working.

There are other locations which we call *power spots* found in nature. These places accumulate special *chi* or energy: waterfalls, river gorges, lakes, mountains, valleys, springs or our own back yards that have a natural magic to them. The magic is similar to the stone circles even when left unmarked. Our circle castings are actually an attempt to recreate these natural power nodes in our meeting places. All of these are places where we can more easily commune with our souls and our deities to create change. When we are there, magic is in the air!

How then do we construct a circle? We can use a number of methods to cast the circle, but in each case the priestess/priest/facilitator visualizes the circle as glowing energy, perhaps of white-blue-violet light starting as a thin line and expanding to a sphere which encloses the group. The celebrants can join that visualization. Whether people experience circle casting as an exercise of the imagination or a psychic vision makes no difference. Some will feel the circle energy or hear it instead of seeing it in the mind's eye. In all cases, the group mind strengthens the working. People who have helped construct the circle and can sense the circle, will not forget it is there and crash through the edges without opening and closing passages. Even if we think we are creating the visualization out of our imagination, magic is present. Strong circle casting helps minimize interruptions from outside. Telephones are less likely to ring, visitors less likely to drop by, and neighbors less likely to rev engines or run chainsaws outside. People are less likely to scatter energy by arriving late or trying to leave early.

Constructing strong circles is a learned skill. Practice. I ask my students who set about learning magic and ritual to try all of these methods at different times and test the strength of the energy field each method creates by pushing against the boundaries. For a circle to be truly inclusive, the leaders need to be sensitive to mobility limitations of people attending circle. Remember not to use dance when you have people joining you who are physically unable to dance.

How to Cast a Circle

Joining Hands

The facilitator (who may be priest, priestess or another celebrant) begins by reaching out with the left hand and taking the right hand of the next person on the left. S/he says, 'Hand over hand (heart) I cast the circle,' as s/he meets their gaze, sending love and peace. Be sure to encourage people to look one another in the eye. It increases the group mind and intention of the casting. If the group is using 'hand over heart,' the two of them raise their joined hands over the heart of the person the facilitator has spoken to. When the connection has been made between them, the second person turns to his or her left and repeats the process with the next one. The joining of hands proceeds around the circle back to the beginning. Everyone leaves their hands clasped and in place over the heart if that is the casting being used. When each person has been part of the casting and is knit into the circle, they look around at one another. The facilitator says, 'The circle is cast.' S/he will signal when to release hands. The circle is in place. All imagine the sphere of energy around, beneath and up over them.

Movement and Chant

When there is sufficient room, the group can walk the perimeter reciting a casting chant which gets progressively louder and more dramatic as they go. The group can hold hands and face inward, outward, or follow each other and act out the words:

> *Black spirits and White, Red spirits and Grey*
> *Come ye and come ye, come ye that may!*
> *Around and around, throughout and about,*
> *The good come in and the ill keep out!*
> From Renaissance literature

Alternatively, in a smaller space, the priest or priestess can circle the coveners outside the circle with the broom or staff on the ground. The one casting the circle makes the ring three times in silence, while the group breathes together and grounds silently, or chants, *'The circle is cast.'*

When the room is too crowded to walk around the outside, the priestess or priest can pass a sacred implement such as the staff above the heads of the coveners from inside of the circle. One or three passes is traditional. If using three passes, the circle caster may ring the circle with a magical implement at the feet, at the heart and above the heads. The broom or staff is then laid before the altar. If a sword or sacred knife (athame) is used to cast the circle, it does not touch the ground at all. Steel in the earth is said to be an affront to the world of Faery. Not a good idea. Steel implements can be worn or laid on the altar, or placed in an insulating scabbard or wrapped after their use before they touch the ground.

Adding the Elementals to the Casting

People who volunteer to call the quarters can first walk the perimeter, sprinkling the elements on the ground around the circle: earth, salt or cornmeal for the north; burning incense fanned with feathers for the east or a chime struck repeatedly in time with the steps for the east; a torch or burning candle for the south; water in a shell flicked with the fingers for the west. Indoor circles are cast with sprinkled salt water so the earth or salt crystals do not make such a mess to clean up. There is no crime in being practical with magic.

The ones calling the quarters can stand in place holding something which represents the sacred nature of the quarter while the coven circles the perimeter. Individuals stop at each quarter to receive a blessing or ask a boon from the Elementals through the Witches calling the quarters. North might hold a crystal or a rock. East might shake a rattle or offer a burning bowl of sage or incense herbs. South likely would hold a lighted red candle. West would offer a dark bowl or cauldron of water which reflects up at one looking into it.

Movement and Smudging

The priest walks the circle, inside or out, fanning smoke from burning sage around the perimeter of the circle. The priestess follows him with burning sweet grass. The sage balances the energies of the circle, transforming chaos into beauty. The sweet grass amplifies order and beauty to prepare the circle for the ritual. These substances are typically used by Native Americans in creating sacred space. Because the Web is a North American circle, we honor the plant spirits of our land and incorporate them into our rituals. This use is one of the ways we embrace shamanic workings in Web Wiccan Consciousness. If sage is not part of the circle casting, the celebrants are smudged before they enter the circle as part of our preparations. Where sage and sweet grass are not indigenous plants, circles use other aromatic herbs that are. Selection of these continues the properties of balancing and amplification.

Candle and Flame

The priestess lights the work candle in the center of the altar and raises it in offering to the Gods and Elementals. She then passes the candle clockwise from her right hand to left saying, 'From right to left I cast this circle with light.' The person next to her takes the candle in the right hand and repeats the chant, handing it to the person on the left with the left hand. When the candle returns to the priestess, she states, 'The circle is cast' and places the candle back on the altar to focus attention on the work of the ritual. Because Web circles include children as participants, we have used a lantern lighted with a battery candle so the little ones can help cast the circle. In the southern hemisphere she would pass the candle counter-clockwise from left to right hand saying so as she does it. The person on her right would receive the candle in the left hand and pass it to the right.

The Significance of Ritual Sequence

Smudging, grounding and then casting the circle are triggers for the unconscious to awaken and participate in the ritual. Because we use these steps in ritual every time we meet, they become markers for us who seek to enter a transcendent experience. These triggers both shift the consciousness and stabilize the ego so it does not panic when it is set aside for the hour or so of ritual. The soul then is more able to access psychic insights and merger with the Gods. All of higher magic begins with grounding and the creation of sacred space.

Casting a circle and participating in the group mind requires skill in meditation and shifting levels of consciousness. Some people struggle with that shift in consciousness. To help people step out of ordinary reality and experience direct access to the spiritual vision of perfect love and perfect trust, I use a simple visualization of the psychic grid. This meditation begins a life journey which keeps unfolding. I encourage readers to participate in the practices described in this book. Note that grounding and creating sacred space begin the process. You can read this aloud to yourself as you follow the instructions. You may have someone else read it slowly, pausing at intervals for you to follow the instructions. You may choose to record yourself reading the meditation with appropriate pauses. You may reread it until you know the meditations well enough to direct yourself silently within your own mind.

The Grid Meditation

Calm and center yourself. Breathe deeply and follow the breath to your core. Let the peace of the breath fill your body. Send the breath down your spine to grow roots that strike deep into the earth. Let the tap root attach to the bedrock. Let the lateral roots strike out beneath the soil in every direction around you forming a complete circle of stability. Draw in the earth energy from the tap root and the lateral roots. Fill your body with the earth energy. Let it spout out of your head like a fountain and fall back to the earth to rejoin itself in your roots. Feel the earth energy come up, out, over and back into you in an endless cycle.

Then draw the celestial energies down from the heavens into the body, filling your body, soul and mind with the energy of the Sky Beings. Ground that energy all the way through you and into the earth as a gift to the Earth Mother. Feel the joining of those energies beneath you.

At the end of your lateral roots, out at the drip line created by your leaves and branches, see a beautiful line of energy circle you, creating safe and separate space around you for your working. Let the circle arch up and over you, down and under you, creating a physical place of sacred energy on the earth. Sit in the middle and sense its strength and security.

When you are ready, close your eyes and visualize a grid or web of intersecting lines that exist outside our physical world. These lines all connect at your feet in a psychic circle. This circle reaches out across the universe into infinity. For this moment, nothing exists but you and these lines. Let one line glow with the energy of your ordinary life so that you can literally see your path stretch out before you as a single line of color. Notice the color. Notice how your path intersects other paths at regular intervals like a net. Simply observe this image. Know that the line leads you back to your circle on the earth plane. You will always be able to find it.

Now walk out on the grid following that glowing line of your earth path to get the feel of moving across a dimension. Be at home and comfortable. This is your ordinary walk. You belong here. Remember your breath, your grounding, your circle. When you feel comfortable with this experience, turn around and go back to your starting point. Venture back down your glowing path until you know your way. Be sure to make note of other images, colors, sounds or sensations you experience, and tell yourself you will remember them.

Now go back to the starting point and consciously step on the line one place to the right of your ordinary path. Look ahead and see the same kind of intersections with other paths that you saw before, but in different places. Notice the color is slightly or perhaps dramatically different. Without moving, glance back at your ordinary every day path and see how close it is at the beginning under your feet and how it diverges more and more the farther you go along its line. Remain on the path one place to the right and observe. Remember.

When you are ready, walk along this new path a few paces to get the feel of a new way. See how it is the same and yet different. Get comfortable and at home here too. Notice the color, temperature, sounds if any. Move up and down this line as far as you like, returning to the start of the line where you stood before, when you are ready.

Now consciously step aside two more paces to the right and stand on a third path four paces away from your ordinary reality. Notice the color, feel and intersections as you did before. Breathe and know you are secure. Move out along the grid and see how far you can go with comfort. Return to the starting place and move back out along the path several times to increase your comfort and range. Note any other images, sounds or contacts made as you walk along.

When you are done, return to the beginning of this path and go back to the place you began four paces to the left. You will remember it by the glowing color of your everyday life. Stop and recall what you have seen or felt. Breathe deeply.

Now move three paces to the left of that everyday path. The colors change again. Notice them and their intersections with other paths. They all stretch out into infinity from a single point. Move out into the grid on this path, as far as you can go with comfort. Turn around. Can you see the beginning point? Does it matter? Don't panic. You can will yourself back to your center starting point whenever you want to.

Return to the center path and feel the energy of it. Then turn around, observe the different colors or sounds of the other paths on the grid. Pick one very different than your ordinary path and explore that one as far as you dare. Understand you are moving through levels of awareness, and that these levels connect to each other. Observe everything. How far out do you go before the path feels truly different? At what point do you feel discomfort? Why is that? Can you go out farther?

Now return to your center and turn back to the path which is ordinary reality. You will remember it by its color and feel. Connect firmly with that path. Walk back and forth on it, remembering who you are. When you are centered in yourself, come back to your consciousness in your own physical circle at home. Open your physical eyes and see where you are, that it is familiar—a place where you belong. Be aware that you belong every place you walked in your visualization.

When you are ready, release your grounding. Return the power of the celestials up from the earth, keeping what you need and sending the rest back to the sky. Slow the earth energy coursing through you until the fountain falls back through your head. Let it sink slowly down your body keeping what you need at every level until the excess is collected beneath your body in your roots. Send the excess energy down your roots to the bedrock and out of your lateral roots into the soil. Place your hands on the ground and complete this release of excess energies. When you feel balanced top to bottom, side to side, back to front, thank Gaia for her power. Withdraw your roots back to your body, the tap root from the bedrock and the laterals just beneath the soil from the drip line. Draw them back into your body. Then focus on the glowing sphere of energy around you. Fold it back on itself until it is a single line of blue light ringing you a few feet away. Dim the blue light and erase it a piece at a time. Start in front of you and move your focus widdershins (counterclockwise). Turn the blue light back on itself until it is a single point of light shining in front of you. Clap your hands sharply. With that sound, the light is gone.

Journaling on the Psychic Grid

Think about this experience and make any observations you wish in your BOS. You may wish to return to the psychic grid many times, exploring different lines until you understand the experience with your body/mind/soul.

Daily Practice

I encourage everyone to ground each morning when getting ready for the day. Shower time, giving thanks for breakfast, looking out the window to check the weather, any simple routine can include a grounding exercise. Frequent practice makes for a quick grounding. Then I encourage everyone to draw that earth and celestial energy around the body as a shield before leaving the house. I believe the universe is a safe place. I also believe that there are difficult ways to go through life and easier ways. Shielding tips the balance in favor of the easier ones.

A Martial Arts Story

A friend of mine studied martial arts when he was young. He admits to being something of a smart aleck as a teenager. When the sensei attempted to teach the class to walk in balance as a way to avoid trouble on the path of the wise, my friend irreverently asked if, in a drive-by shooting, he would then be able to catch a bullet in his teeth. The Master looked at him patiently and responded. 'No, you will not be able to catch a bullet in your teeth. But when the bullet is fired, you will not be on that corner.'

Daily grounding, centering and shielding protect us from the corners where the worst things happen. Our lives are not free of care or pain, but we are secure and protected. For that reason I say, these are the most important things I have to teach. There is no need to be on the corner.

Chapter 6

Confined to Quarters

I think of the quartered circle every time I cut a pizza. One line runs vertically across the pie through the center. The other runs horizontally. I even put a piece of pepperoni in the middle and try to cut it evenly. I then turn the pizza 45º and cut a second equal-armed cross so I have eight equal pieces. Well, in theory they are equal. Somehow my pizza slices are larger than those for the other people at the table, unless they notice.

Woden's Sun Cross

A circle divided into quarters actually combines the energy of Ouroboros with that of the equal armed cross and creates a powerful joining of male and female energies. This symbol as the Sun Cross or Woden's Cross represents the compass points in a circle. The celestial energy of the sun is embraced by the four winds of the horizon. Two of the cardinal directions hold female energy (creative, intuitive, heart centered) and two hold male energy (inventive, intellectual, mind centered). Those dichotomies exist in each soul, not in separate genders. The circle unites them in our male and female selves.

In Jungian terms they stem from our anima and animus within the human personality. Inside the circle we are reunited with our same sex and opposite sex self in order to be complete. We are both creative and inventive, intuitive and intellectual, heart centered and head centered. We indeed can and do have it all.

Drawing and Finding North

To fasten this concept of gender unity in our minds, I ask students to sit facing north and draw a Woden's Sun Cross on a separate page in their BOS. We select magnetic north using a compass. Magnetic north is on the move at about 35 miles a year. In the beginning of the

20th century it was in Arctic Canada. At the beginning of the 21st century it was in the Arctic Ocean moving across the sea toward Russia. Magnetic north is shaped by the earth's core and marked where the lines of magnetism dip into the earth (the dip point). People rarely guess correctly when asked to identify magnetic north.

Alternatively students may go to a north window or outside to find the North Star. The earth axis points at that celestial. We sit facing that star, whether or not we can see it from our work space. This is likely as close as we can get in identifying true geographic north. Even that is imprecise given the earth's wobble on its axis. The North Star changes over a cycle of about 26,000 years according to the precession of the equinoxes. Efforts to establish true north are hampered by its situation in the ocean rather than on land. Measurement from the nearest land about 400 miles away is not as precise as we pretend it is, because even the land masses shift on earth. So I encourage students to create their own north reality. They are present with north by intention.

In drawing the sun circle we again have choices. We can work free hand in a meditative state as we did with the enso. The brush stroke will be different than before as we inscribe the circle. It always is. Those differences are meaningful. We notice and honor them. Then we divide the circle in half with a vertical line and in quarters with a horizontal line that cross at the center point. If students wish a different mathematical experience, they use a compass and draw a geometric circle. Using a ruler they make the arms exact and straight. A third possibility exists in tracing a round object of the size needed. We then employ a stenciled cross or a protractor to draw the axis. These are three different experiences, all of them valid. As a reader, select the one that fits you, or draw all three in your BOS and sense the differences.

Next we label the four directions placing north at the top of the page. We set the other cardinal points at the tips of the cross. Then I instruct students to add what else they know about the directions. West and north are seen as feminine; east and south as masculine.

There are connections with the magician's tools. There are traditional colors: green for earth and north; yellow for air and east; red for fire and south; blue for water and west. There are also variations of those colors in different traditions. I ask students to find the meaning of each direction in a color that is significant to them whether or not it is the traditional color. I also ask them to include a symbol of themselves in the middle of the circle, selecting something that is meaningful to represent their individuality.

For example, on a personal altar I use deep purple for the north because it is the color of the shadows at midnight on the snow. I use mauve which I call skybluepink in the east because that is the color of a muted dawn. I use red, yellow or orange for south because the fire is all of those. I use jade green for the west because it is the color of Otisco Lake where my aunt and uncle had a camp. How I came to these is a story I will tell with a poem later.

Most of us enter Wicca out of balance. We let heart rule head or *vice versa*. We claim we are not creative. We rely on our feelings without engaging our rational judgment. In cutting ourselves off from parts of our whole persona, we participate in life without all our skills. Perhaps when the priestess leads us in grounding, we find connecting with the stable earth difficult. When she draws down celestial energies, we may wall them off because they seem uncomfortably super-charged. Where we set our limits depends on who we think we are. Our gender identity as male or female can preprogram us into some sex-based characteristics that only partly suit us. Entering into the balanced quartered circle challenges those assumptions about who we are and what we can do. We all have the healthy potential to balance grounding and magic, wisdom and emotions in our physical body. Our entire life is a balance of many elements living in harmony when we allow this to be so.

For example, my partner Merlin is a tall, broad shouldered, powerful male with skill in mechanics, carpentry, agriculture, electrical and plumbing repair—a general Jack of All Trades. He also wears his hair long, favors Hawaiian lava-lavas instead of jeans and does not fear the color pink. His chosen field after college was early childhood education. He was the director of a Head Start program for pre-school children. He loves teaching children how to do things with a patience and respect I wish I could emulate. In adult classes, Merlin works behind the scenes with individuals during breaks and meal times. I frequently say he has more mother-nurturing in him than I do. That balance between the masculine and feminine is born out by psychological testing in which he lands securely in the middle of the scale.

I on the other hand, am a short round motherly looking woman with skill in cooking, decorating, design and communication—a typical homemaker for all appearances. I do not, however, spend my time in the kitchen nor in fussing about the house. My chosen field in college was literature, history and language arts. I prefer children when they are teenagers, old enough to think and reason in the abstract. As a community organizer I gathered like-minded people and challenged the police and mental health professionals in their old biases. I was a leader in the startup of two crisis intervention programs for survivors of sexual assault and domestic violence. I like to shake things up. I am a public speaker, planner and head teacher.

We both combine our anima and animus to reach across gender stereotypes to explore careers uncommon for men and women in the past. I like being in touch with my dominant assertive Aries sun sign. Merlin prefers to work in the background, one on one within the comfort zone of his Cancer ascendant. Our personalities, like everyone else, are a mix and match of traditional male and female characteristics. We have no obligation to suppress skills and interests because of our biology.

Exploring the quartered circle as an expression of our whole persona is an act of magic. What parts of the traditional correspondences attached to the north, east, south and west fit you? Which ones do not? We humans are fascinating combinations of light and dark, male and female, known and unknown. Exploring the quarters of the circle opens us to our many selves in surprising ways. First, of course, we must know what the quarters represent. We begin with the male and female correspondences. Water and earth are feminine; air and fire are masculine. We have them all.

In discussing trance states, Starhawk points out that our perceptions fit into our frame of reference. We see visions in the context of our familiar world. Our symbols in meditation extend beyond the known according to our ability to stretch so we may see smells or hear texture. She explains that our meeting with guides in meditation may be aspects of the self or entities from the 'other'. The source of these visions are many but, as she points out, 'a Witch might call them the two linked motes of consciousness with the Deep Self, and "see" them in female and male human forms that glow blue.'[23] Subsequently Starhawk concluded that any discussion of gender was unhelpful since maleness and femaleness overlap and must include transgendered variations. Men and women still work in bodies that are perceived as one or the other for the most part. I find gender helpful in exploring identity, even when it is limiting. The limitations we accept or even defend are informative about who we think we are.

Inner Work: Meeting Your Other Selves

Meditation introduces us to our inner selves, both the male and female. These selves are Jung's animal and animas. I have shaped these meditation for Web Wicca classes because they are a deep healing practice. You will need a hand mirror to gaze into your own eyes. The meditations can be entered within a full ritual or as a separate meditation. Cast a circle and work before your altar to help ground the work. Connect with the earth and the celestials.

Meditation with Your Same Sex Self

> Begin to seek your same sex self by gazing in a mirror, eyes locked with your reflection. Let your gaze soften. Open to yourself and merge with the image you see, even if you have

thoughts that wonder how you came to look like this. Still them and focus on your eyes.

Sense a doorway opening in the mirror. Match your size to the doorway by enlarging it. Then pass on through, moving toward your own image and into your eyes until you stand on the other side of the mirror's door. Your physical eyes close as the mirror door opens and you enter the other side of the mirror. The figure of a person approaches as if from the back of a room. Watch them walk. Observe. This is your same sex self who has known you all your life. Now s/he wishes to be known and speak with you. As s/he comes closer, notice how different his/her appearance is different than yours on the earth plane. Note those differences without judgment so you will remember them. Let this introduction expand who you think you are. Be aware of any elemental colors, symbols or designs which are connected to this self.

Greet each other. Share names and information with each other. Embrace. Offer gifts from your pocket and receive something in return. This gifting is spontaneous and significant. What you offer and receive means something. Make a date to meet later. Make plans to share things together you enjoy, like movies or food or long walks in nature. You may meet in meditation through the mirror or in other ways as often as you like. When you are finished, take your leave. Your alternate self turns and leaves the way s/he entered. You return to the mirror and find the door. Take a deep breath and walk through it. Shrink the doorway down and let it disappear. Open your eyes and gaze at your reflection. Breathe. Center. Ground.

Journaling on the Same Sex Self

Write about your experience in your BOS. Sketch your same sex self or find a picture that looks similar in coloring and clothing. Paste that in your BOS. Note any information you learned about the elements. Think about what this means and sit with the new wisdom for a time before you enter the next meditation.

Meditation with Your Opposite Sex Self

For some people in western culture, where male and female are divisions we experience as opposites in a dual universe, the idea of becoming the other gender is disturbing. Men often feel their own sexual identity is threatened when they are encouraged to go within and find their inner female. Women reject inner masculine identities because of their feminist strength and abhorrence of machismo, or because of their overly feminine identification with the 'I enjoy being a girl' crowd. Transgendered and intersexed people find the experience of seeking the opposite sex self a double blind test of, 'Who am I really?' which is either great fun or very uncomfortable.

Wicca challenges us to confront our hesitancies and walk into the unknown in the belief that the universe is a safe place. We are stronger for knowing that we are both male and female in our manifestations. We are wiser for knowing that in the Great Spirit, we are all one. The sexual divisions are both real and illusion—just as time and space are both real and illusionary.

Stop and think about that. Some have suggested that in Atlantis we were fully intersexed (having both male and female genitalia) and that part of their technological hubris separated the people into two lonely genders which we have been trying to correct ever since.

> To contact your opposite sex self, enter a meditative state by gazing in the mirror. Allow the doorway to appear and expand. Pass through it as you did before. Call your other sex self to you. S/he approaches from the back, allowing you to observe how different s/he walks and carries him/herself. Again, this one has known you all your life. Greet one another and converse, exchanging names, as you did in the same sex meditation. Embrace. Listen. Ask questions and answer some. Be aware of any elemental colors, symbols or designs which are connected to this self. Find understanding between you. Then exchange gifts. The nature of those gifts is symbolically significant.
>
> Remember all of this for your Book of Shadows. Think about

it deeply and see how these two inner selves, the male and the female, help you understand who you are. Make a date to meet later. Make plans to share things together you enjoy, like movies or food or long walks in nature. You may meet in meditation through the mirror or in other ways as often as you like. When you are finished, take your leave. Your alternate self turns and leaves the way s/he entered. You return to the mirror and find the door. Take a deep breath and walk through it. Shrink the doorway down and let it disappear. Open your eyes and gaze at your reflection. Breathe. Center. Ground.

Journaling on Your Opposite Sex Self

Write about your experience in your BOS. Sketch your opposite sex self or find a picture that looks similar in coloring and clothing. Paste that in your BOS. Note any Elemental information you learned. Know that the names and identities given at first may grow and develop over time as you learn more about yourself. The selves behind the mirror also change and reveal more about themselves as you are able to understand their inner workings. Think about the four questions you were asked when you began this journey. How did this experience help you answer them? This introduction to other aspects of you is part of your growing understanding of who you really are.

When we examine our selves within the quartered circle we see strength in some areas and challenges in others. Our alternate selves who came to us on the other side of the mirror may reveal we are very grounded or perhaps unstable. We may easily see through illusions and have visions. Perhaps we are head blind and handle abstract ideas clumsily. We may have fiery energy and enjoy action and decisiveness. Perhaps we are lethargic and having a hard time making choices. We may be introspective and full of love. We may be cut off from our feelings and lonely. Our other selves share those characteristics with us, or reflect the opposite ones, as if they hold our strengths and weaknesses for us until we can hold them in our physical bodies. Building a friendship with our other selves reunites us around the circle into one.

The Compass Points

The four compass points of north, east, south and west have standard Elemental correspondences in Wicca. These directions also have relationships with certain deities. There are many deities to meet, but I ask my students to start with one for each direction.

North represents the earth in the northern hemisphere. North holds feminine energy which nurtures and protects us. The earth is the Mother or Gaia. Earth forms us and creates our bodies. This is the physical reality of being human. Mother Gaia holds her children.

East represents air. Think of the dawn breeze which freshens the day, though the prevailing wind may not be from the east. Air is the swift God Mercury/Hermes/Thoth, God of Knowledge and the Mind. He carries the caduceus as we have seen, a phallic blade or wand, so the east holds male energy which is intellectual and wise. This is the intellectual reality of being human. Mercury communicates knowledge.

South represents fire. Think of the heat of the equator or the high noon sun directly overhead at midday. Fire is found in the forge of Vulcan/Hephaestus which is that creative inventive quality I name magic. This is the human will and source of our invention and creativity. Vulcan is the sacred smith who helps us forge our lives.

West represents water. The seas wash in tides of emotion through our salty blood and are pulled by the moon. Water is the Goddess of Love and Passion, Aphrodite/Venus born of the sea on a clamshell, so water holds feminine energy. This is the human heart, our love, our passion and all our other emotional responses of mad, sad, glad and scared. Aphrodite/Venus helps us open our hearts as her birth opened the clamshell.

Journaling on Your Sun Circle

In your BOS, add this information to your sun circle in as much detail as makes sense to you. Certainly use different deities if you have made previous connections among them and the elements. Look up the stories of those I use if they are unknown to you. Adding key words from the same and opposite sex meditations to the masculine and feminine areas of your sun circle further personalizes the diagram. Your notations there are quick memory aids as we continue exploring the quartered circle and our identity.

Variations with the Correspondences

I generally recommend sticking with the common associations of the elements and cardinal directions. One of my students asked if alternative interpretations might make better sense based on local geography. They might. Directly north of our home is Lake Ontario, a very large inland freshwater sea. The nearest ocean is to the east. There are mountains to our east and south. The prevailing wind is from the west. We could scramble the traditional meanings, but would it help us ground and discover who we really are? Does it help make sense of the quartered circle? Does it join us with other Pagans who share similar paths? I think it confuses the issues. In our rush to be individual we lose the sense of connection with others who celebrate the quartered circle. There are plenty of opportunities to interact with the spirits of the land where we live without trying to literally re-create the magical wheel for local reasons.

Variety does exist. Some traditions reverse air and fire. Those directions still hold masculine energy but the air/blade then corresponds to the south and fire/wand corresponds to the east. For me that is unsettling. I have to work harder to connect with the cardinal points in that framework. Another variation is found in The Goddess Temple in Glastonbury UK. They rotate the directions one click so north is air; east is fire; south is water; and west is earth.[24] I have a representation of their Wheel of the Year on one of my altars and maintain it in accordance with their vision, but I still need to look at it to keep it straight in my mind. I call the quarters according to the traditional connections.

In the southern hemisphere, some reversals make sense. The equator is in the north. The ice crystals of winter are in the south. Summer feels northern. Winter feels southern. The sabbats follow the sun, not a global calendar printed on paper. Christmas is December 25th because the calendar says so. Winter solstice is in June because the sun says so. Becoming aware of the energy of the sun in each season will shed light on our identity as well as that of the sun and its festivals. When we are so immersed in the power of the circle that we can feel the wheel turn, we know there is no other choice than for Yule to follow the sun. Understanding that then allows for the hemisphere variations as we look into the quartered circle.

Ancient Roots

Each of the four cardinal directions is, as we said, associated with one of the four elements: earth, air, fire and water. In Wicca they are personified to stand as Elemental Beings in their quarter of the circle. Their role is of trickster, Guardian, magician, wise one or all of these titles at once. Other Pagan traditions may see the Elementals standing in different places, but nearly all of them experience these as the four Elemental Energies. (The Chinese shamanic tradition is an exception, recognizing five elements.) From ancient Sumeria through the 17th century CE, people of western culture understood all of life and matter was made up of earth, air, fire and water.

After the 17th century the scientific world birthed chemistry out of alchemy and the periodic table of elements, currently 1 (Hydrogen) to 118 (Ununoctium), out of the four humors. More discoveries at the far end extend the scientific chart of elements. The precision of modern chemistry does not negate the value of our alchemical past. We still change with the seasons and dance with the four Elementals. We also understand we drink liquid water made of two gases combined in a two to one proportion as H_2O. Clear thinking does not exclude either science or magic. It combines them.

In exploring the quartered circle, we return to ancestral wisdom that pre-dates the Christian associations with the cross. There are many significant examples in Bronze Age carvings such as those in Bornholm, Denmark (around 2000 BCE).[25] Clay examples of the solar cross were excavated in Troy dating back to 1500 BCE. Some identify the sun cross as one of the earliest symbols used for spiritual purposes since it appears cross-culturally in Asia, Europe, the Americas and Australia.[26] It is associated with the world tree (*axis mundi*) connecting the upperworld, the earth and the underworld.

Nicholas Mann points out that the Avebury Stone Circle complex created a quartered circle which represents the Milky Way bisected twice by the four causeways.[27] Mann sees multiple crosses throughout the complex which follow the seasons, the phases of the moon, and the connections between the northern and southern constellations associated with the cross.

Marija Gimbutas identifies the quartered circle with the cosmic egg and snake of creation.[28] Elsewhere Gimbutas also identifies the encircled cross connecting the cardinal points and agriculture. The circle represents the earth's journey through the seasons and with the cross represents the cycle of life for humans, animals, and vegetation. The cross in hieroglyphics represents the symbol of continuing health and happiness.[29] Seeing the sun cross as a fertility symbol and experiencing it as the union of our own masculine and feminine qualities opens us to deeper self-knowledge. From there we can experience greater creativity in the arts, in spiritual practices and our relationships.

Chapter 7

Elemental Encounters

In the previous chapter we saw that each of the four elements can be associated with Elemental Beings and with various deities. The correspondences associated with a direction and element keep spinning out until students are very confused. For that reason, we proceed slowly to delve into the significance and personal connection with the four quarters.

Each Elemental realm is populated by its nature spirits which are similar but different from others of the same element. A water spirit, for example, may be associated with a particular lake. Another may inhabit a waterfall. There are troupes of the Fey air spirits and each has its leader. Although all rocks are one rock, the Elementals associated with each will resonate differently. Granite is different than lava, than pure quartz, than sedimentary lake rocks. Given their differences, it is wise to know Elemental spirits can provide stability or trickery, depending on their propensity and our need.

Beyond the Elemental spirits there are four Elementals named in traditional ceremonial magic and alchemy: Gob, Paralda, Djinn and Necksa. As we enter into the realms of the Elementals, we will seek out a spirit who will self-identify with the rocks, air, fire and water. Since a visitor to a new country rarely approaches the leader, we will politely ask for guides willing to answer our questions. The Elemental Rulers are rarely those who appear in our initial visits. Be patient with that, even if you have worked with the Elementals for years. We are going to meet them with wisdom and both eyes wide open. Students experience these encounters as literal meetings or visionary insights. Our perception of the Elementals as real or imaginary is one of our many projections. Either view brings us instruction in the other worlds.

The North

In the north where we expect to find the spirits of the earth, we discover the Gnomes or Goblins and their King Gob. Gnomes are small humanoids sometimes referred to as Dwarves in fairy tales and video games. They are engaged in subterranean mining, protecting crystals and guarding crystalline secrets. They are everywhere, generally suspicious of humans and likely to take offense at our assumptions of superiority. I have heard their attitude is well-rooted in experience with human treachery and greed, though I cannot say for sure.

Stories and Myths

In Barbara Donley's retelling of Arianrhod's portion of the Mabinogion,[30] we find a full account of the Goddess Arianrhod and her mentor Bronisen who loved the Dwarf Ebolas.

> It seems that in her youth Bronisen met a charmed young man named Ebolas and fell deeply in love. After much fretting, Ebolas confessed he was, in fact, a bewitched Dwarf. He could not return to the underworld until he gathered three things: birds that could live beneath the ground and sing, the light from the sun, and the respect of humankind. Bronisen agreed to help him gather his treasures in return for marriage, to which he readily agreed.
>
> All was well between the happy couple for a year and a day, but at the end of that enchanted time, Ebolas started to look peaked. He no longer thrived on the air and light of the earth's surface. He asked Bronisen to find his treasures so he could return to his home else he would die. So great was her love of him she readily agreed, even though it meant she would lose him to the underworld.
>
> Bronisen knew the ravens well, so the first treasure was simply arranged. She could direct certain ravens to live beneath the earth, at least part of the time. She had an idea for the

sunlight. If she froze a river so solid it would never thaw but rather cling to the earth as a great glacier, then the Dwarves could dig out the roof of a cave and enjoy the brilliance of the sun as if through a giant window. Bronisen had magic of her own and knew she could do those things.

But to restore the entire race of Dwarves to respectability? There had been a war with humankind. The Dwarves had lost it, as much through their own trickery as through the mortals' military might. Bronisen shook her head. This task was much more difficult. Enemies are enemies. Both Dwarves and mortals carried grudges. Bronisen stayed up all night considering the problem but found no solution.

In the morning she consulted with her husband. Ebolas was thrilled by the ravens. He was sure the window on the world would bring them light and joy beneath the earth. And he had an idea. He told Bronisen he would give her precious stones from his homeland, each with their own magic. She must use them to create understanding between the mortals and the Dwarves. Bronisen nodded thoughtfully. With such fine stones she was certain she would find a spell to make it so, even if it took her all her life.

Together she and Ebolas rode to the cave entrance to the underworld. Ebolas went on alone to find the stones. Bronisen waited because she could not enter the realm of Dwarves. Ebolas, helped along by the ravens, went home with his treasures. His people were pleased. A window to the sun and the graceful ravens were exactly what they wanted. They agreed the magic Bronisen applied to her tasks could win them stature in the mortal world. They offered rubies, emeralds, topaz and pink tourmaline for Bronisen's magic. After three days, Ebolas emerged from the underworld and rejoined his lady love at the cave's mouth to bestow the gemstones on her. She saw him as he was, no longer spelled as a handsome mortal man. Ebolas was short and ill-proportioned with large hands and feet. His ears stuck out and his nose was red, possibly from three nights of celebration with his family beneath the ground. Bronisen did not care. She saw him with her heart as she always did, through the eyes of love. With tender tears, they parted for a year and a day, when she would return with her magic spell.

After careful consideration, Bronisen spoke with her Lady Arianrhod. Together they made a magic plan to weave a golden veil. The veil would bring healing. The women meant the veil to create a compassionate forgetfulness so that Men and Dwarves might once again have harmony between them, though they were unsure how that might actually work.

In one corner of the veil they planned to weave the emeralds to bring wisdom to those who saw the veil. The emeralds would promote peace of mind with the veil's touch. The hearts of mortals influenced by the veil would work toward the Dwarves' best potential good. And the Dwarves would do the same for mortals when they held the veil.

In another corner of the veil they intended to weave the rubies. Those who saw the veil would feel great love toward everyone. Those who had the joy of holding the veil would become vital and healthy mortals and Dwarves. They would extend compassion to all the beings of the earth and under it.

In the third corner the women would sew the brown topaz. Those who saw the veil would feel calm and happy because of the topaz. If they held it they would be healed of old grudges and affronts. The agitation from ancient wars and tales of battles would dissolve. The expectation of betrayal and trickery would vanish.

In the fourth corner they would place pink tourmaline. Being in the presence of the veil banished evil thoughts. Holding it restored their dreams and brought them peaceful sleep. Nightmares filled with violence and death would cease. Imagined dangers and threats of war would fade as groundless fear. Taken together the power of the gems could change both

Dwarves and mortals. But how would Dwarves and mortals come to hold the veil or even see it? Exactly how the women would present the veil was still unknown, but they were confident they would come up with something.

Arianrhod spun the golden thread. Bronisen wove the sacred veil and attached the rubies and the tourmaline. But as the end of the year approached, she grew sad. If she gave the finished veil to Ebolas, he might not come to see her ever again. Bronisen balked. Unbeknownst to anyone, she took the veil with her to the cave but on the way she unraveled two thirds of it. She laid it out on the ground with the tourmaline and rubies woven into two corners. She begged for another year to finish it. Ebolas was so pleased he readily agreed. The tourmaline and rubies worked their magic and his love for his mortal wife increased. They spent the night together, Dwarf and Human. They fell beneath the spell of gemstones, happy and content in love.

When Arianrhod saw the veil unfinished, smaller than it had been when her mentor left, Arianrhod laughed.

'What trickery is this?' she thought, but kept her own counsel.

And so it went. Year in year out, the veil was nearly finished. Then it was undone so Ebolas and his lady love could tryst before the cave enjoying love and passion. But after seven years, there was no help for it. The veil was finished. All had seen it and admired the fine stitching and the jewels. The veil hummed with love and power. What could Bronisen do but give it over?

Then before the day of Bronisen's last meeting with Ebolas, Arianrhod had a need. She had denied her son Lugh a wife, but he was young and virile and pined away for love. King Math and her brother Gwydion fashioned a flower maiden to wed Lugh, but she remained a lovely work of art, no human woman. The men could not give her life, no matter the spells they worked. Lugh pined for the flower maiden and brought the sun to shadow in his grief.

Arianrhod loved Lugh, despite the trouble she had given him.

She saw a way to help both her son and the Dwarves. The veil was exactly the talisman to use. Setting off with the veil she transported herself magically to the king's court. She summoned Ebolas and Bronisen, so all could see the wonders worked by the Dwarves' veil. When all had assembled, with pomp and fanfare Arianrhod waved the veil about. She showed it to each man and dwarf, inviting them to feel the fine stitching. When all were suitably impressed, she instructed her son to cast the veil across the flower maiden's body, holding the pink tourmaline in his hand for love.

The young man did as he was told for once, and to his joy the lovely girl began to stir. Her greenish hue turned to glowing skin, translucent as lilies and snowdrops. Vines transformed to earth brown tresses. Her red lips smiled. She opened her eyes and saw her blond courtier loving her through the golden veil. It was love at first sight.

'Arise Blodeuwedd,' called Bronisen and Ebolas, which of course she did.

Arianrhod made it known that this miracle was the making of her mentor and the Dwarf. The King, his court and all concerned found joy, good thoughts and healing from the veil. The harmony between the races of mortal and Dwarf was restored. And the flower maiden lived happily with her prince, until she didn't. But that is a tale for another time and place.

Earth Elemental Meditation

Lay out the rocks you collected previously. Set them in a quartered circle, if you have enough. Otherwise a simple circle will do. Run your hands over them to identify which one offers to work with you in your earth Elemental meditation. You might feel a temperature change or a tingle when you pass over it. You might feel your hand drawn to a specific rock. Trust your instincts and pick it up. This meditation is a shamanic stone reading.

We enter into the stone's consciousness by grounding and stilling ourselves. Use the rock as a connection through which you send your roots down into the earth to touch the bedrock. Remember, 'All rocks are one rock.' Draw the rock energy into your body. Feel this merger. You will become heavier and stable. Your systems will slow as you connect your consciousness with that of the rock, which is much more deliberate than human awareness. Take as much time as you need to make this connection with the rock. Then select one surface of the rock and gaze at it.

Ask the rock: *What is rock? Who are the spirits of the earth?*

Wait. A symbol will appear in the rock surface. You will be surprised you didn't see it before. Gaze at it until you fully understand what it is. Remember the symbol. Turn the rock to another surface: the back or one of its sides.

Repeat your question. *What is rock? Who are the spirits of the earth?*

Another symbol will appear. Gaze at it again until you understand. Turn the rock to a third surface and seek a third symbol the same way. Then find a fourth. None of these symbols were evident in the rock when you started. They are not the result of the chinks or crannies or veins in the surface of the rock. They are communications from the Elemental earth spirits. Thank the rock. Ask if there is anything else it wishes to say. When the Elemental contact fades, offer the rock sacred water, oil, cornmeal or tobacco. It may have a preference. Then unless otherwise instructed return all the rocks to their basket.

Breathe deeply and remember your grounding. Open your eyes and return from the rock state of consciousness gradually. Stay still and write down the four symbols which appeared on the surfaces of the rock. Explain as much of their meaning as you received. Allow additional insights to surface as you write and include them. This is automatic writing of a sort. The earth Elementals may be giving you information that helps you understand them, so allow the process to unfold. You are simply remembering what you already knew. At least the part of you that is the stone already knew it.

Now ask how these four symbols fit together in learning about the nature of the earth. Make note of that in your BOS. Be grateful.

The East

In the east we have the Sylphs also known as faeries. The Sylphs in alchemy are led by King Paralda. Faeries are associated with Oberon and Queen Mab. However, there are many faery kings and queens. Sylphs can appear in the sky as clouds and tricks of light or angels. Faeries appear as small humanoids, made of light and nearly translucent. They are pictured with wings because they can levitate and move through the air with the wind, though if you see them they may not have wings at all. They are engaged in blessing the natural world of plants and the supernatural world of magic. They are everywhere. Additional faery kings and queens exist to lead the various troops of the Fey. Shakespeare's *Midsummer Night's Dream* is a common reference to the mischief faery magic can make when we become caught up in its jealousies and miscues. The faery Puck exclaims to Oberon, 'Lord, what fools these mortals be!'[31] I suspect that sums up the opinion of humans held by the Fey.

Stories and Myths

The Fey live in our house and are more reliable than legend would indicate, at least to those who behave honorably to them. We have a sunroom with lovely plants as big as small trees, tiny faery houses hanging among the plants, mirrors and rocks. The Fey seem to like it there. You can see the cats watching them fly across the room. My partner Merlin's particular patron is Queen Mab who made herself known to him in the woods in Wiltshire when he was young enough not to question the possibilities. She is present with us in the house. Her gift to him is protection and in some cases (I speak from experience) vengeance. If there is an argument involving Merlin, the end result is in his favor, right or wrong. Fortunately we have little to argue about, but when I dig my heels in because I know I am right, I am apt to trip over my shoelaces. Merlin swears it is not his doing, which I believe. She clearly spoils him and opposes those who would give her 'little boy' difficulty. He is careful in invoking her attention to his needs. He remembers quite clearly the lessons learned in Wiltshire.

During the London bombings of World War II Merlin's family moved from Greenford, Middlesex, to Calne, Wiltshire. They eventually found Cowage Cottage, a 16th century stone duplex in the woods on an estate where they could be safe together. Living a mile or more from the road, Merlin roamed the woods from the age of five or so. It was there he met Queenie, his not so imaginary friend. Because petrol was rationed and his mother did not drive, they walked three miles to town, a long distance for a five-year-old, even in a land where people often go by foot. In those days it was not uncommon for neighbors to offer a woman and child a safe ride if by chance they were going in the same direction.

One day Merlin and his mom were walking along the Calne Road when a shiny fast car whizzed by, taking little notice of them and offering no ride. Merlin scowled at the tail lights and said to himself, 'I hope he gets a flat tire!' They kept on walking. Down the road, around the curve they found the shiny car pulled to the side. Indeed the tire was flat. His eyes grew big and he felt shamed. Did he do that? He began to build his strong personal ethics right there on the road to Calne. Be careful what you wish for, especially if Queenie is your friend.

Air Elemental Meditation

To meet the spirits of the air, I use a moving meditation similar to the Buddhist *kinhin*. Kinhin means to walk with spiritual teachings. Slow or fast, the pace is deliberate and in tune with the principles under consideration. Sometimes after extended seated meditations, the individual walks to stretch the legs and regain circulation without disrupting the connection to higher consciousness. The eyes remain soft. The steps are taken in harmony with the inhaled and exhaled breath. The feet are placed deliberately in alignment and rocked from toe to ball to heel as they are set down, and peeled up from the floor from the heel to the ball to the toe. The movement is deliberate, so it is well to move slowly at first. The steps are small, only about six inches apart, heel to toe. The energy of the left foot should match the energy of the right foot in rhythm and spacing.

In kinhin, the walker moves in a circle or oval so no decision need be made about direction. The destination is inward. In Chapter 4, I referenced this practice in our discussion of the cursus in Britain near Stonehenge and in other locations when I suggested these were paths followed by the priests and priestesses as they communed with the spirits. It is in that context we begin the air meditation. You might want to practice kinhin walking and breathing in order to center yourself. When the practice feels comfortable, walk with the spiritual teachings of the air. If this method of walking is uncomfortable and distracting, then save that skill for another day and simply walk deliberately with intention for the air meditation. If you cannot walk for the meditation or live where it is not safe to walk in a trance, adapt this working. Sit in front of a window with the breeze blowing on you. Or postpone the working until you can enter a safe place in nature to meet the wind.

But if you can, go out into the wind and walk at a steady pace into the wind, then turn and walk away from the wind. You can choose a pattern to walk in so that you have no decisions to make about where to go. This frees you to chant.

Ask the wind: *'What is the wind? Who are the spirits of the air?'*

Over and over, repeat the chant. Listen carefully. The wind will speak in your inner ear just as the rock gave vision to your inner eyes. Pay attention, and let the thoughts flow without evaluation. Let them make sense of themselves, or not. When you feel the wind has finished, thank the air Elementals, and bring yourself back to ordinary consciousness. Make an offering by throwing cornmeal into the air, or lighting sweet grass or incense left outside to burn to ash.

If the Fey came to you clearly, you may wish to leave a dish of milk or food for them. Ask of their preference and they will tell you, but follow through as best you can. When you are finished communing with the Fey, breathe deeply and ground with your hands on the earth. Stretch. Walk differently. Go back inside, experiencing the door as a portal to ordinary reality. Take in your surroundings without speaking. Find your BOS and write down the wisdom of the air. Explain as much of your connection with the wind as you can. Allow additional insights to surface as you write and include them just as you did with the rock. Draw pictures if you are so inclined, or make a collage of air images.

Occasionally I take shamanic students to the lakeshore where it is always windy. There we can commune with all the Elementals without interruption. A group of us sat facing the wind coming in from the water and combined both the water and air meditations. When we were finished, off to our right a small cursus of seagull feathers stood up straight, blowing in the wind. Their quill tips secured them tightly in the stones. The pattern extended about five feet long. I was surprised because I had not heard anyone move across the stones to collect the feathers and stick them in between the cobblestones. The cobbles make a clear crunching sound as they push together underfoot.

I pointed to the formation and asked who had made it. No one had. They thought I had somehow distracted them while they were meditating and set it up myself. I had not. We were alone in the park along the shore. No one but the faeries could have made the cursus, for I was leading the meditation and remained conscious though my eyes were closed. My rational mind at first convinced me that the wind could set the feathers in the rocks, until I realized that such a thing was not rational at all.

The South

In the south we find the Salamanders, Firedrakes or Dragons led by the flaming King Djinn. Salamanders appear as small amphibian-like newts in a hearth or bonfire. The magic ones appear when you stare into a fire. They are wispy smoky creatures in the flames, not unfortunate newts who were minding their own business sleeping beneath the bark in a log. They guard the realm of fire, both encouraging the cook fire or need fire and defending against wildfire, sparks and conflagration.

Firedrakes and dragons are the reptiles of well-known legend. They are sinuous relatives of the snake, hording treasure and protecting it with their fiery breath. The war between dragon and mortal is well known on every continent. In Christendom they were blamed for withholding the Holy Grail that the brave knights sought. Dragons actually combine the four elements in their mythology: earth/treasure, air/breath, fire/weapon, water/grail. Although they are better known in our culture than the Salamanders, they are not hearth helpers like those smaller Elementals.

In the eastern world the Djinn are powerful magical beings of the fire also known as genies when assuming a humanoid form. The Fire King is named for them. We have so much cartoon and fairy tale attachment to the Djinn, we are apt to underestimate their power to our own peril. The Salamanders and Djinn can aid magical workings in surprising and exponential ways. As with all Elementals, be careful what you ask for.

The Djinn are a race of independent beings in the Middle East with a history and mythology of their own. I suspect both the Elemental King Djinn in Europe and the independent spirits of the Middle East come from some common Indo-European source. Neville Drury defines the Djinn as genii 'daemon or spirit of

Arabian tradition, a higher order of being than humans'[32] which is formed of smoke, ash and fire instead of earth and clay. The Djinn ruled the earth before the creation of humankind and are said to have assisted Solomon in designing his Temple in Jerusalem. Barbara Walker connects the Djinn to the Roman use of *genius* by which a person's familiar guardian spirit was identified.[33]

Authorities frequently fall into the trap of glittering generalities when discussing the fire Elementals. We are cautioned to leave them for last. We are given the Arabian stories of powerful beings which are willful, dangerous and difficult. Some Djinn in Islamic lore are equated with evil demons. Our own pop culture warns of the dangers in associating with the Djinn in video games, of all things. Regardless of the cultural context, working with the Djinn is literally playing with fire. One needs take care.

Stories and Myths

The largest bonfire I have seen is held at Starwood, a summer Pagan festival which connects many traditions. On the final night, they light a ritual bonfire as big and as substantial as a two-storey house. We dance around it all night long, with first, second and third shift drummers blending and weaving sound with the power of the fire. One year, seated out of the way and facing the flames, Merlin and I saw the forms of Salamanders the size of a cat or dog run harmlessly along the burning logs. Ceremonial magicians have said the size of a Salamander is dependent on the size of the fire.

That year there was a large hollow log placed upright in the flames, a chimney log if you will. The sparks shot out of the top of it. The fire burned through the knots along the length of it and the King Djinn entered there in the fire. His profile with a strong Arabic nose was clear. His eye found me. It was indeed a magical communion.

As the chimney log was consumed he rose up out of the flames and re-formed in the dancing smoke and sparks in the sky. Merlin and I were touched by him for many hours. Prior to the festival, the two of us had been threatened by chaos. After the festival the chaos passed from our lives, but not easily. We cannot know if the journey was shorter because of the Djinn. Neither can we say for certain it was more tumultuous than it might have been without his magic. I suspect both are true.

Our spiritual community has found the faces of Djinn and fire spirits in ritual bonfires at home. They stand among the flames and wait for us to notice. Photographs reveal the same Elementals ready to make magic with us. It is true of course, the ancestors use the flames to speak to us, so every figure is not an Elemental. Fire gazing opens the third eye between the eyebrows and shows us those who wish to speak to us, shade or Elemental.

Building a Fire

Fire gazing is an effective meditative tool, especially after dark. The meditative practice begins with building a sacred bonfire by yourself without the aid of lighter fluid or paper. This requires you to work in harmony with the fire spirits. I have no objection to matches or butane lighters, but a purist would strike flint to make fire. You can choose as you wish. Most people living in an urban setting find building a fire sufficient challenge with a dependable starter flame. I ask that you build a fire because it is a meditation all its own. Ground and center. Work with the fire spirits. Be intentional in your choices. Here's how:

First, select a safe place for your fire. Think three dimensionally. Which way is the wind blowing? As the wind changes direction, what is nearby? How high will the flames reach and what is above you? How dry is the ground and surrounding vegetation? You can scrape the ground and lay the fire on the dirt if you need to. Have a hose or bucket of water nearby. Fire moves fast and can surprise you. Make sure you are 15 feet from a tent or a building. Make sure if the ground is covered with dry organic matter, you dig down to the soil and put a ring of rocks around it. Make sure the rocks are not sedimentary rocks with moisture in them (they explode when hot). Be safe!

Next, gather dry wood for fuel, kindling and tinder. Avoid fresh cut trees; they have too much sap and will not burn readily. Treated wood gives off toxic gas. Old wood with lead paint does too. Think about the fuel. Each wood has properties in spirit. Sense them. Look them up if you wish to call in a special magic with your firewood. If this is your first fire, you likely have enough to think about without concern about the magic of the wood.

Find some tinder or shave wood curls thin to use as starters because you are not using paper. Dry plants, moss, crunchy leaves and tree bark will make good tinder, but they cannot be damp. Gather dry twigs for kindling, or split some smaller pieces off your fuel wood. If you are splitting wood with an ax, you stand the wood upright and embed the ax into the cut end. Then with both hands on the ax handle, you pick it up and strike the chopping block with the embedded wood. The ax moves safely through and splits the wood. Keep your fingers safe.

When you are ready to build this small ritual fire, lay some kindling on the dry ground, some on top of each other with room for air to circulate around the kindling. Air is an important part of fire! Place some tinder (with air spaces) in amongst the kindling and on top. Don't choke off any airways. Look and see where the air should pass through the wood. Then build a small tipi of your thinnest fuel wood around the kindling so the flames will reach it. Again you leave spaces for the air to move around. When the fire blazes it will catch the fire wood. As that burns and drops into the blaze it will feed the fire.

When you have a nice stack of fuel, kindling and tinder in front of you, light the tinder. As it catches, blow it gently to encourage the flame. Remember to turn your face away when you inhale. Encourage the flame to catch the kindling, and feed it more twigs if it needs them to catch the fuel wood. Always work from small to larger wood. The more dense the wood, the longer it needs to ignite. Work slowly. Too much kindling and fuel at once will choke the fire. Too little starves it. Starting a fire is enhanced with elemental communication, but use nice words. Swearing at it does not help!

When the fire is going strong, you can relax and meditate. When you have finished your meditation, stay with the fire until it burns out. Enjoy the peace and crackle of the blaze. You may find more spirits than you expected. If you must leave, then put the fire out. Scatter the ashes with a stick and be sure they are out. Wet them down. Bury them. The Djinn are tricky. You need to engage them in the process of extinguishing the fire. Give yourself at least half an hour to put the fire out from coals to dead ash. As you cannot rush the fire building, you cannot rush its dousing. Working with fire is a lesson in magic.

Fire Elemental Meditation

You and your fire should have a strong rapport by the time you have it blazing. Stand before the bonfire, center and ground. Connect with the energy of the fire. Dance around the fire, encouraging its leaps and sparks with your dance. If the smoke curls out toward you, wind it around your arms and twirl in it as you move through it. Three circles around the fire are usually sufficient to build the connection, but more or less may suit your fitness. When you are certain the fire understands your presence, sit on the south side and gaze into the flames. Watch for the Djinn or the Salamanders to appear. Be aware of other spirit shapes that emerge from the flames. Draw the flame into your third eye between and above your eyebrows. Establish a two-way connection between your third eye and the fire, letting the energy move into you and back freely.

If your living situation makes fire building impractical, a candle meditation will do. Light a candle in a darkened room. Place it so that you need to look up slightly to see it. Unfocus your eyes, and concentrate only on the flame. Draw it into yourself through your third eye, feeling the energy move back and forth from the candle to your brow and back.

When the energy flows easily between you and the fire—

either candle or bonfire—ask: *'What is the flame? Who are the spirits of the fire?'*

Let the answers come to your consciousness. Stay with the meditation as long as the Salamanders are present with you. Get up and dance again when you feel them leave. When you finish, return all the fire energy to the flame with thanksgiving. Ground. Look away from the fire into the night. Bring yourself back to ordinary consciousness. Observe the sky and the stars if you are outside, or the furniture and artwork if you are in. When you return from the fire meditation, take some pictures of the blaze. When you look at them the next morning you may find some fine surprises. Think carefully about what you saw. Write it down or draw it in your BOS.

I have seen my partner Merlin fire dancing as if the fire were a partner. He stays safely in the circle surrounding the fire, out of reach of the flames. He then moves with the drums and the flames, turning and beckoning the blaze higher. In the Grupple Dome at Brushwood, he coaxed a dying blaze built with unseasoned wood into a roaring fire. He held the flames with his gaze and motioned them higher with his arms, slowly, deliberately and without a doubt. People stopped and stared at him. He did not know that.

He danced joyfully with the flames in much the same way at SummerFest at home. People were circling the fire, dancing for the music and social fun of it. Then Merlin began his dance. The flames leaped higher and higher to answer with him. When he finished he sat to enjoy the fire. An African American woman stopped to talk with him. She had recently returned from the villages of West Africa where she had taught midwifery.

'You were invoking Chango,' she said matter of factly. He shrugged, non-committal.

'I saw that dance done in Africa, just the same way. It is the dance for Chango,' she insisted. Merlin nodded. Chango is a fire Orisha. There are specific ways to address any fire spirit. If one is in tune with the blaze, one knows. Our guest was amazed white people knew how to call Chango. What Merlin knew was how to call the fire spirits. The Elementals teach us what we need to know. It is intercultural.

The West

In the west we have the Undines or Nixies led by the Sea Witch I know as Morveren and by King Necksa. The word Undine is akin to undulate, a root word for wave. I know the Undines as sea serpents like the Loch Ness monster (you should forgive the pejorative expression). Some sources identify Undines with the Merfolk which include Selkies, commonly confused with seals. Others find in them the water nymphs of fresh water rivers, falls, and lakes. These creatures govern lunar energy, tides, love, feelings, fertility as well as birth and death. They assess the soul and mete out consequences. They sing and seduce.

Stories and Myths

The tale is told of the beautiful maid who rose up from a German lake amidst a storm and attached herself to the household of an elderly couple. They were bereft of their daughter who had disappeared, perhaps drowned in the lake. The young woman claimed her name was Undine and would answer to nothing else. She was merry and spoiled despite the best efforts of the old woman to train her in the ways proper to her age and eligibility. Undine simply had no will to do anything but what she wanted.

One day in late autumn, a handsome knight with a story of his own sought shelter in the cottage by the lake during a severe and unexpected storm. Undine was delighted. He was strong and sexy, exactly the man she might desire. The storm raged harder than any storm ever had. The creeks flooded the lake and tore down trees in the forest until the spit of land where the cottage sat was cut off from the land and became an island.

Undine flirted with the knight until she won his heart.

Eventually, despite his promise to wed another back home, the knight agreed they should be married. When had he ever seen a more beautiful woman? Her hair flowed like water over her shoulders. Her laugh was as musical as a waterfall; her touch as soft as spring rain. But they were cut off from land. There was no boat. The lake surface churned and refused crossing. How could they wed?

One night as the storm, which had never really ceased, raged as furious as it ever had, they heard a voice cry for help. Undine and the men rushed out to see who might be there. To their amazement a holy priest of the church was dragging himself through the storm, bedraggled and half drowned. They helped him stand and took him to the cottage. As he was fed and dried by the fire, they heard his tale. He had been rowing across the lake on a fine calm day with casks of good wine to deliver to the abbey when suddenly he was caught up in a storm. His boat was smashed on unseen rocks. He and his casks of wine were flung ashore with nothing else. The men determined they would find the casks in the morning. Meanwhile, the priest agreed he would perform the desired marriage ceremony.

As one might predict, the knight and fair maiden were married and all went well. The storm ended, though the island remained cut off from all travel. Finally when the food supplies and wine were depleted, the housewife confided in Undine she did not know what to do. They could continue to catch fish for meals, but what bread could she bake with no flour? Undine nodded wisely and said she would go to the shore to see what might be done. The housewife did not like the thought of that, having had her own daughter disappear in just such a manner, but Undine always did exactly what she wished. She told everyone what she would do, and that no one should follow her.

Of course her husband disobeyed. He took his great sword and tracked his wife down to the water thinking she did not know he was there. He watched as she walked to the end of the dock where the boat had once been and called out over the water. A wave rose up in greeting. It splashed across the pier and left a man standing in its wake. He was very tall, ageless and aged all at once. His hair and beard curled like whitecaps around his head. The knight was alarmed and raced forward brandishing his sword.

Neither Undine nor the stranger was surprised. Husbands the world around behave in such impetuous fashion when they are new and untamed. The older man stepped forward to meet the knight who swung the sword sideways as if to cut him in half. But the sword passed harmlessly through him as it would through a waterfall and the man disappeared. As the knight stared agape, the older man reformed from the water across the dock and stood before him taller than before.

It was then the knight learned he had married an Undine, a water spirit. She had summoned her uncle who was master of the lake to ask for help. Now that he had been attacked, Undine's uncle was in nowise interested in helping the mortals. He was even less pleased when he learned Undine had married one. Eventually, however, he was convinced he should assist them all to leave the island and return to the knight's manor where the old couple might buy supplies and celebrate the wedding in fine fashion. Undine swore her husband to secrecy. He was never to tell anyone the truth of her or speak in anger less she leave him and return to her family beneath the waves.

The old water spirit was true to his word. The floods receded. The island once again became a spit of land jutting out from the forested shore which they walked across without getting their boots muddied. Many misadventures beset them as they traveled inland with the priest, usually whenever they neared a waterfall or creek. Few of Undine's family approved of her mortal connections, but neither she nor her husband explained the reason for their difficulties.

Finally they returned to the manor, a fine stone fortification fit for royalty. Undine was well pleased. The knight's former fiancé was not. After feasting and celebration, Undine tired of trying to win over the friendship of this plain and jealous girl. She banished her to the kitchens and told her to busy herself making supper. Then Undine ordered the construction of a beautiful fountain in the courtyard. When it was finished, it sparkled with lovely falling waters. Their sound was like music, something Undine sang whenever she went out to sit in the garden. Some said it was as if the fountain spoke to her, and of course it did.

Years passed. Undine seemed harder to please. She was rude to the old man and woman who thought of her as daughter. She was imperious to her husband. She never let that annoying jealous girl out of the kitchen. People did not like Undine despite her beauty. For her part, she found her human associates dull and unimaginative. Her only solace was her friend the fountain whom she had known all her life.

One day in an attempt to placated Undine's moodiness, her husband planned a trip to the king's palace where there would be music, dancing and fine wine. Undine perked up a bit. Anything, she thought, would be better than the hovel they lived in with its dull food, dull wine and duller people. The entire household boarded riverboats to sail down toward the sea and join the king for May Day.

Undine was delighted. The water sparkled in the sun. She trailed her fingers in the waves. The waves caressed her hand with love. The knight worried about his wife. She leaned too far over the edge of the boat. She was careless. He told her to step back away from the rail. He chided her for her recklessness. Undine gave him a straight look and continued to do as she pleased. The knight grew frustrated with her ungratefulness. He had arranged this fine trip all for her pleasure and still she was head strong and set on her own way. He raised his voice though he never had before and spoke in anger.

'Undine, do as I say! I am your husband!'

Shocked Undine turned to look at him. Her back straightened. Her hair coiled around her shoulders as if blowing in the breeze, but there was no breeze. She smiled with no joy or humor before she replied, 'Not anymore.'

With that she poured herself over the rail and disappeared in the river. They heard a joyous chorus of water waves and music, the sound of many voices. Undine was gone. Of course people looked for her for days. The old man and woman cried. The knight sat silent in shock. All the company gathered together to console them, including the plain brown haired girl from the galley who had once been the knight's promised lady.

When people dried the tears from their eyes and looked again, the little cook seemed quite transformed. She was beautiful. Her hair shone like polished chestnuts. Her eyes were sweet and loving. She seemed bewildered at her coarse attire and flour dusted apron, which she removed and snapped sharply in the breeze. With the snap of the apron, she started as if awakened from a spell. Where was she? Who were these people? And why were her parents unhappy? When she addressed them in soft tender terms and called them by name, the old man and woman's tears turned from grief to joy. Their daughter stood before them, grown and beautiful.

Mortals tell this tale as a warning. Stay away from the Undines. They will trick you and make you unhappy. Undines tell the tale differently. They say they brought people only what they desired in their hearts. They restored them to happiness and showed them love with no strings attached.[34]

Water Elemental Meditation

Of course the best water meditation is on the shore gazing out on the ocean, lake or river. Sitting before a waterfall might be a similarly strong location, though I have not tried that. Better yet, perform this rite at sunset or moonrise.

Ground and center. Then with your inner senses seek out the Path of the Shining Ones across the water. Breathe in through your crown from the stars and out from your heart along the sparkling pathway as you call to the water Elementals. Listen to the waves break on the shore. Breathe in time with the waves as if they are messages from the Undines. They are.

If you cannot go to the water, using a dark bowl of water as a dark mirror to see through the physical world to the other side will work. I often do the bowl meditation next to a fountain so I can hear the water. Sit staring into the dark waters, breathing deeply and relaxing. Listen to the water sounds and drift with them deeply into the pool in front of you. Settle down into yourself and ask: *What is the sea? Who are the spirits of the water?'*

When you finish, draw back from the water, blinking rapidly. Return from the Path of the Shining Ones. Feel the shore under your feet, or the furniture in the room around you.

Breathe deeply. Ground and center. Thank the water for its inner vision.

This meditation works to pierce through your consciousness and go into a wider dimension of reality. This changes YOU, which is the point of all spiritual endeavors. That is why you need to have some idea of who you are before you start tinkering with your impressions and definitions of self.

Water meditations often take us to the underworld to connect with people who have passed on before us. When we learn that the realm of the west is the land of the dead and the human unconscious we are transformed. These things bring us face to face with our deepest fears and also introduce us to our greatest joys. That is how many religions use the rite of baptism: to connect the initiate with life after death through the element of water.

On the other hand, some Christian denominations and followers of Mithras (a pre-Christian Christ figure) see baptism as a rite of salvation and thus entry into the next world. Baptism is also a rite of association or membership, connecting the initiate to the group and a rite of passage through the stages of growth. Hindus use immersion in water as a purification ritual, a practice also shared with the Celts. Ancient Druids practiced baptism as an act of protection.[35]

Communing with all the Elementals through these meditations is like baptism initiating us into the rites of grounding, visions, magic, belonging, healing and protection. Through our meditations with the Elementals we are marked as individuals connected to the wind, fire, rain, lakes and streams, mountains or crystals. The Elementals recognize us as initiates into the mysteries of spirit. As we evolve, repeated Elemental meditations mark our journey from untutored to adept. By entering into their world, we are purified from the limitations of time and space. By befriending them, we become their friend. We are protected and secured from random terrors and malevolent fate. We are also forewarned. If the Elementals feel the need they will resort to trickery. They will remove those things from us they judge to be stumbling blocks. They will be arbitrary. They will be powerful. They will accept no excuses. They will be amused.

Putting it Together

My Elemental meditations over the years have provided all those associations and protections. Sometimes the meditations were a mystery at first. Perhaps yours were too. I share those from January 1995. They make more sense to me now than they did in 1995.

North/Earth (a stone reading): We are the spirits of physical manifestation, which is to say misdirection and the illusion of permanency. 'For the things which are seen are not real and the things which are not seen are real and shall last forever.' We are the dreams of the Gods who are made.

East/Wind (a walking meditation): We are the spirits of being. We are tree dancers, cloud movers, weather men, the creative forces of destruction. We bring the expression of life from the breath of the Goddess, for All That Is.

South/Fire (a fire gazing meditation): We are spirit energy—that is what makes a soul. We are the core, Kore, the heat and power of focused intention. We are graceful, seductive incubus, succubus, Forger of Souls, Immortal Power, Pele! We are the touch of God. Know that hellfire would never be punishment for it is in the fire we are created.

West/Water (a dark water scrying): We are the spirits of complexity. We give variety, multiplicity, sensuous joy of change. We spin the ageless cycles of infinity in all their masks. We are the ebb and flow of currents, undercurrents, layers of the truth. We are the filters that sort the complexity of God into individual manifestations as a resister-reducer-transformer, changing the energy to visible, tactile forms and back again. We are the Life of the Goddess.

I saw the essence of their Elemental grandeur in action in a storm at Brushwood Folklore Center in Sherman NY. A young man called the Elementals with chant, dance, poetry, gestures and mental intention. Here is what happened. A group of us were gathered under a large semi-permanent tent around the stage for a blessing circle. The thunder storm rolled in unexpectedly. We opened the circle and sent people scattering to secure their campsites and save their bedding. The storm intensified.

When everyone returned to the circle, one fellow went out in the rain to dance to the storm. No one could stop him. He whooped and hollered, stomped his feet and danced energetically to encourage the storm. I have no idea what he thought he was doing. What he did was increase the interplay of all the Elementals at once. The storm strengthened in response to his call as certainly as the bonfire responds to Merlin's dance. The wind came up in answer to his voice crying out in the air. It blew harder and harder. The thunder answered as he yelled for more. The rain surged into a true downpour and the earth turned to mud in answer to his pounding feet as he splashed joyfully in the puddles and bathed in the rain with the Undines. As his arms waved around the lightning flashed fire across the sky. All the Elementals were there, giving him a wild madness as he danced and called them to join him. They answered with a ferocious storm, more intense than we had seen all summer. The rest of us watched with our mouths open, protecting the dancing fool from the lightning he invoked. The storm passed as quickly as it came. The dancer was exhausted.

None were hurt and the campsites were intact. Yet the experience is indelibly imprinted on my memory. If we seek them, they appear. Their values are different than ours. They wonder why we are not thrilled by burst water pipes that made such a pretty waterfall. They are impatient with our fear of fire or earthquake. They are surprised when we scurry indoors out of the wind. On that occasion at Brushwood, those of us who understood what had happened thanked the Elementals for their display of might and beauty. It was an elegant storm, after all. We also grounded the energy we held for them, and sent them on their way safely out of the campground back to their own realms. They were willing to go. It had been an intense but brief experience which could have ended differently.

Chapter 8

Sitting in the Circle's Center

Encounters with the Elementals help define us. Our identity is expanded along with our experiences. If we meet the spirits of the earth, then we are people who can converse with the Gnomes. We are visionaries who can find truth in rocks and crystals. We can ask questions and receive answers from Dwarves and their treasures. If we meet the spirits of the air, then we are people who can converse with Sylphs and Faeries. Our lives are significant enough to receive aid and protection from the realms of Faerie magic. We are worthy of that attention. If we are bold enough to see the Salamanders in the fire or speak with the Djinn we are protected. Our hearts' desires come more easily to us. We truly shape our lives and call the fire of creativity to them. If we are deep enough to commune with the Undines in the water we open our hearts to hear their songs. We can dare to love with abandon. This is who we are and dare to be.

On the other hand, folk tradition and ceremonial magic are filled with cautions about direct dealings with the Elementals, as if we were not having daily interaction with them already. We are warned that wayward spirits can overtake us and make our lives miserable as they did the false prophet who cast out demons in the New Testament.[36] Short of that, initiates are warned if they are filled with self-importance or gullible in their beliefs, they will be troubled and unstable because they cannot learn High Magic.[37] People fear possession, madness and ridicule when they begin to encounter Elementals. The answer to that fear is in wisdom, grounding and deep thinking. When we understand the universe is a safe place, when we work within the quartered circle, the most frightening beings we encounter are ourselves.

All of these Elemental encounters bring us new allies in our venture through ordinary reality. We have made their acquaintance.

They offer us assistance in each of their realms of expertise. Having meaningful connections with the Elementals changes who we are. No longer head blind, we can imagine ourselves in more dynamic lives. We have begun our transformation into mature magical humans. These meditations connect with our identity as humans through our five parts: Body, Mind, Will and Emotions in the four directions of the circle and with the fifth direction of Soul or Spirit in the center. These segments of our identity contain more surprising insights. They are not as obvious as one might think.

Imagine a matryoshka doll. You may know of them as Russian nesting dolls, that set of hollow wooden figures placed one inside the other. The original ones start on the outside with a woman, dressed in a long, shapeless peasant dress and head scarf. The figures inside are graduated, each a size smaller than the one before. They can be male or female and dressed differently. The smallest doll is an infant turned from a single stick of wood. The artwork is elaborate and follows a theme. I have a set of nesting Santas. For this chapter I purchased a set of blank nesting dolls. Then I decorated them to fit the soul and spirit, will and magic, intellect, heart and physical body.

In your Book of Shadows, make the exploration of the five bodies concrete. You can draw the nesting dolls in two dimensions as we work together. You can make a set of three dimensional paper dolls out of graduated cones so one fits inside the other. Draw the face at the tip of the cone. If you want to create a round head for each cone, attach a ping pong ball covered in a scrap of stocking gathered at the neck. Insert the ends of the stocking into the tip of the cone. You will need to create the cones large enough to fit the scale of the ping pong balls. If your imagination and creativity are sparked by the project sufficiently, you can purchase blank nesting dolls from most craft stores or online.

The Physical Body

With five dolls nested one within another, the smallest represents the physical body. This body is connected to the earth element, the Gnomes and the rocks and crystals in the north of the circle. Imagine the doll with all your physical characteristics. What does it look like? You are freed from the tyranny of a perfect body image because all nesting dolls look like bowling pins! But apart from that hour glass figure women wish they had, and the well-muscled wedge shape men envy, what does your littlest matryoshka look like? Sketch it out with hair, eyes, a smile and typical clothing that represent you. If you have health issues, include them on the doll, perhaps as a healed and transformed issue. We frequently use dolls to represent and promote our healing, so consider including your healing in the doll.

As you plan the doll, remember your body is one that can talk with the Gnomes and Dwarves. Maybe you wear a crystal. Maybe you have a special ring. Let your personal magic and beauty show in this doll. Include your wishful thinking and your humor. Spend time with your sketch and describe it in words. You can make a list of words or write a poem as you wish. Does your description favor your positive self-image or a critical list of faults? Why is that? Think about it and add any insight you have into your personal assessment of your body. Be honest.

There is a second aspect to your physical body. Around your skin there is a bluish energy band called the ethereal body. You can see it if you hold your hand against a light-colored wall. Spread your fingers apart and soften your gaze. The movement and faint color you see is not your imagination. It is your ethereal body. How to represent this on the doll or drawing requires some creativity. A coat of glaze or a faint blue chalk outline are two possibilities. You might wrap some sheer fabric around the doll. The ethereal body balances external energy with internal energy, drawing chi in from the natural world and sunlight inside to heal and protect us. It is also a place where pain or caresses, touch or wounds, and physical sensations may be stored as a physical memory. The ethereal body or astral body is also called the etheric twin. When we travel in dreams or trance and leave the physical body behind, it is often this ethereal body that ventures out. Because it is a twin you may wish to indicate its presence and allow your doll to represent both at the same time.

When you think you have it right, transfer your ideas onto the fifth doll. Some sets have more than five dolls which include some very tiny ones. We want to select a doll big enough to decorate appropriately. This doll is your physical body. S/he is the least permanent one because our physical bodies live one life. The rest of us continues on.

Like all projects, the actual manifestation of your doll is something different from the plan or intention. These differences are important clues to who you really are. The 'mistakes' you make are the best parts. The surprises bring a message which we need to honor. Is something crooked or out of proportion? Don't change it. Ask why and open yourself to the wisdom of it.

The Emotional Body

The next largest doll is the emotional body. This body is connected to the water element, the Undines and the lakes, rivers and oceans in the west of the circle. Imagine the doll with all your emotional and physical characteristics. The four basic human emotions are: mad, sad, glad, and scared. The rest of them are subsets of the basic four. You feel giddy? That could be glad or scared. You feel apprehensive? That is a level of fear. Some psychologists indicate feeling tender or loving is a separate category. Others identify shame or contempt as separate. I find the fewer categories the better. Your emotional body contains all the feelings implied by the basic four, but which ones predominate? Are you usually sunny and chipper, expecting the best of life? Are you sad, stuck in a round of depression that may even have rooted itself in the physical body's biochemistry?

In our culture, feelings and emotions are often masked by thoughts. We say *I think* when we mean *I feel. I think today is going to be a good day,* distances us from our own happiness and optimism in case the day goes sour and disappoints. It was only a thought, not something from the heart where we actually dared to feel hopeful.

We also say *I feel* when we mean *I think. I feel today has been wasted on trivia* is a mental assessment. We may feel frustrated by all the things which prevented us from our intentions, but our thought is the day slipped by and is lost. Part of our process in finding our emotional bodies and later our mental bodies is to differentiate between thought and feeling. As you describe your emotional body, pay attention to the different feelings which relate back to mad, sad, glad or scared. Pay attention to the thoughts, opinions, evaluations and attitudes attached to them, but set those aside for use later.

When we describe our feelings as physical symptoms, we are connecting the physical and mental body. *I feel tired* is a physical state, a symptom of the body. It may be connected to any one of the four basic feelings. We can be tired because we have wrung ourselves out with anger. Ranting and raving or suppressing rage takes our energy and creates fatigue. We can be tired by grief. Fatigue and depression often go hand in hand. We can be tired because of fear. Looking over our shoulder, protecting ourselves from ill will can be exhausting since our imagined fears are much greater than the real ones. We can be tired because we are happy and used up all our energy in play, laughter or good works. The body has limits. It needs rest and nutrition. Understand the difference between a physical response to feelings and the feelings. In your BOS make a list of words that describe your emotions today.

I feel...

Add the physical responses present in your body if you wish to explore the emotional and physical body connection, but guard against distancing yourself from your feelings by confusing them with thoughts or analysis. Judgments have no place in our explorations yet.

Emotional Body and Chakras

The matryoshka doll representing your emotional body connects to the physical body through energy centers or wheels called *chakras*. There are hundreds of chakras. I include the seven main chakras located in the torso in my study of Wicca and identity because they are windows to self-knowledge, healing, and balance. There is ample evidence to convince me that our ancestors in Europe knew of eastern philosophy through the travels of the Druids and through common Indo-European roots.[38]

Also included in our emotional body is the aura. The emotional aura is made of the colors which swirl around our physical bodies with clues about our physical health, mental balance and emotional well-being. From that statement you can conclude that the emotional body connects the physical and mental aspects of the self. Many psychics can see either the chakras and/or auras, and even more can scan them with their hands or scrying tools.

How do you wish to represent your feelings, chakras and auras on your second doll? Again take some time to think about the possibilities. If auras and chakras are new subjects for you, do a little research to extend the brief description included here. Remember chakra is a Sanskrit word meaning *wheel*. The chakra system is a series of energy wheels aligned in the body as spirals arranged as plates of color along the front of the body, coiling like a spring in concentric circles through the body to attach at the spine. It is my understanding that the colored auras of the energy body which surround us are extensions of the chakras.

In eastern thought, the chakras are represented by wheels. They are also depicted as lotus flowers with a varying number of petals: four in the root chakra and one thousand in the crown chakra. Each chakra has a tone, a color, and related psychic skills, among other correspondences.

The root chakra is red. Located at the root of the body it is connected to the tailbone from the perineum and faces downward, though many diagrams face it outward from the body for the sake of illustration. There are four petals to its lotus flower. The root chakra represents our life force and vitality. The tone which makes it vibrate is C on the piano, often sung on the syllable Lam (pronounced lahm). The psychic skills related to past life recall stem from the root chakra.

The belly chakra is orange. Located in front of our womb-place, whether or not we are male, female, intact or not, it is connected to the spine at about L-1 the first lumbar vertebra. There are six petals in its lotus. The belly chakra represents our sexuality and some aspects of our emotions. The tone which makes it vibrate is D sung as Vam (vahm). The psychic skills of clairsentience stem from the belly chakra.

The solar plexus chakra is yellow. Located in front of the stomach, it is connected to the spine at about T-8 the eighth thoracic vertebra. There are 10 petals in its lotus. The solar plexus chakra represents our identity by revealing how we create or manifest the lives we live. The tone which makes it vibrate is E sung as Ram (rahm). The psychic skills of manifestation and connection with the Higher Self stem from the solar plexus chakra.

The heart chakra is green or pink. Located in front of the physical heart in the center of the chest, it is connected to the spine at about T-1 the first thoracic vertebra. There are 12 petals in its lotus. The heart chakra represents our compassion and love for the Divine. It empowers our ability to heal and be healed. The tone which makes it vibrate is F sung as Yam (yahm). The psychic skill of healing stems from the heart chakra. Healing has a direct relationship with Divine Love, which of course is a heart chakra attribute in sending and receiving love to and from the Goddess.

The throat chakra is sky blue or turquoise. Located in front of our larynx in the mid throat, it is connected to the spine at about C-3 the third cervical vertebra. There are 16 petals in its lotus. The throat chakra represents our communication and creativity. The tone which makes it vibrate is G sung as Ham (hahm). The psychic skills of clairaudience and telepathy stem from the throat chakra.

The brow chakra is indigo or purple. Located at our third eye, between the eyebrows and up slightly, it is connected to the pituitary gland. There are but two white petals in its lotus. The brow chakra represents our knowledge and intuition. The tone which makes it vibrate is A sung as Sham (shahm). The psychic skills of clairvoyance stem from the brow chakra.

The crown chakra is purple or white. Located at the top of the head, it is connected to the pineal gland. There are a thousand petals in its lotus. The crown chakra represents our connection to the deities. The tone which makes it vibrate is B sung as Om (a-u-m). The psychic skill of channeling stems from the crown chakra.

The transpersonal point is white or crystalline light. Located about two feet above the crown, it is our direct link to All Being. There are either an infinite number of petals in its lotus or it shares the thousand petals with the crown chakra. The transpersonal point represents our connection with the Universal Grid. The tone which makes it vibrate is C sung as Lee. Alternatively this chakra can be opened by singing all of the chakra mantras in succession. The psychic skill of merger, shapeshifting and oneness stem from the transpersonal point.

Herein is an overlooked mystery, that the lotus and chakras are understood to be representations of the female genitalia (yoni), a tradition Georgia O'Keefe followed in her floral paintings, and Judy Chicago in her three dimensional art. Both artists used rich floral colors in pinks, oranges, reds and purples with petals folded back and over each other around central openings in the flower, which then appears deep, moist and mysterious. A familiar Sanskrit mantra associated with Kwan Yin is, *'Om mani padme hum.'* A rough, inadequate translation is, *'How beautiful is the jewel in the lotus,'* which in tantric circles is praise of the clitoris cushioned in the labia. Certainly this is a different way of thinking uncommon in polite western society but typical of Pagan and neo-Pagan thought. The body and the feelings are beautiful and nestled within each other.

It is no surprise, then, to realize the chakra system is complex; sensual as well as spiritual, invisible as well as physical, ever-changing and layered. We can study the chakras in terms of colors, symbols (including the number of petals in the lotus), tones, sounds and pitches, fragrances, crystals, and pure energy we can feel with our hands. Think about how to represent those things in art or symbols which are meaningful to you. Then include them in your matryoshka sketches.

Emotional Body and Auras

The chakras feed the aura. Around our physical bodies and extending outward up to two feet are the colored auras residing in the emotional body. The predominance, clarity or absence of a particular color is significant though the actual reading of an aura may be very individual. For some people, bright red in the aura shows a high energy life force. Murky maroon shows compromise in the life force. Our vitality or health may be clouded by anger, depression, or fear. Bright orange may show a sensual *joi de vivre*. Cloudy burnt orange reveals discontent and separation from others. Bright yellow signals clear connections to the Higher Self, high self-esteem and confidence. Cloudy mustard yellow dims the connections to higher energy and creates space for sullen self-doubt. Bright green indicates healing love and balanced compassion of the healthy heart. Murky blue-green shows pollution in the waters, misused sympathies and perhaps manipulation. Brilliant blue displays our creativity and clarity of communication, our sense of being heard. Darkened grayish blue shows interference and static in our lives. Clear pulsing indigo points to an enriched divine connection of intuition and insight. Dark opaque indigo reflects our closed eyes and poor psychic vision. Deep purple exposes our own divinity and wisdom. Dim or lighter purple shows our resistance to the Goddess or rejection of the Divine and influence of the ordinary ego in place of the Gods. White and crystalline auras validate our transcendent nature which is both human and divine. Muddy occluded light indicates we are stuck on the logic of the earth plane, perhaps denying our own divine nature.

Some psychics have computerized photography which shows the aura and the chakras. This picture is a useful tool in learning more about one's self, though it is only a snapshot. How the emotional body displays itself around us changes constantly with our feelings. I have several of these photographs and none of them are the same, given they were taken years apart. I have confidence in this computer system because of my partner Merlin.

Ever the tease, Merlin decided to consciously flare his aura when we had a set of these prints taken. He pulled the earth and celestial energies through him as we described in grounding. Then he flared them out of his third eye as the photographer was ready to snap the picture. The photo shows only a man's torso dressed in Merlin's clothing with the head nearly obscured by blinding white light. The unsuspecting psychics (yes psychics are surprised too) had no idea what to make of that. Apparently they were used to the usual seekers at a psychic fair who did not know how to direct or control their energies and the energies around them. After much dithering about, they admitted they had never seen such a thing. Merlin then confessed he had done that purposely to test the equipment. On the same occasion, my aura showed brilliant red and orange around my head and shoulders with highlights of yellow and white. The pattern was much more typical. There was nothing wrong with the camera.

Artists who make spirit art can draw us with our auras. Aura readers can describe the colors dancing around us. Or we can sense them ourselves. If you cannot see your own aura, but had to describe it, what color(s) would you choose? What emotions are reflected by those colors? Mad, sad, glad, or scared? What are your chakras telling you about that? What shades of the assigned colors are they? What size? Very often, the first answers which come to mind for those questions are accurate. Then our thinking brain cuts in and edits our replies. If you can catch yourself not thinking, you may find out a great deal about your auras and chakras without seeing them.

In preparing your second smallest doll to represent your own emotional body, use color, symbols, chakras, or other indicators of your emotional well-being or needs. Use as much or as little detail as you like. You may make an abstract doll of bright and dark colors without features. You may line up all the chakras in the body and color them in. You may create a featured doll that speaks of some secret emotional aspect of your true self. Or you may end up with a representation that looks exactly like the loving, caring, worried, overworked creative you that everybody knows. The choices are all yours, but work carefully. Be honest. If you are aware of body issues which have an emotional connection, think of a way to represent that on your doll.

For example, I suffered a severely stiff neck some years ago. I woke up with it. I was so sore my neck refused to turn to check for oncoming traffic. I had Merlin drive me to work for a meeting. I had assembled a gathering of powerfully placed professional people to ask them very hard-hitting questions. Determined to tough it out, I had not even admitted to myself how nervous I was. Stronger than a bull dog, I powered through the pain and led the meeting. When I walked away, the job was done. My fear was confronted. The pain disappeared before I returned to my office. If I were to represent that on my emotional body doll I would paint the right side of my neck that hurt so badly a brown muddy red. Red represents the pain, the alarm and fear at what I had to do and anger at myself for being cowed by professionals looking down their noses and over their eyeglasses at me. The snapshot was accurate for only a few hours until the job was done, but for the space of time I suffered with that stiff neck, it was no less real. That story reminds me of essential parts of who I really am.

A similar thing happened when my mother was dying. Frantic, grieved and beside myself I had an appointment with my chiropractor, a very witchy psychic woman. My whole body felt out of joint. She put me back together as best she could and heard my grief and helplessness. I wanted a miracle I could not produce. Catherine said something very wise. She said my five-year-old self was peeking out of my eyes, terrified of being abandoned. What I needed to do was sit with her, hold her in my arms and be the adult. The five-year-old would always have our mother and she would always have me. The other part of that truth is that the adult me always has our mother too. She is only a breath away. I did not know that by experience then, but it is true. Death is another one of those very real illusions of separation which the Web Consciousness can resolve.

If I were to represent that fear of abandonment on my doll, I would cloud the heart with grey green tear drops. But underneath the teardrops would be a brilliant emerald green heart surrounded by circles of pink love like rose petals. As long as you can perceive color, using it on your doll is important. It speaks to the soul on a very deep level. If your color perception varies from the charts, that does not matter because these are your colors. If you perceive the world in black and white and shades of gray, then the shading will provide some of the same experience. You may want to add textures in place of color. String, thin gauge wire, pieces of mixed jewelry or beads can create patterns and symbols which speak to the spirit and soul.

The Mental Body

The middle-sized doll represents the mental body. This body is connected to the air element, the Sylphs and faeries on the east side of the circle. What does it look like? Few psychics can see the mental body. Those who do describe its aura around the humanoid form as an oval of white, blue and silver light with some pastels mixed in—faery colors. This egg of auric light reaches out about five feet around the physical body, depending on how strong the emotional field is. We expect the mental field to reach out further than the emotional field.

The mental body is both the mind found in every cell of the body and the activities of brain located in the skull. What is the difference? The brain is a specific organ within the physical body. It has three levels of ordinary consciousness: sleeping, dreaming and wakeful working awareness. Each has distinct and measurable brain waves. All of those mental activities are part of the mental body by way of the brain.

Additional levels of consciousness, also with measurable brain waves, are reached through meditation. We reach the deeper mind which exists in every cell of the body through contemplation. The mind is in the brain and everywhere else.[39] The mind infiltrates the physical body but exists, in my view, beyond the physical body within the mental body.

In many ways consciousness is a mystery. How do we prove we exist? Is there a physical reality or are we projections of the mind? Is the solid flesh reality or illusion? Is the oval egg of white light as real as the body or more so? Is the glass of water we drink real because it is in our hand? Or is it real because we think it into being? I am content to leave these questions in the realm of mystery for now. How we individually resolve them shapes us as we explore identity. The questions are part of the journey, whether or not the answers appear.

For our purposes in depicting our mental body on the nesting doll, it is enough to consider the mental body in terms of intellect and brainpower on one level and wisdom and intuition on another. In our mental body we explore on one hand our knowledge, cognition, attitudes and beliefs and on the other hand our discernment, insight and character. The intricacies of those aspects of our being will unfold naturally throughout our journey into identity. Rather than struggle with an academic discussion of these high minded concepts, let's think about three questions:

What is the best idea you ever had, whether or not you acted on it? The very best one. I had to sit with that question for some time before the obvious answer floated up to my consciousness.

Once I thought of it, there was an 'Aha!' moment. Of course that is the best idea I ever had! How obvious! It is the inception of the Web PATH Center, my spiritual community. Several of us dreamed it up together, but it is the most profound, best intentioned idea I ever had. It has changed me dramatically. It has helped hundreds of people make sense of their lives. A person's best idea does not have to be large. It does have to be deep.

What is the worst idea you ever had, whether or not you acted on it? Fortunately this is not an interactive book. Your worst idea can remain secret with you as mine will with me, but finding it amid all the camouflage of denial resident in the mind is an important bit of self-knowledge. The worst idea I ever had seemed like a good idea at the time. How many times I have said that to myself! I am repeatedly amazed at my naivety. I am astounded at what that idea revealed about me and everyone I knew at the time. I still look in the mirror and shake my head. That woman reflecting back at me does not look like an idiot, and yet there I was.

I can laugh about my worst idea now. That is a sign I have healed from the grief, trauma and the therapy sessions necessary to get me back in an upright position. The worst idea I ever had changed me as radically as the best idea. Both of them involved cognition, rational thought, and evaluation. Both of them involved insight, wisdom and intuition. The thinking part of my mental body was fully engaged. In my best idea, I had sufficient insight to carry the plans through. In my worst idea, I miscalculated and misunderstood. The intuitive part of my mental body was fully engaged in one and underutilized in the other.

Would you make the same choices if you could do it all again, knowing what you now know? I certainly would found the Web PATH Center all over again. It has been a wonderful leap of faith and learning. Sadly, if I knew then what I know now about my

> worst idea, I would not have the courage to try again. Both of these ideas blew my mind open. Both were important opportunities for soul growth. I value the journeys through both paths. Still, a dumb idea is a dumb idea. I would not repeat it.

In preparing your middle-sized doll to represent your own mental body you can use the faery colors suggested by the mental aura or any others that seem appropriate to you. In the center of a light body you can represent a humanoid body. Significant symbols or words will represent your best and worst ideas and experiences. The name of your *alma mater*, your favorite books or philosophers, even movies or other dramas can represent your beliefs and attitudes. Use as much or as little cultural detail as you like to show where your ideas come from. You may make an abstract doll of shining colors without features. You may create a stack of books in the brain area. You may choose significant mathematical or physics formulas. You may create a doll with a wise face that speaks of some secret knowledge held by your true self. Or you may end up with a representation that looks exactly like the bright, clever insightful you that everybody knows. The choices are all still yours as long as you are honest.

My mental body doll has a jagged broken heart on her chest. This is not an emotional representation. It is a mental reminder of the price I paid for not listening to my inner wisdom. The break is mended, but the jagged scar shows. Sometimes I think of this as a lightning bolt descending from my brain to my feet. My doll also has a lovely eight armed spider web adorning her dress. This is a reminder of my community, the Web, which sustains me, challenges my thoughts and encourages my education under the tutelage of Grandmother Spiderwoman.

The Magical Body and the Will

The fourth doll represents our will or magical body. The magical body is inspired by the fire element, the Djinn, Salamanders, candles, flames and wildfires on the south side of the circle. What does it look like? The magical body includes our creativity and imagination on one level. On another level it includes our will and decisiveness. The trick is to balance them.

I know, I know. The common human refrain is, 'I am not creative.' But that is one of those lies we tell ourselves. That lie itself is creative. We made it up! Creativity comes from our inner spark. Our will fans the flames of the creative spirit so the spark catches the imagination and fires it up. With creativity we are able to focus our thinking and feeling to help us truly become who we are. The expression of our imagination and our creative impulse is a gift we give ourselves. If we insist on being who we really are, we will be creative, joyful, magical and real. Creativity and magic are expressions of the will.

To the person steeped in pain, dis-ease, chaos, dissatisfaction and general crabbiness, the realization that by taking life by the horns we open the way for our creative and spiritual juices to flow sounds much like blaming the victim. How can we be creative, make magic, dance and celebrate the seasons when our bodies hurt, the bills are piling up, gas prices soar and the world seems destined to flip over on its back, belly up? How indeed! It is not by disciplined will alone that we should do anything, but by sheer joy. There is no reason for us to exclude joy if we also experience pain. There is no reason for us to choose suffering if we also experience financial stress. There is no reason for us to be dissatisfied or angry if we also experience challenges and difficulties. The will operates more freely in the context of joy.

We are indeed the creators of our own dreams and dreamers of our own realities. If we do not like our lot in life, we are free to change ourselves. To change ourselves we may change our mind, our living situation, our attitude, our job, our expectations, our friends, our health, our choices about food, smoking, exercise, meditation, ritual, visualization, or thought patterns. Each of these are our responsibilities, no one else's. Each of these is a magical transformation created by the will which focuses the desires of the heart (feelings) with the daydreams of the mind (thoughts). Consciously combining thoughts and feelings creates magic.

I'll say that again. *Consciously combining thoughts and feelings creates magic.* We have not been encouraged by the institutions in our western culture to create our life choices and experience through our consciousness, but the fact is we do. Instead of seeing ourselves as the victims of life, we can imagine changes that creatively express joy in our daily experience. Imagining is the first step. Naming them is the second. Naming is a creative act that gives us power to shape and direct our lives. If we are unhappy with our economic situation, we can name what we would like: *rags to riches*, perhaps. If we are fearful of crime in our neighborhood we can rename what we would like: *homeland security*, perhaps. Saying what we want is an act of will that starts the magic and can counter naysayers and negative connotations in ordinary reality.

Creativity and joy need the direction of the will. We can call this self-discipline, but those words are steeped with joyless determination. Better named decisiveness, the will takes action to focus the wishful thinking intellect and the wistful dreaming feelings into success. Being decisive about our lives requires a strong will. We willingly commit to our dreams and wishes. We spend time, attention, training, and work in order to create magic and achievement. We overcome self-doubt and lethargy. We set aside distraction.

A Nike Story

All this decisiveness, commitment and action may sound impossible to people with a poorly developed sense of Self. The motto of the Web PATH Center is, 'Just do it!' Let me explain.

Back in the 1990s when Merlin and I were imagining a Pagan ritual and teaching center we had no place to meet. The house was too small, though we had big plans for it. We were certain we lived in a conservative rural area where there were no Pagans. We worked at full-time absorbing jobs that ate up our days Monday through

Friday. How? When? Where? The vision of a spiritual center seemed very far away from us.

One summer weekend we went to the Sterling Renaissance Faire in Upstate New York not far from our home. Wandering up and down the hills through the forest we sampled their food, watched the jesters and laughed at the washer women with their racy humor. Then we stopped at the Gypsy Camp to have our palms read, as we did nearly every year, by Zut.

When she saw us, Zut let out a welcoming whoop! She had been waiting for us, psychic that she was. Zut was one of the few who would read for us as a couple, and do so without looking at our palms. She waved our hands away, claiming she had seen them before. Then she waited for her guides to speak. I didn't tell her that the Web Center was on my mind, but I was hoping for some brilliant idea on how to create a place where people could build a sense of family and practice their spirituality. After a bit, Zut sat back puzzled. She scowled at us.

'Why am I seeing a Nike Swoosh?' she demanded, referencing the logo for Nike sports equipment. I cracked up. Their entire ad campaign that summer had involved the logo and their motto: *Just do it!*

So we did. As an act of creative will, we found some Unitarian churches that would give us free space to teach in. We put a creative fire under a remodeling project and made space to use at home. I overcame my reluctance to work in an unfinished house. We ended up with crash space for up to 20 people, a huge kitchen they could create healthy meals in as part of their education, and a dedicated ritual room. Ten years later, the group grew to need its own space. As I started this book, I had no idea what they might choose but I knew by Nike they would make a decision! Halfway through this manuscript the Council rented a store front as an act of faith. I find our progress exciting.

As it turns out, Nike is the Greek winged Goddess of Victory. Clearly then, my nesting doll depicts the will as a winged Goddess.

She has some attributes of Rosie the Riveter and The Little Engine that Could. She is dressed in purple, gold and white as a tribute to the suffragettes of my grandmothers' era. This strength of will is easy for me. I am an Aries. For others, being decisive and taking action is much more difficult. Depict your will honestly. Select the colors with an appropriate intensity. Find relevant symbols. Add encouragement for your creativity and magic. Then, just do it!

The Spiritual Body

In the center of the circle is the fifth element: ether, also known as spirit. For our purposes I combine the soul and the spirit in one, though such an idea is controversial. Thomas Moore,[40] psychotherapist, and James Hillman,[41] heir apparent of Carl Jung, both define the spirit as being connected to universal truths and the afterlife. In contrast they see the soul working in the trenches of our physical lives, beset with challenges and difficulties. They warn that keeping the soul and spirit separate can lead to the sort of fundamentalism the various monotheistic religions have fallen prone to, and yet they describe them separately.

As a Witch, I see the soul and spirit working together, intimately connected to the rest of our being on a mission of exploration. As time and space are illusions, so are good and evil. The soul and spirit are eternal. They know everything any part of us has ever known and can help the physical brain access that information. It is the soul and spirit which connects the dots and brings us that 'Aha!' moment of epiphany.

Most authorities agree that the soul and spirit are eternal. Some go to great lengths to explain they are connected to different chakras and through them to different physical organs. I find such esoterica tiresome. What is practical? How can we make the abstract concepts of soul and spirit solid enough to comprehend? Having done that, what possible physical depictions might be added to the largest nesting doll? If we have encouraged our creativity and magic sufficiently, perhaps individually we will find answers to those questions. How do we reach our epiphany?

I begin with the understanding that we are our souls. We cannot seek to find our souls. We cannot lose our souls. We cannot save our souls. We are our souls. True, souls can be battered, bruised and fragmented. Portions can hide in our shadows and need retrieval through shamanic work or psychotherapy or perhaps spiritual healing. Nevertheless, we are our souls and they are us.

As the nesting dolls suggest, all the pieces of a human are incorporated together with our incarnate being (body). Four of the auras of that single incarnate being extend out beyond the physical body. The spiritual body is the largest and most extensive. In fact it intertwines with everyone else and connects us to the universal grid. Through the spiritual body, we are connected to our other incarnations outside time and outside this dimension. We are connected to the Gods and Goddesses. Beyond them, we are connected to All Being through that spiritual body. On the other hand, through the spiritual body we are also connected to our emotional aura, our mental body and our physical incarnation. The same is true of the soul. This soul is connected to all souls.

Spirits and souls are constantly growing. Their evolution is one of the reasons why we are here in Earth School. It is one of the reasons why our spirits and souls are anywhere: to learn. We have an unrealistic sense of souls being made perfect, and having arrived at perfection they remain static. Not so! Souls survive not to be perfectly still and static. They would find that as boring as would you or I in our ordinary consciousness. Souls survive to learn from experience, to grow and play with the infinite variety of possibilities. All their learning is expansive. Our souls are growing every day.

I often say to my students, *'The possibilities are endless.'* I hope from that they take in the vast limitless realities open to them from the physical body through all their parts to the spiritual body. By opening to the evolving nature of perfection we can embrace our mistakes, embarrassments or failures as steps in the staircase of perfection. Notice I said 'of perfection' not 'to perfection.' Perfection sits on every step. We are perfect for where we are and what we know today. Tomorrow we will also be perfect but we will know different things and stand somewhere else. Such awareness increases our compassion for ourselves and others as we stumble along doing the best we can with clouded awareness and incomplete information. The soul and spiritual body offer us the opportunity to clear up some of the fuzziness.

In *The Third Jesus,* Deepak Chopra says that 'the soul is the highest form of the self' and that the soul works behind the scenes to shift our consciousness into harmony with All Being.[42] Chopra gives no option in this. Even a determined materialist with no thought for spirituality is involved in the co-creation of reality, intentionally or not. For him, it is simply how the universe works. Our natural state is at one with the Divine. The soul is the part of us that is free from the anomaly of pain.

Seth through his channel Jane Roberts says the soul is our 'most intimate powerful inner identity'[43] which is growing and changing across dimensions. He points out that the ego acts as if it is in charge. It clouds input from other parts of our multi-dimensional being. We are, however, never cut off from our souls, never out of touch. The communication flows back and forth all the time. We are free to tap in at any point to receive psychological, psychic and emotional commentary on our many lives. The soul is strongly conscious and eternal. Seth insists we neither lose nor save our souls, that they are 'the part of you that is indeed indestructible.'[44] He later identifies our spirits as consciousness as well.[45]

Seth refers to our souls as 'incipient Gods'[46] and later develops the God concept in ways traditional religions find alarming. He indicates we as humans fulfill our own prophecies. When the world need arises the avatar steps forward as a soul deeply connected to the Divine, yet is not far different than the rest of us. All our souls connect the Higher Self and the Divine with our four Elemental bodies as represented by the nesting dolls. The connection among our Selves is woven in a spirit of love and compassion. On a soul level we remember everything from every life without judgment and without excuses.

Not all our Selves are human. Seth remembers one life as a dog and another as a tree. At one point in his history with Jane Roberts, a higher energy form which was still Seth appeared. That manifestation of Seth had never been humanly incarnate. It had some difficulty holding a human projection to speak with Roberts and her husband.

Working shamanically, I have learned that all things have consciousness: humans, animals, rocks, trees, and everything else. The accessibility of that consciousness to our waking brain can be muted. Working in trances induced by drums or rattles sheds light on that access. We can communicate with souls which are hidden in rocks or trees. In an animistic community, membership extends beyond the tribe of humans into the geography, flora and fauna. The understanding of Oversoul allows for this extended family through the phyla and species. This connection with All Being is concrete, specific and accessible. We communicate our truths across the boundaries set around human consciousness by our skeptical culture and our scientific endeavor. All Being includes the miraculous and the scientific. When miracles and science are in opposition, then we need more information. The facts are not all known. Our souls and spirits, however, have it all figured out through experience. They have been there in touch with the animate and inanimate and they are in the process of phoning home. The question is, did we leave the phone off the hook?

With that integrated understanding of soul and spirit reaching out and through everything that exists, 'The Song of Amergin' from *The Mabinogion* translated by Robert Graves makes more sense. Not only beautiful poetry, the poem is a soul song, that piece of sound given to the human spirit to sing to the guides and guardians of our journey. Bridges are built across the abyss into the Other Worlds by our song.

The Song of Amergin

I am a stag of seven tines,
I am a wide flood across a plain,
I am a wind on a deep lake,
I am a tear the Sun lets fall,
I am a hawk above the cliff,
I am a thorn beneath the nail,
I am a wonder among flowers,
I am a wizard: who but I
Sets the cool head aflame with smoke?
I am a spear that roars for blood,
I am a salmon in a pool,
I am a lure from paradise,
I am a hill where poets walk,
I am a boar, ruthless and red,
I am a breaker threatening doom,
I am a tide that drags to death,
I am an infant. Who but I
peeps from the unhewn dolmen arch?
I am the womb of every holt,
I am the blaze on every hill.
I am the queen for every hire,
I am the shield for every head
I am the tomb of every hope.[47]

The soul and spirit knows we are a stag and a salmon, a hill and the wave of the sea. We are the tear of the sun, which is a name for the Moon Goddess Niamh. There is a literal truth here that pulls us beyond the limitations of the rational brain into the presence of our beloved souls. We are the secrets of the dolmen arch if we would listen and remember.

So how to represent all this on our fifth doll, the largest one, which represents our spirit and our soul? To finish your project of representing your many selves through art, you need to know who your guides are. What are their symbols? Their colors? Do they have animal familiars? Do you? What connects you to the Divine. How are you integrated into All Being?

If your rational mind rebels and screams back it is not connected, understand that is how everyone's ego responds at first, either out of defiance or out of despair. The truth is we are connected. The ego has nothing to fear. We have always been connected to All Being. The ego has suffered nothing for that. In fact it has gained health and comfort from it. There is nothing to rebel against because the connection to All Being is who we are already. We are One. The ego has nothing to mourn. We cannot lose our souls because we are our souls. We cannot be denied this connection because we are the connection. We simply need to open our awareness and remembrance. This is true.

If the soul and spirit connection between you and All Being still seems abstract and unreachable, draw what it is that would bring the connection to All Being close enough to touch. Use your imagination. How do you build a bridge like that? Who could help? What memories are already there that you can dig up? Trust yourself and call out for help. Then remember to listen. This is a deeply sacred connection you are making by finishing (for now) your dolls.

My spirit and soul doll has my shamanic animal guides on it. They carry me to the lower world, to the upper world and throughout the middle world in trance and meditation. The doll has symbols of my dance with Christianity on it because I spent many years learning about the New Testament Christ. Those lessons were certainly part of my soul growth. The doll has representations of my Divine Patrons: Lamia, Grandmother Spiderwoman, Manannan, Morveren, and CuChulain among others. And there is a representation of my shamanic journey to death which is not to be forgotten. Perhaps above all others, it was that 'AHA' moment that helped me understand who I am.

One of my symbols on the spirit soul doll is a river. For a time my passage in the upper world of shamanic work was blocked by the river which flowed between the place where I arrived in the upper world and the other shore where a beautiful temple and a spirit guide waited. I was told when I could walk across the water I could approach. I refused. Obviously I could not walk across the water. Jesus did that, maybe some other avatars. Not me.

One day in ordinary reality, I was walking down a hallway of black and white checkerboard tiles, very esoteric symbols themselves. It occurred to me that the tiles were empty space made up of fast moving atoms, and a predominance of empty space. In my illusion of physical reality, walking on tiles, earth or concrete was no problem at all. I could do that because in the convention of this middle world reality, that is what people do. What about in the upper world? In the convention of that non-ordinary reality, could I not walk on water? Was that perhaps simply what people do?

Turns out it is! In my next shamanic journey I approached the river and stepped out in faith. Gleefully I walked, then ran across the water as if it were solid ground. My very wise and patient guide simply smiled. I know. It took me long enough.

Later his teaching involved the river in its whole length, from seeping spring out of the ground, through wetlands, channels and into a babbling brook. The river grows, rushes through narrow channels, passes slowly by land and tumbles over rocks. It changes and flows around many obstacles. I swam in the river and learned to become the river. The shapeshifting from woman to water to fish to water to Undine to woman was again mind blowing. Reality is so much more than we are taught by our earth institutions. I am the river. It is both symbol and reality.

Clearly all of these dolls change as we grow. The drawings we make now are but snapshots of who we allow ourselves to be. None of us knows who it is we shall become. Making a conscious effort to work with the Elementals and spirit from the center of the circle shows our sincerity in understanding who we really are. We are all these things, all these beings. When I sing the familiar elemental chant, this chapter is what lies in and around the truth of it. Perhaps now it will for you as well.

Air I am, Fire I am, Water, Earth and Spirit I am.[48]

Chapter 9

Guardians, Watchers and Angels

Our identity now includes an expanded view of ourselves. We are physical bodies but we are emotional, mental, magical and spiritual bodies too. All those aspects of self are a single entity like the nested matryoshka dolls. Remembering that beings can seem very different and yet be part of the larger whole is a key concept for our studies of identity around the quartered circle. We are both *I* and the *other* equally and at the same time. So are other manifestations of spirit.

For example, the Elementals are planet-based spirits of earth, air, fire and water who also live in the lower world of Faerie. They have other aspects as fully connected to them as our emotional body is to our physical body but who live in the akashic realms of the upper world. They appear to have separate identities. We can study them separately or we can study them as different octaves of the same energy but part of the same unified being.

The music metaphor can help make this concept clearer. Suppose we have a multi-voice choir of sopranos, altos, tenors and basses and we ask them all to sing the note C which we then strike on the middle of the piano. Altos and tenors will likely match that note exactly because it is comfortable for them. Sopranos may jump up an octave and hit the C which is eight full notes higher than middle C. Basses may drop an octave. We then have three different versions of C but they are in unison. They are the same note. The physics of that note shows middle C vibrates at 256 cycles per second, and doubles to 512 for the next octave. It halves to 128 for the lower octave. Singers select notes in their range. These notes are in different octaves and are the same notes because they are in a 1:2 ratio to each other.

On the other hand, the singers all have their own timbre or sound. Two sopranos singing the same octave of C have different voices. Each singer's tone will have a distinct quality or color to it. That is the timbre. They can bring their tones into sync with each other in a cooperative effort or they can increase the differences in a diva's effort to be the star and stand out. One way increases the cohesiveness of unison and the other diminishes it. Neither changes the fact that the sopranos are in the same chorus singing the same note. Souls and spirits can do the same thing when they work together or if by way of human ego they compete for power.

The Elementals we have already met are Gnomes, Sylphs, Salamanders and Undines. They are the spirits located in the earth, in the wind and clouds, in the fires and volcanoes, and in the sea, lakes and rivers. Who else are they? I believe the Guardians of the Watchtowers, angels and archangels, the watchers, the dorajuadiok and the dakini are all beings in the same continuum of Elemental energy, each resonating on different octaves of the same note, to follow the musical metaphor. Their vibrations have a different range and timbre. Understanding they are the same helps us reach out to them. Understanding they are different helps us value them in all their personae. There are important similarities and distinctions to comprehend.

Some Elementals are creators of ordinary reality. They make or become the rocks, trees and streams. Others protect and defend the creation as angels and archangels. Others interact with the created beings (human animals and others) as teachers and guides, typical work for the Guardians of the Watchtowers. Some conduct surveillance and keep records as the watchers. Others intervene with miracles and transcendence as the dakini. Still others stand in the unknown to reveal mystery and push us into higher levels or consciousness as the dorajuadiok. Then again, any of these beings may trade off and engage in encounters more typical of another's work because as we already know: *One thing becomes another....*

Guardians of the Watchtowers

How can we experience these various levels of Elemental energy in practical everyday life? When we cast a circle and call the Elementals, we understand we are creating sacred space. We acknowledge the presence of the Fey in the four quarters of the circle. We draw pentacles and set up altars that reflect their essence in each quarter. We also open the pathways into the astral and akashic worlds. Our actions in drawing that pentacle and addressing the four directions are as if we unlock a gate through which we travel outward between the worlds. The gate also opens the way for other spirit beings to travel inward and join us in the circle.

In the Web rituals, we particularly employ this exchange between the worlds at Samhain with the ancestors, at Yule with the new Sun King, at Imbolc with Brigid, at Litha (summer solstice) with the inner court audience before the invoked Lady and Lord, at Lammas with Lugh and at any full moon. The deities in the upper worlds, the ancestors in the lower worlds, and any inhabitant of the world of the Fey may traverse the boundaries between the worlds to join us in a ritual located in someone's living room in ordinary reality. This expectation is lost on inexperienced celebrants who may not notice the ritual space is crowded with spirits.

The new celebrant thinks the priest and priestess are doing all the important work. That is an incomplete vision of what is actually happening in ritual. The participants from the other worlds complete the ritual workings that the humans begin. There is a high level of energy exchanged within the ritual between the seen and unseen. Magic happens as our energy transcends time and space. Seasoned Pagans, facilitating priest and priestess and the man-in-black all create a secure container for the energy raised by the merging of time and space across the normal boundaries. We see behind the curtain, so to speak. Rituals are created as vehicles for this exchange.

To prepare the ritual space for this reconnection of human and spirit beings, we follow the processes identified in Chapter 3. The area is cleansed with sage and sweet grass. The participants ground and draw earth and celestial energies through themselves for the working. Then the Elementals are called to stand in the quarters.

They inspire and energize the working we expect to perform. They participate, but so do their higher octaves who we call the Guardians. Either at the point in the ceremony when the Elementals are called or prior to the celebrants' entry into the circle, designated people call the Guardians of the Watchtowers as sentinels of the gates in those towers.

Many people, in reducing ritual to its lowest common denominator, treat the Guardians as if they are the same as the Elemental spirits. Again, they are the same. They are different. Both. The Guardians are another octave of energy, more refined and light-filled than the Elemental energy and certainly more so than the human energy of the circle. I sense the Elementals rising up from the earth plane traveling on the wind, moving through earth or fire and riding the waves to join the circle. I sense the Guardians arriving in sacred space from outside this dimension. It is as if they approach the circle from beyond the earth-based boundaries and reach the gate to help open it from the outside. They then stand there in the opening to vet any spirit approaching with the intent to observe or join the ritual. They have power sufficient to bar access if need be. In a circle, there are four Guardians just as there are four Elementals, one in each cardinal point. The Elementals work within the rim of the circle. The Guardians stand at the outside of the rim of the circle.

Dr. John Dee's 1584 Renaissance diagram of the 'Vision of Four Castles' inscribed on a gold disc now housed in the British Museum sets out the angelic hierarchy and fortress of the circle.[49] Square towers stand in the north, south, east and west of the circle; these are the four Watchtowers. Pathways between the coordinates form an equal armed cross through the circle dividing it into quarters. Dee and his associate medium Edward Kelly channeled and transcribed the diagram together with a great deal of material relative to the angelic hierarchies and Enochian magic of the Renaissance. While Web Wicca does not follow the elaborate rituals and correspondences of Enochian magic, Dee's influence is behind most Wiccan practices and elemental correspondences. I see the towers and the

Guardians standing in the Four Gateways when I envision a circle. Dee's image is similar to a medieval keep, though it is a circle instead of an irregular walled city or square bailey yard. The diagram is also similar to a Hindu mandala, many of which show a palace and inner courtyard with gated towers in the cardinal points.

Raven Grimassi connects the tower image to the Guardians and to an ancient Roman practice of building four small towers at a crossroads with an altar at each corner for the *lares* who are guardian spirits of ancient Rome.[50] Regardless of which cultural image strikes the celebrants of ritual as most appropriate, there are deep roots in the practice of calling in Guardians to strengthen the security of the circle. The Guardians also amplify the magical energy raised and help direct it.

The Guardians of the Watchtowers are connected to the stars. Raven Grimassi states that in the early star cults in Mesopotamia the four royal stars were associated with the four directions.

Aldebaran governed the east and spring equinox.
Regulus governed the south and summer solstice.
Antares governed the west and fall equinox.
Pomalhaut governed the north and winter solstice.

These stars were called *watchers*. Each had a tower or ziggurat built in the honor of the watcher of that direction.[51]

Like the Web, Grimassi teaches that in setting up the circle and calling both the Elementals and the Guardians of the Watchtowers we are setting a circle within a circle. The path between the two is the world between the worlds. The inner circle is set with the Elementals at each cardinal direction. The outer circle is set with the Guardians of the Watchtowers at each cardinal point where they oversee access from the astral plane. Grimassi notes they are appropriately associated with spiritual teachers, celestial beings, Elemental rulers or angels. In his view they should be called for every circle for the success and effectiveness of high magic. Otherwise the gate to the astral plane is either closed or unguarded.

In fact Grimassi connects the Guardians, the watchers, the grigori, faeries and egregores as beings co-created by humans and the Gods. The process he describes begins with a mortal image of a spirit being. We create that being as a thought form. The more life we imbue in that being, the more it takes on. At some point the archetypal Gods and Goddesses take note and meet us half way. They provide an eternal spark of life to create a lasting being, assuming that is also our intention. There are thought forms and egregores created by humankind for temporary service that are not enlivened by the Gods. Grimassi states in the context of Diana's creation of the fairies in *Aradia: Gospel of the Witches*, 'Italian Witches believe that the Grigori (Watchers) are such an ancient race' that they might be the faeries referenced by Leland in his book.[52] If that is so, then all the Elementals and Guardians may have their source as created beings in ancient magic.

The Watchers and Grigori

Identifying the Guardians with the grigori or watchers is significant. Two books by Andrew Collins, *Gods of Eden: Egypt's Lost Legacy and the Genesis of Civilization* and *From the Ashes of Angels: The Forbidden Legacy of a Fallen Race* explore the possibilities of our star connections in great detail, even though in those texts he repeatedly shies away from naming the stars as our origin. Collins postulates the existence of another human race of very tall beings with elongated heads and serpentine facial features known as the watchers in the *Dead Sea Scrolls* and other ancient texts. He theorizes the watchers brought agriculture, astronomy, metallurgy, divination, herbalism, and other technologies to very primitive homo sapiens. Collins indicates their teaching is revealed in the great leap forward of the Egyptians and before that of the Mesopotamians at a time when other tribes were nomadic Stone Age clans. Collins makes convincing arguments that the four rivers flowing from Eden described in Genesis are the headwaters of the Tigress and

Euphrates rivers in Iraq, or more accurately Kurdistan. He surmises the stories about a fallen race of watchers was a racial memory of events which happened around 9000 BCE after the last ice age. Whether or not this is the source for other stories about fallen angels is unknown.

What is known is that the priest-shamans, as Collins names them, observed some form of bird or vulture cult. They wore bird cloaks as a sign of their office. These cloaks represented kites, vultures or other scavengers which were associated with early underworld or lower world death/destiny cults. In eastern Turkey there are 36 underground cities including Derinkuyu which have layers of streets, tunnels, housing, and community spaces all safely beneath the ground. They descend a quarter of a mile beneath the surface with adequate ventilation so they are able to be sealed. There are stone uprights on the earth's surface marking the air shafts. These were constructed as long ago as 9000 BCE. Oddly, the deepest layers are the ones with the tallest ceilings, ample for nine foot tall watchers. Collins surmises these cities were protection for an advanced society of watchers from the ice age, floods and volcanic eruptions. Myths from Iraq and Iran indicate their ancestors had escaped climatic cataclysm by building a *var,* a word denoting an underground city. He states also that the word for city in Persian is *ark.*

Make of that what you will. Did an Elemental race of watchers actually live on earth? Were the Tuatha de Dannan actually in the land of the Celts? Were there bird tribes who visited prehistoric humankind from other planets? Are the Guardians and watchers among the Gods and Goddesses of ancient myth? Are the angels or archangels part of that genus? Our search for our own identity is shaped by how we answer those questions.

According to Collins, Diyarbakir, in Turkey, is surrounded by a wall shaped like a fish. The wall rivals the Great Wall of China in size though it only extends out for about three miles. Why a fish? Collins postulates that this is in deference to the constellation of Cetus, the whale or fish which is in the Eridanus chain of stars as they appeared at dawn on the spring equinox in 9000 BCE. Collins says these stars and constellations were later associated with the Goddess Tiamet whom we know also appeared as a water Elemental and was slain by the patriarchy at which point her history was rewritten as that of a sea monster instead of a Goddess.

In Babylonian myth, Tiamet was cut into pieces by the God Bel-Marduk after threatening to drown the earth. One part of her slaughtered body became the earth which covered the subterranean waters known as the Abzu. More significantly, the tears she shed were said to have become the sources of the Euphrates and Tigris rivers, which flowed through ancient Sumer. In addition Collins describes an owl-shaped bone with tears found at Çayönü Tepesi, Turkey, which dates back to 7000 BCE. He believes this is one of the earliest relics of Tiamet and her people.

One wonders how Tiamet could have been pre-dated by the watchers who lived at the source of the four rivers and also have been the source of them herself. Who were Tiamet and the watchers, really? What does this all mean? The answers are among the great mysteries which archeologists uncover and then puzzle about. Calling on the watchers and Guardians in ritual or meditation opens the akashic record so we can study the meaning of our history with them. The evidence is scanty and inconclusive without the insights gained through trance or ritual. Of course in studying the clues to *Where did I come from?* we ask the same of the Gods and Guardians. Where did they come from? We can easily be trapped into illusions of time and space as well as of those made by logic and imagination.

In the Iraq-Kurdistan-Syria area not far from Çayönü Tepesi is Harran, destroyed by the Mongols in 1279 CE. Harran was the seat of a Pagan population variously known as the Chaldeans or Sabians who were deeply steeped in astrology and possessors of Greco-Egyptian religious texts on which the *Hermetica* of the Middle Ages was based. These were the supposed writings of Hermes, who was the Greek God related to the Egyptian God Thoth, God of the Moon and my personal protector. Perhaps all of this interests me because I have a past life that connects with Genghis Khan, a patron relationship with Thoth, a long standing obsession with the ancient mysteries, and a sneaking suspicion that monster Goddesses like Tiamet had bad PR from the conquering patriarchy. These Goddesses would not submit. I can relate to that.

But beyond my personal connections, I think there is a deep secret here about human origins and the meaning of history, and perhaps the possibilities of the future. We find it in Stonehenge, in Medicine Bow and in the pyramids. The sacred geometry of the spirit has been marked on the land by someone. The land is connected to these symbols, not only in the sacred geometry that is drawn or constructed on its surface, but also in the rock, soil and water itself. The openness of a meadow, the box of a canyon, the triangle of a mountain, and the V of a gorge speak a symbolic language to our souls. In our ventures out into sacred space, we remember this and listen for the words of Gaia with the inner ears of the brow and throat chakras where we can communicate in symbols. Then we see how myths and history weave a pattern in our consciousness.

Angels and Archangels

The Guardians in western mystical traditions are often represented as four of the archangels: Michael, Gabriel, Uriel, and Ariel. They are the same archangels found in the world's holy manuscripts. *The Book of Enoch* appears to be the earliest text and cites seven of them: Gabriel, Raphael, Michael, Uriel, Ariel (Zerchiel or Araqael), Raguel (Ruhiel, Ruagel or Ruahel) and Remiel (Jermiel or Jerahmeei). Other archangel names appear in the world's religions, so the number is not certain. The archangels, like the other Elementals, have creative responsibilities in making and repairing the earth. Some are involved in healing. Others are protective and defensive combatants and peacemakers. They challenge, teach, and initiate. The archangels do not fit neatly into any categorization that is familiar to us. Some people assign them to different elements than I do or to several elements. You may wish to talk with the Guardians individually to come to your own understanding of who they are and what they represent.

The correspondences of the archangels, as I understand them from a Web perspective, are these:

Raphael, whose name means 'God has healed,' is allied with the needs of earth and north because he is involved with healing the earth and the people of the earth. Admittedly some connect him with the east and air.

Gabriel can also be identified as the angel of the earth because among the archangels he visits the earth plane most frequently, intervening in earth history on the side of justice, i.e. the parting of the Red Sea for Moses so that the people of Israel could escape slavery and the armies of Pharaoh, or calling Joan of Arc to rescue the Dauphin of France. Theosophists explain Gabriel's interest in mundane politics through his role as consciousness raiser. They refer to him as the angel of vibratory transformation. Gabriel is also identified as the trumpeter at Doomsday. I suppose there is a certain balance in calling upon the helper and champion of earth to pull the plug when we finally run out of options. His name means 'God is My Strength.' Some people associate him with west and water.

Michael stands in the east as the 'Prince of Light,' a warrior angel of the sword, our tool of the east and air. He serves as protector and defender of those he champions on earth as well as of the truth. His name means 'He who is God' as an indicator of the Elemental and divine concurrence. Some people associate Michael with the south and fire because he has governance of the sun. They also then assign the sword or athame to the south and move the wand and staff to the east. Then again, there is John 'I'm not that kind of an angel'

Travolta[53] who played Michael as a very earthy, hard-living angel with a sense of humor and interested in the wide range of human experiences.

Uriel stands in the south with fire in my circle because his name means 'Fire of God.' He is often depicted as an open-handed angel holding a flame. He is the other governor of the sun, associated with erupting volcanoes and earthquakes. He is a source of mysticism, a translator between mortal and divine, as keeper of the greater wisdom and secrets. Some associate him with the north and earth.

Ariel stands in the west as one of the rulers of water. An androgynous being, his/her name means 'Lion of God' and s/he is in charge of Pagan spirits of power and trickery (aka the Elementals). For that reason various authorities connect Ariel with the air, with Raphael and the earth, or with fire (southern lion and the quickness of magic.) She/he is sometimes avoided by ordinary mortals because of his/her association with magical spirits. Hers/his is the watery realm of the unconscious, sleep and death. Ariel's name is also synonymous with Jerusalem. This is the same spirit found in Shakespeare's *The Tempest,* appearing as a female sprite and advisor to the magician Prospero. Ariel assists in psychic development. S/he is associated with both earth and air by some authorities.

I realize that for some Pagans including angels in a discussion of Witchcraft and Wicca is uncomfortably Christian. St. Thomas Aquinas said 'angels transcend every religion, every philosophy, every creed. In fact angels have no religion as we know it ... their existence precedes every religious system that has ever existed on earth.'[54] Most religions have highly evolved winged spirit beings who serve as both guardians and messengers. They are analogous to the watchers discussed by Grimassi and Collins and referred to in New Age literature as the bird tribes.[55] A number of us have seen them in our shamanic journeys and been given feather cloaks. Before taking a firm position against the possibilities of angels in Wicca, stop and consider all the connections we can make about angels as the Guardians.

Both archangels and Guardians of the Watchtowers have Elemental correspondences. They are associated with color and sound. They provide protection and defense in ritual space and ordinary reality. They live in a higher dimension, visiting earth for specific purposes. Although we call them Guardians or angels, they can be understood as Elementals and as Gods. They are powers working in the earth plane for the benefit of the whole globe: natural world, animals, humans, history and politics. They have enough power and sufficient authority to wipe us all out, but they do not. Their myths tell stories about Guardians gone bad and angels who have fallen. Because of those stories, humans have demonized some of them into evil spirits bent on conquering and corrupting the earth. Nevertheless, even in our oldest myths, spirit beings were seen as Guardians: genii to the Romans and daemons to the Greeks.[56] These beings inform the European tradition of Guardian spirits, lares, genii and angels.

Angels are also recognized in Asia. The *dakini* or helping spirits in James Redfield's contemplative novel *The Secret of Shambhala* are Buddhist angels. Redfield uses fiction as a vehicle to describe lessons in consciousness which he has learned in ordinary reality and trance. The main character has to learn to respond without fear in order to be open to angelic interaction through synchronicity. They appear as helpers at exactly the right time to use their powers of supernatural intervention. At one point when Redfield's main character is in the ruins of a monastery in the mountains in a blizzard, he thinks he sees another person. Responding in fear he is nearly crushed by an avalanche and the crumbling ruins. By stilling himself and opening through what he calls the first extension or positive prayer field, he is able to perceive and accept the help of the dakini. He explains:

> The temperature was falling and I knew I had to stay inside. I spent several minutes imaging the stones staying in place... I pictured myself sitting beside a warm fire....I walked out to look over the rest of the monastery. I had only reached the hallway when ...I could smell smoke...When there was only one room left [to explore] I peered around the doorway. In the corner was a burning campfire and a store of wood.[57]

The miracle is provided by the dakini who manifest what he imagined. When he was fearful and imagined crumbling ruins and avalanches, they also complied if only to teach him to ask for what he needed. Redfield continues:

> ...in the half-light I saw a tall figure standing at the edge of the doorway. I tried to focus on him directly, but I could see him only at the peripheral edges of my sight. I realized it was the same man I had seen in the snow when Yin had pushed me from the Jeep. I tried to focus on him directly again and he vanished... I had imaged a fire and then it had manifested. But it was too much to believe that my field could be that strong. There was only one explanation. I was being helped. The figure I saw was a dakini.[58]

We all have access to spirit intervention by these beings. We may call on them by the title Guardian, dakini or angel or any other we understand. In any case, we always begin by being still and forming positive images of ourselves and our need.

I would be remiss to leave out the tantric aspects of the dakini.[59] These Guardians meet many human needs including sexual ecstasy. That highly evolved spirit beings are able and willing to engage in sexual merger with humans is a scandalous secret in most human spiritual institutions. In Christianity such spirits were those of the succubus and incubus (based on gender and partnering). They were described as highly suspect demonic spirits who were guilty of corrupting holy men of God or women of God. Their angelic reputation was smeared by the inability of the Christian church to imagine sex as a sacred expression of divinity. Some of that washes over on contemporary Pagans. To the degree we see sex as slightly sordid, a titillating and forbidden erotica, then to that degree we will limit our interactions with spirits and deny their sexual identity. This topic deserves more exploration than I can offer in this text, but suffice it to say the dakini are erotically attractive to Pagans who can accept that the universe was born in ecstasy otherwise known as 'the big bang.'

In addition to sexual ecstasy the Elemental Guardians and angels bring us through life to our destiny and on through death. When I originally wrote this material on guardians and angels for a Web Wicca class, Eh'Lorhylii who is one of the Webwomen found a black and orange northern oriole in the road. After retrieving his body she went to look him up in order to discover his significance to her, knowing the synchronicity was important. However, she inadvertently found *Oriel* whom she explained was the angel of destiny whose name is from the French for *golden*. She had already spent part of the day discussing the healing powers of angels and angel feathers in an online Reiki forum. As a bird watcher she perfectly well knew how to spell his bird name, but it was important she discover his angel name. When she told the story, we realized her teaching was our Wicca IV teaching as well. The Guardians bring us to our destiny. If we are unclear about why we are here we need to ask our Guardians for information. If we are frightened by our destiny, we need to ask them for help.

Shamanic Applications

Compare this not only to the discussion of angels but also to *The Reluctant Shaman* by Kay Whitaker. In the 1970s Whitaker was a wife and mother who returned to college to complete her degree. Unexpectedly she was chosen by two South American shamans as an apprentice. Her book is about her training as a truly reluctant shaman. One of the earliest lessons her teachers gave her was a vision and meeting with the personified figures of death and destiny. Those figures certainly can be understood as angels though they were not so named by the teaching shamans Chea and Domano. They used this awareness of death and destiny throughout Whitaker's education reminding her to 'honor them [death and destiny] as ...trusted elders.'[60] Through this encounter Whitaker learned that death and destiny arrive here in this incarnation with us and stalk us all through life.

We must be at peace and connected to the power of both death and destiny, balancing the power with the raw fear our ego experiences when confronted by either. In fact, Whitaker's experience was so traumatic that it was explained as her death by her teachers. Her body continued, but her soul had been so shaken that she was entirely different. She knew something that shattered the illusions from her life and let her see the fabric of infinity and truth in a way which was totally foreign or unknown to her. Chea and Domano told her 'you tore a little hole in your web and fell off.'[62] I challenge students to do that as they study. We tear off the limitations we impose on ourselves to seek the larger reality.

In answering our big four questions about identity, the angels of death and destiny bring events into our lives to make the reasons for our incarnation clear. In my case my destiny is found in teaching people how to love with both an open heart and an open hand. I have not always understood how that destiny fits into daily life, despite being aware of it as my *raison d'etre.* For me hindsight is indeed 20/20. If we are to profit from our interaction with the Guardians of death and destiny, it is smart to pay attention to synchronicity.

Our work with the angels includes great synchronicity. At the same time Eh'Lorhylii was experiencing her Oriole revelation cited above, Suzanne, one of the women in our 2005 Wicca IV class, reported repeated harassment by a black and yellow goldfinch. It attacked her car, pecked at her windows in the house, flew in an open car window, hid its head in the window gasket material of the car and generally made a pest of itself. None of that is typical goldfinch behavior. When we looked at *goldfinch* in *Animal Speak* by Ted Andrews, we again found the archangel Auriel (same one as Eh'Lorhylii's Oriel spelled differently) bringing a connection to nature spirits. This was during the time the class was seeking out sacred places in nature where they would be contacting nature spirits. Andrews defines nature spirits as fairies, elves and devas rather than goldfinches or orioles. He explains:

> The presence of goldfinches usually indicates an awakening to the activities of those beings that are normally relegated to the realm of fiction. Goldfinches can help you to deepen your perceptions so that you can begin to see and experience the activities of the nature Spirits yourself. This deepening of perceptions is reflected in the black cap—an awakening to that which is normally hidden from view.[63]

Andrews goes on to say the undulating flight of the finches can be used as a rhythm pattern in meditation to assist in astral projection. At that point we were simply astonished to see the task set for the class reflected in the goldfinch behavior.

Then in 2008 I was using the same material to teach a shamanic intensive *Living Inner Visions*. I realized the very week of that seminar I had had an encounter with a female goldfinch brought in and released by my cat Magic. After catching the cat and shutting her in the bedroom, Merlin and I rescued the goldfinch. I was privileged to hold her in my hand and feel her fly off out of the window to the trees, a happy little bird indeed. Between the time I told the story about Suzanne and the goldfinches in 2005 and my experience releasing the goldfinch in 2008, Suzanne had died. This catch and release of a goldfinch was nothing short of a spirit communication both from the goldfinches who remind us that consciousness makes us all One, and from Suzanne to remind me of her wisdom and evolution and of mine. It was also a cheery greeting from a valued friend. I was happy to have rescued the finch. In the true expression of synchronicity I must always remember the cat's name was *Magic*.

As I teach, I ask myself and the students in the silence of our souls to release our limiting beliefs and walk into the unknown silence with an open heart. We face our destiny as manifestations of divinity. We face the annihilation of our mortal limits, a death of our illusions. In the course of her experiences described in *The Reluctant Shaman*, Kay Whitaker finds out just how far that annihilation of mortality goes. She becomes a spirit walker, astral traveler and one aware of the gates or portals open to her from the Otherside of ordinary reality. The angels, dakini, nature spirits, Guardians or Elementals are our guides and protectors in this journey. There we will find our reason for being and our courage to face the Infinite. Once there perhaps we will finally remember who we really are. In greeting the Gods of death and destiny we discover why we are here.

The Dorajuadiok

I find another representation of the Guardians of the Watchtowers in events described by Hank Wesselman in his shamanic books *Spiritwalker, Medicinemaker* and *Visionseeker*. In these biographical accounts, Wesselman spontaneously connects with a descendent 5,000 years in the future. That man, Nainoa, is wandering the post-apocalyptic world on an exploratory mission during which he is taught about and meets the *dorajuadiok*, a word Wessleman learns from the future. Nainoa's shamanic teacher William explains the dorajuadiok are spirits who are immensely powerful, able to control or direct other spirits at the shaman's request including the Elementals. They are able to assist in shamanic healing and soul retrieval. However, they are also capable of stealing souls if they are not properly directed or are directed by one with ill intent. A few of our Webfolk have encountered these beings in their spiritual education.

Wesselman identifies the dorajuadiok as immense beings of pure awareness with no features. One was an arrow shape. They appear as black spirits, black because they are from the light and appear as a shadow or photographic negative in this reality. When seen transitioning between the worlds they offer glimpses of a very bright light. They are from The Void and the source of eternal power. Their purpose is to reveal the patterns and connections between the worlds and realities. They are activators without form but are perceived as shadows. They transport the soul into the universal grid to experience the deepest connection with All Being.[64]

Wesselman describes one telepathic connection with these most powerful spirits:

> The towering Spirit appeared in the visual field, as if to emphasize with its presence all they had seen. Then for the first time its own alien intelligence touched theirs—and offered that the matrix itself could be the creator, that they might think of the 'creator' as 'the created,' as the 'already manifested,' as 'the formed experience of everything within it'...They felt a sudden sense of unity with the dorajuadiok as it included them in its company with the next thought: 'We are the creators of our part of the great pattern. All the personal God-selves, deities, Spirits are formed in reflection of what we do and become on the level of action. They did not create us. We created them. They come into being in response to us and what we become.'[65]

After further instruction Wesselman understood that the dark and light side of the dorajuadiok, and by implication all consciousness, are each halves of the same awareness. I understand this to mean that the evil we identify in ourselves and others is the other half of our enlightenment. Through it we reach out to create our own salvation by becoming aware, by remembering who we are. When we, like the great bodhisattvas, understand the pattern and connection between the light and the dark, then we also teach others to relinquish their fear of the Abyss, of the dark and of judgment. Exchanging fear for wisdom opens us to merge with the spirits. We evolve into the beings that humankind are destined to be in order to take our place among the stars.

A Summation

From this study of the Guardians of the Watchtowers in their many forms we can make several conclusions. First, the cardinal points around the circle are key entry points for the ritual. If the celebrants formally enter the ritual space, they should approach through one of the gateways. Different traditions cite preferences for different gateways. The practical matter of that is determined by the physical layout of the room.

Second, the spirits enter through those gateways, usually through the one that relates to their nature. Spirits carrying messages and teachings for the mind enter from the east. Spirits of deep feelings enter from the west. Spirits of the crystals come from the north and creative magical spirits from the south.

Third, the spirits acting as Guardians appear cross culturally around the world. There are common characteristics associated with their guardianship including bright lights and colors or conversely inky darkness, transparency, flight or wings, protection, provision for our needs, challenges for our souls, and unconditional love.

Fourth, these spirits incorporated both the light and the dark and what humans conceive of as good and evil. That truth is alarming to some who have yet to understand the intimate connection between those principles. Interaction with these spirits can be equally alarming because their power is magnified beyond our experience as humans on the surface of the earth. Interaction and exchange with them requires us to open ourselves to higher levels of energy. We must risk our ego identity to find out who they are and by extension who we are. All of our ritual exploration is a matter of spiritual enlightenment about the nature of the unseen and a path of self-discovery in identity.

Calling the Spirits

Once we accept we are manifestations of the Divine Creative Force and related to All Being, how do we consciously call the Guardians and stand with them in the quartered circle? Which spirits are interested in standing with us? With whom are we able, in our current vibrational field, to stand? We can find a variety of ceremonial approaches to the Guardians of the Watchtowers, but truthfully they are someone else's words. We can repeat them as we 'summons, stir and call' the Guardians, but that is a bit like a form letter. I would not send a form letter to an intimate partner. On the other hand, I also word love letters very thoughtfully, weaving my own voice into the words. It is important to me for the Beloved to know it is I who speaks, so I use my own words and encourage my students to find their own voice.

In *The Reluctant Shaman,* Kay Whitaker learns to communicate with Elemental spirit beings by singing or weaving her heart's song with them in a natural setting. She is given this task as homework and chooses to go outside and practice there. Inadvertently she sings to the waterfall in an isolated ravine and thereby calls a river spirit.[66] We know that to be an Undine. The spirit does not appear immediately: Whitaker is first approached in a dream. She asks for help in understanding this dream and learns from her teachers what she has done. They are somewhat amused. They had opened the door for her to merge with a wind spirit, but had thought to postpone her merger with a water spirit because of the difficulties involved. Chea explained:

> Normally you would not be approaching water spirits for several years... They are highly complex and require an enormous amount of concentration and commitment to bond with.[67]

Both the wind spirit and the water spirit are described as friends who will work with Kay Whitaker for the rest of her life as long as she honors them. The water spirits are seen as the most pure and nurturing among the spirits associated with the elements. Bonding with them can take several contacts as one focuses and forms an impeccable intention toward this connection. Such a merger has its dangers but, as Chea said, 'You know who your enemy is now—your own thoughts and fears.'[68]

Whitaker was instructed to practice her spiritual gifts until she was able to hold her center without capitulation to fear or extraneous thoughts. When she could be brave and focused she could seek out the physical meeting with the river spirit. She makes reference to her four gifts used in the encounter but what they are remains unclear. Evidently her accessibility to her gifts may vary with time and place. A close reading of the text suggests the abilities needed are these:

The ability to center no matter what is happening around us,
The ability to sing one's song from all the energy centers (chakras),
The ability to send our song out with focused intention, and
The ability to be taught in dreams and to dream one's reality into manifestation.

According to these teachings, fear travels with us even when we are centered. It keeps us keen and respectful of the spirit entities we seek. Our song opens the way for us to hear the song of the Elemental and to blend the breath and song together. We learn the calling sound of the Elemental and realize we have entered into a commitment. The wind moves quickly so the ability to focus is less demanding. The water moves more slowly and the necessary focus must remain until the connection is secure. When we prepare for this journey, we learn what is necessary in our dreams. It is important that we remember them.

I understand the personal song reference in this book as one's power song used in shamanic practices. Wicca does not emphasize the discovery of this song, at least not in most beginning references. Yet contacting spirits requires a shift in our energy which is assisted by sound or singing. People who have yet to discover their own song need to take that as their next task. We may dream the song. We may drum and let it come spontaneously out of our mouths, releasing it as a channeled blessing. We may suddenly sing it when driving along alone in the car or walking in the woods. We may sit in meditation for hours or days until it arrives. In any case, a personal song is a spiritual gift which we must long for and desire. If we expect to receive it we will. The song may come without language. It may come with rhymed lyrics. It may be a familiar tuneless whistle repeated by an elder at work that returns to us unexpectedly as a power song. Once it rises to our consciousness, we keep it private. A personal song is never shared. Success with much of this spirit communication with the Elementals and Guardians depends on it.

Whitaker contacted both the wind spirit and the water spirit. Of the experience with the wind she writes:

> There was no doubt ...that the wind keeper could kill me at any time, more easily than we would squash an ant. But I knew she wouldn't...then she was all around and blowing straight through me. There was light everywhere... I could feel her surging through me like an electrical current. She was one of many like her that controlled the atmospheres at different locations... We would be friends for the rest of my life.'[69]

Her meeting with the water was more difficult. She traveled to the ravine and waterfall where 'the mist of the waterfall pulled together and created the form of the woman from my dream.'[70] However, even though the spirit took her hand, Whitaker lost her concentration and ultimately the contact. She was aware the water spirit only meant good for her, but had to postpone the full merger for another day.

Whether or not we can hold our center, focus, chant and sing to the Guardians or the Elementals from all our chakras and meet them face to face is a matter of individual courage. When we desire this contact, our intent must be clear. We create sacred space in the wild or in our normal magical working environment. We sing from and through all the chakras. Following Whitaker's example, we open our arms wide and embrace the spirit as we are also embraced. This spirit will protect us, help us find people and meet up with them, and give us revealing dreams or necessary information directly. In communication with these entities, it is wise never to promise anything we cannot fulfill. If we pledge to work on air pollution, we do it. If the spirit asks something of us, we consider carefully what to say. This is an ecstatic union which might inspire us to think we can and will do great feats of daring. Remember in disappointment she might squish us like an ant without thinking about how permanent that seems to the ant.

Another means of connection with the Guardians is through meditation on the seven rays of color, one at a time. We used these meditations in an advanced class seeking out an archangel connection. We stayed with one color until the archangel energy approached us through the traditional hue. Typically this meditation consists of a series of sittings. One Guardian appears with the ray of color and communicates with us in meditation. One at a time is sufficient dynamic energy for a session. In this meditation, I advise selecting a color based on a pull toward that specific visual spectrum. This affinity indicates who approaches.

In my first effort in 2005, I was selected by Zadkiel whose name means *prayer*. Dressed in purple, he is an angel of solace, charity and gentleness. His appearance at that point was recognition of my need for a deep comfort in the soul. From his perspective, he saw disturbing events which had already wounded me and future events which were then about to become disruptions in the Web but had not yet occurred. In addition, Zadkiel also encourages our yearnings for enlightenment, individually and collectively. Zadkiel holds the powers of invocation which are necessary for calling in the Guardians and the deities.

His female counterpart is Amethyst. Together they champion our efforts to create justice in our world. They offer individual liberation from political oppression, drug addiction, or an abusive relationship, work to which I had already dedicated significant portions of my professional life. Their magic is alchemy and transmutation, which is to say transcendence above injustice and chaos. They mean to change things. The great value of the violet ray is in its ability to erase the past and cleanse the mind and memory of clutter and pain. That was then. This is now. Nike! Zadkiel and Amethyst assist in clearing up karma so that we can merge with the Divine. These are very valuable helpers.

Since my life had been spent in organized advocacy fighting for women's rights, economic justice and later investigating discrimination complaints, I have to conclude both Zadkiel and Amethyst had been present in my life all along the way. In fact they must also have had a deep relationship with my parents. Back in the 1950s in the days of legal segregation in the American South, our family lived in Florida, transplanted from New York State and set down amidst unbreachable class lines defined by race and color. White people like us were expected to treat black people with distain. Walking down Main Street with my mother we observed two white women push a black woman into the street with vicious threats that she should remain in the gutter where she belonged. Without even thinking my mother marched up to them and hip-checked them off the curb into the street and stared them down with words to the effect they should know all about the gutter since they seemed to have slithered up from there themselves. I cheered my mom, not realizing people could be killed for less. I was seven.

My dad had similar incidents at work and was threatened with termination from his job if he did not stop telling off the rude white men who ridiculed the men of color who were customers. We only stayed in Florida a year. I suspect that Zadkiel and Amethyst had worked overtime to bring us all through that unscathed.

The other obvious means of calling the Guardians is with the spoken word, a method which works well in ritual. In some contexts this is called prayer. In others it is called channeling. Because Web Wicca intends to create a human-spiritual partnership between the celebrants and the Elementals, Guardians and Deities, we work around the usual phrases and relationships found in grimoires and instruction manuals to speak individually. This happens in two ways, one initiated by the humans when we speak from the heart with the spirits and listen for their replies in interactive prayer. The second is in opening our own energy fields to spirits so that they can speak through us as channels. Our channeling may occur during drawing down rituals and shamanic circles. Channeling also occurs in private sessions offered as readings for one another or in artistic expression. Satira is likely the most adept channeler I have ever sat with, in the Web or elsewhere. Her guides speak in unknown languages and then translate their loving messages to us so we can actually benefit from them.

For us, direct communion with guides and Guardians is essential. There is no need for high priests or high priestesses acting as intermediaries. Each Witch or Pagan builds relationships with their patron deities, guardian spirits, power animals and ancestors and in some cases spirit lovers. The web of human and spirit entities becomes increasingly multidimensional for every celebrant as they open to their individual possibilities. This is the universal web of consciousness in dynamic interaction for which my spiritual community is named. Every human on earth has the potential of remembering how they fit into the universal web. The greater the number participating in this universal consciousness, the better our hopes for the earth.

Journaling with the Guardians

When I teach, I ask students to call the Guardians of the Watchtowers by speaking from the heart. In one class exercise, they request the Guardians' help in channeling a ritual invocation of the four Guardians of the Watchtowers and the Elementals to use in a group ritual. People who had no idea they could write rituals or poetry have produced beautiful results. Most of the people I have worked with write with pen or pencil on paper. Several of us have started using a computer in the process. The spirits seem fine with that. Here is how this kind of channeling or automatic writing is done. I hope you try it.

In solitary practice, state your intent to yourself. What is it you wish to write? Who is it you wish to call? Find your own words right from the start. Then set up a simple altar with sacred things you find soul stirring. Include at least one candle. Instrumental music or drumming can help people who are inspired by sound rather than distracted by it. Remember you are to hold your focused intention no matter what happens. Cast a circle, ground yourself, center and breathe. Call the Elemental quarters, the Guardians and the Goddess and God you desire to work with using simple and direct phrases. Tell them about your intention to write or channel a ritual calling for the Guardians. Ask them to teach you about it as you write.

Gaze at the lighted candles for inspiration and be still. Let the spirits join you as you repeat your purpose and intent in your mind whenever your focus or center wavers. They can sit beside you for inspiration or they enter your being. You can set your limits based on your readiness. Not many people wish to immediately become indwelt by spirits they are meeting for the first time in their consciousness. On the other hand, people who have long associations with these spirits may feel very comfortable taking the next step and merging their consciousness if not their bodies. Simply state what it is you are ready for and ask them to respect that.

Then begin to write as if you are alone. Let it flow as automatically as you can, not censoring your words or worrying too much about the grammar and spelling. Just write it out. When you feel the flow ease off, go back and read what you wrote. You can make obviously needed corrections and ask the spirits for clarity where what you wrote does not seem to make itself clear. Be still and listen for the answer. It may surprise you. When you have completed this first draft, ground your energy. Open the circle with thanksgiving in the usual manner.

It is okay to go back at a later time and edit. I find spirits use too many prepositional phrases. They favor some awkward sentence structures. English is not their first language. Help them out. This is a collaborative effort between you and your muse. The spirit who helped write your work is as interested in it as you are, so share your thoughts. They will tell you if your edits go too far.

Students have discovered deep personal connections with the Guardians by writing out these invocations. They have also built bridges across the dimensions so the paths from the other worlds to this one become clearer to them. I suspect that our circles grow in magic and transcendence with the experience of people who are involved in prayer and channeling in their solitary practices. Paganism in any of its forms including Wicca and Witchcraft is a way of life, not a simple series of celebratory circles for special occasions. Communicating directly with the Guardians, Elementals, and Deities is a key part of one's soul growth.

The invocation of the Guardians of the Watchtowers included at the end of this chapter was the first channeled poetry I helped create. Reading it over to include here, I was again struck by the mystery described in these lines that was surely not part of my education and conscious knowing when I wrote this in 1989. I can still sit with the poem and learn something which seems new to me. I would ask you to do the same, meditating on the vision to see if the Guardian Women will speak. When you think about who I am and the work I was doing in human rights in 1989, it is no wonder the Guardians chose to appear to me as powerful women. That is not their only form. Nor are their colors the usual Elemental colors. The ones they used here are very personal to me. When I set an altar these are the colors I use. Note that earth, air and fire have a winged or star connection. Water comes from beneath the surface and is surrounded by mists. As I recall, the edits I did related to line length and the number of lines in a stanza. Otherwise, the poem is largely as dictated. Because it is a long invocation, I only use it privately or for special ritual occasions. You are free to try it out, though I am sure your Guardians would rather hear your voice than mine.

Invocation

Guardian Woman from the snows
With hair of white whipped by North winds,
And clean steel eyes that pierce the skin of reason,
Sort and measure truth from our lips,
Intensions from our minds,
And purpose from our souls.
Purify us inside out with killing cold
Before which no one stands but you.
Dressed in grey furs from beasts who loved you,
Fastened with leathers from their hides,
Adorned with polished stones
Hand chiseled from the Mother Lode of God
And set about you like the stars,
Accept our homage, people separated
From the fields of power She ordained
And you have tamed.
Stand in the North's Gateway.

Guardian Woman of the dawn
With hair of palest light,
Stirred gently by the morning breeze,
Eyes wide open, innocent of evil,
Knowing All-There-Is.
Hold us in your wise detachment,
Teach us lessons of Infinity,
And raise your sword against us

To cut away the fear of daily life
Dressed in golden gauze that glows with sunrise
You cast a halo through which I dimly see
Three strings of creamy pearls
Resting intimately on your breasts,
Wings stretched out behind in iridescent light.
Accept my awestruck wonder at this morning vision
That you and I are God.
Seal the doorway of the East.

Guardian Woman from the fire,
Flame hued hair tied back with bronze barrettes,
Your eyes reflect the dancing sun flares of your aura.
Heat us into finished vessels,
Strong, resilient and polished.
We rise from the simple clay, merge with You
As art work of the Bird Tribes.
Pass the wand around us.
Blend our wills inside the sacred space.

Dressed in cloaks of feathers from
Fantastic birds, you breathe the Goddess fragrance.
I see you shimmer through the smoke,
Leather bands around your wrists and ankles,
Belt inscribed with names and spells burned on.
Accept our envy. Mountains fire at your word.
Guard the Southern path.

Guardian Woman from the Western Sea,
Black hair damp from underwater worlds
Turn your dark eyes of hidden dreams toward us.
Reveal the secrets held within the cup
You hold before your heart.
Pour out each one in turn that we may name ourselves

More clearly. Passion. Courage. Fear. Hope.
And not drown before we understand our names.

Dressed in sea green gown crossed with silver bands,
The mists surround you like a shroud,
And here we learn of sex, and death, and sleep.
Protect us from the madness of the isolated soul adrift,
And steer us into shore.
Accept our love, for that we understand in part.
Watch carefully the Western port.

Join hands about us, Guardian Women,
The beautiful Amazons of Higher Power.
Form the sacred circle, sacred space,
Above, below and both sides 'round,
North to East to South to West,
Touch the Star, the Knife, the Wand, the Cup,
And all be present in the body, mind, the will and heart,
Our every aspect vitalized.

So mote it be!
Dorothy L. Abrams, 1989

Chapter 10

Personal Security

Having met the Guardians of the Watchtowers and called them to the circle as defenders of sacred space, we might well wonder what other protection and defense they offer in the guise of guardian angels. The dakini rescued Redfield's main character in *The Secrets of Shambhala,* but that was a novel. As ordinary human beings can we expect the same in ordinary reality? Indeed we can. Their intervention may be less miraculous and more behind the scenes. As I mentioned earlier, I suspect my family benefited from intervention by the Guardians when we acted as ordinary citizens in the cause of justice during a dangerous time in the American South. We were unaware of such protection, but that hardly negates it.

In two other personal examples of guardianship I can share these examples. My partner Merlin describes a family crisis in which his older brother was severely burned as a small child. An ancestral grandmother appeared as a spirit by his hospital bed to hold his energy in his little body and to reassure his family he would survive. He did. I experienced a life threatening respiratory illness in 2004 during which a soul stealer stood in the doorway of my room in Intensive Care, waiting for me. One of my Guardians stood at the head of my bed as a pack of protective spirit wolves circled my bed widdershins. They remained in place until I recovered sufficiently to defend myself. Obviously I survived, soul intact. I believe spirits maintain our personal security without our awareness or calling.

Nevertheless, I advise protecting yourself and property before a crisis occurs. When we leave home, I quickly and consciously spin a circle of light around our vehicle to keep us safe. I imagine it as a cushioning buffer to keep the car secure from other drivers. It is also an infiltrating energy source designed to keep the mechanics in running order. One evening Merlin and I were driving home from work, headed into the setting sun. Suddenly we found ourselves on a narrow stretch of road sandwiched between a bicycle and a tractor trailer. There was not enough room for our speeding vehicle to pass between them without hitting the cyclist or the truck. Merlin steadied the steering wheel, trying to avoid the inevitable. I silently cried out to the Guardians 'No!!!!' Then we were in one piece on the other side of the incident, safely through the eye of that needle. There was not enough room, but there was. Remembering the occasion still makes me close my eyes and catch my breath. If we are alert and remind ourselves of the experiences we actually have, all of us could easily fill a book with these interventions. Most of them go unnoticed or unremembered and so they are also unappreciated.

By calling on Guardian spirits, we benefit from protection against the unbalanced energy of random events, which is the usual source of our difficulties. Occasionally another person's ill will is involved. Sometimes that ill will focuses intentional harm sent toward us. More often it is a burst of anger or fear that creates the potential for pain or injury. Those bursts of negative energy come from criminals as well as friends and foes. Nations engage in wars in which harm comes to all concerned through battles, incendiary devices, destruction of homes and the scars on the heart and soul suffered by both combatants and civilians. The existence of danger is a complex subject which I would prefer to address before entering the discussion of how to set up wards and protection about one's life and property.

The Universe is a Safe Place

One of the principal values the Web PATH community holds is that, 'The universe is a safe place.' That belief seems contrary to the facts. Obviously people are maimed and killed by violence, war and auto accidents. Houses burn down. Robbers break in and steal our stuff. For people who have been victimized by violence, assault, abuse or other manipulations common in our culture, we seem naïve. Who can deny there is rape, or war, or other horrors on this planet? We appear to be blaming the victim if we are not clear about how traumatic events develop out of human and divine energy. If we create our own reality, why are we not all rich and healthy? Surely no one would create a disaster if they had a choice.

Furthermore, there are events related to global warming which we call Earth Changes. The Japanese earthquake, tsunami and nuclear disaster of 2011 piled crisis upon crisis. Technology broke down in 2005 when Hurricane Katrina caused wind damage and severe flooding, worsened by the failure of the levees in New Orleans, Louisiana. Along the same coastline in 2010, the Deepwater Horizon oil platform was the source of a destructive oil leak which was then mishandled and misunderstood so that the damage to 500-1,000 miles of the Gulf Coast was magnified. The Icelandic volcano Eyjafjallajökull covered homes and farmland under several inches of ash as it disrupted air travel all over Europe in 2010. Christ Church, New Zealand, experienced back-to-back earthquakes in February and December 2011 in the 5-6 magnitude range. Australian drought and flooding hit the news at about the same time. How can we feel safe in the face of natural and technological disasters?

The entire belief that the universe is a safe place is predicated on the understanding that all existence is a manifestation of the great creative energy we call Mother Goddess or All Being. This literally means that each individual, as wonderful, annoying, uplifting or dangerous as s/he may be, is a manifestation of that great creative energy. So are all animals. So are all rocks. So are the star people and other dimensional spirits. This belief in the great creative force also means that all spirit entities are aspects of the Goddess—another guise of her. Do you feel safe with Brigid or Diana? Kali, Pele, and the Morrigan are her disguises. Are you comfortable with the Gnomes, Sylphs, Salamanders, and Undines? Christian demons are their other faces. There are no beings apart from those which exist in the collective universal consciousness.

All Time is Now; All Space is Here

The second understanding on which our safety is built is that all time is now; all space is here. We know we have experienced and lived through fearful events. Those times and places are with us here in this warm, comfortable safe place where we sit protected by friends and family. When we were in the midst of disaster, this warm comfortable safe place was present with us then whether we felt it or not. Time (chronology) is an illusion which is convenient to our bodies so we can make sense out of our perceptions. We have agreed to accept it as an interpretative device on the earth plane. It is so convincing we can scarcely see life without it. Yet there are glimpses behind the illusion. Learning to navigate separately away from time is part of the magic of trance work and healing. It is also part of the magic of being safe.

The same can be said for space. Our separateness is a convention that creates geography as an interpretive device for physical beings. We experience geography chronologically because that is what the rules are here. We agreed to them, so we move in linear fashion from one place to another. Those rules do not govern dreams, trance, astral projection and magic. Whenever we perform effective magic, we step out of this linear thinking useful in ordinary reality, but limiting in magical pursuits.

Consequently, if all beings spin out of the great central creative force that is All Being, then all parts are working together to produce our experiences. I believe our life events are for a divine and evolutionary purpose that I can trust. My life history, my reading of the great sacred texts and my ritual and trance experiences all point to that conclusion. A universe which is about love and oneness cannot fail me. My conviction in this belief is a matter of faith, but it works. I am safe on a soul level, and so is everyone else.

Change Your Mind

I do not mean to say that understanding time and space as illusion is a simple matter; nor is trusting in a safe universe. We need to work at changing our perception of everyday life to include awareness of time and space and danger as an illusion. How can we get these ideas into our awareness?

Meditate on a regular basis. When we have merged with the universe in a meditative state and feel ourselves stretched across all time and space, dispersed and yet intact, we finally realize there is no end to existence. We may morph from one manifestation to another, but we continue.

Investigate past lives. When we have viewed our death and rebirth even once, we are unalterably changed. When we have seen ourselves as male and female, old and young, loving and spiteful, black, white, brown or as alien or earthling, we understand how indestructible we are.

Use shamanic journeys to resolve your fear of death or pain. After adequate preparation with a shamanic teacher, embrace the shamanic journeys of dismemberment and the journey into death. Both are deeply revealing experiences which assist us in unlearning the fear of death and what might happen to our bodies. Those journeys taken after laying appropriate shamanic groundwork enable the soul to fully enter into the peace that surpasses understanding.

Trance experiences separate our consciousness from ego which appears to be the part of us that is vulnerable to fear, abuse and damage. The ego is useful in survival for the human manifestation, but must not have veto power over growth and new experiences which assist us in learning about identity and consciousness. Our ego is not identity and consciousness. We do not need it to survive across time and space. We do, however, need it to survive daily life in this time and space. Therein is the crux of the matter of fear and loss. On one hand we are eternal souls able to survive any disaster and keep on going. On the other hand we are finite human bodies apt to be injured, killed and harmed by the events on our planet. We are both.

In any event, the universe is safe when we are prepared for it. When we are unprepared, it is scary enough to keep us away from our soul's wisdom. Individually we may be terrorized, physically injured, blocked or barred entry into some insights of enlightenment. The soul and the spirit always survive and gain from the experience. The ego, body or mind may not care for the experience and in the end the earth plane part of our existence does not survive. When I think about that I respond with courage. Courage also is a choice that the soul makes. When I am challenged by fear, I ground and center and remember one of my favorite quotations from Shakespeare's *Julius Caesar*:

> Cowards die many times before their deaths, the valiant never taste of death but once. Of all the wonders that I yet have heard, It seems to me most strange that men should fear; Seeing that death, a necessary end, Will come when it will come.
> *Julius Caesar* II ii 32-37

In contrast, when we are prepared for the surprises of the universe represented by hurricanes, earthquakes or assault, even our bodies are safe unless on a spirit level we have agreed to the challenges caused by physical pain or injury. Accidental injury, illness and disability are legitimate life lessons. Most of us have written some of them into our life scripts. Our souls agree to take on illness, trauma, and war as lessons for ourselves and for others. Ultimately, of course, we all agree to die because that is the birth process into the next life.

Are human beings able to walk through life prepared for these challenges? Yes. Do we? Mostly not. Being human means being caught up in time and space, unaware of the connections between the manifestation of 'I' and the manifestations which are the rest of us. When we can maintain awareness of our connections across the web of consciousness, we are safe. What does this awareness look like?

It is awareness without bias. We jettison our prejudices and biases against others to operate in a spirit of love and compassion.

It is awareness without anger. We release our desire for revenge, allowing the love of others and trust in karma to handle judgment on those who have hurt us. We experience our anger and play with it; we are not reduced by it. We do no harm with our anger.

It is awareness unshaped by fear. We experience our fear and wisely laugh at ourselves as we play the role of a three dimensional being in a blockbuster movie. When we feel fear we dig deep and come up with courage, not folly.

We live in the full knowledge that we are more than race, gender, ethnicity, history, culture, achievements, emotions, bodies or spirits.

Now obviously in this dimension, we will still fall off a building if we step into the air. We will still burn our skin if we step into the fire. We will still drown if we try to breathe under water. We will still be maimed or killed by rocks thrown at our heads. But if we are killed, we still exist. We will continue to live outside this dimension. We will have access to those in this dimension by spirit communication and reincarnation. That understanding of how things work is perfect love and perfect trust. That is faith. In acknowledging the dichotomy of fear and faith, Starhawk wrote the chant, '*Where there's fear there is power*.' When we address our fears and continue anyway, we find our power.

Stand in Your Power

Having said all that, how can we create a physically safer environment where we work and live in ordinary reality? How can we defend against physical or psychic attacks? At the risk of sounding like a broken record caught in an endless loop, I repeat: ground, center and stand in your power. A person who is connected to the earth and the celestials has an active spirit-based defense system in place. A person who has the faith to expect that defense system to work and who knows even a portion of the answer to '*Who am I?*' is standing in his or her power. This is not power over anyone, but of one's self.

Physical vulnerability is a fact of life for a human body. There is always someone bigger, badder or stronger who could do a body harm. Addressing such concerns with physical prowess is only helpful in a limited fashion. Carrying a club or other weapon may seem to make sense in the dark, but it invites trouble. Like attracts like. I recall Merlin's experience with the aura camera. He flares his aura as a powerful bright light in a threatening situation and the threat moves on. I have learned to do the same. I have no idea what people see or don't see when they look at us, but they move on. We had a recent experience with that kind of self-protection.

A couple weeks before I wrote this chapter we were leaving a theatre after the show. Most of the crowd had disbursed. Our car was right across the street. As we waited for the traffic light a group of loud, bold teenage boys came around the corner near our vehicle. There were half a dozen, maybe eight of them laughing, swearing and poking at each other. They seemed good-humored enough, but they also seemed unpredictable. My hackles went up. So did Merlin's. I grounded quickly, flared my aura and stepped boldly toward them and my car. I also sent out peace and good humor.

A couple of them nodded respectfully and they all kept on going down the sidewalk. Were they harmless kids out for a good time, well behaved and well-raised to be respectful of their elders? I have no idea. I simply know we both felt the same thing at the same time and responded in the same way. Was there spirit entity backup behind us? Could be.

How does one flare an aura? Merlin says he begins with gathering the aura around him, drawing it in around him like tightening a cloak close to the body. He uses his diminishing aura to disappear in plain sight. Then he pushes energy throughout his auric field to extend it out several feet to shine like the sun. He plays with this skill just for the fun of it, so the ability to use his aura to pass unnoticed or dominate a room is second nature. Because he is a very grounded person, he does not consciously ground before doing this. Being grounded as a state of being means he is ready to use his aura on an instant's notice.

We would be wise to follow that example. If on the other hand, something has so unnerved us that we have not grounded and lost our connection with the earth and celestials, then quick attention to that before changing one's aura is a good idea. As I say repeatedly, we do not want to do magical work of any kind using our own energy without it being replenished and charged by the earth and sky. When Merlin teaches this process, he always starts with grounding and centering. He emphasizes this skill especially with young women, who have not discovered the depth of their own identity.

When I flare my aura, I reach down to my root chakra with my consciousness, knowing the root chakra has roots to the earth. I then draw life force energy up my spine, and out of my heart, hands and head to shower out and over me. I experience something akin to a kundalini rush, which verifies to me that the process is genuine. Then I hold that energy stream, imagining myself in the midst of a sphere of brightening lights and colors. I have not measured my flare with photography as Merlin has. He has his effort documented on film and also in a class by an observer skilled in aura readings. Nevertheless I can feel it.

Shield and Repel Negativity

When negativity is sent out to us as energy and not a direct physical confrontation then we begin with the same defense as we use on the street: ground, center and stand in our power. A psychic attack of this nature is an energy onslaught thrown by another being—usually human. The attack can be by intent or reflex (without intent). Someone does not have to be a skilled magician in order to throw energy about. Sometimes we enter a room to find the atmosphere is so thick with emotion we can feel it on our skin. That is energy being projected outward quite unconsciously. People do this all the time. We can pick up this energy whether or not it is directed at us, if we are in a vulnerable state that is ungrounded, unprotected, or ill.

Someone who is angry at us for very mundane reasons may throw their feelings in our direction from a distance simply because they are so furious. We may do the same in unguarded moments if we do not ground our anger and resentment, resolve our disputes and speak honestly about our feelings. We need to be very aware of what we wish for when we are angry, especially if we live by the maxim 'harm none.'

Diane Stein associates specific chakras with specific psychic skills. The belly chakra located between the pubis and the naval is the location of clairsentience among other psychic skills, according to her book *All Women are Psychic*.[71] What this association means on a practical level is that we take in other people's emotional energy and physical states through our bellies. Clairsentience is not quite the same thing as empathy, which is a heart-centered psychic skill of compassion. The impressions received from people around us are less filtered in clairsentience and have the potential for changing our mood or making us feel ill. I find this skill of clairsentience valuable in shamanic healing when I need to know how the client feels. I can experience it first hand in my gut. However, I also need skill in grounding and transforming those feelings so they do not root in my own body. Clairsentience is not such a welcome skill when one is in class or attending a party. It is a disorienting nuisance in a crowded concert or other public event.

To address this vulnerability to other people's stuff, we partly close down our belly chakras to limit the amount of emotional energy that can pass through that opening. This narrowing of the aperture also reduces our availability to other people's projected anger, fear or grief that is directed personally to us. One effective means of protecting the belly chakra is simply folding one's hands over it. That makes us unavailable to the feelings careening around us in volatile situations. Then we can imagine the chakra working like a camera lens or the iris of the eye. The center of the chakra closes down to about a quarter of its size. Notice the chakra does not shrink; the center of it twists to reduce the opening. This smaller opening is usually enough to allow us to relate to people's cues about their feelings without being at the mercy of them.

When we work in a volatile environment we may find we need passive protection over the belly chakra so we do not have to be constantly on alert. One of my chiropractors suggested I wear a white silk camisole or T-shirt as a passive shield when I was working with distressed and angry clients. Apparently I was picking up the chaotic energy around me. My body then translated it into sciatic pain and lower back issues. The clothing must be long enough to cover the belly chakra. White cotton will do in a pinch. Man-made, chemical-based fabrics are not appropriate or effective. I returned to that advice when I felt someone battering at my defenses a few years ago. I was physically ill and not able to attend to my own security as well as I wished. The white camisole did that for me. A similar clothing shield can be apparel with little mirrors stitched in the fabric. I have a vest of that nature, though it shields the heart and not the belly. Admittedly some people think mirrors on one's clothing make an odd fashion statement.

Night terrors can be an example of psychic attack. Not every bad dream is a psychic attack, but some of them are. Sometimes we are our own worst enemies. We create havoc and chaos in our lives through inattention, depression and negativity. Filling ourselves and lives with love and beauty will change bad dreams—both those we have asleep and the daydreaming we do awake. I am not surprised that many people asking for healing or protection fill their leisure time with violent video games, negative magic fantasies or slasher tales in books or movies. A little of those things will do no harm. A steady diet may distort perception.

On the other hand, there are people who will attempt to send out ill will for hire. Years ago I had crossed a woman who likely had a legitimate complaint against me. I had behaved badly I admit. She had friends who knew how to practice 'roots' which is herbal spell magic from the black American South sometimes referred to as Hoodoo.[72] Rootworkers offer healing, divination and problem solving. Their work is most often positive, but also includes effective hexes. For an amount of money, these individuals can gather negativity with perhaps some base spirits and send them off against the foe of a client.

In this instance I woke up suddenly in the middle of the night terrified of what? I had no idea. I simply was in the midst of raw terror. That was very puzzling and unlike me. When I finally realized this was external energy, I sensed its direction. It was pouring in through my bedroom windows. Quickly I threw up a reflective wall of white light and bounced the negativity back the way it came using a positive spirit chant. The fear disappeared immediately and did not come back. I did not wish anyone ill, but I did insist it stop. Of course once I figured out the likely source of the incident, I took responsibility for my own behavior, though not as soon as I might have. As a typical human, I wallowed around in denial and blaming before I arrived at the admission my behavior was blatantly wrong.

The beginning of our personal security lies in our own ethics. We need to live up to our expectations of others. Otherwise, we will have repeated opportunities to practice shielding. The intrusion in my bedroom by a rootworker from a distance was that kind of opportunity. I am grateful for the lesson in shielding and the reminder to harm none. Frankly, I made myself vulnerable to that psychic attack through my own actions. People who have a lot of trouble getting along with others do well to consider what energy they send out themselves. Living in light and love is much easier than being on the defensive all the time. Nevertheless, we are wise to be skilled in psychic self-defense, the basis of which is the quartered circle.

Shielding with the Circle

Negative energy, gossip or an out-and-out psychic attack may hit its target or simply muck up the atmosphere, depending on the focus of the sender. We can avoid being the target or getting mucked up by the atmosphere around us if we shield adequately, unless of course we deserve a kick in the head to get us back on our right path.

The circle or sphere of light is the most common shield. Ground, center and cast a circle of white light to stand in just as if it were a sacred ritual circle. Extend the circle to become a domed roof overhead, a domed floor beneath our feet, until the shelter encloses us in a complete sphere. Let the light brighten and solidify as a shield which protects from all harm. Let this be a portable shield which moves with us. Renew the visualized shield as needed. Picture the light absorbing and transforming harmful energy as it comes near the perimeter. We can add intent to our circle spell that as any energy approaches the shield, the shield becomes stronger. If this is part of our daily meditative practice, we are ready to face unexpected challenges of all kinds.

A visualized sphere of mirrors is used to repel energy and send it back to its source. We create a sphere of mirrors in the same way we constructed the sphere of light. Again we start by grounding and centering. Then we make the sphere of light. When that is clear in our mind's eye, we change the sphere's surface to reflect like mirrors. This mirrored ball could look like a geodesic dome with each triangle a polished mirror, or like a mirrored disco ball from a dance floor. We may attach the surfaces of the mirror shield to a psychic computer programmed to adjust the angle of refraction so that the energy returns to its source, not to a random target.

If we do not attach the mirror shield to a self-adjusting mechanism so the source receives the returned energy, we may surround the mirror sphere with an energy catalyst like a cloud or a ring of fire set several feet away from the mirrors so what is reflected is also enveloped or consumed and then transformed. This is responsible magic and also completes a circle of energy from onset of the protection ritual to transformation at the conclusion.

Setting Wards

At times we sense our property, home, office or vehicle needs specific protection beyond everyday shielding. Maybe thieves have targeted a neighborhood at night and taken electronic gizmos from parked cars while the owners slept. Maybe they entered empty houses during the workday. Maybe we are leaving on an extended holiday and our teenagers foolishly announced it on Facebook.

In those cases we set secret wards around our environment which will protect everything within the space from intrusion. As in all magical workings, we need to be sure we state this is for the universal good, that it harms none. The wards are spiritual constructs described as egregores in the previous chapter. They will be located either above the space being protected, or in the four Elemental directions of the quartered circle around the space.

We can directly approach the Guardians and Elementals for assistance in this matter. The direct approach is effective if we have established a personal relationship with them. When we request their assistance in this manner, we state their limitations as well. We do not want wards that overreact and maim or kill on our behalf. I love my computer, but it is not worth having an Elemental electrocute a thief who tries to steal it. We want the wards to discourage meddling, move trouble away from the property, and encourage troublemakers to think better of causing us harm. We also do not want Elementals to decorate our homes with waterfalls spewing from burst water pipes or electrical fires leaping out of the walls (so pretty, don't you know). Personally I am more comfortable with Guardian intervention than Elemental help for exactly that reason. The earth-bound energy of an Elemental is very direct.

The strength of a warding is found in its unpredictability. Any warding we can set can be dismantled by someone of skill who can guess what ward we might use. For example, because I am a Witch, someone would readily guess I would call the spirits of earth, wind, fire and air. Protective spirits not so easily identified are a better choice. Such wards set for protection of property are active egregores which have the ability to act independently according to the charge they are given. Be sure to include 'it harms none!' Our wards might not limit their responses to spiritual and emotional pressure if not directed to do so. Not only is this being responsible with our magic, it is the right thing to do. Remember, what goes around, comes around.

In setting wards I might call in four animals, one for each direction, which people would not likely guess. If our group totem is a coyote and everyone knows it, I would choose something different. If the Patron Goddess of the Web is Grandmother Spiderwoman, she may guard the property, but the wards would be secret and placed in addition to her presence. Some groups create icons, pictures or collages to ward the collective group space, though they are less secret. In my opinion warding symbols or sigils should not be displayed, though they can be cleverly represented in art or collage and who would know?

How do we set wards? In a ritual setting, I move to each direction in turn, carefully visualizing a ward in place in that quarter. I see it clearly. If this is a group working, I describe it aloud so everyone can help visualize the thought form working its protective magic. We speak and listen. The ward receives its charge for protection in the universal good, with harm to none. I explain the period for which I call the ward to service. I then link the four wards so they strengthen each other when challenged. They may jointly hold a knotted cord that encircles the property, the knots reinforcing the protection charge I stated. They may hold different pieces of the same picture that fit together to create an image of peace and security. They may all wear a similar crystal or cloak. By linking the protective spirits in each of the directions, anyone unmaking the wards strengthens them in the attempt.

A ward can be sealed with a sigil, rune spell or symbol. We may repeat one image in all of the directions or set different ones. That image can be the energy link among them. Think of this as a mental puzzle exercise. We are creating a lock with a very specific key which only we understand. The sigil can be drawn in the air and then unmade the same way. Remembering the details of the making gives us the key in unmaking. Otherwise, the ward may misinterpret our attempt to unmake the thought form as an intrusion from the outside. I am clear they work cooperatively with me as the coordinator over a limited term of service.

Wards hold up about 30 days on their own. I strengthen, renew or replace them as needed. If the ward is for a temporary service such as a weekend campsite, I create a releasing ceremony with thanksgiving and let the ward dissolve back into its source. Gratitude is important to our defenders (and everybody else). It is important we do not thoughtlessly abandon our wards when we leave. The next person who rents our campsite may find it decidedly unfriendly because our warders are still at work.

Notice I use a vocabulary that reflects group effort, co-creation, and consensus. The magical literature from the past uses patriarchal terms which reflect power over the egregores or spirits. Western mysticism even referred to them as demons, which they are not. Web Wiccan Consciousness builds an interwoven network of shared power in the 21st century. This is not our grandfathers' Wicca. We stand as partners with the Gods and Goddesses, not so skilled or powerful as the deities while we are mortal humans, but at their side nevertheless. I do not wish to be commanded. For that reason I do not command. I direct and discuss. I listen. I respond. I set limits and goals. I stand in my power. I also know what the limits of my power are and agree not to overreach. I am open to guidance and differing opinions from the spirits. I am empowered to disagree if I have cause.

My personal experience with setting wards started when we were camping at Starwood in Sherman NY. Not wanting to sleep on the ground anymore, we had an old motor home. After a few years, the door locks no longer worked. Although the festival was remarkably free of crime, there were a few instances of theft. Anyone with a big motor home and lots of gear inside surely looked like a promising target for a thief. Besides that, we traveled with a large group from the Web who camped around us. People left their personal effects in camp chairs, on tables and on the ground around our bus without thinking much about security. To protect ourselves and their stuff, we cast a permeable circle and constructed wards in the four directions. This was a private ceremony conducted by Merlin and me and perhaps a couple of the other teachers.

The wards were different every year. They were not made of traditional Wiccan symbolism. One year we used Hawaiian correspondences. Another year, we called Hindu spirits we had worked with. Another year one of our campers volunteered to set the wards. He later told us he used Christian symbols figuring no one would think of that! I suppose he was right. In any event, over a period of about 10 years we lost one box of Merlin's ear cuffs. Why that and nothing else I have no idea. No food, no money, none of my crystals, no equipment disappeared. We always expressed our gratitude in the releasing ceremony.

Chants and Charms

After practicing at Starwood, I learned to set wards using a chant to protect our home from extreme weather. This incident was a direct teaching from the spirits. It happened one afternoon as a thunderstorm was brewing. I was napping with my dog—a big Gordon setter mix. Suddenly spirit woke me up and urged me to protect the house before the storm broke. Blinking the sleep out of my eyes I spontaneously sung:

Protect this house and the barn, keep us all safe from harm.
Protect the trees and the land, hold them safe in Gaia's hand.

I had never heard the verse or the tune before but that seemed to be the correct action. I settled back into my pillows, not knowing what to expect. All of a sudden a clap of thunder exploded overhead. The poor dog rose straight up off the bed, several feet in the air, looking at me as though it were my fault. We ran outside to see what had happened. Ozone smelled sharp in the air. Lightning had struck the nearest utility pole across the street, sent a three foot shard of the pole flying up the road, and knocked out our electricity. Our water pump, breadmaker, and some other appliances were fried but the house, barns and trees were safe on the land. The dog, however, never slept through another thunderstorm, poor thing.

The next time I felt the need to ward the house with my chant, the wind split a tree across the road, dropping it into the street. The tree knocked the transformer off the utility pole, but we were safe. In the Labor Day storm of 2001, the wind, rain and lightning blew through our county, leaving everything intact at our house, but uprooting trees in the nearby town as if a tornado had struck. They called it a straight line wind. People north and south of us had severe damage. In the ice storm of 2003 we lost branches and tree limbs and electrical power, but the generator kept us warm and the house, barns and trees themselves were okay. In the thunderstorm of 2007 our trees stood while seven of the neighbor's trees across the road went down. I am always impressed with the power of this simple song and the second verse that goes with it. The guardians have given us a great gift for which we are thankful. Nevertheless, we had the weakest of the old maple trees growing at the front of our house taken down this year with proper ceremony. Her wood is recycled as firewood to warm the house. Suddenly, the need for the song seems less urgent, though last week when the winds hit 70mph I sang my heart out. We were fine. I am confident we always will be.

Knowing when to remove an old tree, lock a door, or walk around the block instead of to the car is part of the common sense of personal security. When evaluating potential danger or psychic attacks, we add wards to secure the perimeter, remembering *the universe is a safe place*. The powers that might cause harm are allowed to do so only with our complicity, which is based in fear, ego, ignorance or inattention. I find psychic attack, now that I understand it, to be more annoying than anything else. It is a mistake to be superstitious about our supposed enemies because we do manifest friends and foes alike from All Being, even the good, bad and the ugly.

Protective Plant Spirits

Some of the weeds people exorcise from their lawns are actually protective plants. Burdock, dandelion, red clover, mullein, thistle and comfrey plants can be charged with protective spells. Ornamental plants such as feverfew, cedars, holly, red anemones, blackberry brambles, raspberry canes and roses all protect property. A walk around our house and barn reveals multiples of these botanical volunteers standing watch. We do not use weed killer. When we mow their tops and flowers off, we tell the dandelions and clover to come back stronger. Thistles and burdocks need no encouragement. I attempt to limit their freedom, but they are more stubborn than we are.

I sing to these plant protectors as well as to the warding spirits who protect our home. Although rituals and chants for protection are available in many books, I encourage my students to write their own in the belief they are both more meaningful to the beings involved and less predictable to mischief makers who might want to get around them. Writing or singing original chants strengthens the partnership between the Witch and the wards. Personal protection needs to be personal.

Crystals and Crystal Grids

We can use crystals to ward our property. They can be linked in a crystal grid on an altar that will not be disturbed, placed individually at doorways and windows, or left in a car out of sight. Any crystal left in the sun will fade so I limit windowsill crystals to those that are clear or white. Crystals to ward personal property and those we wear as protective jewelry should be cleansed and charged under the full moon each month. For that I use a spring water bath and place them overnight in the moonlight with my intention to protect the house (or me) for the good of all and harm of none connected to it. The charge can be done verbally or in writing depending on the strength of my focus and attention to the working. One can get more elaborate in the preparation of a grid and charge it by using salt water, protective herbs like cinnamon, cloves, or cumin and in burning sage and sweet grass, or other protective incense which is meaningful to the warder.

For a particularly strong link with the Guardians, we can create a protective grid with a set of crystals. The simplest crystal grid uses a set of matched crystals. To promote white light energy we select clear quartz. To promote love we choose rose quartz. To promote healing and wellness we work with green citrine or malachite. To promote connection with the Divine, we gather amethysts. To promote clairvoyance we combine lapis lazuli, aquamarine and blue topaz. People with more skill and knowledge of crystals use a combination of crystals to achieve specific purposes. Obviously the crystals do not have to match, but they need to be placed intentionally. We pay attention to where each one belongs relative to color, quarter, and the layout of the house. For example, we may need particularly powerful crystals near the front and rear doors. We may want the most beautiful crystals near our altar.

The shape of a crystal grid depends on the purpose. We may shape them in harmony with sigils in use by the warders. We also recognize practical considerations like the number of available crystals and the space in which the crystal grid will be set. For a basic protective grid, I use nine cleansed crystals, four in an equal-armed cross representing the Guardians, with one representing the center and four more crystals to complete the circle around the center. These crystals are set at the same radius as the four representing the Guardians so the circle is true. Nine is a good number for protection since it is three times three.

When I have placed the crystals in the desired formation, I

approach the task as any sacred working. I ground, center and draw the power of the earth and celestials into my body. Then I send their power down my arm into my wand. I usually use a crystal wand for this working as like speaks to like. Then as I repeat the charge and intention for the grid, I begin with the center crystal representing spirit, and touch each stone in order, beginning in the north and then returning to the center. I move from the center deosil to the northeast and back to the center and so on around the circle. I then complete the grid by going around the circle from the north all the way around to north again, touching each stone with the wand. I then take care that nothing moves or jostles this grid as long as it is empowered.

When I dismantle the grid, I begin in the north working widdershins around the circle, then center north center, center northwest center and so on around the circle. Then I select one stone and displace it. The grid is dismantled. I can sense that by placing my hand over the grid. When it is empowered it literally hums under my hand, inaudible but palpable. When it is dismantled, it is an interesting collection of stones with potential power. The people who originally taught me to create crystal grids indicated we could simply move one stone to dismantle the grid. We quickly found that despite being grounded and centered, that action gave us a backlash of energy. Some people got psychic headaches from it. A formal dismantling to match the manner we used to set up the grid avoids that reaction.

Remember, people working with a grid in the southern hemisphere reverse the course, starting in the north and moving widdershins to the west and around the circle to set the protective powers. They work deosil north to east to release them.

In addition to magic and protection, we have used crystal grids to enhance our ritual altar on the sabbats. We place a grid under the altar table where it will be safe from being disrupted by candle lightings, wands and athames that are used during the ceremony. One of our priestesses thought to make a three dimensional grid by placing one under the altar, one on it and one on the ceiling. We found that was more power than we bargained for. We never set the ceiling grid. After that we were content with one grid under the altar. It is wise to figure out how much energy we can reasonably channel and direct at one time. Human bodies can be overcharged and burn out quickly if we overreach. In my opinion working with crystals and ritual is not a fancy set piece suited for the stage. We are working with occult power, spirits and magical human beings. More is not always better.

For a Witch, how to set up an individual crystal grid and the selection of the crystals is a spirit teaching. We can check our information with books and experts. However, our interaction with the guides and Guardians focuses our intent for a specific protection set up in our own space. The matter of receiving direct information about crystals from the spirit world came to me some time ago when our community had regular Wednesday healing sessions. We were working with a friend doing chakra clearings and Reiki when we were told by spirit she had a need for rhodochrosite and aquamarine in her heart chakra. I had some handy, so we quickly cleansed them and placed them on her chest. At the time we did not know why that was important, but we trusted the spirit guidance and followed directions.

We later learned those stones directly address personal protection and the releasing of one's fears of attack. They also address heartbreak. Our friend was vulnerable to both heartbreak and potential domestic violence at the time. Specifically, rhodochrosite is a pink to salmon-colored stone of love and compassion. It encourages positive attitudes and heals relationships. It is particularly helpful for people feeling unloved or bereaved, including those recovering from sexual abuse.[73] Interestingly I purchased a raw rhodochrosite geode with quartz crystals in the vagina-like opening years before this healing session to use in healing work with women. I did so just because it felt right without having known the rest of the properties of the stone. Since then I added a larger rhodochrosite to our entryway at home.

Rhodochrosite also helps us integrate heartbreak in our emotional bodies and keep the heart open so in the midst of our pain we do not close people out. At the same time, the crystal prevents us from the denial of our feelings. With rhodochrosite we have to be honest with ourselves. Clearly, embracing our pain without shutting people out is not so easy! When we can remain open though hurting, we clear the root and solar plexus chakras in a gentle fashion. Some of our gut level problems with health including colitis and painful menses can be related to emotional pain and stuck energy from shutting down our connections to people who can help.

Rhodochrosite helps us identify patterns in our lives and why we repeat the same themes, events or relationships so we can understand the teaching and go on to the next thing. The energy of this stone will be challenging if we are repressing old or not-so-old stuff and trying not to talk about it, so be advised. For example, rhodochrosite might help us address our fears of other magical people whom we believe walk the left hand path and abuse power. In learning to deal with them, we experience our own power and understand they cannot harm us if we protect ourselves. That might be a difficult lesson if we are frightened by the dark or shadows, including our own. Rhodochrosite helps create a positive can-do attitude, lifts depression and lightens the life spirit when we allow its full flower in our hearts, but that takes courage.

Aquamarine is either green or blue, or blue green. It is a stone of courage which calms energies, reduces stress, quiets the mind, and counteracts the 'forces of darkness' or those who would think to use them. It helps us break up old behavior patterns similar to the workings of rhodochrosite. Aquamarine helps us find closure in old issues, helps in communication and opens us to higher states of consciousness in a safe manner, clearing the chakras and shielding the aura.[74]

In terms of physical health aquamarine addresses autoimmune diseases and allergies, which can be the body's over-protective response to perceived threats from outside. Those threats might be in the form of psychic attack, gossip, emotional blackmail, destructive criticism, or agents of dis-ease like viruses and bacteria. Diabetes, lupus and arthritis are among the body's overactive self-protections, though there are many causes for those conditions.

To activate the energy of these stones in response to personal threats and danger, we communicate with them as we did the rock in the elemental meditations in Chapter 7 and let them teach us. If we have several small pieces of these stones we can set up a crystal grid using the pattern of the quartered circle. Other patterns are also effective should we wish to incorporate more stones. A pentacle pattern, a sacred square or triangle placed in a circle are among the effective consecrated symbols we have used in ritual grids.

Journaling on the Crystal Grid

In your BOS, plan a practical experience in setting wards with a crystal grid. You can work with any crystals you may have. Cleanse them first with spring water, a smudge or moonlight. Then meditate on the crystals and research their esoteric meaning to figure out how they fit into a protective ward. Listen to them. Record what you learn in your BOS. Then practice setting out the grid. Remember to ground and center, create sacred space and call your guides and Guardians. Work within the quartered circle. Then link the crystals with your wand as described, in the northern hemisphere working clockwise to set the grid and counterclockwise to release it. Work in the opposite directions in the southern hemisphere.

Sense the power of the grid with your hand. Ask other people to do the same before you describe the working to them. Make notes about your intention, the crystals, the grid, and the energy sensed in it. You can leave the grid in place if it is secure from nosy cats and relatives or you can dismantle it as directed. If you leave the grid in place, recharge it on the full moon or dismantle it on the waning moon. Remember to sense the change in energy after you remove the links among the crystals.

Ritual: Setting Wards

Create a protective ritual to set wards and record it in your BOS. If you decide to call animal allies to ward your home, first identify them in your BOS together with their correspondences. What do they usually protect or enhance? What are their favorite colors? Which of the directions or elements do they most often address? A hawk, for example, usually stands in the east and provides vision and knowledge. Researching the animal spirits you wish to call and creating the ritual will give you practice and skill reinforcement. Set your wards in place on the dark moon and leave them up until the full moon. Then ritually remove them. Test the energy around the space you warded before and after each ritual to convince yourself this made a difference. If your spiritual practice does not normally incorporate rituals, I have provided an outline to follow. If you are experienced in this kind of working, follow your usual practice.

Ground

Cast the Circle with a Chant. This one is similar to works by Doreen Valiente, but based on lines from William Shakespeare in *MacBeth* and Thomas Middleton in *The Witch.*

Black spirits, white spirits, red spirits, gray;
Come ye oh come ye, come ye that may.
Around and around, through out and about;
The good stay in and the ill, stay out.

Call the quarters: Specifically call in the Elementals and the Guardians of the Watchtowers to witness the work and stand in the Gateway of the Astral.

Prayer: Ask for help and guidance in your workings. Speak from the heart or use sacred writing which suits you. I recently changed the poem I use to this one written especially for the times:

I ask the Shining Ones, the Beings of many Dimensions
To reach across the veil and touch us
That we may see through earth's illusion
And into the magic of being one and many

Together, you and I Bright Holy Ones of power.
Help us create love where there is fear
Hope where there is sadness
Peace where there is anger.
As we call you, return to our world;
Enter through this circle.
And be at home.

Invocation of the Mother Goddess: Select a Goddess of Protective Magic.

Light the Goddess candle.

Invocation of the Lord, Consort to the Lady: Similarly you want a God who works as the partner of that Goddess and who also strengthens your magic.

[Isis and Osiris, Bel and Belit, Fand and Manannan, or Cerridwen and Tegid Foel are examples of sacred pairs who could help. If you are unfamiliar with any particular pantheon, you can call the Lady and the Lord. Again, your selection of deities is best made with ones who are paired in their stories, who are known to have worked cooperatively and have good intentions toward humans. We call both a Goddess and a God for balanced polarity. People who work with the Goddess Diana as the divine virgin may call her brother Apollo as the male balance to her power.]

Light the God candle.

Speak the Ritual Intent: Be clear about the reason for your ritual. Add that the working is done for the good of all and harm of none.

Construct the Wards: Do this from four directions as described above.

Raise a Cone of Power to Strengthen the Wards: The cone of power is raised from the root connection up through the earth, through the body and outward to the egregores(s) called in as wards. Acting out that gathering and release, increasing it with the inhaled breath and releasing it with the exhaled breath empowers the magical working with the energy raised in the sacred circle.

Grounding: Once the cone of power is released, place your hands on the ground and balance your energy. Take everything you do not need for health and stability and release it back to the earth and Gaia.

Release of the Lady and the Lord
Release of the Four Quarters
Open the Circle

So far in this book we have seen the quartered circle is a sacred form which marks energy nodes on the earth. It holds us in ritual space and contains the energy of the working. It is a quieting place for meditation and creativity. It is a transitional place between the worlds where we meet spirits and deities. It is a protective space that keeps us secure at home, in our work places or on the road. Now we will continue to explore the quartered circle and its relationship to us by looking at it as a healing circle, a place of celebration in the arts, a doorway to transformation through sacred geometry and finally a genogram to explore more about who we are.

Chapter 11

Circles for Physical Healing

Healing practices and the chances of a positive outcome are enhanced when we work within a circle and balance the quarters of energy within the body. Each of the aspects of our many selves is affected by illness. Involving all of them in the healing processes is part of a magical intention for wellness. Illness begins in any of the bodies that are our identity and reach into the others nested together in us. Healing does the same.

Physical Healing from All Four Quarters

Heart disease, as an example, is the number one killer of women in the US. Physically the deterioration of the cardiovascular system is implicated by poor diet, lack of exercise, smoking, genetics, and age; all part of our physical body's development. We can visualize that as processes occurring in the north of the quartered circle. Healing there begins with physical actions. We stop smoking and change our diet. We take medication. We may opt for surgery. We lose weight. All of those actions work, but none are 100 percent effective. One of the reasons for ineffectiveness is that the other bodies are left out.

Stress, worry and negative thinking damage the mental body and are a contributor to heart disease.[75] Our hearts are wrung out by the ruts we dig with compulsive thoughts about our painful lives. We can think of that as misery in the east. We can address that with prescription drugs which treat the mental component of heart disease as a physical problem. We enter therapy to understand our mental pain and resolve it. On the other hand we can approach this dissonance through the body/mind connection. In the quartered circle we learn calmness through ritual and meditation. Stress fades and the heart heals when we calm our thinking. We can combine the physical and mental healing with yoga or tai chi as moving meditations. The mental healing enhances or initiates the physical healing.

In western society, our magic and our creativity are cut off from our physical health experiences. We deny our creativity which heals the heart if unleashed. We live without intervening in our own fates as if there were nothing to be done about our challenges. Life happens to us and we plod through in a soulless manner, enduring depression and undercutting hope and joy. Our lack of spiritual connection to the arts and magic leaves us feeling abandoned by the Gods. Our physical bodies are disconnected from our infinite possibilities. Our will seems paralyzed, unable to act for our own good, even when we think we know what it is. Our spiritual bodies are ill in their heart centers so we experience heart dis-ease.

The medical doctors tell us to lose weight and stop smoking to heal the physical heart. The counselors and psychiatrists tell us to seek calmness and meditate as we learn to reframe our stress to benefit the rational heart and physical organ. We ignore the doctors because we lack the will to take hold and heal our bodies and minds. We can think of that as a drought in the south. Healing of the will comes from expressing our creativity. We engage in the laughter of the arts and joy of spiritual practice when we empower our will to act. When we reconnect with the part of ourselves that makes magic and beauty, our will strengthens to find the purpose of life. Our ailing hearts regain power both as physical pumps and as connectors to All Being through the heart chakra. Our hearts regain the will to live in the south quadrant of the circle.

Our emotional bodies live in a sad-scared-mad emotional spectrum too much of the time. We say our hearts are broken and we grieve losses without healing them. We believe our wounds are so deep we can never find joy again. Sooner or later this lack of self-love is reflected in the physical organ. These unbalanced emotions damage the heart in the west. They also reflect the damage already incurred by the heart in the other three directions. Emotional wounds benefit from therapy. They also benefit from love. Finding out who we are and loving ourselves opens the door to other people—both those who are incarnate humans and the others. Their love is allowed in to heal the heart and restore balance in our mad-sad-glad-scared human hearts.

Whether our wounded heart began with high cholesterol (physical body), with short-circuited ideas about our identity (mental body), with ineffective spiritual connections (spiritual body) or with an unfaithful lover (emotional body) makes little difference. The healing can begin in any of those places. Using western medical skills, cognitive therapy, meditation, spellwork, art, journaling, spiritual practices or human compassion and relationship together will heal the heart. The heart will not be fully healed if we leave any of these quarters out. Working as an alternative healer and priestess, I encourage people to look at the whole picture and build a healthy intention in all their bodies. Fortunately healing does not need to occur in all of them at once. Healing can begin in any of the bodies and spread out through the circle. Then when we face the final healing, which is death itself, we are wise and at peace.

By addressing ailments as part of the quartered circle we should see that healing combines western medicine, eastern therapeutic practices, spiritual celebrations and loving human relationships. Each of those pathways has a place in the health, recovery and ultimate demise of the body. How does that work in the Web Wiccan Consciousness? When we in the Web are asked to work healing interventions for someone, we do so without charge. This working is part of our spiritual practice. It is a gift from the heart to people who are part of our community. Nevertheless, we need the client's permission and everything they know about their ailment, especially the medical diagnosis and treatment.

The opinion of the physician does not limit my expectation of the outcome, but it certainly shapes that of the client-patient. Medications change bodily response. We cannot and should not work against the advice of a physician. Our choices as alternative healers need to support and coordinate with the medicine they are receiving. If the client's sleep patterns, dreaming and ability to experience meditation or trance are changed by medication, one of us may need to shamanically do that work for them.

Sometimes clients express doubts about their physicians and treatments. We will help them read their medical reports and seek options. We can coach them in what to ask their doctor and when to seek a second opinion. A doctor and patient need to be partners in the healing. Neither of them should be comfortable in accepting a power-over model for their relationship. If the doctor's will dominates the patient's, then it may be time for a new physician. That, however, is an act of the patient's will and decision-making. People who are sick often revert in their fear to a 'fix me' state, which is not realistic. The only one who can actually implement healing is the person who lives in that body. The rest of us are facilitators.

Occasionally a person will ask for healing instead of seeking medical treatment. This is a tricky area. Our work does not replace good medical advice. On the other hand a person has the legal right to refuse medical advice. We tread carefully. Energy healing like Reiki is always appropriate because the healing energy will act where it is most needed. Sometimes that working is on the client's mind to seek out western medical treatment.

I never conclude sessions with those stubborn patients without reminding them they need to see a doctor. That has happened a couple of times with friends who had a diagnosis of diabetes. It seems that is one of those labels people deny. To their own peril they ignore the numbers, skip their meds and eat inappropriately despite intellectual knowledge of the dangers of doing so. Chakra clearing and balancing has a significant balancing effect on blood sugar levels, but it is temporary. The deep healing necessary is in the area of the will, spiritual practice and creative arts resident in the spiritual body and the southern quadrant of the circle. Medication and monitoring glucose levels help the individual read what is going on in the body while protecting internal organs.

On the other hand, sometimes people who are compliant with

nutrition, exercise and medication still experience unstable blood sugar numbers. There is an emotional component to blood sugar levels. High stress, frustration and strong emotional reactions on the sad-mad-scared end of the scale interfere with diabetic control. Chakra healing in ritual space a couple of times a month helps even that out. Then we teach clients how to balance their own chakras and send them off with homework. Daily work by the client helps even more. Individuals who learn to commit themselves to their own wellness later embrace better dietary practice and find in the end their need for medication is reduced.

The issue of working with permission is important as we set up our circle of healing intent. Even when the individual has asked for healing, I still look them straight in the eye and ask for permission to touch them and to work healing energy on their condition by the name of its diagnosis. I want to connect with that inner self that the thinking brain may have silenced. If I see a shadow of doubt reflected in their eyes, we talk about that until the shadow agrees too. We have all the time in the world. No medical director is trying to get them in and out in 15 minutes, which is what happens in an American doctor's office. Our work will be more effective if I know what their hesitancy is. Maybe that fear is the first thing we need to offer healing.

In distance healing, I need to know the client is really a client. Sometimes well-meaning relatives want a person to benefit from spiritual healing even when the patient's own beliefs would never allow it. I suppose they think since we never meet, their relative will never know. Even a cursory knowledge of healing and spiritual communication should tell them that is false. They may not know what is being done or who does it, but they will sense the healing as an invasion of their personal space. Sneaky healing is not healing at all. It is taking power over someone who is already in trouble. That is bad karma and bounces back on everyone involved.

Every Pagan, Witch and Wiccan should have at least one healing modality at which they excel. Becoming proficient at alternative healing requires a good deal of study, practice and even an apprenticeship or formal education. People hesitate to call themselves healers because of the responsibility that implies for their own health and for intervention in times of crisis. Certainly when we step up to become healers we stop playing at magic and start creating it. In the Web spiritual community, the second level class offers a Reiki I instruction and attunement together with the Initiation of the Healer. In the curriculum we introduce selected modalities chosen from community healers who practice chakra and aura healing, sound vibrational healing, shamanic healing, acupressure, reflexology, kinesiology, body work and massage, crystal healing, herbal first aide, nutritional healing, aromatherapy, or healing visualizations. The modalities for any particular class are selected by the teaching team assembled for that seminar. Our expectation is that the students will continue to explore the various modalities until their area of specialty is clear. We then hope they will become expert enough to return to teach us what they have learned and to offer their services to the community as needed.

In this chapter, I focus on how healing is offered within the quartered circle since a full exploration of alternative healing and its place in Pagan spiritual practice would take a set of bound volumes. Within the circle, our effectiveness as healers for ourselves or anyone else begins with our self-knowledge and our personal roadblocks on the path to understanding who we are. As we ask ourselves those familiar four questions (*Who am I? Where did I come from? Why am I here? Where am I going?*), we also ask where do we get stuck most often? As we explore our identity, we find that the answers to our questions unfold in some areas more easily than others. We might find information readily rising up from our hearts about who we are, and about our origins but not so freely about our life purpose or our destiny. On the other hand, we may have a good idea of what our work is in this world and what we believe about life after death, but still not have a clear understanding of our soul's origins or that of human kind. The places where we find our insight blocked and our beliefs unclear make patterns of stuck energy which repeat themselves in our lives in many areas, physical health among them.

Scanning the Energy Field

We can find the physical location behind these blocked places in our lives by reading and scanning our energy fields. The man-in-black in a ritual circle does this during any ritual as a means of assessing the well-being of the people participating in any high-energy magic raised during a sabbat or esbat. It is the same in a healing circle. Any participant can sense the auras or chakras of their friends once they step out of their own ego and join the collective energy of the universe present in spiritual endeavor. Some of us will be able to see the auras or chakras. When we assess our health as individuals or for someone else we pass our hands through the aura or use a pendulum to find places where the energy flows freely or is constricted. Some call this dowsing. Scanning the energy field of a client enhances our perception. The energy around the body may make the pendulum swing erratically or stop altogether where the body is hurt. Scanning with an open hand may reveal injury or pain by a change in temperature, either hot or cold on the palm of the scanner's hand. Balanced feathers, tuning forks or drums beat softly around the body can reveal the same thing.

Testing our accuracy using several scanners, each with different methods, is always interesting. One person may report a chill around a person's left knee. Another will see the pendulum respond at the same point. A third person might hear the resonance of their drum sound duller around the knee. A fourth using a balanced feather might see it dip or turn over the knee as the feather is held lightly across the index finger. What all this means depends on the report from the person attached to the knee, but for the rest of us our scanning revealed something of significance constricts the energy at that point. Having a good sense of human biology, anatomy and body chemistry helps interpret that.

Listening

The explanation from the person seeking healing is more important than anything the rest of us have to say. A good healer is a good listener. Although the individual may have an arthritic left knee for a reason s/he does not know, hearing what they do know helps shape the ritual or healing response for them and around them. If the person who seeks healing is not part of the planning, then the healing will not take deep root in his or her life. That lack of the client's connection to the healing process is one of the weaknesses of western medicine. A patient shows up, presents a problem and expects a pill or surgery to fix it without much input from the patient. How frustrating that must be for the medical doctor who knows changes in lifestyle, habits, diet or exercise will reinforce the medication or procedures so the problem is actually resolved! Without involving the person mentally, emotionally and physically to the healing of the knee, the symptoms may disappear only to reoccur in another form—perhaps in the other knee.

A healer addresses the whole person. When our bodies give us a medical problem to solve, they are also presenting clues to our needs as bodies, souls and spirits. It may be that a sore knee needs appreciation for its work. A knee is a metaphor for kneeling, supplication, submission, flexibility, service, and oppression. It also has an erotic connection as a tentative first touch of familiarity from a potential lover. An old fashioned marriage proposal starts on bended knee. The knee is one of the most vulnerable joints because of its biomechanics, so pain there can be related to security. It is also one of those body intersections where pain and dis-ease are telegraphed from some other place.

Any or all of these could be hiding behind an arthritic knee. Following the beginning of energy issues around a client's arthritic knee or any other ailment is a process of discovery which we may be allowed to join if we are loving and trustworthy listeners.

We are fools if we jump to conclusions about that sore knee in the absence of the knee's owner. We are oppressors ourselves if we insist we understand the significance of the energy blocks around that knee when the individual is stuck and unable to voice their pain. Finding their voice is part of the reason they need healing. Learning to speak their truth is far more important than getting rid of knee pain. Our job as alternative healers is to open the door for that story and to hold it open until they are able to walk through it.

Certainly a sore knee can be a matter of a torn cartilage. I would be the first to urge someone to have it fixed rather than suffer. However, if one has surgery one needs also to honor that process with meditation and ritual so that all the bodies are present in the process and all work together for healing. That is a little different than what is usually done by physicians or energy healers. I believe when we experience the best from western medicine, which is very good at surgical intervention and emergency care, we need to back up our treatment with the alternatives which we do equally well. The various healing modalities, including western medicine, work together effectively to reconnect the physical, emotional, mental and spiritual bodies. That is what the elders mean when they say walk in balance.

The Wounded Healer

We as healers are wise to feed our own health and positive energy in the aura circle around us. Herbs, nutrition, fitness and yoga keep us healthy with a strong immune system. Although the concept of wounded healer is true, we do have obligations to ourselves to stay well. I am always startled by stories of medical researchers being diagnosed with the very diseases they study. There is something about our intense mental focus on a disease that creates opportunities for that dis-eased energy to concentrate in our bodies. Keeping our energy circulating freely through our bodies may prevent our fears from creating illness. Being positive about who we are and where we are going helps prevent illness. There is no need to pick up other people's illnesses either through the transfer of bacteria and viruses or through fear and vulnerability. We do that, but we do not need to.

How can we avoid becoming a wounded healer? Well, the truth is we likely cannot since we all have wounds of one sort or another. Acknowledging our own physical, mental, emotional or spiritual challenges keeps us humble. We present ourselves as a helper-healer, not some super spiritual guru on a pedestal. We assist people as they find their healing at the same time as we seek our own. This balancing of healer and wounded has a long history. The wounded healer is another Carl Jung archetype going back to the myth of Chiron who had both an emotional scar and a physical wound that could not be healed.

Chiron's Story

Chiron was the son of Cronus—as were many of the Greek heroes and legends—and Philyra daughter of the Ocean. Cronus, one of the Titans, sought out Philyra who as an oceanid (aka Undine) could shapeshift as well as he could. She transformed into a swift mare and fled the lusting Cronus who pursued her as a stallion. Might overcomes right in their story. The stallion Cronus caught and mounted the unwilling mare. The two conceived the composite child Chiron who carried his parents' physical forms of human and horse, known as a centaur. When he was born, Philyra was aghast her son appeared as such a monstrosity and appealed to the Gods to be relieved of the responsibility to raise him. She transformed into a linden tree, known for its sweetness. Chiron might not have agreed with that characterization, since he experienced her rejection as a deep wound in his heart. His father had no interest in him either, so his uncle Apollo befriended him as a foster father. From Apollo and Artemis Chiron learned hunting, archery, astronomy, botany and the arts.

Rather than following the debauched and raging reputation of the other centaurs, Chiron grew to be a noted healer and teacher. His 21 students included Achilles, Herakles and Asclepius. However, fate can be unkind. Married with several daughters,

Chiron lived in good health through the ages. He inherited immortality from his parents, despite their rejection of him. One day, however, his former student Herakles was embarking on his fourth labor to retrieve the wild boar from Mt. Erymanthos. Herakles stopped for rest at the home of another of the centaurs and unwisely opened a cask of their wine. A rowdy herd of centaurs smelled the grapes and stampeded toward it. They brandished clubs and threw rocks at Herakles who fought back with arrows and firebrands. The gang of centaurs ran to Chiron's cave to hide, but the fight carried on. Chiron was wounded by a stray arrow in his knee. Herakles attended to the wound promptly, but the arrow was tainted by the blood of the Hydra. The wound could never heal. It caused the immortal so much pain he longed for death.

In compassion for his mentor's pain, Herakles arranged for an exchange among the immortals to release Chiron from his agony. Prometheus was undergoing daily torture for having brought fire to the mortals. If Chiron agreed to relinquish his immortality and descend to the underworld, Prometheus could be pardoned and Chiron could die. The deal was struck with Zeus. At his death, Chiron's spirit was placed in the sky as the constellation Sagittarius.

Death as Healing

With death, we step into the center of the circle, the place of soul and spirit and descend into the Void as did Chiron. His final act of teaching as the wounded healer was to open our understanding to appreciate death. In our human minds, that sounds frightening indeed. Part of our purpose in studying the quartered circle is to find out how to enter the Void and to return. We seek the meaning of death. Like Kay Whitaker, we confront both destiny and death.

Many times we feel we have failed when a client dies despite the best effort of the community to intervene in the course of an illness or accident. Merlin and I felt that way when we worked with my mother in the 1990s. As a victim of an auto accident and likely poor medical treatment, she struggled from April to August in the hospital. In partnership with the medical staff, we fixed one thing after another but it was not enough to save her life. She knew in June she wasn't going to get well. I failed to listen. This was my mother! I was unable to let go. All of us were focused on her survival in this life. Generously, she stayed until we were worn out by the effort. Only then could we agree to let her leave us physically. I still have moments when I think I did not do enough, or say enough. I hear her voice chiding me for that. She had many aches and pains and problems in addition to the trauma to her lungs from that accident. Her death healed all of that. I still struggle to honor her wisdom in knowing what I did not know about death as a healing. She thinks we succeeded. We think we failed. I suppose that is how most of us feel when a friend dies. For that reason my mother sent me a message in the clouds three days after she crossed. In a mackerel sky in block letters she wrote my nickname followed by 'Wheeeee.' Seriously, she did. She had been a cloud reader all her life, and that is what she did. Death is a healing.

Ritual Healing

Healing within the quartered circle offers the protection found in any ritual space. It also strengthens the healing energy as an act of magic, which is the purpose of most ritual circles. In addition when we call the Guardians of the Watchtowers, we are joining with higher energies associated with the archangels. You may recall that of the archangels, Raphael was known as the healer, Michael as the protector, Uriel (or Oriel) as the mystic and Ariel as the ruler of the unconscious, sleep and death. We incorporate the healing each of those realms provides.

In setting the Guardians for the quarters of a healing circle, we can ask Raphael to heal the wound in the north, the place of the body. We can ask Michael to protect us from illness in the east, the place of the intellect. We can ask Uriel for the mystic ability to understand the healing and illness in the south, the place of spirituality and will. Finally we can ask Ariel to join Raphael in healing the wound, providing rest, healing the unconscious aspects of the wound and finally, in assisting in the soul's transition when the healing involves physical death in the west, the place of emotions and dreams. Whether or not we work with the archangels by name, we can ask the same of each of the Guardians of the Watchtowers in setting a healing circle.

The Healing Ritual

To proceed then, once we have discussed with the client the healing, diagnosis, treatments and care they have already received, we invite the client to ritual space with a chair or massage table in the center depending on the work we mean to do. We have several bottles of spring water for drinking placed on the altar. We come to the circle after ritually washing our hands to remove any contaminates, both physically and energetically. When we enter the ritual space, we smudge ourselves and the area unless the person objects because of respiratory conditions. In that case we may use a crystal wand to clear the area.

We ground with the person so we are all working with the earth and celestial energies.

Then I again ask the client for permission to proceed. I remind them they are in charge and may ask questions or direct our touch as they feel they need to.

We cast the circle, honor the ancestors, call the Elementals and Guardians and request help from our healing deities.

We scan the body and identify energy blocks. Then we work on removing them. We may work in silence or speak depending on the direction of the healing spirits present in the ritual. Much of this work is in partnership with our spiritual mentors. Some of what we say is channeled.

We may have healing music playing in the background. Remember sound vibrations heal too.

We ask for feedback from the person receiving healing. We remind ourselves that the healing response may increase gradually during the ritual and for days afterward.

We wait until we feel the presence of our healing guides begin to withdraw. They signal the session is finished for the day. We give them thanks.

Then we ground again. We return the person's power to him or her, seal the aura and then step back. We make sure we are individually able to release the energy of pain or illness back into the earth. After testing ourselves to see how balanced we feel, we keep any energy we need and send our elevated mental and spiritual energy to the earth and sky.

We thank the Guardians and Elementals as we release them.

We thank the ancestors and deities and release them.

We open the circle and drink the spring water.

Healing Modalities

Within the ritual we can offer a variety of healing skills, none of which is a substitute for medical care. Any of them may succeed in ways which will surprise the medical doctor. Each Witch or Pagan is challenged to learn at least one modality well and use it freely for the good of all and harm of none. This generosity is the essence of community and connection among us.

Removing Energy Blocks. What modalities remove energy blocks within the sacred circle? Our choices are directed by the spirit guides. As a team, we collectively or in turns use one or more of the following:

Physical Touch. Laying on hands we hold the physical connection with the client while we draw energy through our bodies from the earth, moon, or stars and send it into the client until the blockage flows out of their field and into the ground. The earth and celestial energy flows as if through a one-way valve. The pain or illness does not rise back through us.

Physical touch can involve extracting negative energy from the client similar to shamanic healing practice. In that case, the energy worker imagines throwing the extraction into a small green fire that burns the energy blockage and changes it into healing love. Alternatively, the energy worker can send the blockage into a pool of healing water, a spring of Brigid or a physical cauldron of pure water. Once I collected some persistently troublesome negative energy into a box to be physically buried. The disposal of the negativity is an important part of the healing process and protects the workers from picking up the illness they are removing.

Body Work. Even if we are not professionally trained massage therapists, physical body work in which we are linked to our spirit guides is highly effective. Note that even where massage therapists are licensed, we cannot accept payment for this healing modality. As I said before, we work for the common good without remuneration and are ministers, priests and priestesses of our faith. Obviously the healers and the client need to plan ahead so the client can disrobe in a changing room and slide under the covers before everyone joins them in the circle. We maintain a person's modesty with good sheet coverings and reinforce the client's control over the intensity of our muscle stimulation and pressure. We follow the same limits and guidelines licensed therapists follow. That addresses the legality of hands-on healing and body work in our jurisdiction. We also have considerable training in musculature, physical technique and energy healing in addition to having had regular work done by professionals in the field. Our own professional massage therapist does wonderful things to keep us healthy. That is qualitatively different than body work done in sacred space by a group of healers. I recommend both. I do not think I need to reinforce that body work is neither sexual touch nor foreplay, but there. I said it.

Acupressure. We have learned simple effective cures for headaches, colds, flu, back pain, sore legs, toothache from using charts and books. No needles are involved. Acupressure follows the same 14 meridians as acupuncture. By stimulating or quieting specific points on a combination of meridians, the healer is able to restore balance and energy flow in the client's body, or their own. I rely on acupressure treatment for sinusitis both in and out of ritual.[76] We have a favorite acupressure procedure for pain relief which does not treat the condition but does reduce the pain.[77] Another routine reduces emotional stress and physical fear responses including increased blood pressure. Details on that protocol are described in Chapter 14 of this text.

Reflexology. Using charts, flash cards and even reflexology socks we learn to stimulate the areas on the hands and feet which correspond to our major organs and body structures. Reflexology enhances body work or acupressure for muscle tension. The area along the inside of the foot below the great toe and along the arch, for example, is helpful in reducing back pain and sciatica, a common complaint in modern life. Further relief can be encouraged by running up both sides of the foot and ankle for several inches and by pressing on the underside of the foot near the little toe.[78]

Kinesiology. Using anatomy charts we can test various muscles for strength or weakness and then use the acupuncture meridians and trigger points to improve the balance in the body system which corresponds to symptoms and dis-ease. Kinesiology is a remarkable tool to understand feedback from the body. Without the client knowing what works or what is needed, the body sifts out fact from fiction. My favorite resource in working with muscle testing and the meridians is *Touch for Health*.[79] Donna Eden's books and videos are also very helpful.[80]

Sound Vibrational Healing. Another method of releasing tension and pain in the body involves sound. We sing tones into the blockage or set tuning forks over them. In chakra balancing, we may also tone the seven main chakras on a scale starting at the root with 'C'. Tuned crystal singing bowls create the same effect for a group. A full set of them will tone the entire scale. In one of our Web classes, Soft Moon Rising taught how to sing one's chakras. Willow Woman, a woman in her 70s who sometimes used a walker to get around, began practicing daily chakra toning on herself. Later Satira taught a class with a full set of crystal singing bowls. Again Willow Woman worked with the tones and sounds. She found the bowls had a profound impact on her physical body. The sound healing together with nutritional changes created a change in her that is noteworthy. She walks unassisted now. She climbs stairs. She has lost a good deal of weight and she returned to work part time providing human services to mentally challenged adults. Later she fell in love and started an entire new adventure in her life. Recently she reported her success in a three-mile hike in the Catskills. When I asked her about her personal practice she said she can feel the tones resonate in her body which tells her even without the bowls or tuning forks she is on the right pitch and working the right healing.

Crystal Healing. Crystals use their natural internal vibrations to clear the energy flowing in and through the body. They are soundless to our ears, but they are also healing vibrations. We can lay them on the body or use them as wands over hurt places. They can be set in a grid under the chair or massage table to enhance the healing.

I suppose I was one to underestimate the power of crystal healing until I had this experience. Merlin and I were working on our friend Stonelight Weaver in the ritual room, removing chronic pain she had after an old automobile accident. We had soft music playing and a few candles around the room. It was very peaceful. Because we are all old friends, she choose not to bother with sheets and covers and lay face down naked so we could work on her sore back. I was at her feet working with reflexology. Merlin had loosened her neck and shoulders with acupressure and body work. We are both Reiki masters.

Working in concert with his guides, Merlin picked up an amethyst crystal point, one that is about four inches long, and lightly touched points down her spine simply following the directions of his guides. I was not paying much attention to him, concentrating my thoughts on our friend's healing and her feet until he called my name and gestured to her back. A thin white light had extended straight down her back to her sacrum and then split into a V across her buttocks. Then it extended down the back of her thighs. Doubter that I am, I thought he had marked her dry skin, until he told me what had happened. The two of us simply held the energy at her head and feet at that point, until the light faded. I can only explain those lines of light in terms of the body's resonance with the crystal as it seeks its own healing. In effect, the crystal created its own grid. Crystals and bodies do that. When I asked our friend for permission to use her story she said the healing felt like a cool white laser releasing tension between her bones and muscles, lowering her pain level. Her pain stayed at that lower level for years until the rest was released through massage and Reiki. Her healing remains. That pain is gone and she expects it will not return.

Reiki. Those of us who are initiated healers at the Web all have our Reiki attunements given by a Reiki master. Reiki is a hands-on system of healing from Japan which works in harmony with all these other modalities. For a Reiki master, offering any of these healing practices is unconsciously combined with Reiki. We would find separating them very difficult. At his request, I use Reiki and energy healing nearly every day on Merlin's extremities. He has peripheral neuropathy in his feet and legs related to old back injuries. I lose sight of what impact our

> daily Reiki sessions may have, since like the rest of us he is a wounded healer. I keep thinking the neuropathy will disappear and it does not. However, when he has a check up with a neurologist, the assessment is always positive. They wonder why he functions so well, since western medicine can do nothing to help. They think people in his condition are disabled, perhaps relying on wheelchairs. The truth is Merlin has full mobility, cuts firewood and goes to exercise class at the local pool several times a week.

All of these methods have one basic thing in common. The practitioner opens himself or herself through the crown chakra and allows the universal creative force of love to work through the practitioner. This may be a very quiet presence we sense in ourselves, something that says, 'Ah! Be still. I am here.' Or it may be a powerful overwhelming arrival that reverberates throughout our bodies, sometimes taking on a sexual charge of kundalini energy. No one can dictate what it is or should be. A healer trusts the inner knowing. The outcome is left to the wisdom of the healing guides and the client's many, many selves.

In a sacred circle, when the healing work is complete, we return the client's hands to their belly chakra as a symbol that the vulnerability they shared with us has finished for the day, and their personal power is restored to their own hands. Then, with one healer on each side, we gather the aura and seal it back up around them like a cocoon, laying our hands on top of the client's hands, alternately stacked and including each healer. Then we remove our hands and step back. We give thanks to the spirits who helped. We ground the energy we have raised, giving thanks to Gaia for her assistance in keeping us all well and stable. We release the healing guides and helpers, the Elementals and Guardians by name. Then we open the circle with a chant or by walking widdershins around the space.

By that time the client has likely returned to ordinary

consciousness and is ready to sit up or stand, wrapped in a blanket if need be. We caution them to take their time. They have been between the worlds, usually for an hour or more. We offer them the spring water we brought to the circle to drink and partake ourselves. Then we leave to ritually wash our hands to complete the cycle. The client remains in the ritual space alone as long as they need to. If the client needs to dress, they do this once they are ready to reintegrate into ordinary reality. Again, privacy is always protected.

Confidentiality

Privacy and confidentiality are important issues of trust. The individual who seeks healing has often been commandeered by the medical profession and well-meaning relatives telling them what to do and how to do it. Our work as sacred healers is to be a facilitator of healing. We recognize that any healing that occurs is the client's work in partnership with Spirit. We may be invited into that partnership, but we are not primary partners. For that reason, we have no business telling other people's stories without their permission. We certainly have no business revealing their identities. Willow Woman, Stonelight Weaver and Merlin all agreed to share this part of their stories, or I would not have been as specific.

People who come to us for help in the quartered circle must be able to trust us with their secrets. Truth be told, as we work inside the spiritual, mental and emotional auras, we are apt to find out things the client has not recognized. We are telling them their own secrets. We need to do so in a gentle and tentative fashion.

For example, in working with a client we may recognize that although they seem placid on the outside they are filled with rage. I would not reveal that in a group healing effort unless I could ask facilitating questions that the client can choose to answer or not. With my hand over the part of the body that is ailing, I might comment, 'I'm feeling a lot of roiling energy caught up here. Can you identify it? You don't have to name it aloud, but it might help us.' The client can shrug off the question or take the opportunity to explore his or her feelings within the circle. The choice is truly theirs. If a client speaks about anger and its source, then all the assembled healers agree to keep the information confidential. No one shares the client's illness, secrets or breakthroughs. If a person cannot be trusted with secrets, then s/he cannot help with the healing. Confidentiality and respect are that important.

I had a personal experience which underscored for me the importance of confidentiality. I was going through a rough patch and needed all the help I could get so someone brought this man, a friend of a friend, to my house. In the process of scanning me, he asked publically without any ground rules, 'Do you have any idea how angry you are?' I gave him a straight look and answered in monosyllables. The healing session was over as far as I was concerned. He could not be trusted nor did he have good sense. That put the rest of his skills in question. I suspect if he was sensitive enough to know I was angry, he also knew my anger spiked at his bluntness. We were not working in a sacred circle. I did not know what to expect or what he really was prepared to offer. My resistance to him was based on the source of my anger sitting within hearing distance of his question. Time, place and confidentiality all need careful choices in a healing circle. Had I not been so sick, I would not have participated in the first place. I was trusting the wrong people. I do not trust him to have kept his insight to himself afterward either.

The Circle of Healing

There is more to the circle of healing than creating ritual space. Some of it is a mystery rooted in sacred geometry. In the process of what happens during a healing session, the healers are also healed. There are many times, more than we can count, when someone has made an appointment with us for a healing session, then the day and hour arrives and one of us feels our wounds more keenly than usual. We wonder if we should back out, but a commitment is a commitment. As Woody Allen the film director and actor said, 80 percent of success is just showing up.[81] We have consistently found ourselves healed, our pain reduced, and our mental state improved by participating in the healing energy raised for someone else.

This healing response is not universal among alternative healers. Professionals in the field report feeling drained or becoming ill after healing sessions. I say that only to encourage new healers to be consistent with grounding and channeling energy from the earth and the celestials. Feeling exhausted and depleted after healing sessions are indicators that too much is taken from the body of the workers gathered in the ritual. Headaches, symptoms carried away from the client by the healer, or disorientation are all warning signs that the cycle of energy has not been completed between the earth, moon, sky and human. Working with energy and illness is not an area we can afford to be casual about. Like contamination from bacteria, energy drains and unshielded exchanges can make us seriously ill.

My healer friend Soft Moon Rising says she looks internally whenever she feels ill or imbalanced, particularly in connection with a healing session. She focuses on the physical problem and asks if it is hers. If the answer is no, she sends it away with words and gestures. Because she is experienced and working in concert with her guides, the problem leaves immediately. If the answer is yes, she starts her own healing right away. She is one of the healthiest women I know.

Shields and Other Magical Arts

To maintain our own health or to guide another person through their own restoration to health, making a physical representation of the circle can be a magical reinforcement of our personal balance. The ways to do this are only limited by our own creativity. We can make a physical shield using shamanic symbols, heraldic symbols, Pagan symbols or other objects of power. This can be as simple or complex as one would like. These circles are explorations of identity and connections with the spirit world.

Shields are more familiar than you might think. They are

repeated over many cultures as medicine wheels, Celtic knots, pentacles, mandalas and even in scientific diagrams of the solar system or of atoms. Science is, after all, another culture with its own values, languages, mores and customs. We are familiar with these maps of atoms or solar systems organized around the sun, a nucleus or an empty center known as the Void, but not necessarily with the concept of a shield.

Shield making is criticized as cultural appropriation of a Native American practice. However, every culture had shields covered with symbols and used to protect the shield bearer and to identify him or her. European heraldic devices revealed lineage, family or clan and oaths of fealty in Europe. They appeared on shields, banners, crests, tunics, and badges. These devices were tied to family identity and their history. Understanding who you are can be revealed by the symbols you or your family chose. In my case, one of my family lineages is the Clan Fraser of Scotland. In combination with the head of a stag, their motto on the badge is: *Je suis prest* (I am ready). Merlin has asked me for years '*Es que tu pres?*' (Are you ready?) whenever he was prepared to leave a place. Little did he know I and my family have been ready for centuries. These little synchronicities are significant in our healing because they help us remember who we are.

In our Web Wicca fourth level class, which lasts a full year and a day, each student prepares a circular artwork as their initiatory project. A shield drawing about one's chosen healing practice follows a rich tradition, though other themes for a shield help the student equally well. So do other media. StoneLight Weaver prepared a sand painting with colored sands and sacred objects. She told an earth healing story as she created it for the class. When we had has sufficient time to meditate on it, she swept it away as an indication of the temporal nature of our creations.

Ravija drew a pastel of a sunrise she had seen on the way to work. The sun rose muted by the mists. The light created a full circle of luminosity around the sun stretching far out away from the center. The clouds reflected the radiant colors. She caught it all with her palate of pastels in a poster sized work of art which credits the connection between beauty, identity and balance in our healing. These two women caught the magic of it in their projects.

I have next to my desk a leather shield fastened with sinew to a willow hoop. It has feathers, stickers, crystals, drawings, beads, and shells. I made it years before I understood what it meant. There is a spiral of energy in the center. Stars pass through that spiral and become circles as they descend to earth. The shield is about the birth of human souls from the stars and the interplay of the Elementals with them. My shield exudes a quiet healing to me as I write beneath it. Suzanne looked at it the first time and declared it 'real art.' That is true in so far as the balance between the soul-body-mind-spirit is contained in its roundness. The willow frame connects to itself like Ouroboros. The entire shield helps me remember who I am.

An Art Project

To participate in the quartered healing circle, create a work of art that represents balance and wellness. Oils, pastels, water colors, clay, mosaics, fabric art, string, wire—anything can be the medium for a healing experience. When I made my shield, another woman used an embroidery hoop as her frame. Her shield was created in needlework. A quilter who taught our class in death and dying used fabric art to make comfort quilt squares to hand out as she led the discussion of those difficult subjects. They can as easily be round.

In each case, the maker finds things spontaneously placed in their healing circle artwork that surprises them. The meaning is deeper and more personal than expected. This is the magic of pulling all the pieces together to make ourselves whole. We have to do it, not simply think about it. I encourage all artists to create in sacred space, sitting in the presence of their guides and guardians. This act energizes the will to heal through the creative arts.

A Dolphin Story

Sometimes healing comes through our connection with the natural world. Merlin discussed his reading about cranial sacral somatic responses at the time I was writing this book.

> John Upledger, D.O., O.M.M., worked in Clearwater FL in the 1960s and 70s where he developed an admiration and friendship with the wild dolphins in the bay. They seemed to him to share his capacity as a healer which he later incorporated in his work with people with disabilities. What seemed significant to our discussion of the circle as a sacred figure in healing involved an author friend of Upledger named Timothy Wyllie.[82] Wyllie who also lived on waterfront property along the Florida coast decided to test the intention of the dolphins that typically swam with the regulars who live on the beach and played with them in the water. Specifically, Wyllie decided to test the stories of dolphin rescues and his own sense that they were watching out for him. He feigned distress in deep water to see what they would do. The dolphins swam in circles around him as if assessing the situation but did not intervene. Apparently they were not fooled.
>
> The next night Wyllie pushed the test further than a rational man would. He swam out into the Gulf as far as he could without reserving anything for the swim back. The dolphins were there, circling around him as he started going down. Apparently they realized his distress was genuine. Three of them brought him back to shallow water; one on each side offering a flipper so they could tow him, one alternating under and behind him. They waited at the three foot depth to be sure he could stand and wade ashore before they left. The rescue, which was genuine, started with a circle of dolphins swimming around him.[83]
>
> Later, when Upledger started working with patients in the water, wild dolphins circled them as a group several times. Then one would break out of the circle as the others continued swimming in which looks to me like a group holding the energy

> for the working. The one would come to either the therapists or the patients and use touch with its nose, a contact that lasted several seconds up to a minute. The touch stimulated a rush of energy that the therapists could sense, given they were used to sensing energy fields. Many times the patients were measurably better when they left the water.

Whether the circle is created by nature, the dolphins or humans, healing breaks out within the circle. The quartered circle is not a replacement for conventional medicine, but it does restore balance to our bodies on levels medical doctors cannot reach. Each of our bodies—physical, intellectual, volitional, and emotional—needs strengthening when we are ill. Each of them helps maintain wellness when recognized and nurtured. For that reason, working with the four directions, the Guardians and our multiple selves creates continuing health in the circle of our lives. These connections also help us emerge from the underworld where we rest ailing selves and psyches. We can change our habits and wounds as surely as we repair our bodies. This change is built into our cells.

Chapter 12

Mind and Heart Healing

As we have seen, our physical healing is securely connected to our emotional, mental and spiritual healing. Circle magic is not always sufficient to create physical healing without our willingness to understand how our heads and hearts are involved. Full healing often requires new ideas about old beliefs. We find ourselves reframing the past and digging deeper into the shadows to find hidden treasure in our memories and in those things we refuse to know. Individuals expecting easy access to the hidden self may well be disappointed. This journey is one filled with dead ends and illusions to hide the shadow selves one believes to be unacceptable within our circle of family and friends. Healing our hearts and minds exposes what we dare not tell ourselves about our selves. It is an identity quest which relies on finding clues in our life patterns and repeated themes.

The Shadow Knows

Carl Jung said, 'The shadow is the invisible saurian tail that man still drags behind him. Carefully amputated, it becomes the healing serpent of the mysteries. Only monkeys parade with it.'[84] I love that imagery. Jung is remarkably Pagan in his psychic insights despite what his religion and education made of him. Essentially, the mental and emotional healing within the quartered circle forges connections between our opposites of light and dark, male and female, angel and demon. Our task in Earth School is in building bridges between our conscious and unconscious selves so the lizard tail becomes a caduceus, the serpent of healing as we first suggested in Chapter 3. The known meets the unknown in the process of individuation. Our illusions fade and we meet ourselves.

A friend who has walked long years on this path in Jungian

analysis suggested that the journey takes a good deal of humility and the ability to laugh at ourselves. Even then, she suggests, we only see the patterns made by the shadow, not the shadow itself. This shadow quest reminds me of the dorajuadiok of Hank Wesselman's shamanic writings.[85] The dorajuadiok appear as black shadows because their light is so bright we would be blinded. So does Wesselman see the pattern or the spirit? Our unconscious selves or shadows are like that. They are both hidden and (we think) shameful. Jung calls them golden because of the gifts they bring us in self-knowledge and healing. When we see ourselves playing with our own negativity for the sake of the experience rather than possessed by it, we are able to smile about our fears and limitations. They are roles in the drama of our own biography. Some dramas are tragic and others comic. We are more than these roles. We can view them safely. When they are integrated as part of our story, we have created some alchemical healing of our own. Then we hold in our hands the opportunity to remember who we really are.

From that it should be clear the shadow is not our evil twin. Parts of us relegated to the shadows include some very strong characteristics which were not encouraged in our lives so we stuffed them away in the closet. Here Jung will roll over in his grave, since he had rather set views of masculine and feminine, but I as a woman identify extreme femininity such as the damsel in distress as part of my shadow. I frankly have difficulty seeing any part of her in my history. As soon as I remember an incident where I might have been in such crisis that I needed rescuing, I feel my awareness turn away and look at something else. The pattern surfaces in my humor, my selection of movies and books, my friends and my politics. The mythos of Dorothy is 'I'd rather do it myself!', which is a phrase I used often and was praised for throughout childhood. For me, the damsel is buried deep. I do not recognize her. She is clearly not a bad woman, but she is in my shadow.

Similarly, my friend Fey identified athleticism as a part of her shadow. Her family focused on the arts and resented sports. Our families' beliefs are a large part of our shadow formulation. My father said so often 'I can't stand a helpless woman' I assumed they were bad. Fey assumed girls should not have muscles. Those normal parts of our personalities were sent to the shadow self, unquestioned.

In our soul growth, both of us needed to learn the value of the shadow. The feminine damsel can accept help from the knight in shining armor without rolling her eyes. She can admit when she is over her head. She can accept tribute to her femininity without losing her identity and independence. The artistic soul can also play tennis or run a marathon. The mature self-actualized adult can still hear the parental voice that says, 'In our family, we don't do that.' That freedom is the goal of integration in the personality.

Hug Circles

Sometimes what we learn from family or experience are deep negative shadow messages. Violence, abuse and incest might create a perennial victim or an unconscious abuser. Relearning how to connect with people who are not abusive is difficult when the boundaries have been breached. Picturing how that works can be helpful in rebuilding our sense of safety.

I once had the privilege of teaching with Oreida Anderson, a sex education counselor from Indiana in the US. She worked in the field of relationships and sexuality, particularly with disabled populations, until shortly before her death in 2011 at the age of 89.

In the 1980s we were training crisis advocates for the sexual assault victims' intervention program known as SAVAR in Auburn NY. After a particularly difficult time with one of the women in the program, Oreida told me she was going to ask her exactly when it was she had been sexually assaulted. It was clear to her that the woman's erratic behavior was based in fear, grief and anger typical of a rape survivor—or perhaps incest. If Oreida had that conversation it was in private and I never learned the outcome. What she added to our studies that weekend was a lesson on personal boundaries and the hug circles commonly used in educating special needs children and adults. More recently a number of people have developed the circles curriculum[86] and marketed it. I footnote them here since they hold the copyright on printed and video material. However, I learned it 20 years earlier from Oreida.

Essentially what Oreida taught us that weekend was to conceptualize our personal boundaries as a series of concentric circles. The inner circle is the circle of intimacy. That is a private circle for myself and when the time is right, for my lover. Additional people need not apply. It is inappropriate for parents, friends, or funny uncles to transgress my boundaries into my circle of intimacy.

Outside and concentric to the circle of intimacy is the big hug circle. Parents, good friends, dates, family members can all belong here in the big hug circle. Pagans often end a ritual with a big hug for people with whom they have celebrated the sabbat. Connecting with big hugs shares our spiritual family connections, as long as we are agreed hugs are appropriate. Insisting on hugs is not. In some circles a hug includes a kiss. For others it does not.

Stepping further out from the center is a third circle; this one is the casual hug circle. This might be a one armed hug, pat on the back, or quick two armed hug. Oreida described it as the hug we give a friend we pick up at the airport when we haven't seen them in a long time. People in a ritual circle who are somewhat uncomfortable with hugs and do not want to open themselves to the intimacy of a spiritual family, may use this more distant and casual hug.

There is a fourth circle outside the first three called the handshake circle. This is the business person's greeting, or the how-do-you do at an introduction. We know the person's name and a bit about them, but they are acquaintances not friends. In this circle, people remain at an arm's length, literally. Without trust building and time to get to know one another, it is inappropriate for an acquaintance to crash through into a hug circle uninvited. It is also inappropriate to invite them before we have evaluated their character—there are a lot of creeps out there!

The fifth circle is the friendly wave circle. We know these people by sight because they go to the same places, shop at the same stores or live in the neighborhood. We might even know their names. They are not people we know well. We have little information about them and we give them a smile and a friendly wave. They do the same. Neither is an invitation to more intimacy. If someone from this circle tries to push past our boundaries and claim a hug or kiss, we back off with a straight look and say no. If they are kind and well balanced we will learn more about each other and build trust together. If they are interested in holding power over us, our instincts of flight or fight kick in.

Outside these circles are the strangers. We have not been introduced. We do not know where they live. We know nothing about their lives. Some of them in the helping profession will shake hands. Some in medical professions will need to examine us. They should always maintain professional demeanor. Once I had a doctor behave too fondly while he was checking my throat glands for swelling. He complimented my earrings and asked who gave them to me as he pushed back my hair from my forehead. That was definitely a violation of my boundaries. I was really sick with bronchitis so I breathed germs on him as I claimed they came from my boyfriend who was 6ft 2in, someone I assured him he would not like. He stepped back and left me alone. The earrings actually came from my mother, but he did not need to know that. He was not my regular doctor in the HMO so I did not see him again.

When we have well-defined boundaries based on the fact we know who we are and who we are not, then calling someone on inappropriate behavior is relatively simple. We trust our instincts to know when someone's actions feel odd. We are unblinking when they try to turn it back on us as if we imagined it.

Difficulties arise when we are unclear about who we are. Sometimes that lack of clarity comes from having our boundaries broken by people who refuse to accept our sense of self. Well-meaning family members who think we should hug and kiss Aunt

Clara because they know her even though we do not may start the process of confused boundaries. For people who are sexually violated or physically beaten and abused in their childhood, the boundaries are ripped up in tatters before the child has a chance to ask the question '*Who am I?*' When people we would normally trust in our big hug circle push into the intimacy circle with either sex or violence or both, the damage to our identity is significant. Healing the boundaries where they were torn down is an important step in the emotional and mental circle of healing.

Boundary Repair

How can our boundaries be healed? First, the survivor of abuse needs to understand what healthy boundaries are, that they have the right to live with good boundaries and demand honest relationships. People who have been abused have usually been lied to. They have been told lies about their attractiveness and their desirability. Frequently they believe they are ugly and no one will love them, particularly if they tell their secrets. Relearning the truth about their own worth and that they have right to keep unwanted people out of their inner circle of intimacy is a difficult step for a person who has been abused. Healing that inner circle may take time and patience. Ritual can help.

Second, the person needs to learn who belongs in which outer circles. That doctor belonged in the stranger circle. I put him back there in a hurry. Someone I met in a bar last night does not belong in the intimacy circle. Someone I have dated for a time might, when I am comfortable with that. Someone I am married to generally does belong in the intimacy circle in a loving and affectionate manner. A married partner who is violent and rapes or beats me loses the right to intimacy as well as the keys to the house. For me that sounds simple. For a survivor of abuse, clear decisionmaking is not so simple. Drawing the circles and putting names in them may help make it simpler for people in the process of reconstructing their boundaries.

When Oreida wondered when it was one of our SAVAR advocates had been sexually assaulted, she based that on the woman's inability to work within boundaries that made sense. The woman demanded best-friend status from people she knew only slightly and then complained that they pulled away from her. She behaved rudely toward people who were her close friends, making unfounded accusations as if she wanted to pick a fight. She switched sides in the middle of a discussion claiming no one understood her. She tried to manipulate people involved in the training weekend and sowed discord among friends. Her temper flared unpredictably at people who were at best in her handshake circle. No one could please her. No one knew where they stood with her. After I learned the hug circles, I kept trying to guess which circle she had me in at any given moment. I was rarely able to predict that.

Healing our lives means we understand we are wounded and we will the wounds to heal. We integrate our history with our present. In saying who we are, we include *'I am a survivor of broken boundaries,'* whatever they may be. We do not stop there. We include all the manifestations we claim in this life. That is the point of integration. We are not only survivors. We are also parents, children, teachers, students and much more.

The point of healing the hurts is to see the whole picture as best we can. I remember a student from many years ago. The class assembled. Many of those in the circle, and we always meet in a circle, were names to me but not much more. We passed the talking stick and introduced ourselves, one by one. Nervously, a young woman took the stick and blurted out that she had ADD and ADHD and was the spoiled brat of the universe. No one yet knew her name. Because the person who holds the talking stick is the center of the universe, no one interrupts. No one else speaks. She finished with her detailed diagnosis and passed the stick. We still did not know her name. We didn't learn it until the stick came all the way back to me and the introductions were finished. Then as gently as possible, I started the teachings about *I Am*. We learned her name then, where she worked and why she was in the class. I hope she remembers that lesson as fondly as I do as an illustration of our complexity and the power to name ourselves.

Third, we use crystals to heal our boundaries. The aquamarine and rhodochrosite we studied in Chapter 10 can be of use in a circle of healing for people with damaged boundaries. Both stones, as we learned, help us identify patterns and themes in our life events. When we repeatedly select friends and lovers who harm us, we know we are seeing evidence of a shadow self that has accepted victimization. If we repeatedly hurt the ones we love we see the shadow of the abuser rising in us. If meanness comes out of our mouth when our intention was to build a relationship with people we like, the defensive shadow is reacting on autopilot for us. If those are the shadows we intend to heal, a crystal grid of aquamarine and rhodochrosite set up in ritual can help the broken heart. Jewelry charged in ritual and worn over the heart can carry the healing with us for as long as we need it. Sacred jewelry of that nature needs to be cleansed and charged with the full moon because it is working full time. People working with therapists might carry these stones in their pockets to help maximize their sessions.

When we understand we have emotional wounds to heal, we must also understand we have strengths. We are people with a wide history, a complex history and multidimensional selves. We are not always the same. We do not always come from the same emotional quotient.

Meet Your Bus Drivers

Another way to look at the complexity of human identity is found in *Who's Driving Your Bus?* by Earnie Larsen and Jeanette Goodstien[87] and *The Dark Side of the Light Chasers* by Debbie Ford.[88] Both help us understand that we are many personas all at the same time. This does not mean we are schizophrenic. It does mean that we are multi-dimensional, multifaceted beings—even if we simply consider who we are on the earth plane in this time and space. So let's start there.

If I were to make a list of my various roles in life, I would include activities as grandparent, partner, ritual leader, poet, builder, cat mom, writer and on and on through all my various duties, relationships and hobbies. Each of those aspects of ourselves can be in charge (drive the bus if you will) at any given time while the rest of the facets of self sit back and enjoy the ride. Understanding who is driving our bus at any given time helps us understand our reactions to the people around us, the ones who make our life wonderful and the ones who dance on our last nerve.

As I have used this concept to help people understand their identities, I have learned that some of us readily list our very best qualities and some of the quirky ones we are secretly proud of. These folks are slow to list the negative qualities in their personality, traits like being short-tempered, self-centered, critical, or being procrastinators. In fact, my teaching experience has been exactly that—people are reluctant to hang out what they see as dirty laundry. Consequently, a class sometimes fails to be real. Until we recognize all of us have shadows, we cannot find the gifts these gray characters bring us. Finding clues to our shadow identities and their gifts is a large leap in our healing and self-knowledge.

On the other hand, I have also learned that some of us can pretty accurately list our presumed negative qualities such as being depressed, being manipulated, or being the perfect Pagan on the outside and miserable on the inside. These folks are slow to find the positive qualities in their personality, like being compassionate, creative, smart, wise, analytic or highly organized. I suspect that individuals who cannot name the good in themselves have boundaries to rebuild and abuse to heal. Unconsciously, they have taken their innate goodness and stuck it in the shadow.

The truth is that we are the heroes of our stories. We are heroic. But we are also the villains in our stories. We are the success and the failures. We came into this incarnation to learn success and failure, joy and disappointment, love and betrayal. Most of us are right on schedule. That does not mean we have no need of healing. We came to be wounded and we came to heal. A key step in our healing of emotional pain comes in accepting all the aspects of self and finding the gifts. We are not all sweetness and light. We are perfect for where we are today. Tomorrow we will be different but we will still be perfect for the time and place. In our today and in our tomorrow we are gloriously flawed.

Accepting the total busload of characters that make up our human personality is important. A repressed, denied or feared aspect of self gets even. It pops up in unexpected ways in our own personality. It shows itself to us in the behavior of other people who act as mirrors for us until we understand. If the people around us are a bitchy, difficult complaining lot then it might be because that is the story we need to pay attention to and find within ourselves. Their behavior is actually a set of clues in the mystery of *Who am I? Why am I here? Where did I come from and where am I going?* I understand this better when I think of the Rule of Three. The energy we send out (The Bitch is unacceptable) returns to us threefold through the actions of others. They are mirrors of our internal prejudice. Our internal prejudice frequently comes from a piece of ourselves we find unacceptable, also known as our shadow.

Journaling on Your Bus Drivers

In your journal or BOS, start a list of your bus passengers, any of whom might be called on to drive. Include these personas as a beginning, but don't limit yourself. Keep going. Give them names like Facilitating Phyllis and Touchy Tony.

Who is driving your bus when you successfully mediate a dispute in the family?

Who is driving your bus when you pitch a hissy fit and yell at the people you love the most?

Who is driving your bus when you get up in the morning and go to work even if you don't want to?

Who is driving your bus right now?

To make this practical, consult your list of people who drive your bus. Check off the ones who were in charge this week. Add any who are missing. I spent a lot of time cleaning up and straightening the house. I refer to her as Sally Homemaker, and I have to remind myself to appreciate her efforts. Sometimes I resent the work she does and that too often translates into resenting her.

I also spent time writing. I call her DL Salinger, using my own initials and the surname of the reclusive American writer. There is something about retreating into my office and refusing to come out and talk to people I find appealing.

I spent an inordinate amount of time reading because I had a new novel I simply could not put down. I call her Bookworm.

I spent time being the Researcher, the Translator, the Travel Guide, the Navigator and of course, Kitty Mom.

When I originally did this exercise, I sketched out 35 stick figures with symbols that delineated their titles. Bookworm sat on a stack of books. Shamanic Worker beat a drum. They were arranged on a winding trail leading up to the bus in a sort of potato-shaped figure. The implication that they wandered around without much pressure to get on board was important in my drawing. People who have shared this exercise have made straight lines, concentric circles, squares and boxes. Each shape is revealing on its own. Think about who is on your bus, where they sit and how often they get to drive. Then make a sketch. Be as elaborate as you like. Mine is in full color and posted on the wall.

Once I had finished my sketch and showed it to my teacher Julie McCarthy, she praised me generously. Then she asked me where the shadow figures were. I had left them out. All the people on my bus were creative, healthy shakers and movers. I went back and made a second drawing. This one included thirteen people in a circle dressed in varying shades of gray and black. They also were stick figures carrying symbols of their identities. Lizzie Borden II carried an axe and represented my rage. Lazy Dottie lay in a bed and refused to get up.

When I finished I felt that someone should stand in the center of the circle to pull the images all together. A picture flashed quickly through my consciousness. I did not fully understand it but I knew it was right: El Zorro! The 19th century action hero in Spanish California who fought injustice and marked his victims with a *Z* slashed in their clothing by his epee was exactly the man for the job.

My bus murals are as whimsical as my descriptions of them. I enjoyed drawing them and making fun of myself. I also opened whole chapters about who I am, why I am here and my origins and destiny by looking at all the parts I play as I go through life. The Lizzie Borden II personality is instructive in those discoveries. Lizzie Borden was a 19th century woman in Massachusetts who was accused of killing her parents with an axe found in the basement of their home. The crime occurred in 1892. After a media frenzy she was tried and acquitted. The murders were never solved. She had been portrayed as a rage-filled murderess but there was no blood evidence. The axe could not be identified with any certainty as the murder weapon. While I am not consciously murderous, I experience the same rage and outrage that everyone else does from time to time. Maturity has mellowed it, but I recall my mother giving me a dressing down for throwing a shoe across the room because I didn't get my own way. Tantrums did not happen in our family. That is why Lizzie is in the shadows.

The fact that my rages were disapproved of in my birth family context is key to pushing Lizzie back in the shadows. The fact I recognize her traits and remember my parent's words are clues to an important aspect to my own shadow self. Apart from well-structured introspection, if I were asked if I am an angry person I would quickly deny it. The denial would be a reflex. I am a good person and in our family we do not throw our anger and rage about along with our shoes. That belies the fact that anyone is capable of anything. All the pieces are there in our physical and chemical make-up. The fact we maintain control and learn to behave appropriately in most circumstances is a wonderful tribute to our soul strength.

What is the gift of my anger? Anger spurs me to action. I no longer feel the need to have my own way in domestic life nor to throw shoes, but injustice, discrimination and basic unfairness make my blood boil quickly. I am a political animal. I know how to organize effectively. After all, I was one of the founding mothers of the sexual assault victims' advocacy center I mentioned above. A group of us started that service as volunteers in 1978 when a series of women were assaulted in public housing. The center still exists and is a funded agency which has survived politics and budget cuts. That spur to effective community action is the gift of my anger and that of several others.

The downside to my anger illustrates how closely the mental, emotional and physical bodies are woven together. In the 1990s under the Clinton administration in the US there was a strong opposition force in Congress, similar to the situation seen under the Obama administration. Heading up that opposition to the Clinton administration was Newt Gingrich, then Speaker of the House of Representatives. My anger at Speaker Gingrich in 1994-1995 went out of control, particularly when he effectively shut down the government over a budget dispute. I do not know him personally, but I was so outraged at the cuts in social services and efforts to limit product liability by manufacturers, I got sick. I did. Within a 30-day time period, I went from being a healthy 40-something-year-old to having acute gall bladder disease requiring surgery. I roll my eyes and laugh at myself now, but at the time it was not funny. I was so galled at what was going on in Washington, I sacrificed my gall bladder.

Fortunately I caught the significance of my physical response to my emotional state and fixed it. I grounded and healed my physical body after surgery with light and love. I lit candles and turned the national situation over to spirits who might be better prepared to deal with big issues than I am. Spirits assured me I would like what happened. In 1999 Newt Gingrich resigned in disgrace from the office of Speaker and from his congressional seat. He had been forced to face charges of ethics violations and misuse of tax exempt donations. The charges were dropped once he resigned which paved the way for his resurrection as a political candidate in 2012, though that was futile as it turned out. Having learned about angry Lizzie, I am not left defenseless in the face of political attacks on the programs I have valued and helped put in place. I have learned to wait and see what happens next instead of letting my emotional body wreak havoc in my physical one. I have every expectation I will like what happens this time too.

I tell my stories about the people on my bus to demonstrate how much in common all of us have. We share the same mad-sad-glad-scared spectrum of human emotions. We all have our public personas and our shadows. Any of us can be wise or foolish. When we identify our complexity we see there is no absolute good and evil in us, only energy in balance or not in balance. Then we can allow ourselves to see the gifts brought to us by our own presumed villainy. When we can do that, then we can step outside of our judgments about ourselves and other people and see that we are indeed part of the total web of consciousness, and that I am you, and you are me.

When we first taught emotional healing as our working in the west, we thought we were ritually and magically finding ways to resolve our difficulties and rid ourselves of problematic aspects of personality. That was never very satisfactory, even though the closing ritual attempted to do just that in a healing way. In fact, we never rid ourselves of our Lizzies because they have an important protective work designed to help us take care of ourselves. Lizzie pushes us to create solutions and structures that address the source of our anger. When we refuse that aspect of ourselves, or on the other hand unleash, encourage and celebrate that ability without restraint, we fall out of balance. On one hand we become wishy washy, pretending we are not angered by injustice. On the other hand we become difficult or dangerous to live with. That is true of every aspect of self that we are uncomfortable with or embarrassed by.

Debbie Ford quotes Carl Jung to describe why we experience so much shadow when we think we are seeking the light. Frustrating difficulties and personal betrayals occur, not because we are being punished or are secretly so awful we cannot find the light. Rather as Jung puts it, 'One does not become enlightened by imagining figures of light, but by making the darkness, conscious.'[89] Our connection with our own darkness can drive the white lighters into a tail spin. I had one apprentice leave over the assignment to seek the dark moon wisdom after we had worked with the full moon wisdom. What we deny has power over us. I have often regretted my subsequent hissy fit when she broke her oaths as an apprentice. I avoided having people make such promises as a result. Eventually I learned that if we do not do the rituals they do us. My short term apprentice did not want to deal with the dark side of herself so I obligingly and unconsciously gave her an experience with my angry shadow. That is truly how life works.

Since that time I have paid attention to the balance created by my shadow Lizzie. Nevertheless, even when I think I am speaking softly or holding my tongue, people have found my shadow and experienced her anyhow. That is not a bad thing as long as I harm none. Our efforts to be light workers means we understand our shadows and can dance with them in a healthy affirmative way. That is what it means to be a Witch—one who holds both the shadow and the light in hand.

People who have not danced that dance find our witchy freedom from guilt unacceptable. They project their shadows on our dance.

The late Native American seer Sunbear taught his tribe that guilt is a useless emotion.[90] Merlin and I have taken that to heart. Guilt is an energy sink that leaves people spinning their wheels over the past. As Sunbear saw it, if we feel bad about something we did, we have a responsibility to fix it. If we took something, we give it back. If we owe a debt we pay it. If we spoke harshly we apologize. If it is something we cannot fix, we pay the price. If we harmed someone we help them heal. In the meantime, we chop their wood and carry their water. If we broke the law, we confess and take the punishment. If our actions hurt someone and they reject our help, but no laws were broken and there is nothing to be done, we let it go. Bemoaning our guilt, wringing our hands about the past, is no use to anyone.

Freeing ourselves from guilt is not then the same as freeing ourselves from responsibility. A soul which seeks deep emotional healing and union between the conscious and unconscious is a brave soul indeed. As we approach our emotional healing within the sacred circles, we find the unknown shadow lurking around corners and hiding behind vague memories. When we get close to the truth, our minds lapse into familiar coping skills, habits so common we do not see them in action until someone points them out. Frequently a helpful observation from friends is met with hostility. The hidden aspects of self are things we do not want to look at. They are also the source of our pain and dis-ease. They are the barriers which undercut our happiness and success.

Defense Mechanisms

The shadow self typically uses three common techniques to distance the conscious from the unconscious self: avoidance, denial and projection. Distancing can be a valuable part of the soul's defense against 'too much, too fast, too soon.' No one needs to be in a hurry to rip the masks off the soul and expose the shadow. Small steps in tolerable doses make a wise path. On the other hand, using these defenses to distance the soul from growth leads to stagnation. Here is how the distancing techniques work:

Avoidance means exactly that; we divert our attention and activity to keep the truth away from ourselves. We are too busy with other activities to spend time writing about our shadow self or sketching silly pictures. We suddenly find the demands of work and family more time consuming so we drop out of class or put the book away. We get sick. In Wicca III where we tackle these difficult aspects of identity we have about a 50 percent attrition rate, mostly from unexpected colds and flu.

We pick fights with people holding up the mirror to our shadow so we can avoid them and, in so doing, avoid ourselves. We blame our friends for making us too angry to sit down with and reason. We nitpick about the details and definitions of the shadow, the soul, of Wicca or Witchcraft, of anthropology and theology. Academics do that all the time to keep the discussion hypothetical instead of allowing for personal growth. Students ask off-topic questions to change the discussion away from uncomfortable reflections on where their blind spots might be. Even among people who are committed to the shadow quest, procrastination can distance them from their discoveries. After all, what can be avoided does not have to be acknowledged.

Denial also is what it seems to be. When confronted with a difficult truth, we dismiss it. Usually this denial is vehemently asserted with lots of exclamation points. Unconsciously we deny the truths about ourselves because out internal judge would not have our unacceptable shadows exposed. What if we were rejected by the people we love for being someone we do not love ourselves? That our family might already love us in spite of our disagreeable nature never occurs to us. We see denial at work when people responsible for a rumor deny they started it. Someone who knows they caused a problem between friends assures everyone they would never hurt a soul. When confronted about words or actions they lie. *I did not do that!*

Sometimes we are so good at denial we fool ourselves. We deny responsibility and point fingers at others. We take on inappropriate responsibility for making other people follow our rules and micromanage them. We ignore issues which are causing severe problems in our families or groups. We misname the problems in order to minimize their importance. Often we deny the truth so quickly it is an unconscious reflex which effectively hides the shadow. Addictions and domestic violence are two problems that hide behind denial, but certainly not the only ones.

Projection is an outward displacement of truth. Like a movie camera that projects a story on a screen, the soul takes the internal source of our difficulties and places it on someone else. When we pick other people apart for failing to meet our expectations we are usually talking about ourselves. Again this is an unconscious act. When we project our issues on someone else we feel convinced that we have been betrayed, let down or hurt by that individual. That the responsibility or source of the problem comes from within ourselves never occurs to us. We end up assigning motives, feelings and roles to people who have no connection to our beliefs about them. In fact they are astonished when confronted about their imagined wrongdoing.

When I was active in the Christian church we used to talk about pitchfork and shovel sermons. Someone would hear a homily that touched a nerve, but rather than take it in for themselves they thought, 'Isn't that just what Mr. Jones needs to hear!' Then they mentally pitch the message in Jones' direction. Later they would hear something else that might be a bit challenging. They quickly think, 'Ah! That is just what Mr. Smith needs to do to straighten out his life!' Then they mentally shovel it off in his direction. Nothing can ever take root at home because of the quick-witted use of the pitchfork and shovel. Avoidance, denial and projection are the pitchforks and shovels of the shadow quest. It is up to us to catch ourselves using them. I regularly look back at myself whenever I want to complain about someone else. What is that soul so generously reflecting to me about myself? What clues to my shadow self do I need to observe?

Finding the Gold

How do we turn the serpent's tail into the healing caduceus? We can never eradicate the shadow. Our goal is to appreciate it and find its strengths. We balance the conscious and unconscious self with soul healing, which is with a self-examined spirituality that satisfies our needs. Because we are 21st century Pagans, we seek resolution with our shadow selves through ritual, meditation, magic and the arts, particularly in storytelling. This is an ever unfolding process. The more we discover and integrate in our shadow quest, the deeper the layers appear to be. I open our seminar on transforming our wounds and discovering the shadow through storytelling with this tale. It is based on an old tale from Taoist China. See where the shadows hide and where is the wisdom.

The Old Man and His Horse: A Favorite Story

Once there was an old Chinese man who lived in a village far from the places of commerce and power. He had little material wealth and few personal possessions, but he did have a fine horse. After a time, the emissary from the warlord who controlled the village came to see this fine horse and if it were all it was said to be, to buy it from the poor old man. The horse was strong and brave, a regal animal if ever there was one. The emissary offered a princely sum for the horse but the old man turned him away because the horse was his friend. One does not sell one's friends. The emissary was impressed with the old man's loyalty to his horse and rewarded him with four small pieces of gold. Then he left without the horse.

The villagers came to the old man, admiring him. They said, 'Old man, you were right to love your horse and keep him for yourself. You stood up to the emissary and now you have four pieces of gold. Could I borrow a bushel of grain?'

The old man shook his head and said he had no grain to lend, but he gave the man who asked a small basket of grain seeds. Then he told the rest of the villagers, 'Let us say I did what I could for my friend. Whether it was wise or foolish we cannot know. We do not know the rest of the story.'

Sometime later, the old man arose to greet the morning sun. He went out behind his house and the horse was gone. He looked all through the village to see if someone had borrowed the horse but no! There was no stallion waiting for his hand on his neck and a treat from his pocket. The villagers immediately gathered around to see the empty paddock. As one they shook their heads. 'Old man!' they warned. 'We knew it was bad luck when you sent that emissary away without the horse. Now you have no horse and only a few gold pieces when you could have had many.' The man who had received the seeds asked, 'How many pieces of gold do you still have?'

The old man shook his head and said he had no idea how many gold pieces he had, that it was not important for him to know. Then he said to the rest of them, 'Let us say I had a horse once, and now I do not. I could not sell a friend nor can I keep him forever. We do not know the rest of the story.'

Of course the old man had sorrow because he did miss his friend the horse. One night when the old man was sleeping, he heard a familiar nicker and whinny. Then he heard hooves. Then he heard lots of hooves. When he went out to greet his friend the horse, there he was with 16 wild mares! The villagers heard the horses too and came running to see what the commotion was. As the old man closed the gate of his little paddock on 16 beautiful horses of every imaginable coat and color, his neighbors came close and clapped him on the back. 'Old man!' they cried. 'You were right! It was good luck that your horse ran away for a little while because he has come back with many mares. You will have foals and your fortune will grow! This horse is your best blessing!' The man who had borrowed the grain and kept track of the gold shook his head. He agreed it was lucky the horse came back but observed that now the old man would have to build a bigger pen.

The old man laughed, clearly glad to have his friend return with such a herd of mares. 'Well, it is true,' he admitted. 'Now I must build a bigger paddock. But let us say I now have 17 horses. We do not know the way of luck nor what happens next.'

The villagers went away shaking their heads. How could an old man be so blessed and not brag of his good fortune? The man who borrowed the grain would like to have hated him for his good fortune, but even he found it hard to be jealous of one who was crazy.

So the old man called his son who lived in another village to help him build a larger paddock and a shed. When their work was done, the son stayed on in the old man's little house to help him gentle and tame the mares. The son was skilled in befriending horses in whispering in their ears and quieting them. Yet even with all his skills, one of the mares threw him off her back when he tried to ride her. He sailed high in the air and landed on a rock which bruised and crushed his spine. He was crippled, unable to move about. The old man and the villagers brought him into the little house that was hardly big enough for two and made the son as comfortable as they could. The wise woman came and gave him herbs and roots to help him sleep but she could not give them hope he would walk again.

Predictably, the villagers stood around the old man's door, muttering about his fate. They said, 'I do not know what to think, old man. It may seem lucky that you have 16 horses and that some of them will give you beautiful foals, but look at what bad luck this is. Maybe you better get rid of those horses. Your son is crippled and what will you do?' The man who had borrowed the grain offered to take one or two of the mares, in order to help out.

The old man thought of his son in the house and the horses in the field and shook his head. 'Let us say my son is injured and I have many horses. We do not yet know what will happen.'

All the villagers left, with the exception of the healer woman. As they went to their homes they thought, 'What a crazy old man who cannot see the truth of anything.' The man who borrowed grain went home and hugged his sons glad they were well and safe. But he did not have any horses. The healer woman stayed for many days, cooking food with healing herbs and helping care for the injured young man.

Now at the same time the warlord whose emissary had not been able to buy the horse engaged his province in an ill-advised war which was not going well for him. He had lost many warriors in battle. There were too few soldiers to protect his lands from those he had attacked. So again he sent out his emissary, this time with a small group of armored riders to take the young men of many villages away to fight in a war from which many would not return. The man who borrowed grain was beside himself in grief and cried on the old man's shoulder because all but one of his fine boys were taken to be warriors.

The villagers followed him to the old man's house which by this time had two new rooms, one for the healer woman and one for his son. 'Old man!' they cried. 'You are so lucky. Your son is crippled and cannot go to war. You will have him with you always. Our sons are well and strong and they have gone away to be killed!' But the old man would not be moved to one side or the other by his fortune. He shook his head because all his neighbors still did not understand.

He said, 'Let us simply say my son does not go to war and yours may yet return. We do not know the whole story.'

Chapter 13

Healing the Creative Will

We address our emotional healing around the quartered circle in some detail through the next several chapters. Our hearts and feelings in conflict are complex. Their issues and wounds are not easily resolved. The best we can do is begin with a will to continue, so first we visit our hearts in the south, the quadrant of our willfulness, decisiveness and creativity. If we cannot make a clear decision to find our healing, it will continue to elude us.

The Will to Be Well

Celebrating our own creativity is a good beginning for heart healing. When we teach emotional transformation in Wicca III, we always warn people that it might be a rocky road. Apparently our guides and guardians take the dare seriously. One man fell off scaffolding at work and had to find a new career. He is a professional psychic now. Merlin declared his key value to be rooted in ethics. Immediately he was charged with ethics violations at work. The charges were thin fabrications, but their appearance at exactly that junction was an unmistakable challenge from the spirit world. One of my values is seen in the frequency with which I tell people to remember who they are and speak their truth. After a Wicca III class, I nearly died of a respiratory illness that was rooted in my identity and breath. Healing our creative will, our minds and hearts is tough stuff.

All of us have the ability to decide and to create new things out of old ones. For some of us those skills are unrecognized. We dither about making and unmaking decisions, unable to choose what is best. Others of us are certain we were behind the door when creativity was passed out. We claim we cannot carry a tune or draw a straight line. Fortunately neither is required to be creative.

Creativity is simply working with our imagination, a skill we use every time we ground or cast a circle. Creativity is moving energy through our bodies and out into the physical dimension to form something meaningful: touch, healing, beauty, innovation, repairs, construction, needlework, cooking, stories, explanations, lessons, music, love making, joy, wisdom… The list is infinite. People are put off by the expectation that creativity must be new and original. Singing someone else's song in our own voice is original. Finding a way to fix a broken table instead of chopping it up for firewood makes it new. Creativity at its simplest and most profound is problem solving. These are the ingredients and tools I have. Where do I go from here?

My favorite references to use in opening up creativity are the SARK books. Susan Ariel Rainbow Kennedy, founder of Planet SARK has written a series of books with marker pens and crayons to encourage ordinary people to dare their own healing and creative change. All of her writing is about *empowerment,* that third kind of power Starhawk defined. She approaches transformation and healing as a joyous explosion of creativity. She tells her stories of abuse and then re-writes them to reveal her healed self. In her recent book *Glad No Matter What* she explains: 'I don't actually know which story is "true", but the body doesn't care, and my spirit and emotions are practicing living and telling new stories.'[91] That healing of the body, spirit and feelings is our goal. What she writes is true in one dimension or another.

In the Web, we tell stories in ritual as an art but also as a lesson in healing. Through them we rewrite our own stories and the myths of our ancestors to understand the world of opening consciousness. That is one reason I have included so many stories in this book as an example in healing. Despite being written on the page, our stories cannot remain the same. We move on and change our stories.

Our myths must do the same, else the Gods are static when everything else evolves. That limitation on the Gods is by far too Christian a concept for my faith. The Gods are not immutable. They evolve with us from jealous, vengeful, bloodthirsty warriors to something else which we have not yet seen. Remember the principal discussed in Chapter 12, that the people around us reflect truths about ourselves so that we can see them more clearly? They mirror our inner being when we are head blind to our truths. So do the Gods. Our friends, our foes and our Gods play roles to raise our wisdom. When we catch on, we free them to change their roles.

Perhaps it is difficult for us to see Isis or Diana differently than their ancient selves. Yet the Egyptians or the Romans who wrote about them during their own cultural empires were writing reflections about entities older than their civilizations. They described stories in terms they understood because the stories resonated from within them. Our resonance is different in our time and place. Because the ancients lived in a cult of war and separation, they have left us a legacy of conflict and duality. The challenge for us in the 21st century is to heal the rift and embrace our immanence. We are one, the Gods and mortals, dressed in different energy fields but springing from the same core. Our stories have become tales about how our rifts are healed.

In telling the story of Lamia in Chapter 3, I changed several significant events. Lamia is the archetype of the bad mother. In the original versions, most of her children were killed by the jealous Hera. In some versions Hera forces Lamia to devour them. In her grief Lamia then ate the children of Libya. She seduced and killed her lovers. There are threads in the tale about her eyes. These references are contradictory and related to guilt or prophecy. When I began writing this bloodthirsty tale, I asked Lamia how she wanted to shape those issues. She admitted to culpability for many deaths in childbed, miscarriages and suicides, but not to cannibalism or murder. She admitted neglecting her children, of hating them because they reminded her of Zeus. Together we explored the sensationalized story for what might have happened. Her interference with the lives of women to prevent them from bearing living children and easing both mother and child into death was connected to a madness certainly. However, in her delusion, she believed she was saving them from a fate worse than death. Her life as an immortal filled with the pain of loss, betrayal and crushed dreams distorted her reason. She no longer believed in love. Her beauty and seduction drove her lovers mad, but she saw that as justice. She projected the behaviors of Zeus on every man she met.

In my telling of the story, Lamia is a shapeshifter, one who took the form of a snake willingly in hope of a respite from pain. Through that form she found healing in confronting the truth of what she had done and who she had become. The snake comes full circle. The bad mother works through her pain. She learns the lessons of her shadow and finds their gifts. Then through the gifts of Thoth she is transformed back to her beautiful female form and sent to make amends. This story is for us in the 21st century, a place where we can seek transformative healing. We see our shadow as our work in progress and know we too can be changed. How that may come about is part of the story we do not yet know.

The stories we tell about our Gods and ourselves are part of our identity quest on a healing path. When I teach these lessons in a classroom setting and in ritual we look at our personal beliefs and stories in six areas of our lives: body image, personal relationships, family history, sex, money, and death. Once we have mined our stories for our personal truths we finish with an uninterrupted autobiographical story called *hearing into being* as used by the American feminist Sonia Johnson in the 1980s.[92] As readers of this book, we can write our stories or connect with others to speak them. I prefer the latter since uncovering our identity is an exercise in finding our voice. Speaking our truth requires deeper commitment to our memoires than writing them to be hidden away in a desk drawer. Our voice needs hearing and respect.

Storytelling

People tell stories without thinking about how to do that. We tell jokes, family anecdotes and work narratives to make our lives interesting. Our stories connect us to our community of friends. For some reason, when we turn the spotlight around and begin speaking of ourselves in a class we freeze in stage fright. I encourage students to consider each monologue a one-man or one-woman show; an early life review if you will. Because we are telling stories within the quartered circle, I ask people to create a safe and sacred place at home where they can talk out loud to themselves. Crystals, artwork and sacred objects enhance the circle of personal space. There we hear our story develop without interruptions, distractions or editing from family and friends. My car served as such a place while I drove an hour to work each day. I ask people to tell each story over and over within the privacy of their sacred space. In the repetition we let it grow and change. The more we tell it, the deeper it digs into our shadow.

In addition, I ask people to meditate on each story they tell about themselves. Storytellers see the natural flow and chronology of their story through meditation. Outside the meditation, they can check facts if need be. High school yearbooks, scrap books, old diaries all hold their secrets. In ordinary consciousness and in trance storytellers firm up what they know about their story. As storytellers, we work in our mental bodies to recall our truths. We keep talking to ourselves, honoring the sad and scary parts of our story, seeking out both our anger and our joy held by our emotional bodies.

Lastly, I tell my students to listen to their own story as if they were the audience at a dramatic presentation. What voice, gestures, pauses make the story clearer? I ask them to keep telling it until they know it by heart, knowing this story is important to them and the people who love them. When they know the story well, they act it out, using voices and making faces.

Fourth, in the sacred private circle the storyteller evaluates the story. They ask the story: *Why are you here? Where did you come from and where are you going?* They do this as often as is needed because the repetition is not a performance. It is practice. It is experience. It is identity.

Finally, the story comes to a conclusion. Even if the story still needs work, I tell the students to conclude what they are doing. Every story has a beginning, middle and an end. If the ending isn't done yet, the storytellers create some closure that is satisfying to them. Adding the ending helps identify the story rhythm. It is also a healing step. As storytellers, creating our own endings reminds us our lives are really in our hands. This step is empowerment.

When we are developing stories and healing from them, we tell ourselves our story every day or two until the story is an organic part of our thinking. We know when it is complete. Then we can record it; write it down for future generations if we want to. We will not forget this story, and we will never tell it exactly the same way twice, because we will not have to. Tom Cowan the shamanic teacher said, 'Some of our best personal stories are like the sacred stories of indigenous people: learned slowly, sometimes part by part, as a process of initiation over the years from childhood to adulthood. They revealed their secrets piece by piece.'[93] We remember that as we tell our stories. We think about stories as lessons from Spirit.

In finding our voice we are initiated into our Selves. Telling our stories heals us. We find courage in speaking. Our creativity is opened up wide. Our wisdom shines through. People from the Web have transformed their own lives with the healing of the heart and mind. They are able to reframe their stories by observing themselves in the telling. They are able to gain insight into the other players in their stories, which challenges assumptions. The outcome is never final as long as there is breath in us. The ending can shift into gladness no matter what the story line. Just ask SARK.

Student Interviews

Through a series of interviews with former students, I tested my premise that our storytelling created not only a surge in creativity but also an emotional healing for the students. Elise indicated she had taken the class after carefully checking us out on the internet. Then on the strength of another student's comment about how much his life had been changed she decided to jump in, beginning with Wicca I even though she knew a good deal about Wicca from other groups and many books. By the time we reached storytelling and emotional healing in Wicca III she knew she both wanted and needed that deep emotional healing.

Elise referenced one of the first meditations we did in class though I have no real memory of it. I apparently set them on the shore of a lake. She then climbed into a Narnian boat and sailed out in the water, only to have the side of the boat open up, take on water and capsize. She went down with the ship. After the meditation I gave students time to share their experiences. She chose not to, though the meditation was understandably troubling. Then I said to the class that it would not be unusual for people to experience a capsizing boat. She still said nothing, but concluded that she was supposed to be here and would be descending into herself. We both laugh at that synchronicity now, but at the time such an apparently offhand remark striking at the core of a secret would make anyone blink.

I asked Elise what happened after the class. Was she changed? Did she find healing? Elise credited her experiences with this class for her immediate transformation in recognizing she was closed off and isolated inside even when surrounded by people. Our class was the first time she was asked to, and allowed to, open up about herself and her feelings, which kick-started other things that had been fomenting beneath the surface. One of those other things was to ultimately seek counseling, which she had previously resisted. Elise took all this emotional and creative work to heart, found balance and healing, learned how to say yes and no and now teaches students to do that, both in her own Wicca classes and in her workplace where she supervises more than 20 people.

When I asked how her heart has been healed by storytelling, Elise said she was allowed to love. That unfolded more afterward but through class meditations and rituals she discovered loving was not something that she was good at. By the end of class she said she knew she could be loving if she wanted to be. Through counseling since then she has learned she can love difficult or damaged people in her life without fixing them. That in itself was a breakthrough.

Stonefinder, a man of few words, also evaluated his storytelling and healing experiences through our classes. He said all three levels of Wicca classes changed his life particularly as a healer and psychic. He is more compassionate and caring to both dogs and people. Where he was angry, guilty and blaming, he is calm and grounded. He cited his work with the Wicca classes as creating a complete turnaround from where he was with no way to know what would have happened to him otherwise.

Peg, who teaches our class on death and dying, explained that telling her stories and delving into the books of Wicca III created an opening for her own history of abuse to surface. She spontaneously channeled a poem that allowed her to speak of her own pain. She learned to tell her truth. Since then she says she is more the owner of her body and person. She not only learned how to be heard, she came into 'being as a Witch.' When I was too ill to lead the Drawing Down the Moon ceremony, she stepped in and channeled the Goddess. Peg not only learned how to speak for herself, she learned to speak for the Goddess.

As the head teacher, I have been molded and shaped by the storytelling classes as much as the students. The creative work is transformative. Spirit took the opportunity to strip away my illusions, remove people from my life, add a second career as a writer, deepen my experience as a psychic and heal my childishness. When I review the work we do in emotional healing, I wonder how it is we dare. Elise encouraged us to continue. She also advised we keep the warning label so people know this is important, difficult and life-changing work.

Meditation and Chant

To make this transition from where you are now to where you will be, learn the words of this chant. Sit with them in sacred space. Light a candle for the fire of inspiration and creativity. Sit in the south of your circle and repeat the chant until the words take root. Write them in your BOS along with any other thoughts you have about your will and decisiveness.

I will be gentle with myself, I will love myself.
I am a child of the universe, being born each moment.[94]

When you are finished chanting, continue your journey of remembering who you are within the safety of the quartered circle by beginning to speak your story. It will grow and change. You will revise it, but begin now. Tell yourself who you really are.

Chapter 14

Body Awareness

In telling our story, we need to explore our body-mind connection. The fitting together of the physical reality with its creative in-house source is the point where transformation of our reality will occur, if it occurs. I begin with the understanding that the mind is in every cell of the body. It is not simply encased in the brain. The brain and its neurological impulses and synapses send conscious and unconscious thoughts throughout the body. True. But the mind is more than that. The mind contains the electronic messages of our genetics, our histories, our incarnations, our magic and will. This knowledge is accessible through our meditations and trances. We enter the knowledge with our ritual work and our dreams. It is also accessible in our memories and in our bodies. Neuropeptides are molecular chemicals which carry emotion, related thought and memory to every cell in the body.[95] We have what is essentially a thinking body but one which is largely ignored by healers, physicians and resident souls in the body. We treat the body as if it is only along for the ride much of the time.

We can test the connection between body/mind with acupressure. Current emotional distress can be released by stimulating seven pairs of acupressure points in the arms and seven more in the chest which have nothing to do directly with our brain. We begin by making a private note in our journals about what is distressing right now. Mad, sad, or scared? How intensely? What is the source of those feelings? Which people are attached to them? We identify our distress and place it on a scale of 1 to 10, 1 being the least and 10 being the most distressed. My question is not about what we think but what we feel. Our bodies will respond when we get it right. We make a face. Our breath changes. Muscles tighten. We record those physical responses too.

Next we stimulate each point described below on each side of the body. We always treat bilaterally. The point will often be a depression under the skin, a slight bunch of energy making a little bump or a tender ouchy spot. These points move around slightly and will not always be where they were yesterday because they are part of our energy field. Not all of them will be sensitive every time we have a disturbing emotional reaction, but many of them will be.

Emotional Release Points

Points on the hands and arms are on the Large Intestine (Li), Lung (L), Heart (H) and Pericardium (P) meridians.

Li4 Joining the Valley (not for pregnant women) and *L10 Fish Border*. These two points are in the web of the thumb and index finger. Li4 is on the top of the hand up into the muscle. When we press that with the thumb of the opposite hand, the index finger will automatically reach L10 on the underside of the hand.

Li11 Crooked Valley (or Pond) and *L5 Marsh at the Bend*. These two points are at the elbow. Li11 is on the outside of the elbow where the crease ends when the elbow is bent. L5 is on the crease of the inside of the elbow on the thumb side.

H7 Spirit Gate. This point is on the heart meridian at the underside of the wrist on a line down from the little finger and located on the largest crease at the wrist.

L9 Great Abyss. Find the point at the inside wrist at the base of the thumb.

P6 Inner Gate. Also on the wrist, this point is located in the center line tracing up from the middle finger and two thumb widths up toward the heart from the largest wrist crease. The point is on the underside of the wrist/arm.

P4 Cleft Gate. This point is up the inner forearm along the same midline as the Inner Gate, but located 1/3 of the way between wrist and elbow.

Li 15 Shoulder Point. This point is located by running the hand over the cap of the opposite shoulder toward the arm. Li15 is located centrally in the depression beneath the bone at the point of the shoulder.

Points on the chest are found on the Lung (L), Kidney (K), Stomach (St), Pericardium (P), Gall Bladder (GB), and Spleen (Sp) Meridians. Again, these are located on both sides of the body and should be treated bilaterally.

L1 Letting Go. When seated, the thumbs fall naturally into a depression on each side of the chest when your elbows are resting on the arms of a chair and you fold your arms up toward your chest. L1 is on the lung meridians which run parallel on either side of the sternum and over the breasts.

K 27 Elegant Mansion. You find this point under the clavicle (collar bone) in the depression on either side of the sternum. The thumbs fall naturally into those depressions if the hands make loose fists and are placed knuckles down on the sternum touching one another.

St 16 Breast Window. This point is central to the breast, about where it starts to swell between the 3rd and 4th rib located down from the collar bone (clavicle). The stomach meridian is toward the arm further than the kidney meridian, and toward the centerline further than the lung meridian.

St 18 Breast Root. Following the stomach meridian over the breast and underneath, you locate St 18 on the chest wall between the 5th and 6th rib.

P1 Heavenly Pond. This point is up a couple of inches from St 18 and outside the breast between the 4th and 5th rib. (Split the difference between St 16 and 18 and move outside the breast).

GB 22 Armpit Abyss. This point is nearly parallel to P1 but further around the body under the arm and down one rib.

Sp 17 Food's Cavity. This point is parallel to GB 22 but back toward the front of the body a couple inches, not as far as the P1 point.

When you have finished, assess your feelings. Have they changed? Did you at some point feel a release of the distress you had? On the scale, what number would you assign to the intensity of your distress after stimulating and calming the emotional release points? This release is likely temporary. If we have not addressed the root of the problem, it comes back to finish teaching us the truths hiding behind it. Nevertheless, it is helpful to feel some ability to guide and direct our emotional roller coaster while we are trying to figure things out. When our emotional distress is mild, we can select those points which tend to be the most sensitive. When our distress is acute we need them all.[96]

Muscle Memory

Our minds remember old emotional events and store them in our bodies. Sore muscles, back problems, any tension-related condition can be investigated in terms of memories stored in the body/mind. Psychic massage releases the stored stress out of the muscle into the blood or lymph systems to be removed from the body by natural excretion. Drinking water assists this process. Knowledgeable healers can balance our body-mind and release the negativity stored in our tissue. Our physical realities give us clues about our heads and hearts.

This storage system works for old physical wounds as well. Energy cysts hold the pain and associated feelings of a physical injury at the site of a scar, broken bone or healed injury or at the point to which it telegraphed. Chronic fear, anger or grief may be tucked away with the memories of what happened. In his book *Your Inner Physician and You,* Dr. John Upledger explains that injury to the body carries energy into the tissue which may in fact travel beyond the initial impact of a wound or accident. A body which is strong, flexible and balanced can rid itself of the impact energy. A body reacting in fear or grief and which is less vital may hang on to the gift of extra energy created by the wound. The energy becomes concentrated and compressed into a cyst of stagnant chi which will in time create medical or emotional problems. Massage therapists, particularly those who have been trained in Upledger's craniosacral release, can resolve that problem.[97] When we are stuck in healing pain or illness, expert assistance is needed.

Rune Clues

One of the methods we used to explore body clues to the source of our strengths and challenges is in seeking out runes left on our skin by scars, birthmarks, moles, freckles, even by the faint blue of blood vessels beneath the epidermis. Some of these are temporary and others more permanent. If you are not familiar with the runes, you may need to research them. There are several versions, even a set of Witches' runes which bear no resemblance to the Nordic runes. You can select one that suits you. If you prefer you can use the standard English alphabet. Writing words involves *spell*-ing. Our alphabet is no less sacred than the runes. Alternately, people well-versed in esoteric symbols can use those. Your spirit guides can show you what you need to know in any of those symbols. As you might expect, I have a story.

The Runes: A Story of the Wasp

A few years ago I was picking up a pile of books and magazines which had scattered across the floor. It was a lazy sunny fall day when the air outside was cool, but the solar heat inside was toasty. I felt a needley pricking on the inside of my upper right arm where the magazines rested, but thought a staple or paper clip was sticking me. When I put the reading materials down on the table I saw a drowsy yellow jacket fastened to my arm, stinging me repeatedly in an attempt to survive and escape. I pulled him off and threw him across the room, a quick reflex but

> not quick enough. He had stung me eight or nine times in an 'S' pattern as he wriggled around under the books in my arms. There were little droplets of blood oozing out of the wounds, and then they started to hurt. A little ice, a little lavender oil and a couple of aspirins later, I started to reflect on the pattern and wondered why he had tattooed an 'S' on my arm. Leja suggested it was for the rune Sowilo; a reminder to look to myself and see what needed attention, what I was denying. This rune represents our life force, health, success goals, and our connection with the Higher Self, wholeness and power. The wasp's tattoo stayed with me halfway through the winter. Every time I showered, hot tubbed or dressed, there it was, reminding me of me.
>
> After that, Rosewycke suggested we all had runes on our bodies, etched in scars, wounds, wrinkles, veins, or other marks that carried messages. She noticed it first in the back of her hands—each hand was different. We decided to add rune markings to our exploration of body image to see what spirit messages were written on our skin. This is a no-touch experience, to promote self-awareness and self-love. In some classes we worked skyclad in front of mirrors to find our runes. In others we did that at home and brought in a report of our markings. In either case, we sat as a group and discuss our bodies with frankness and honesty.

Both approaches to our bodies serve our purpose in pushing our limits to discover our Selves and our manifestation in physical reality, in the minds of others and in our own hearts. We want to pull together our physical bodies with our emotional bodies, mental bodies and spiritual bodies to heal the disconnection we have from our Be-ing. Admittedly this can be very difficult work for some people. We provide deep level support for each other, and focus not on what is wrong with us, but what is real and perfect as it is. The spiritual premises are many:

We are perfect right now. We do not have to change to be perfect. We do not meet any charts or external ideals to be perfect. We do not have to criticize anyone else to be perfect.

Areas of our dis-comfort and dis-ease are gifts and mirrors for us to use in understanding where we have been pulled off center. These are areas where we can learn more about our souls.

We can change our bodies by changing our minds. This is not to meet some artificially imposed goals, but to heal the separations between our bodies and souls.

Journaling on Your Runic Observations

Create a sacred circle in front of a full length mirror where you will not be interrupted. Stand naked in front of the full length mirror and find your body runes or symbols. Resist any negative messages you typically tell yourself about your body. Today you are on a search for clues from your body about how it connects to the rest of you. Notice the shape your belly makes and appreciate it. Flat bellies are few and far between. Round ones resemble the moon. Look at your sides and if you can arrange mirrors to do so, observe your back. One of my friends has the most charming little heart arranged by bone, skin and muscle right over her sacrum which is at the back of the belly chakra, the seat of sensuality. You would not want to miss something so important on your own surface.

As you identify your marks, sketch them in your journal leaving room to meditate and consider the message they carry. Be as honest and clear as you can. This is a peek at your personal challenges, strengths and reasons for being here. When I had that wasp tattoo I wanted to go straight into denial. The wasp marking an S on my skin could not possibly mean I had any illusions left! Fortunately, my rational brain knew better. Eventually I figured out I was pursuing a mission of self-discovery behind the scenes that my brain had not acknowledged. I was challenging my illusions about love, relationships and loyalty outside of myself. It took years to see the whole picture. Give yourself time. Allow this exploration to be a beginning of your body's story.

Obviously, viewing our bodies in this way skirts around the issue of form and fitness. Weight, grace and musculature are reflected back at us from the popular media constantly. We are challenged with questions about our adequacy because hardly anybody looks like the movie stars. American youths are severely overweight according to health charts. Pregnancy stretches female bellies leaving scars and expanded waists. Men and women pass middle age and find their firm bodies sagging. Joints stiffen. Hair turns gray and some of it falls out. What are we to think of ourselves if our bodies are so different from the film ideal?

The answer to that question is also part of the clues found in our bodies. Being gentle with ourselves and loving ourselves as children of the universe reflects the love that the Divine gives us. We are loved not in spite of our physique but because of it. Our physique reflects the truth of our lives and the truth of our story. Punishing the self through the body by neglect, addictions or poor nutrition is like shooting the messenger who arrives with news we did not want to hear. How much wiser it is to decipher the code and figure out the best thing to do with our new information!

Tell your body story to yourself until it flows naturally. Use the runes as a framework for the story. Include your medical history, child bearing, injuries or physical training and strength. Repeat the story moving from top to toe or right to left. When you know the story well, and have a healing ending to the story (which is not the same thing as the end of your life) find a trusted friend from your big hug circle and ask them to keep your confidence between you. Then tell your story. Ask them simply to listen without comment and hear your truth. You will likely end by sharing that big hug. Then go out and celebrate with a walk in nature. Note your insights in your journal.

Chapter 15

Money Stories

Investigating our money stories is a journey of both the north and the east. In the north, money represents the physical world of treasure, gold and hard work that digs ditches, grows crops and manufactures goods. In the east, money represents the mental world of education, career and management. Our attitudes toward money are learned beliefs. They are born in the east as mental constructs. They can be changed. We learned our attitudes from experience, example and books. We can learn new ones. When I embark on a money journey, I select a crystal to help me understand my relationship with money and set it in the north of my altar. I meditate with that crystal when I am confused, ill-at-ease or need to make a financial decision. I also light incense if I need to change the atmosphere around me to be more positive and generous. If I am working kitchen witchery, I burn cinnamon and nutmeg scents in the east. If I am working a deeper magic for success, good fortune and psychic ability to mold my future I use copal.

Money is a power issue that impacts on our health, our stress level, our relationships and love life. Money opens the door to higher education. It underwrites our recreation and our ability to move about the world or stay in one place as we choose. People talk about their own money situations even less often than they talk about their medical history or sex lives. Grandmother Elspeth of Haven in West Virginia[98] used to refer to money as 'that dirty green stuff' until she embarked on a study of money and how it interfaces with our spiritual lives. Whatever we do with our money or believe about our money, we ought to be smart about it! Our experiences with money form our beliefs about it. We know what we 'should' think about money or at least we imagine we do. But what do we really think? Clarifying our thinking about money addresses what we think of ourselves. Being clear about money allows us to stand in our own power, which is another healing journey.

I ask students to tell me what their first reaction is when I say *money*. When we have listed their thoughts and feelings about it, I ask for the second and third reactions because money is a complex subject. Our real beliefs are often well-hidden in the shadows. Some people agree that money is filthy lucre. Others think it is a necessary evil. There are those who love it. Some see it as a tool. People who are seeking more money expect it to bring happiness. People who have a lot of money claim it makes them miserable. These are beliefs and emotional reactions learned from environment or experience.

Because we are studying spirituality, people are surprised when I tell them money is neither good nor ill. There are no wrong or right beliefs about money. I suppose the commonly misquoted maxim 'Money is the root of all evil' shapes their expectations. Actually the correct quotation is: '*The love of money is the root of all evil.*' (1 Timothy 6:10).

That is a Christian value and may or may not apply to our identity as Pagans. The things we love are our teachers as much as the things we hate. The negativity or oppression expressed in the world as evil is also a teacher. 'I've been rich and I've been poor. Rich is better.'[99] Bea Kaufman, Sophie Tucker and many other entertainers are credited with that adage. No matter who said it first, it is true.

I have worked for economic justice all my adult life. Because of that experience I have learned the quest for financial balance is as important as any social reform. Our experience with riches, want, poverty, desire, compassion and charity forms our beliefs about money. As the body was a teacher about our wounds and healing, so is our experience with money. Our bank balances, debts, employment history and education all teach us about power. They reveal our financial wisdom or lack of it, and our ability to make good decisions. Handling money teaches us deep truths about living in a physical dimension, about our responsibility for our lives, and about sabotage from institutions and the power elite if we fail to use our psychic gifts and intellectual acumen.

Money Memories

In order to explore our experience with money, I ask students to describe what they remember about the role of money in the family where they grew up.

Did people argue about how it was spent?
Did people save money?
Did people who worked outside the home share their earnings with people who worked inside the home?
Was the sharing equal?
Did children and teenagers have money?
Was it an allowance or earnings?
Who decided how children saved or spent their money?

Once our family experiences are shared around the room I ask what people feel when they think about their own memories. What happens in their bodies? Does the heart beat faster or do they hold their breath? Are they tensed or relaxed? These physical clues point at hidden feelings about an open discussion of money and family. Frankly I am much more interested in the feelings and physical reactions than in the justice or injustice of how money was handled at home.

My Memory

Unless of course we are talking about my home! I grew up with the story of my mother who as a young bride told my father off in no uncertain terms when he sent her to shop for groceries and then stepped in to pay for them. She had no money of her own in their marriage, at least initially. Because she had been a young working woman living with her parents and paying room and board to them prior to her marriage, she found her status as unpaid wife unacceptable. She instinctively knew this was a power issue that needed to be discussed early in their lives together. Their solution was for him to give her a percentage of his earnings for household expenses and her own needs. They decided together how to pay the bills. If money was short, she kicked some of her money back into the common pot to cover them. I am not sure how my father felt about that, but he saw the justice of it.

Because my parents' story is important to my beliefs about money and power, I cannot separate them from my feelings and physical reactions. I know my mouth gets tight and I scowl at my poor young father who had no idea that such a thing would be an issue. I know I expect him to have known better, to have read my mother's mind and been proactive. I also know I am projecting expectations from the 21st century onto a guy who married after World War II and thought he was doing my mother a favor by taking care of her. My reactions to an old family story reveal far more about me than they do about my parents who worked things out as best they could between them. My reactions reveal my fervor in defending the value of work in the home. They expose my belief that women need their own money and are safer if they earn it in a job. They are part of the explanation for my work history and career choices.

Jobs

In exploring our history with money, we also examine our experience in the workforce. Students and teachers discuss their first real job as an adult and how much they earned. Then we remember how we felt about the job and the money and when that changed. We describe our most important paid job as an adult and the earnings attached to that. Then we disclose our dream job and what we were paid to do it. I ask people who have never had that dream job what has kept them from pursuing it. For people who are currently not working for someone else or who are retired, unemployed or on disability I ask what they do to pay the bills and is it enough? Then I ask them all how they feel about the experiences they have disclosed. Talking about money honestly is a difficult challenge. The group must be committed to confidentiality.

Depending on the group I may include a discussion of financial security. I encourage people to be as open or private about that as they like. Then I ask about their savings, investments, IRAs, money markets or other pockets of money set aside for a rainy day. Have those accounts lost or gained money in the current economy? How do students feel about their future security? What plans for retirement do they have? What kind of impact do those feelings have on daily life? I conclude with a question about how they feel about my questions. Some students have never considered how they will support themselves in old age.

A surprising number of people are working in jobs for which they are compensated inadequately. They are living pay check to pay check and try not to think about what would happen if they lost their jobs. In our classes, we have a number of people who have faced unemployment, lost their homes, or experienced other financial disasters. I point out that people who feel financial need work no less hard than people who have enough money. Sometimes they work much harder with their bodies and court injury and disability. It is a myth to say the poor are lazy.

There is usually another truth happening parallel to the money story that prevents people from reaching financial success. They need more education; they are experiencing discrimination; they make unwise choices in taking a job or leaving it; they are ill or injured. Changes in the economy can close plants, end jobs, diminish the value of savings or drain investment accounts. Part of my money story is about my parents' expectation that social security would be enough for their retirement and that they would be able to keep working odd jobs to supply any additional needs. They underestimated the economic forces at work in the last 30 years of the 20th century. They did not anticipate the ravages of aging for a generation who smoked and ate heart damaging foods. If they had known better, they would have done better. That is a piece of street wisdom that applies to many things. The complexity of people's financial lives is daunting. What is key for us is to heal the wounds and realize abundance and prosperity are possible.

Journaling: Begin Your Money Story

Outline your money story before reading any further. Identify your own feelings about money. Recall your earliest childhood memories about family money discussions. Include your own employment history. Assess your current financial security or insecurity. Identify your feelings about money. Ask yourself: *What is the wisdom hiding in the shadows?* Answer any or all of the questions raised above. We will use this outline later in our money healing.

Information and Object Lessons

One of my objectives is to provide more information to help students shape new attitudes and beliefs about money. I use the book *Simple Abundance: A Daybook of Comfort and Joy* written by Sarah Ban Breathnach[100] to educate and inspire the class. This text encourages people to heal their money stories by opening up to the possibilities of fiscal security. Breathnach faced that point when she realized that working hard all the time, trying to control everything in her life, and driving for perfection was not getting her anywhere. She took stock of herself and changed her life. In the foreword to the book she explains that money was an emotionally charged issue that she had given control over her ability to be happy. She counted as accomplishments only the things that gained her money. On the other hand she desired to be spiritual, authentic, creative and whole.

With these values in conflict (valuing only what earned her money versus being whole, spiritual and human) she contracted to write a book about abundance. The book she finished two years later was quite different than the one she started, because on her way to putting her thoughts on paper she changed. One day she woke up 'a happy woman experiencing more moments of contentment than distress.' In her quest to balance her way of being she learned to base her life on intangible things like gratitude and joy instead of her bank balance. She writes: 'I've made the unexpected but thrilling discovery that everything in my life is significant enough to be a continuous source of reflection, revelation, and reconnection: bad hair, mood swings, car pools...overdrawn bank accounts... exhaustion, illness...'[101] Everything. In walking in this authentic awareness of the relevance of everything, she found that an authentic life is the most personal form of worship. She made everyday life her prayer.

Interestingly, Breathnach's bubble burst. She had tremendous financial success with her several books, but her fiscal skills did not keep pace. She ended up divorced, broke and living with her sister. Somewhere along the line she forgot the basic lesson of keeping it simple. Her new book *Peace and Plenty*[102] tells that story. There is a lesson in the reversals a public person faced, who had it all, lost it and then faced facts to overcome ruin. I reference this story because of that lesson and the insight it gives into *abundance, sufficiency* and *scarcity*.

Abundance means an ample profusion, wealth, plentitude, riches, and more than enough. Our belief in abundance is why we play the lottery, but our disbelief in it is why we have not won. The spiritual secret about attaining abundance is in realizing we have an abundance of personal power to manifest as much wealth as we need or even want. Are you aware of that? The downside of abundance is that it implies, in economic terms, that there is a natural imbalance in wealth: that there are *haves* and *have nots*. Is that necessarily true?

Sufficiency means enough for everyone to share. We may not have an embarrassment of riches, but there is enough to meet our needs, both in the present and the future. A commitment to the possibilities of sufficiency means being deeply grateful for what one has. It may mean finding a deep satisfaction in simplicity and understanding how less can mean more. Sufficiency means accepting real life as is; we embrace our circumstances and settle into the feeling of being who we are. From there we can build anything. What do we need to have so we can accept that this is our life? What do we need to know to accept that this is enough? What do we need to do to make this life enough?

Scarcity means shortages. There is only enough for some people and not enough for others. In other words, there is only enough to fight over. Working economically with the law of supply and demand, we create scarcity. The ebb and flow of supply is artificially manipulated to drive prices up when the community envisions scarcity. The power to manifest enough for one's own needs is handed over to others who control the 'means of production' or the market futures.

We can readily observe this scarcity mentality at work in oil and energy pricing. One of the OPEC nations threatens to reduce the supply and prices skyrocket when nothing has happened except that the collective imagination has panicked. The oil suppliers raise prices. People who can hoard do. Who really controls whether we can get what we need to live comfortably? Sarah Ben Breathnach writes: 'There is no scarcity except in our souls.'[103]

In our mad-sad-glad-scared spectrum of emotional responses, scarcity creates fear. Abundance and sufficiency create gladness. We can reverse our emotional reaction to shortages and begin to cultivate gladness instead of fear. Our scarcity will be replaced by having enough to share. In creating our emotional healing, we must know where we live in our hearts most of the time. If we are fearful we reinforce our lack. If we are grateful we reinforce our abundance and sufficiency. We can direct our feelings and choices to give us what we want. How that arrives in our lives may be a surprise.

A Student's Story of Abundance

StoneLight Weaver's story is a prime example. She believes in abundance and that the universe is a safe place. It is a part of her essence and how she perceives the world. A few years ago, after finishing her Master's degree in nonprofit corporate administration she bought the perfect house to live and retire in. It would be paid for when she was 52. This house had a wonderful garden, great neighbors and was a steal! She was expecting a raise although she was interviewing for jobs in line with her new degree, employment that would not restrict her talents. She had several good prospects.

Then her world collapsed; she was laid off before she had unpacked the boxes in her new house. Being an optimist she could see the benefit of a couple weeks off work to get the house in order and re-decorated before accepting one of those wonderful job prospects. Life was still good.

StoneLight Weaver began positive affirmations and started asking for abundance in her life as she settled in. The only abundance she found was time to rest. The job opportunities did not come through and the job market dried up. Her unemployment benefits ran to the limit and ended. She could not afford to live elsewhere as economically so she used her retirement to support herself; she went to work for day labor as a supplement to her savings. Then her body gave out on her. Ill, tired, in constant pain she slept 20 hours a day.

Needless to say, she lost her wonderful house. It looked like after 30 years of work she would be homeless, sleeping on a friend's couch or living in her car. With prayers and affirmations, she fought back against despair. She worked on acceptance, saying she was exactly where she was supposed to be. She believed nothing happened without a purpose. Those beliefs kept her spirits from crashing as she packed a lifetime in boxes for storage in a friend's garage.

Then a miracle happened. Her sister whom she had not seen

in years called to offer her use of her rental property—rent free! Her sister saw no justice in StoneLight Weaver being homeless after all those years of hard work. Both of them expected the better employment opportunities in a new town across the state would give her a dependable job quickly.

Imagine her delight in moving into a fabulous upscale house located in a very posh community. Rejoicing in her new abundance and a safe universe, StoneLight Weaver continued to work as a temporary day laborer. She was still quite ill and overwhelmed with this roller coaster ride. She wanted to return to her beloved career in the helping professions, not only for job satisfaction but also for relief from the physical nature of the work she had to do. Again, she allowed the universe to find the best path to an adequate income with work she loved. Having learned that these things come in unexpected ways, she trusted and waited.

She did not have to wait long. In the middle of winter she fell on the ice and suffered a traumatic brain injury. With no other choice, she applied for disability. Her application was miraculously approved in record time. She says it sounds terrible to say, but she was injured just enough to be unable to handle a 9-5 job anymore but not so much that she is on the shelf. She was removed from the stress of finding work or working piecemeal. Her short term memory is severely damaged but she can engage in the joys of reading, the arts and outdoors. With good notes, she can teach those on a spiritual path the truths she has known all along which are part of her long term memory. With peace she explains the universe did the job just right. She has more money in her pocket than she has ever had; lives in a beautiful home and spends her days teaching, carving and enjoying the sunrise.

This is abundance, but it arrived in an unexpected way. StoneLight Weaver always had enough to get by, though she lost her house. She learned to accept support from her family. She was willing to work at anything. I saw her working a carnie booth at the State Fair and having a fine time doing it, though it took a physical toll on her. She learned a great deal about the body/mind connection. She also proved she was safe no matter what happened. As she was able to accept that, the pressure came off and the universal Mother took care of her. Some of us would rail against the limits a head injury imposes. StoneLight Weaver has learned gratitude and takes on life with positive expectations for the future. A couple of students studied some of our emotional transformation material with her one weekend and came back wide eyed and mind blown. Our journey is sometimes not at all what we expect.

When we do not talk about money, we find it takes on demonic proportions. We think we are the only one afraid of late fees, overdue bills, bankruptcy, balanced checkbooks, money saved for a rainy day, rainy days, budgets and foreclosures. If we avoid talking about money, we can hardly know if we are in or out of balance with the money fairy. If we do not talk about money, we can pretend we have it all under control. So let's talk about money some more.

Money Types

There are several money personality types we can identify. There are the *hoarders* who still have the first dollar they earned. They may not even pay their bills on time because they are keeping their money. They may have tons of money and never buy a new car or a needed appliance. Their relationship with money is not in balance because it all flows in and stops there. Money stagnates out of fear of what might happen or resentment over what has happened in the past.

There are the *spenders* who let the money run through their fingers. They spend it as fast as they make it. Shopping trips are part of their routine, one of their major recreational sports. Sometimes they buy things for the image of owning them. Sometimes they buy things that are such great bargains they simply could not pass them up, even if they never thought they needed them before. Their relationship with money is not in balance because it all flows out. None of it stops in the bank account. It does not matter how much money they have. The spender spends up to the limit of the credit cards. Money disappears in order to fulfill the spender's emotional needs for joy and gladness.

There are the *money monks* who believe that money corrupts them. They may believe 'money is the root of all evil.' They may live in opulence like the officials in the Roman Catholic Church but claim a vow of poverty. They may give up great wealth to sit under the bodhi tree like Buddha, starving their way to enlightenment. They may beg for money to give to the guru but keep nothing for themselves like the Hari Krishnas. Or they may be like many Pagan leaders who half-heartedly try to make a living as healers or teachers and criticize the New Agers who successfully market their spiritual skills and make a bundle. Some money monks manage to make a decent wage but hand it over to someone else either in an ashram or other spiritual community, or within the family so the monk never has to think about the meaning of money and how it is spent. They are too good to do the dirty work of writing checks or keeping track of the budget. For them, money is a dirty word.

There are the *avoiders* who similarly let someone else handle the money in the family, not because they think they are too good. Rather, they believe they are not good enough. They believe they cannot be trusted to pay bills on time, or to balance the books. This belief may be reinforced by the spouse or parent who maintains control of the purse strings. The avoiders may make a lot of money, but they entrust it to someone else. Sometimes they get cheated. For them money is one more indication of their lack of confidence.

There are the *money moguls* who amass fortunes in industry and business. They may start on a shoe string or with family fortunes, but they can turn a dime into treasury. The money mogul is not just successful, but in love with the game of creating wealth. There is no end to it, no point at which there is enough. There is always another challenge, another investment, another opportunity. They may be very generous with their money, because they know there is always more. For them, the money flows and multiplies, but the process is an obsession.

What then? Is no one healthy about money? Are we all flawed and hopeless? Our love affair with money is an up and down struggle. Some days are clear and some are not. All of us have lessons to learn when it comes to handling money. If we dare to transform our attitudes and habits about money, we will truly heal our lives. If control over money and the power to earn enough has been a problem in the past, we may lack the will to stand in our power and pay attention to the details. We may persist in not understanding how the money world operates or how to go about getting the education or employment needed. We daydream about being rich but have no plan for how to get there. On the other hand we may be too willful about money. Stubborn and hardheaded, we find ourselves obsessing over what we should do and never do it. We have spending binges and punish ourselves by strict budgeting. When we are truly willing to form a healthy relationship with money, then we will get real and find our authentic selves. We will relax, calm down and see things as they really are in our financial lives.

Money is neutral. It does not care what we do with it. Money represents our life energy. That is why we treat it with respect. When Elspeth finished her study on money, she started calling it *green energy*.

A Ritual on Having Enough

Within the healing circle then, we can address our wounded history or we can begin to create prosperity. We likely need to do both. Prosperity spells work better if our fiscal baggage is not whispering doubts about our magic. I have two parts to a prosperity ritual:

Part I: Release the fears and mistakes of the past by burning them in a cauldron or outdoor bonfire; and

Part II: Create new green energy with magic.

We begin by meditating on our relationship with money and the healing we need. Is there a wound from our history that must be healed? Do we have fears or obsessions that drive our bus when we handle money? Are we in a crisis financially or at work? Do we understand the lessons connected to our money experiences? Choosing a single focus for the ritual helps make it effective. We can repeat the ritual frequently to address all aspects of money healing.

Once we understand our focus and an appreciation for our anticipated healing, we decorate the altar with symbols and candles appropriate for the working. We collect onion skins, paper or pebbles to burn, drown, bury or cast to the wind, depending on the Elemental energies that resonate for us. We include a purse, bag or ceramic pot to catch our treasure.

I use candles for this ritual because I like fire magic. Individuals who prefer wind, water or earth can adjust their spell work accordingly around the quartered circle. Fears and mistakes can be infused into flour and thrown out to the wind to change our minds about money. We can write them on paper, make confetti and throw our fears to the wind with equally fine results. We can find a willing rock which will accept our mistakes into its density to rid ourselves of the physical and emotional effects of our history with money. Then we can throw the rock far out into the water or bury it in the earth. There are many ways to release and banish our past as part of our healing process. We should work with the Elementals that are most comfortable to us. In selecting the method, we remember we are communicating with the Djinn, Undines, Gnomes or Sylphs.

Once we decide on the Elemental partner for our spell work, we set up the quartered circle as we always do: cast the circle, ground, call the Elementals, call the ancestors, evoke the Guardians of the Watchtowers and then call on a God and Goddess appropriate to the working. In this book we have not studied divine participation in the quartered circle because that takes us into a different story about our pantheons. Our relationship to the deities deserves a book of its own. Nevertheless, we incorporate a spell with this healing ritual so we should pay attention to our divine patrons. Suggestions for these patrons are found in the next section.

Once we have learned the identity of our patron(s) for this ritual, we ask them for advice about the ritual and the request we intend to make, usually in meditation. Have we deeply understood the aspects of our history we need to release? Do we recognize the emotional ruts we trod along and the wounds which must be healed? Do we truly comprehend the gifts and lessons hiding as the shadow behind those wounds? The outline to our money story which we wrote in our journals helps us discover these answers. In addition we expect the guides and Gods to extend our insight about our money story before we embark on the spell work.

When the circle is cast, the quarters, Guardians and deities called and the meditation complete, we proceed with the releasing. For a fire ritual indoors, we use dried onion skins. Writing with a porcupine quill, we note our beliefs, experiences, embarrassments, pain, anger, and fears about money issue on the onion skins. We tell ourselves the whole truth as completely as possible. There is a work candle burning within a large cast iron cauldron set on a rock or thick tile in case the fire burns brighter than usual. There is water on the altar. A fire extinguisher is within reach though we have never had to use it. One by one we feed the onion skins onto the tip of our athames and then into the flame. We name them and let them burn. We feel them leave, transformed by the fire into heat and light. We give thanks for each one. As the flame flares, each individual asks that the enlightenment be made clear so that he or she will understand.

When the onion skins are gone, we begin the second part of the ritual. Each person anoints a spell candle with olive oil for prosperity. With the tip of an athame or with the porcupine quill, they scratch the name or a symbol for their new green energy on the candle tip. Then we light the candles in the name of divine patrons and set them before us on the altar. We meditate on the flame until all inscriptions have been consumed by the fire. During the meditation we may hear a teaching on how our new prosperity will come.

What is my part as one participant in the ritual? I take spirit instructions seriously. If I am told to give money away, I do it. If I am told to approach someone for a job or to offer help, I do it. If I have a vision of a working for the earth I do that. If something comes to mind that is not possible or would be harmful, I know it is not of spirit. It likely rose up out of my own fears and ego.

As the candles burn, we raise a cone of power over them to signify we have understood. The cone of power also sends the empowering energies out into the world to create the changes we have requested. We usually use the breath starting from a wordless whisper and increasing to a shout which is timed with our hands thrust upward to the sky. We leave our raised hands open, ready to receive our blessings. For me, the working has never failed. I have always had enough once I began to work this magic. I find sufficiency is prosperity.

At the close of the ritual, we release all the energy raised during the ritual. We ground the cone of power back to the earth so that Gaia can take the extra energy and use it for her purposes in healing pollution, empowering other people and protecting those who appeal for help. We release the Lady and the Lord, perhaps with an offering of gratitude. We close the astral gates and release the Guardians again with gratitude. We release the ancestors and Elementals the same way. We open the circle enclosure and scatter its boundaries. Then we share food and drink as a celebration of the spirits, the ancestors and each other. The feast is also another level of grounding that brings us back down to earth from between the worlds.

Goddesses and Gods of Prosperity

In planning this ritual, we can select The Lady and The Lord in an open call to the universal divine. We can select the one or ones we routinely work with. Or we can call the deities associated with prosperity. In class, the students involved in the ritual make that selection. Because the Web PATH Center involves people from many Pagan traditions, the choices are varied. Here are some we have called upon.

Gamelia, the lucky aspect of Hera, was celebrated on January 1 in Greece with bay leaves, palm fronds, dates and figs to invoke her blessings. Burn myrrh incense and carry silver coins. Two-sided items like coins, hour glasses and reversible clothing demonstrates the change from old to new, before and after.

Benten, the only Japanese Goddess of Luck, steers a treasure ship over the seas. She also rides a golden dragon. She is the patroness of gamblers, so buy a lottery ticket! Salt water baths or salt sprinkled around our treasure will enhance our bounty. She also brings beauty and love to women, perhaps because traditionally it is a source of women's financial security. Don't be caught up in relying on a lover for money in the 21st century! But enjoy the love.

Nokomis, an Algonquin grandmother, provides the bounty of nature whether it be food, furs, or precious stones and gold. Corn and gold will draw these bounties to us as we go about our work.

Aditi, Goddess of the Infinite Sky and boundlessness of Time and Space in India is celebrated with butter statues which are then dismantled and shared out with the people in an act of celebration and generosity. Think of prosperity in terms of sharing the wealth as we butter our toast each morning. I'm not sure if that works with artificial, heart-healthy spreads and certainly not with common margarine, but the key here is generosity.

Nerthus, a Germanic Goddess of Spring, was celebrated with bonfires, turning the soil and mixing dirt with milk, flour and water for spring planting. People hid all their weapons in case they would displease her. Draw the prosperity of peace to your home by repotting some house plants, turning up some garden soil, and lighting fires and candles. Wear bright clothing to bring in the energy of spring. Nerthus rode in a chariot, so we clean out our cars and invite her to ride with us to the bank.

Erzulie, a Haitian Love Goddess, fills our empty pockets. Her color is blue and peppercorns are her wealth. We carry some in our pockets, and pass her blessing and love to the people around us.

oShion, a Romani Goddess, rules fortune and fate. We seek out our lucky number and let it lead to the prosperity we need. Eating oranges, pineapples, or strawberries seasoned with nutmeg and allspice invokes her blessings as does wearing flowers and bright colors.

Lakshmi is a Hindu Goddess of Love and Luck who can open the treasures of Heaven to bless us. Rice, coins and basil can seal our appeal to her for success. I have her icon on my altar with those offerings in her bowl.

Annapurna, another Hindu deity. As Grain Goddess, she brings us prosperity from the fields. To call her bounty in, we offer any grain to the north wind and leave it on the ground for the birds to carry away.

Felicitas, a Roman Goddess of Success and Good Fortune, is honored by our wishing others good luck and blessings. Remember by blessing those who exemplify what we desire, we draw those blessings to our own lives. We can send cards, letters, and trinkets out as an act of faith in the Rule of Three. Our kindness to others is returned in multiples. If we scent our cards or letters with pine oil and cinnamon, we attract money and luck respectively.

Henwen, an English Goddess of a Prosperous Harvest, is honored by the annual turning of a stone in Devon England. Henwen is depicted as a pregnant sow who wanders the countryside nurturing cats, wolves, eagles, bees, and blessing the growing grain. We give a special treat to our kitties since the Web is populated by cat people. When we plant seeds, garden or harvest grain, gather honey and eat it on whole wheat bread, we remember who supplies our bacon! We could turn over a large stone in the yard or rearrange our furniture in Henwen's honor. There is a Native American casino near our home called Turning Stone! It might be worth a visit related to our prosperity spells if we ask Henwen to help.

Pandora, whose name means All Giver in Greece, can be honored by creating a wish box into which we put symbols of that we wish to attract. Basil and amethyst added to the box increase our hope. When we make a wish box, it is a good time to remember; be careful what we wish for. It is, after all, Pandora's Box!

Fortuna is the Roman Goddess of Luck, Wealth and Abundance. The wheel is her symbol which reminds us everything changes. However, the cornucopia or horn of plenty is also her symbol. We can anoint the wheels on our cars with almond oil to keep the money rolling in. Wearing bright colors symbolizes what we would attract. Fortuna blesses and recognizes any lucky charm we carry if we dedicate it to her. The Romans made a kind of fortune cookie to give each other blessings of the Goddess.

Tanat, Cornish Goddess of Luck and Fertility, brings our dreams into being. She is a spring Goddess who protects the young. We invoke her energy by dancing with a partner or a group. The more dancers, the more luck. In Cornwall, the people danced through the streets wearing triangles and flowers as they called her name to increase the blossoming of joy. Tanat is a fertility Goddess, so be advised. Children were a parent's wealth in the old world.

Awehai, a Haudenosaunee (Northeast Forest Indians in North America) Goddess of the Sky and Heavens, promotes a prosperous community. She is the sky woman who fell from the stars to land on the back of the turtle which is North America. She carried the seeds and starter plants of all creation to create the great bounty of Turtle Island. To draw in her bounty we eat strawberries and share them with our family.

Saturn, the Roman God of Labor, is a prosperity God of the fields and vineyards who taught the people agriculture. As a harvest God, he brings wealth and bounty. Saturn as the sower is closely connected with Ceres (Demeter) and his worship continued in Rome along with that of Jupiter. Saturn's feast Saturnalia started around December 17th and continued for a week. This was a festival like Carnivale with gifts, merry making, feasting, drinking and general excess. Social roles were reversed but often a king figure was sacrificed at the end of the festival to represent the dying God. Saturn is known as Cronus in Greece, the God killed by his son. For that reason, Saturn is often associated with death and the underworld. However, the sacrificial king offers his life for the land and the prosperity of the people, so Saturn is no more or less a dark God than the Holly King or the Horned One. He is also known as a brooding God. As the bringer of agricultural wealth yet depicted by humans as a demon, he may have a right to petulance. In addition to being an underworld God, a harvest and agricultural deity, Saturn is a healer. We can appeal to Saturn on his day (Saturday) or during Saturnalia (December 17-23) with gifts of wine, olive oil, beeswax candles, and silver coins or jewelry. Gold balls on trees and plants represent the prosperity of the returning sun at midwinter. Red caps remind us that slaves were set free during this festival. He is, of course, the Lord of Misrule so calling him can be a bit like calling Coyote—powerful, unpredictable and surprising.

Vulcan, Roman God of Fire, Valuable Metals and Smiths, was not valued as he might have been because of upper class Romans' distain for hard labor. Vulcan brings us riches from the earth and the sweat of hard work. His feast day is August 23rd. In Greece he was known as the God *Hephaestus*. He is also God of volcanoes and destruction by earth's eruptions, so like Saturn and others Vulcan is also known as a dark God. Yet volcanoes bring up power from the earth. Their hot springs create fertile islands in cold lands and mountains. They are a remarkable combination of prosperity and destruction. A forge is similar. Metals are heated, purified and molded into valuable commodities. His symbols are the anvil and hammer. As the husband of Venus he also responds to love. We eat feasts of fish or Cornish game hens (small birds or animals representative of the sacrifices made in his fires) by candlelight and share a portion in the wild. We ask for blessing and bounty in return.

Mercury or Hermes, aka Thoth is the magician and messenger of the Gods. He is a God of Prosperity, of Crafting and Commerce, and of artisans creating wealth from the beautiful work of one's hands. However, he is not entirely honest, starting his career stealing cows from Apollo and being recognized as the God of Thieves. He gave the cattle back, on the order of Zeus, but Mercury reminds us not all prosperity is honestly gained. The temptation of thievery and cheating exists in the shadow of all of us. Hermes' seat of power was Arcadia. Like Saturn, Mercury/Hermes is known for healing in that he carries the caduceus, which began as a herald's staff but became a symbol of healing. We call Mercury with the staff (wand), orange candles and vervain (verbena) because he is the God of magic, healing and communication.

Lugh is the Celtic God of Brightness, Magic and Creative Work as well as Weapon Skill. In the Celtic view, the strength of the warrior king brought prosperity to the land. When he is weakened by despair or wounded in the thigh the land suffers and crops fail. In our world, we debate the political use and distribution of 'guns or butter' but in the Celtic world, weaponry assured the availability of food. This world view was held more strongly under the patriarchal Gods than it was when the Mother Goddess held ascendancy. We call Lugh with sun symbols, by his spear, by a chain (representing the Milky Way), by a sling stone, by his hound or his horse.

Wen Cai Shen also known as *Bi Gan* is the Chinese God of Wealth or Fortune. He was the personification of righteousness and fairness, having thrown his heart on the floor in protest at the corruption of the king and the trickery of the king's favorite concubine. Living without a heart meant Bi Gan was incorruptible himself. He distributed wealth to the poor and managed wealth with wisdom. Call him with jade or coins on the altar and with money distributed to the poor.

The Horned God/Greenman and Oak King/Holly King pairing represents the father God and source of bounty from the land and forest. Wealth from the hunt and bounty of the natural world are the blessings of prosperity. These also are sacrificial Gods who ritually slay one another as the seasons change; they rise again through rebirth. Forest wood, antlers, acorns, or leaves and growing plants draw them near. Green candles, fruits and nuts and gathered foods honor their wealth.

The Sun Gods including *Ra, Lugh, Apollo,* can be called as Gods of prosperity since the earth's bounty is dependent on the sun, without which life would be impossible. Recall that the atmosphere filters and cools the sun's radiant heat so that we can exist; temper the requests you make of the sun with wisdom and boundaries. In China there were 10 sun Gods, one for each day of their week. When they appeared together they nearly destroyed the earth, and nine of them were slain at the request of the emperor who had appealed to their father Di Jun. When Di Jun could not control his children, he sent the archer Yi to frighten them with his magic bow. Yi then proceeded to kill each of the suns with his arrows. However, the emperor had his agent steal one arrow and thus save one sun to light and warm the earth. Di Jun condemned Yi to the life of an ordinary mortal for killing his children.

Journaling on Ritual, Values and Challenges

Study the ritual components described above and select the ones you wish to use in your ritual to have enough. Write the ritual and on the increasing phase of the moon, celebrate your new sufficiency with this working. When a magical rite like this has been completed, I like to create a record in my BOS. This record serves as a model for future rituals. In addition, I assess my balance in walking through Earth School by the soundness of my health, wealth, rituals, spells and joy. Of course I can be on track for my lessons and seriously out of balance from time to time. Coming into harmony and out into disharmony and back again is a different lesson, one equally important to creating prosperity. I learn more about myself by taking notes.

Discussion Questions

In addition to recording the ritual and outcomes of it in the BOS, we may wish to think on paper or the electronic page of our journals about the teaching materials. These discussion questions on our personal values can help.

When is enough enough? Our society spends large amounts of money and energy seeking more. When does that stop being meaningful?

How can we provide 'right livelihood' for ourselves and our families? Many jobs pay well, but some of them have a psychic cost or moral tax that we hardly recognize because of our focus on finance. Can we work in a prison in good conscience? A nuclear power plant? In telemarketing? In government? For a weapons manufacturer? Should we expect to be paid for spiritual services? If so, why do we call them gifts? There is no absolute answer to those questions. Finding our own center allows us to know what fits us. That helps us know who we are and where we are going. If we avoid asking these questions because we believe the job we have is the only one we can get, then that also is instructive.

What lessons about sex, power, ethics, vision, balance, fear and a safe universe are hidden in the money symbol? Symbolism is individual. Where one person sees a frightening symbol of control and power-over, another sees freedom and empowerment.

The Meaning of Challenges

When we have difficult times in our work life, we are given opportunities to add to our curriculum in Earth School. What can we learn from:

Unemployment?
Disability?
Time clocks?
Bosses?
Pressure to conform, perform and meet deadlines?
Underemployment?
Bias, prejudice and discrimination?
Favoritism?
People-who-drive-you-crazy, who sit at the adjacent work station?

What personal possession do you value the most and why? What does it symbolize to you? How much time or money do you spend on that? Is there anything else that takes up more of your time or money? What does that mean to you about the worth of those things?

What is your gut reaction to the phrase, 'It's only money'? I worked for years to loosen my heart from fear so that I could say in all honesty, 'It's only money.' For me that was the healing I needed in order to respect money and keep it in its place.

Journaling: Finish Your Money Story

Now finish your money story. Use the outline you made previously. Review your answers to the discussion questions. Think about your challenges and epiphanies. Where did you come from in your money story? Where are you going? Identify periods of scarcity, sufficiency and abundance in your history. What decisions influenced those turnarounds in your life? Does your history reflect the world economy? Could you have made different decisions? Should you make different decisions now? What makes you feel powerful when you handle money? What makes you feel generous? What do you expect from your ritual on having enough?

My story starts with my parents' story told earlier. It continues with my college job in a pizza shop. It is fleshed out by the struggle of my whole family to pay my tuition, room and board through graduation.

Then it follows the same pattern with a series of low paying altruistic jobs that allowed for no savings and barely paid the bills. When I graduated from that lesson, I made a promise to myself to double my salary every five years. Somehow, saying it made it so. I was able to do that through my mid 30s. Then my salary grew large enough so that goal of doubling was unrealistic unless I left my field of civil rights work. I made a conscious choice not to do that.

When my salary growth leveled out, I was writing the first of these Wicca lessons which taught me there was symbolism in the stories of our lives. At one point I learned I could ask the Goddess out loud for a sum of money for a specific purpose and she would deliver it within two weeks in odd ways for the good of all. Then I learned she does not do that every time.

I learned no matter what happens there is enough. I learned I have great wealth in friends and in my partner. I learned that money makes no difference in those relationships when he took a lesser paying job and I earned more money.

Twice in recessions, Spirit told me to get my money out of my investments. Once I paid attention. It is only money. The universe is a safe place. I have no complaints at all. My story is nothing special. Every one of us can arrive at the same place of peace and confidence. We can have enough. We can share. We can release fear and greed. We can enjoy our comforts. We can have our requests answered. We can learn all we need to know about our money story.

Chapter 16

Learning From Relationships

Investigating our stories about friends, frenemies and foes is a journey of the west. These relationships take us up and down the emotional roller coaster. The only thing we know for sure is that affiliations change. We may think we are BFFs (best friends forever) but mostly not. Our attitudes toward people are forged from childhood friendships. They are shaped by joy and disappointment. They are changed by chance words, acts of grace, love, hate and everything in between. We learn what to expect and expect what happened before will happen again. Our feelings reside in the west, the place of the heart. Hearts can be healed.

Scrying

When I seek wisdom of my heart, I use a scrying mirror, crystal ball or a dark bowl of water set in the west of my altar. I gaze into that reflective surface when I am confused by my friends or family. This is scrying. At first all I see is the reflection of myself or the room. Eventually the surface fogs over and impressions manifest. They may be images, voices, inner senses of knowing, epiphanies, or normal sensory data. I suspend my rational mind and let it glide along in neutral as I enter an interactive trance. I pose questions and see images as my guides teach and answer. This may require many minutes of quietude. It may proceed quickly and be done.

To try scrying about our relationships in the west, we begin with a centering breath. Then we ground. The process works better if we consciously release our fears and expectations, our experience and ego. Nothing has to happen. Something will. When we are stilled and connected to the scrying tool, we imagine the person's face and call their name. We are aware of the voice moving across time and space, between the worlds to reach them. We sense their attention turn toward us. They appear in the surface reflected back at us, either literally or with symbols.

Their symbols may seem disconnected until we ask the right question. Or we may see a movie of flowing images that clearly relate to each other. We may go into a deeper trance, close our eyes and see the answers in our mind's eye or hear them telepathically.

I do not always like what I see in the scrying surface. It does not always make sense. Frequently I need to write it down and wait for the details to come clear in ordinary reality. A rush to some conclusion is not helpful. When the images stop flowing there is very little point in trying to press on. Cover the scrying tool, ground and give thanks. Then, with the breath, release the grounding and return to ordinary consciousness.

Being open to an unexpected revelation helps us interpret the information we find by scrying. In my experience, I was shown a physical conflict between me and another person. The fight had no relationship to our ordinary lives though we are not friends and I do not trust her. The battle in the crystal ball turned out to be from past life conflicts in which we both were killed. In a different session, I saw a friend's past life as an historical figure with a withered arm. I was stunned at the appropriateness of the connection but also surprised. Later when Merlin met this man, he chided me for not telling him he had a paralyzed arm. We had quite a discussion over the fact that in this life the man was hale and hearty. Merlin did not let me off the hook for that until I told him what I had seen in the crystal ball. My scrying session and Merlin's observations across the room confirmed each other. Our friend's arm appeared to morph between crippled and healthy in a confusing manner, so Merlin was quite convinced the man was disabled. He was, hundreds of years ago. In my experience, scrying brings past life information or messages across time as well as space. Our past shapes our present.

Trust

Friendships and family ties grow in love as we find trust with one another and with the Divine. Yet trust is a fragile feeling if we have been disappointed in love. Broken hearts undermine our self-confidence. Our sense of optimism suffers when we are betrayed by people who appear to have failed in their roles of friend, lover or parent. Because our experiences include the wounds we want healed, it helps to have an accurate vision of trusting relationships before we go about describing our own connections with people. We all can grow in our trustworthiness. For every betrayal of our own trust we name, there are at least as many betrayals we have committed, one way or another. In examining our relationships, we have an opportunity to check our own fidelity.

Trust includes the confidence that our feelings will be respected. The confessions we share with friends must not be used against us at some future point when we raise concerns about unrelated events in our relationship. For example, having shared my story about the wasp my trusted friends will not come back at me at some future time and accuse me of thinking, 'Life is all about you. Even the wasp warned about that.' That is a valid observation. It does not belong in a discussion about my friend missing an appointment or forgetting a commitment.

Trust means we can share our secrets and stories and know they will not be spread about the community or worse yet, on the internet. We can be vulnerable, cry and rage without being told we are silly or overreacting. We can make mistakes without anyone chortling about our pratfall from perfection. We can do something embarrassing and not be ridiculed. We can be wrong and not be rejected. I have regular political disputes with an old friend. Every so often we need to check in with each other and know we still love each other, despite our differences. I have no idea how he can be so wrong-headed, but he is my friend. I am sure he feels the same way. We are standing on solid ground with each other even though we have deep values in conflict.

When people trust each other as friends, we let each other into our lives so we can create relationships on a soul level that are based in mutual respect, universal love, and a readiness to pitch in when we are needed. We have a concern for each other's growth and independence as well as interdependence. If we cannot trust each other, then these relationships will fall apart and disintegrate like so much low-grade mortar. When we tell our stories about money or our families we are open and vulnerable to each other as if we really are family. It is my hope that we are connected as a spiritual family. The Web is a community of people who dare transform their separateness into a oneness, or unity of love, while still remembering who we are as individuals. I believe this is what will represent Pagan communities in the 21st century as we continue to evolve in spirit and magic.

Obviously such high goals are not always fulfilled. We in the Web community have the same difficulties in developing trust that everyone else has. Most of those stem from our own histories of disappointment and betrayal. Some of us are survivors of emotional and physical abuse or neglect, in combination or separately. It is hard for people whose boundaries have been violated to separate the past from the present. Abuse occurs when there is physical and sexual violence. It also occurs when people are denied the right to their feelings or beliefs.

In addition to having boundaries violated by physical or psychological abuse, people generalize their negative experiences with friends and lovers and apply them to everyone. Old hurts build walls to defend against any chance that horrible things will happen again. A series of friends who made mistakes leave us wary of new friends who might make similar mistakes. Mourning over the unresolved death of a friend or lover leaves no room for a new relationship, partly because the new friend might also die. A hostile, bitter breakup is used as evidence that all people fail in their relationships. Generalizations like these build walls not bridges.

On the other hand, some people draw back from relationships because they feel unworthy. Not loving themselves sufficiently they think they have nothing to offer the community. They imagine their participation is insignificant. They find an offering of trust overwhelming because they fear their own failure. They believe they cannot live up to the offered friendship. Some people think they are cursed, bound to be victimized by their associates so they hide. They may even claim they avoid connecting with people because they would only bring trouble.

The irony of course is that what we expect is what we court. Disappointment breeds more disappointment. Isolation creates more loneliness. A loss of hope fosters deeper hopelessness. To heal these wounds in trust and confidence, we need to understand how we are connected to All Being. In our very identity, we are manifesting the Divine and the Disappointing.

The Golden Metaphor

Deepak Chopra uses the Golden Metaphor from the Vedic texts of India[104] in explaining this connection to All Being. Suppose I am a gold ring or a gold bracelet. I could describe myself as a bracelet or a ring based on the form I have. However, if I were re-shaped (re-born, shapeshifted) into a gold tooth or a gold necklace I would still be gold. The basic truth is that I am gold. I am not all the gold that is in the universe. Nevertheless I am gold. We are gold. This analogy works for all of us.

From the Golden Metaphor we understand that individually we are each God and Goddess. We are in the form of individual humans. Each one is different as one bracelet is different from another, but we are all both God and Goddess. We are not all of that which is God or Goddess, but we are still divine. In addition, we are part of that universal God and Goddess which is the world creation. That is how we are connected between and among ourselves. If we carry that truth as we reflect on our relationships and trust issues we begin the healing. Regardless of our life stories, regardless of our human forms, I am you, and you are me.

When we both remember this connection across the web of life, we are encouraged to live with compassion. Our understanding and forgiveness of wrongs perpetrated against us is increased. Healing becomes possible. I frequently remind my friends and myself that the people who have given us the most grief, who incite the greatest anger or instill the deepest fear, are the people who in their greater soul on the Otherside love us the most. That is a hard truth to swallow. Our abusers, our enemies, our failed relationships are people who outside Earth School love us the most. Everything within us refuses to believe that. Nevertheless, I find the idea filled with healing merit.

Think about it. Our crises build a soul connection between the victim, persecutor and rescuer even in ordinary reality. We remember and rehearse the wrongs perpetrated against us. While we are healing, we tell our story repeatedly as if to mark it indelibly in our minds. That is part of the healing process: to tell the story and be affirmed and believed. By the time we finish, the persecutor has taken on monstrous proportions. Our healing is marked in our ability to release that monster and let it go from our lives. We defeat the shadow and turn it into something else. That something else may be our own inner strength, our own guardianship of the self, or our deeper connection with the wisdom of the universe. We are loved and pulled out of that dark despair.

Who is That Masked Enemy?

When we are sent here from the Otherside to Earth School to enjoy the physical dimension and learn something new, people from our soul groups agree to come with us. Each has a role to play in our lives as we do in theirs. The script is very loose, open to constant ad lib and revision. Since we remember very little about the reason we came here, some of the plot twists are horrifying and unexpected. We forge karmic connections with our persecutors and rescuers which destine us to travel together again and again as we work out our relationships from one life to another. Who would agree to play our villain? The villain has that strongest link to our soul. We are stuck somehow in a continuing drama of difficulty. Did we imagine that an enemy would agree to keep coming back and re-working the scene until we all get it right? I think that unlikely. The person who would play that role for us is one who loves us, one who agrees to the agony of misunderstanding, and one who needs the same healing we do.

As a result, people who are toxic to us here in ordinary reality may need to be banished from our lives. They do not need to be vilified. They do not need to be punished, unless of course they break the law and are convicted after due process. Then the state takes care of that. Their punishment is not our job. From a soul perspective, they do not wish us harm. When we can see this larger picture, then we can move away and let them go. We can step out of that victimization triangle to heal our wounds. In that place of light, we can forgive ourselves and the other for being locked in opposition in the first place.

Forgiveness is a transformative experience. When we measure our beliefs and our relationships, we may be moved to let go of some of the old anger or hurt that has given us a mental and emotional experience of mad, sad or scared. Forgiving ourselves and those we believe have wronged us is one method of releasing the feelings, beliefs and memory of what used to be so important we had to poke at the wounds regularly to cleanse them. It is possible to heal the wounds and have no scabs or even scars. Sometimes people proudly proclaim they love their emotional scars because they are lessons they have learned. That is partly true. The emotional scars represent the lessons they have partly learned.

I learned at SAVAR that survivors of sexual assault and invasion often are distanced from their anger and rage. It takes a good deal of work for some people to open up and accept the fury that comes from being betrayed (most such attacks are from people we know), violated and injured. It can impact on the survivor for years. Some people expect sexual assault to change their lives forever. There is no shortcut that bypasses the anger. One simply must experience it in all its fullness to heal the wounds.

When we have wounds in our hearts that refuse to heal, one

reason may be because we never experienced the outrage connected to the event. When this is true of our wounded self, we must go through the anger first. The anger will not kill us. Talking it out with someone prepared to hear our rage is an empowering experience. We do not act on our anger in revenge. We talk it out.

Back in the 1970s I thought our job was done at SAVAR once the talking brought us to the anger. I believed acknowledging the client's anger would lance the infected wound in their psyche. It did not. Many of the clients and many of the crisis workers were stuck in the rage stage. They had neither the language nor the skill to move on. Some of us realized we could use anger constructively to create intervention programs, work on legislation, and advocate for clients within the legal system. One of us even went on to law school and became an attorney and an elected official. All of those were useful uses of anger, which can be a hugely effective energizer and motivator.

On the other hand, when stuck in the overdrive of rage for a long time, we are subject to adrenal exhaustion, burnout and cynicism. There has to be a way of releasing the anger and finding peace. Temporary solutions come in using the emotional release points discussed in Chapter 14. In longstanding disputes the negative feelings return. Our hearts fall back into grumpy patterns. We withdraw. There is a path through those feelings that ultimately resolves them. Oddly enough, that path leads through forgiveness—hardly a popular word among survivors of any disaster.

An Illustration

After a divorce, individuals often nurse grudges for many weeks, months or years. 'I lost my house.' 'I never see my kids.' 'Child support is always late.' 'The children don't like to see their other parent because it confuses them' (read: 'I don't like them to see their other parent because I am afraid'). 'It's all his/her fault because they cheated on me.' 'I wish they were dead and I didn't have to deal with them anymore.' The divorce is over, the marriage is over, but the energy lives on. This is absolutely humanly normal. I have never personally known of a divorced couple who did not go through a period of this grudge bearing (the rage stage).

I also know of no person going through grudge bearing whose life was made happier by it, whose children were enriched by the atmosphere, or whose health was improved. On the contrary, grudges narrow our vision of what might be. We limit our freedom because of the energy put into keeping the grudge fresh and alive. Our children are forced to choose sides between people they love. They learn helplessness and fear power. Truth be told, we also court heart disease, cancer, depression, eating disorders, arthritis and many other conditions related to unresolved rage.

How can anyone then, escape from the rage stage of loss? The rage stage is resolved when we learn to look for the point, the lesson, or the symbolism of the crisis; by learning to separate from the anger and letting it go away, we can allow ourselves to heal from the emotional pain and physical dis-ease. All of us have events in our lives that leave us clutching anger, pain or fear in our hearts. We must decide whom we blame. Why are they at fault? What are we willing to do to end this situation? Are we willing to have a sincere conversation with the offenders and speak of forgiveness? Sometimes it is not safe to do that because the offender is violent. Sometimes it is impossible to speak with them. We can have this conversation in meditation, which is especially important if our tormentors are dead, distant, or dangerous, or if our asking for pardon would aggravate their pain and create another level of harm.

My Story: The Nemesis

I came to the point of being tired of hating and resenting my nemesis. My attitude and feelings only made bad matters worse. My own creativity was blocked. I also could not feel loved by other people because I had blocked my love for this person (it was one of those love/hate things). I could not confess my hatred, for fear of crushing someone who was very vulnerable, so, 'Please forgive me for hating you,' was not appropriate! I could not offer my forgiveness for a whole list of wrongs because there was no awareness in the other person that wrongs existed. In the midst of the personal crisis of my enemy, my list of complaints was not going to raise consciousness. They might have buried the enemy instead—literally. Pushing anyone clear over the edge was not going to work toward my freedom and enlightenment.

This enemy was my father. He was aged, suffering from the initial states of dementia. He also deeply loved me. He was proud of me. What kind of ingrate was I? So I said nothing out loud! Instead, I went into meditation, contacting our Higher Selves. There I offered my forgiveness for each of the hurts I remembered. Some of them were very clear: an unfinished house, tight financial times, worry all the way through college about paying tuition in time for exams, smothering parental love, intrusion into my private thoughts, constant evaluation. Other grievances were less specific and hard to remember even though I knew I was angry about some nebulous event.

I did not want to say, 'I forgive you for…anything,' at least not at first. But each time I said it about something I remembered, I felt more genuine. I felt more forgiving. I made it real. It was equally real when the enemy turned to me in the Higher Self and said, 'I forgive you too.' That I had need of being forgiven shocked me but the truth was obvious. As a youth I had thought our life was all about me. As an adult I had not recognized my ego playing with the facts. When it came to my father, part of me had spent a life time stuck in Erik Erikson's stages of development for toddlers and children: Independence and Initiative.

For days afterward, even though issues came up in ordinary reality as we struggled to live together—the rage stage was gone. Then Spirit finished the other 49 percent in one mighty act of crisis and release. The old grudges evaporated! I felt them go. I believe I laid the groundwork with the meditation on forgiveness, and the desire to be free.

My belief that I had been wronged, that I deserved better, that the world is not a fair place, that the failures of others had power over my choices all contributed to the rage. Without enumerating them, I also released those beliefs by asking for and sending out forgiveness. I no longer believe that any of that spin on my history was true. I know the events happened, but I also know other causes, other purposes and other stories about them now that I could not have heard before. In my case, my father was not a terrible person. Sometimes the ones we need to forgive act like terrible people. Let us just say these things happened. We do not know the whole story.

Journaling about Your Nemesis

To make this personal, identify your nemesis in your journal. You can draw a sketch or a stick figure to withhold the name or you can put it out there in complete detail. Ask yourself what it would take to consider forgiving that person. Let the realizations come as quickly or as slowly as they will, but write them down. Some of them will be in your power to do. Some will not. Be clear. Forgiving a person does not include condoning their actions. There is no excuse for violence and assault. Having survived an attack, we do not need to carry the energy of rage and violence with us for the rest of our lives. We can set that burden down even though we hold the perpetrators responsible for their actions.

More about Forgiveness

We must genuinely set our anger and outrage down in order to forgive. We cannot hide it in our pockets and act as if we are forgiving. A grudge is a grudge. It eats us up inside no matter how sweet we appear on the surface. A faked forgiveness is no forgiveness at all. It will not be assisted by our spiritual guides and mentors. They know better.

The empty chair technique[105] moves us into a place of forgiveness when we are stuck. Try this when you have no desire to forgive. As a survivor, sit facing an empty chair. Pretend your nemesis or perpetrator is in that chair. Spill your guts. Say it all in any fashion you wish. It is an emotional purging. When you finish, probe some to see what might have been too horrible to say. What might have been censored or held back? This catharsis can be repeated if need be until you are ready to stop screaming your rage and are ready to find peace. Then say the perpetrator is responsible for his or her own choices. They harmed or injured with or without intent. In the face of that truth, speak your forgiveness to the perpetrator if you can. Disconnect all the ties you have between them for the events that happened. Physically act that out as if you are unhooking lines of energy between your bodies. Wad the ties up and throw them into a candle fire. Put them into a bowl of water and flush them down the toilet. Get rid of them.

As long as we hold on to our emotional ties to those events we are stuck with our wounding. The perpetrator has hooks in us and we have them in the perpetrator. Acting out your unhooking makes it real. You unhook the lines of energy from your body and the body of the perpetrator. Both. When we burn them or bury them or throw them into the sea or cast them into a strong wind, we hand the hooks and the lines of connection over to be transformed by the Elementals.

Compassion and forgiveness fill the void left by our fear, anger and grief. This exchange of compassion for anger is important. If the empty space where all that negativity sat in our psyche remains empty, then our old emotional and mental habits have a place to return. If we fill that space with wisdom and compassion, there is no room left for them. At this point, the events are truly over. Some of us are fortunate enough to hear the answer to the question, 'Why?'

More of My Story

What was at the root of the pain between my father and me? In present life issues, my dad was overprotective because he had only one child—me. He was so grateful for that he never could let me go emotionally. More than many women, I was destined to be Daddy's little girl for all his life. For too many years I resented that. I wanted to be independent and strong. I wanted to get away.

On the other hand, my father was a short-tempered auto mechanic. He was never rich nor able to spoil me with money and gifts. He scrambled all his life for money to pay the bills, not because he was lazy but because he did not know how to make money work for him. He worked for money. To his credit, he was as honest a man as ever there was. In the end, he did not have enough money to retire on. His care fell to Merlin and me. My parents moved in with us.

In contrast to our family's financial situation, my father chose to raise me in one of the wealthiest towns in our county. The school system was top notch. I received a solid secondary education that set me on the track for college. The chasm between my economic status and my friends' was painful. That pain made me strong. It made me political. It created an activist. It taught me how to build a career into financial security and to move easily between the classes of people from the very poor to the very rich.

When I became increasingly responsible for my parents, I needed help. I found a counselor who could take me back into my past lives to seek out the hidden wisdom of our family. I learned the seeds of our conflict reached back in time to another life. In the Middle Ages, when I had been orphaned by a cholera plague, I went to live with my sister and her cruel husband. The same soul that came to play the part of my father in this life was that emotionally truncated brother-in-law in another. We came back together to balance the scale, to learn more about how to love each other, to make up for the losses. Because I learned to step out of my own selfish pique and forgive my father in this life for wrongs real and imagined in both lives, we succeeded. In the end, no one ever loved me more than my dad, and *vice versa*. Forgiving him was crucial to my own soul.

A Book That Made a Difference

When I was discussing emotional healing with Peg she told me that the best book she ever read for our classes was *I Thought We'd Never Speak Again* by Laura Davis.[106] With that book, Peg was able to forgive family members for abandoning her as an elementary school girl. She learned everyone in the family saw their shared history differently. She understood people could only offer love and protection within their own limitations; sometimes that was far short of what a young girl needed. Even under those circumstances, forgiveness in her heart repaired their relationships sufficiently to re-create a sense of family.

One of the qualities Davis demonstrates in the stories she tells is persistence. The woman she identified as Miriam asks for forgiveness of her children three times in writing.[107] Her efforts took that long to reach deep within the estrangement so she could genuinely name her failures as a mother and speak her regret. People offer poor apologies and are surprised they are not accepted. 'I'm sorry if I offended you,' insults the wounded listener. It implies culpability on the part of the victim. Maybe there is fault there; it takes two to break a relationship. Our apologies need to take responsibility not place blame. An effective apology offers regret for a specific action. 'I am sorry I hurt you when I said ___.' An apology offers no justifications, no ifs nor buts. It accepts responsibility. I did this specific thing and you were hurt. I am sorry.

Davis also shares Antonio's story about being Latino and gay.[108] His family rejected him, but he was persistent in paying his respects to his mother. He called every Sunday. He and his partner visited every Christmas, even in the face of rudeness. Finally he arranged to spend time with his 75-year-old mother one-on-one. He fixed her hair at his salon and took her to lunch. He told her he loved her and he needed to know if she wished to be his friend. She did. They both said they were sorry and cried. The past was over because they meant it. That took courage as well as persistence.

Resolving wounded relationships is among the most difficult

challenges we face. I encourage students to seek professional counseling when they feel stuck or resistant to the possibilities for emotional freedom. This is truly an area where the wounded healer works overtime. None of us are free of relationships which ended in tatters. Many of us still rehearse our woundedness as stories which have no ending. In telling our stories, we are free to rewrite the ending. We can come to a new conclusion.

Journaling: Rewrite Your Script

In the privacy of your own sacred space, write a new ending to a damaged relationship. Make it believable, but make it come out differently. For example, I have an old broken friendship that remains on some level unresolved. Lately I have rewritten the ending. It goes like this:

> After our failed reconciliation dinner, we both go our separate ways because we have new friends and new successes unrelated to the work we shared once upon a time.

That is not the original story. We parted in sadness. When we met again she seemed reluctant to accept my congratulations on her success. On another occasion she preferred not to see me in a crowd. I am truly sorry for my part in our problems. I removed the hooks. Now I say we both live happily ever after. That is my new story and I am sticking to it.

Is that cockeyed optimism? Not if we invoke the rule of three. The energy we send out comes back threefold. I send out regret, forgiveness and a belief we both thrive. That energy blesses her and comes back to me. I feel my heart open when I write that because it is true.

Chapter 17

Sexual Healing and Histories

If exploring our bodies, our bank accounts and our relationships was difficult, imagine the resistance to a class about our sexual stories! People either want to brag or sink into the floor. Our sexual identity is the most intimate and vulnerable aspect of ourselves. Our shadows are deep in sacred sexual bodies. We hide feelings, history, pain, desire, and pleasure away from the light. We hide them away from our consciousness. We create rules and judgments to control our passionate selves. The very aspect that is meant to bring us the greatest joy may be shrouded in fear, anger, guilt or grief. Yet our sexuality is a part of the Pagan spiritual path. We recognize the Great Rite between the Goddess and her Consort as a metaphor for all the fertility of nature, perhaps for creation itself. Sexual healing is a key area for transformation so we can open up to ecstasy in all our bodies and merge it with our souls.

Residing in the west where our deepest feelings flow, sexuality connects the physical, emotional, willful, mental and spiritual bodies. It is shaped by the heat of our willful passions in the south and our physical responses in the north. Therapists are fond of saying our most important sexual organ is our brain, so I imagine sexuality arises in the east. We can work on this transformation in all four quadrants of the circle. To create an altar for this working, set a pink rose quartz or rhodochrosite in the north; rose incense in the east; a red candle in the south and rose water in the west. Then answer this questionnaire in your journal. There are no right or wrong answers. You will not be graded. This exercise is to get you thinking about your real experiences and beliefs. How do you really feel about sex?

Sex and Spirit: A Questionnaire

1. *Describe your current relationship:*
a. Current live-in partner or married
b. Current steady sweetie
c. Single, no current partner
d. Polyamory partners
e. Divorced
f. Separated
g. Dating more than one person
h. Other____________________________

2. *How do you practice spirituality?* List as many practices as apply but only include the ones you really use, not the ones you wished you practice.
a. I don't
b. Meditation
c. Chanting
d. Yoga, Tai Chi, Chi Gong etc.
e. Dance
f. Prayer
g. Reading sacred texts
h. Drumming/drum circles
i. Trance/journey work
j. Intentional solitude
k. Attending services/circle
l. Other____________________________

3. *How often for each of these practices?* Add the correct choice next to the practice in your notes.
a. Daily
b. 2-5 times per week
c. Weekly
d. Monthly

e. Annually

4. *What—in your belief—is a spiritual experience?*
a. Out of body experience
b. Transcending time/place/identity through meditation or prayer
c. Connecting with other people at a ceremony or religious service
d. A quiet mind/stillness
e. Merging with the universe
f. Emotional overflow
g. Energy moving through body/mind
h. Attending a ceremony or ritual
i. Raising a cone of power
j. Invoking/evoking deity
k. Creating music, art, writing
l. Being out in nature, especially ____________(woods, lakes etc. Be specific)
m. Gazing at the moon or stars
n. Other____________________________

5. *How often do you have a spiritual experience?*
a. Never
b. Few in my lifetime
c. Once or twice a year
d. Once or twice a month
e. Once or twice a week
f. Almost everyday
g. Many times a day

6. *Do you consider sex a spiritual practice?*
a. Yes
b. No

7. *What do you mean by sex?* Include as many as you wish in your definition.
a. Intercourse (without penetration it's not sex)
b. Oral sex
c. Massage
d. Fondling
e. Snuggling
f. Masturbation
g. Cybersex and sexting
h. Orgasm
i. Other______________________

8. *How important is sexual fidelity to you?*
a. A crucial issue
b. One-sided: s/he expects fidelity; I do not.
c. One-sided: s/he does not expect fidelity; I do.
d. Not important, we love with an open hand
e. Important within our group; outside affairs break the rules
f. Other______________________

9. *How often is sex spiritual for you?*
a. Never, not even once
b. A few times, I can count them on one hand
c. Maybe a special time, every year or so
d. Nearly every month, sometimes twice a month
e. Regularly, almost every week
f. Frequently, almost every time

10. *How do you and your partner(s) enhance the connection between spirit and sex?*
a. We don't; there isn't any
b. We don't; it has to be spontaneous
c. Yoga practice
d. Tantra practice

e. Creating Sacred Space
f. Sensory stimulation
g. Gazing into each other's eyes
h. Sensuous sacred touch
i. Prayer/meditation
j. Celebrating the Great Rite, symbolically
k. Celebrating the Great Rite, literally
l. Drawing down the Moon
m. Other____________________________

11. *How important is it to you that sex and spiritual experience connect?*
a. It isn't that important
b. It isn't possible
c. It's nice but not crucial
d. It's key to our relationship
e. Connect with spirit or disconnect with me
f. Other____________________________

12. *How much influence do spiritual practices or interests have in your selection of partners/lovers?*
a. None, I can't find anyone like that
b. None, I practice solitary by choice
c. Equally important with trust
d. A lot, sharing spiritual things is a deal breaker/maker
e. Spiritual connections are more important than sexual connections
f. Other____________________________

13. *What is most valuable in maintaining a healthy sexual/spiritual life?*
a. Frequency of sexual spiritual intimacy
b. Love and respect between partners
c. A partner with shared spiritual consciousness

d. My appearance or attractiveness
e. My partner's appearance or attractiveness
f. Time, energy or health available
g. Education and information about the connection of sexuality and spirituality
h. Other_______________________________

Review your answers. Review the questions. What surprises you about this list? Students have found the concept of sacred sex a deep challenge. The younger students are still caught up in youthful impressions that sex is not quite all right. Okay, so are some older adults. Some of the older adults feel they have somehow outgrown sexual passions. A few have described sex as a messy waste of time. Others feel obligated. Some are simply too tired. A precious few are deeply in love with their partners and share a physicality that includes the Gods.

Sexual healing is not easy. When our boundaries have been damaged by clumsy lovers, abusers, or a lack of self-love, we find ourselves closed off and blocked from ecstasy. When our lives are so busy we neglect our sexuality, there may be secondary reasons for that rooted in physical health, or hurt feelings. Healing our several bodies may indeed help our sexual relationship with our spouse or partner. The first step is in becoming open to ecstasy.

Ecstasy

Merlin and I attended a workshop on ecstasy and the maenads led by Patricia Monaghan some years ago at the Starwood Festival. A large crowd had gathered to hear her speak, more people than would fit in a circle. We formed rings of semi circles around her in the wooded lawn by the main house. As Monaghan taught us about the maenads we each made our own thyrsus using a dowel, a pine cone and colored yarn.

At one point Monaghan passed her own thyrsus around as a talking stick so we could each say what we understood ecstasy to mean. I thought the exercise would take a very long time, given the large number of people present. It did not. Most of the people, both men and women, said they came to the workshop to find that answer because they did not have ecstasy in their lives. These were adults, many of whom were married and nearly all of them sexually active. I understand that ecstasy is not only sexual orgasm, but it is at least that. Ecstasy is also the breathtaking sunrise, the swirling noisy storm, the roiling sea, the joyful cry of a newborn son or daughter. Yet at a Pagan festival, the largest on the east coast in the US, two thirds of us could not describe ecstasy from our own experience.

Interestingly, three things happened as I waited for the talking stick. First, a dog came loping through the workshop with her tongue hanging out and tail wagging. She had clearly eluded her keepers and made a run for it. She wandered through the rows of people, stopping to bless specific people with a flurry of wet doggy kisses. When she was done, she joyfully passed out of the circle and took off through the woods, eager to see what other adventures were hers for the taking.

Right after that, a little garter snake came wiggling through the crowd. The day was sunny and warm, and she was looking for a spot to sleep in the sun. Sadly, the people in her way screeched and shrieked until she raised her head up out of the leaves to look straight at them. I could see she was puzzled. *Whatever is wrong with these humans that they should make such horrid noises and run all over the place like idiots? Don't they know they could step on me? I'd better rise up further so they don't.* Fortunately some kind soul near her picked her up gently and took her away from the group to continue her journey in the sunshine. I watched her wriggle happily away over the edge of the hill to a quiet place.

We had no more settled back down to continue our effort to define ecstasy than a little gray squirrel leaped through the trees, chattering at us from first one branch then another. He swung wildly with full abandon on the thinnest perches to the next slim twig, twirling around them, catching hold a mere breath before he might fall. He put on a glorious, fearless display, all the while chattering away as if we were supposed to understand him. We were.

The dog, the snake and the squirrel all came to show us ecstasy of the spirit. They lived with revelry in the moment. It was up to us to catch their meaning and understand. Ecstasy is all around us. We can experience it anytime we wish. The secret is, there is no secret. Joy in kisses, delight in the sensuous sun, pleasure in our bodies' dance through the trees are gifts of ecstasy. If we recoil in fear or are angry that ecstasy interrupted our thoughts, then there is the point where we can begin our healing.

Openness

Sexual ecstasy is the same way. Being open to loving attention, kisses, hugs and touch makes ecstasy possible. In Web Wiccan Consciousness, part of our emotional healing about sex and the body includes hand caresses and foot washing among friends. We use these experiences as safe touch, not foreplay. Working in pairs, classmates hold each other's hands and pet them. Each person is actually seeking their own sensual pleasure in the skin to skin touch, not offering massage or reflexology. In the hand caresses, people are asked to maintain eye contact. In the foot washing they use soap and foot creams that both people find pleasant. These activities are difficult. They are pleasurable, but they bring people into our hug circle who may not have been invited there before. The exercise is not conducted in the circle of intimacy. Understanding the difference can be very healing for people whose boundaries are confused. Knowing that loving touch does not automatically lead to sex or intercourse is an important freedom.

When I asked Elise what the most difficult part of Wicca III activities was, she said the hand caresses. She sobbed from the first touch, to her surprise and that of her class partner Ravija. Ravija is a centered, physical person so she could stay present in the moment, gaze lovingly into her partner's eyes and support her without saying a word. As a result, Elise found out loving touch could be safe; something that was not true for her growing up. Because many of her boundaries had been shattered, she did not know safe and loving touch. All of the sudden it was there. She also readily admits the sex discussions pushed her buttons. This class was a breakthrough for her, a place where she was allowed to be curious without being lewd. In our closing ritual she affirmed she can be a genuine lover to her husband and in return, allow him be her lover too.

Soft Moon Rising agreed that the discussion about sex was the most difficult, but for a different reason. She had spent much of her life being two people. In business she tried to appear like everyone else in a conservative town. Privately she was a woman who loved women. In the Web she could simply be who she is without criticism or judgment. She has gone on to develop a teaching and healing ministry that focuses on peace, shamanic practice and Reiki. Her psychic abilities as a medium and channel are notable. We laughed over her initial insistence that she was not psychic. After too many years of heartache, she has found a stable loving relationship with a healthy woman who loves her more than peanut butter.

Union

What challenged me as the Webweaver and instructor was teaching sexually experienced adults what they do not know about sex. Most students are familiar with the terms kundalini and tantra. A less well-known term from India is *maithuna,* the art of sacred love and the meditation of sex. *Maithuna* is the Sanskrit word for union. I understand this sexual merging to be the model for creating *one out of two,* unity out of duality. Oneness in sex mirrors the oneness in spirit that we experience in the quartered circle, in drawing down the moon and in other spiritually ecstatic encounters. If we have reached out to deepen our sexual connections with spiritual overtones, oneness makes more sense.

Our sexuality is healed by expanding our awareness of ecstasy beyond the 'beast with two backs'[109] struggling under the blankets or on top of them, locked in a sort of contest of orgasmic will. Instead, we create a different sexual image of merger and reconnection between deeply committed lovers.

We at the Web have for years taught that all things stem from the One which is All Being or All That Is, the Source. She manifests herself as an array of Goddesses. He manifests himself as an array of Gods. Each is spun out of the source of All Being. Each has an identity which is played out in the universe, on earth, and as far as I can tell across the many dimensions. Those identities of the Gods are roles in the same way our identities as mortals are roles. These roles are not all we are at a soul level. Those identities are not all the Gods and Goddesses are at a divine level. One cause for this multi-layered mosaic of who we really are is our source. We are all spun out of the essence of All Being.

One of the illusions we play with in the western world is that this oneness is subdivided into two sides, sometimes opposing sides, such as light and dark, male and female, good and evil. You might understand my objection to that dualism as a woman. A dualistic universe supports the illusion of congruence between dark, feminine and evil all of which carry negative implications for our shared sexual partnering. Can any man couple with a dark, evil female and not be soiled? No dualistic religious or philosophical system has been able to explain the divisions as something other than positive and negative (female gets the negative) in any way that is satisfactory.

Consequently, my focus on the greater unity of being beyond light and dark, positive and negative is an adventure in spirituality and science. Maithuna is an alternative to dualism. It is an alternative to sexual conquest.

On the other hand, sexual merging is more than a wonderful idea on how to create unity in a relationship. It is an ecstatic high. With maithuna, making love becomes more than sexual intercourse. It is the communion of souls and of all five bodies: spiritual, magical, mental, emotional and physical. It is the implosion of the four directions into the center. It is our descent into the ecstasy of the abyss. That descent is why orgasm in French is called *le petit mort;* the little death.

Obviously, this merging begins with the physical contact of holding, kissing and caressing. The sexual arousal increases with thoughtful and loving physical contact in which partners open themselves to each other without reservation. The emotional body is engaged sexually when the feelings of love and acceptance and the conscious blending of the emotional aura and the chakras arouse deep feelings of peace and joy and adoration. As the physical bodies merge, so do the emotional bodies.

Most of us have been in a sexual situation where our bodies refuse to engage in the potential ecstasy because we were preoccupied with emotional issues between us and our partner. Too annoyed with our last argument, bitter about unresolved money issues or sad about repeated hurt feelings, we could not park the memories or feelings. Nothing worked the way it usually does. Even some of the touches that are usually most stimulating felt intrusive or painful. Frequently we decide to fake it or live with disappointment. Rarely do we own our own feelings in order to heal them.

There is another choice. We can park our negative feelings, knowing neither of us can resolve those at the moment, and remember we are still a loving couple. Then we can change the physical rejection of sexual stimulation by consciously opening the red root chakra, clearing it and letting it flower under the attention of our lover. When the root chakra is cleared, then we open the orange belly chakra and let it sense the love and passion being experienced by our lover. Through that emotional sexual healing of the first two chakras, we can find joy and forgiveness for the annoyances, bitterness, and hurt and merge with our partner as an equal. If we want to. If we dare. Then we consciously follow with the other chakras, opening the solar plexus, heart, throat, brow and crown in turn, letting them meld and combine in the emotional body.

When the body and the emotions are open to merger, then the mind or mental body begins to dissolve and connect in new ways with the emotional and physical body involved in our lovemaking. Telepathy increases. We know what will stimulate and please the partner before being told. Our rhythm and breath synchronize, and we can even open our eyes and connect together as we create a new One out of the two of us. No one is dominant. No one is submissive. Logical thought becomes irrelevant. Thinking is replaced by knowing. This sexual path is a wisdom path which grows out of being together, not doing sex. Having an orgasm, making love, acting on each other's pleasure zones is surpassed by the merger of being. Orgasm is not the purpose of maithuna.

Finally then magic happens; the spirits merge. The bodies may not even move. The contact is total body, total heart, total mind and total spirit. Pulsing micro movements of the soul move us from one to two, back and forth in harmony and then in unison, experiencing what it is like to be complete in both human forms and in no form. A cosmic explosion rises from our tiny molecules and extends throughout the universe. We are all things and nothing and this thing. This merger is indeed *le petit mort*, but it is beyond orgasm. It is what my shamanic journey into death revealed, in joining the cosmos in the most perfect joy of being and non-being that defies all explanation.

This ecstasy of maithuna is the experience offered to us in celebration of our sexuality, when we dare transform the known into the unknown. This is sacred sex. This is the Great Rite. It is also our right, but it means we are forever transformed, changed and unlike who we were before.

Challenges to Maithuna

Immediately questions arise. What about a person who has been sexually abused; how can sacred sex have meaning or relevance to them? How can one heal the wounds of sexual assault and violation?

If a person's health does not support sexual activity, does this mean they are cut off from the sacred union of sex as a spiritual practice? If a person has no partner or spouse, is celibate by choice or circumstance, how can sacred sex have meaning for them? If a person's partner is shocked by the possibility of sacred sex and rejects any conversation about this, what can one do?

Healing from sexual abuse requires time. Survivors do well to connect with a crisis center which will help them learn the assault was not their fault. Group sessions with other survivors generally assist men and women survivors in finding their way through a flood of emotions. One of the necessary steps is found in feeling their anger, owning it and expressing it in a constructive manner. The balance between feeling anger and releasing it at the right time is an individual cycle. It takes as long as it takes. Storytelling can help. So can meditation and ritual.

When an individual is ready to move on past his or her rage, then clearing the entire chakra system begins the process. Most Web healers learned to do this in their study of physical healing. Chakra healing requires the ability to see or sense the chakras through dowsing. The healer removes all the occlusions possible. This may take more than one session. Old stuff floats up through the layers of the chakra to be cleansed in turn. The healer then sets all the chakras spinning in harmony using sound or chanting as well as healing hands. Chakras which are larger or smaller than the others need energy siphoned off or added to them. Ideally they all are the size of small dinner plates. Chakras should be uniformly bright. Their colors are like stained glass with the sun shining through. Healers add light or balance chakras with white light, corresponding colors and crystals. An individual could clear the chakras in self-healing with the right training, but that is the hard way.

The second part of the healing process comes through learning the sense behind a senseless violation. This search for an answer to the question, 'Why me?' is frequently shelved by crisis centers and counselors. People wisely want to avoid blaming the survivor (victim) in any fashion. Survivors are told there is no answer to find. That is true, from our view point in ordinary reality. No matter if the person who was attacked made mistakes like leaving the door unlocked, trusting an untrustworthy person or walking alone at night in a dangerous place, no one is asking to be raped or assaulted. Sexy dresses do not cause rape. A world of difference exists between feeling joy in the beauty of one's body and having one's face pushed in the dirt, one's clothes ripped and being battered and violated; between running back inside to pick up a folder without locking the door and having one's home invaded and used as a staging area for humiliation and rape; between believing the best in people and having one's caring crushed by cruel hands and steel toed boots. Nothing the victim did can be used to justify assault, rape or incest.

From a soul's point of view, nothing the human experiences was disallowed by the Higher Self. For reasons which may remain unclear to us, our souls agreed we were strong enough to face the unthinkable. We were resilient enough to heal from disaster. We were creative enough to find wisdom in the mud. Some writers like Robert Schwartz[110] and Michael Newton[111] explain that our souls actively participate in between-life planning sessions to set the script for each life, complete with supporting characters and stars. This is not so very different from Transaction Analysis (TA) scripts[112] except that the soul plans the drama before entering this life. In TA, the soul responds to early life situations and drafts a script, often with Jungian archetypal elements. In both cases, a self-aware soul can re-write the script. The first step is to understand there is script; life is not random; we were part of the planning.

I cannot answer the question 'Why?' for anyone. I can only hold the energy for them while they seek it through meditation, trance or divination. I know that part of the answer will be revealed in what the person chooses to do next in their healing journey. When I was teaching crisis advocates at SAVAR I asked a class of women what they did with the anger once they found it. One person blurted out, 'Join SAVAR!' She was right. When survivors have found their healing they are ready to turn around and help someone else. A survivor of sexual assault may find their story helpful to someone else.

A handful of us who were among the founding mothers of SAVAR in the 1970s were given recognition at an annual fundraising dinner in 2010. The plaque is among my treasures. The speaker that evening was Sayeh Rivazfar, a New York State Trooper who in her childhood had survived sexual assault and attempted murder by a serial killer in Pensacola FL when she was a prepubescent child. Her sister Sara was killed. Her assignment now is to work with the State Police and victims of similar crimes. That is a lifetime later after years of therapy, training as a police officer and schooling. Her story inspired me to see the possibilities for survivors. If she can move past the rage stage to speak about her history, so can anyone. The entire banquet hall was spellbound as she spoke. I was humbled. I know a little bit about healing because I have studied it. She is an expert because she lived it.

There is nothing which can separate us from the One because that is the root and core of who we really are. If our bodies or our hearts or our relationships do not support the sacredness of physical sex, we will find our ecstatic merger or maithuna in meditation or with a spirit lover in our dreams. But that is a different story and another book. Believe me, though, the door never closes on ecstasy.

Journaling on Ecstasy and Orgasm

Think about the significance of spiritual ecstasy and orgasm. If you have experienced both, describe the similarities and differences from your own point of view. Assess them from the north and body, the east and mind, the south and spiritual focus (magic) and the west and deep feeling. Is spiritual ecstasy from meditation or ritual more physical or mental? Is orgasm? What is magical about each of them? What are your deepest feelings about yourself, your lover or your God/dess? How can you express those thoughts and feelings in words, music or images? Artistic creativity is ecstasy too.

Chapter 18

Death as Healing

When we understand that we are eternally linked to All Being as part of the One, we are ready for our next adventure in emotional healing: embracing death as a healer. Death is our birth in the journey we take in crossing over from this world to the other. Death as a normal process of be-ing challenges our pretenses, if there be pretenses, in our spirituality. Remembering that denial is one of the methods we use to distance emotional trauma, we observe the death of a loved one as a deep soul lesson—one which cannot be denied. We grieve. We rage. We disbelieve, but in the end we give up on denial and admit they have disappeared.

What is Death?

The answer to that question is the source of humanity's efforts in creating religious beliefs. Is the soul immortal? Does it transcend time and space? Will we, in some form, live forever outside time? If we do, what will our relationships be like? What will we look like? How will we communicate?

The Web Wiccan Consciousness approaches the subject of death through reincarnation. In that light, all of us have something to remember about death. We have walked through the veil at the end of each life to the Otherside. Each time we entered the Otherside, we met the members of our soul circle who preceded us or did not incarnate with us. As we experienced our life review, we re-learned our lessons from the life we completed. We have traveled repeatedly from life to life and back again. Our souls are old hands at this.

But then we doubt. Then we forget. Then someone dies. We get angry, deny that there is anything right about dying, and we grieve our loss. It is the same old story, and so far we have not tired of it. When we do, we will find peace in the midst of pain. We will end our fears. We will find our joy. We cannot do that until we can, and we should not seek to hurry the learning process. Pushing our evolution too hard usually means we miss something important.

In putting together an understanding of death, there are some common spiritual practices to study: mediumship, maithuna, merger with the divine consciousness, near death experiences, meditation on the passage, shamanic journeys, work as a psychopomp and hospice experiences.

Mediumship

Like channeling, mediumship opens our crown chakra and allows us to speak directly across the veil with those who have passed. Channeling usually puts us in touch with a spirit guide whereas mediumship connects us with someone who lived here on earth and has crossed over. That may be an artificial distinction based on our incomplete understanding of the divinity of each soul. There are many books by writers and mediums like John Edward, James Von Pragh, Rosemary Atlea and Sylvia Browne which describe their work and underscore that it is possible to communicate with and see those we call the Dead. When we begin our education in this skill, these constructs help us work ethically and make sense of our experiences.

1. *Always ask the person if you can bring a message from spirit to them.* It keeps the power balance even and helps the receiver maintain their sense of integrity. You are less of an intruder.
2. *Communicate with the spirit world in a consistent manner so they are consistent with you.* Much of the communication is symbolic or so literal it is easy to miss the point. A person who appears at your side at the same level is of your generation, but one positioned above you is of your parents' or grand-parents' generation. Someone on your right is a relative on your father's side and on the left your mother's side. Or not. It is how you understand their symbols. A psychic may

struggle with a client to understand the image of little flying mice angels. The spirit of a loved one could be insistent on the image while everyone else puzzles over it until one person realized that their uncle had a cat that would lay in wait for the bats to fly out of the barn eaves at dark, then leap in the air as if they would catch one. It was one of those odd details relatives from the Otherside will pick up on to let us know who is really there.

3. *Use your best communication skills with the spirits and the humans.* Just because you think the message is about furry fish does not mean it is. However, key phrases will strike a chord in the listener's memory beyond what you could know or guess. A medium once told me, 'Play your cards right,' in a message from my mother. I knew it was my mother because the medium was fanning her clients' admission tickets out in her hand as if she were playing cards. My mother died in ICU after a card game with her favorite nurse. Mom won the game.

   Another gave me a message, source unknown, that there would be 'three more bumps in the road.' I laughed out loud, because it is the exact phrase Merlin uses when difficulties arise, 'We have hit another bump in the road.'

   In a third reading, my father came through and said, 'Tell her she was right! I wished I had known that when I was there, but she was right!' I didn't know what he meant so I asked. The medium told me I was right about spirit communication and that the magic works. Dad had been a fundamentalist Christian all his life and for him to come through with that message was a blessing. I knew it was Dad because she described him.

4. *Don't be afraid.* Fear will close the communication channels in a heartbeat. My great-great-great grandfather used to come to me when I was a pre-school child. He was trying to prepare me for and perhaps protect me from rheumatic fever which I developed in kindergarten. I was terrified by the visitation

which I could plainly see in my bedroom doorway. Obviously I did not know what my triple great grandfather looked like. My parents kept telling me erroneously there were no such things as ghosts, but I knew there was a man in rough work clothes standing in my bedroom door nearly every night for what seemed to me to be a long time. Since no one else would help me, I finally had to screw up my four-year-old courage and tell him he to leave me alone because I was going through that door and he could not hurt me. He stopped coming in physical form. A year later I was very sick. I did not learn who my visitor was for over 40 years. I am thankful for the love that moves across generations even when we fail to understand it. Grandpa Isaac and I still have a close emotional relationship. By the way, I healed from rheumatic fever with no ill effects except for a minor heart murmur which we healed 30 years later.

5. *Accept that what you see and hear is real.* When I started on this path, my great grandmother Louisa spoke to me through her photograph. She showed me my fears so I could release them. I had to accept that the photo moved, that her expression changed and that animals could appear and change shape in the folds of her dress. Everything in my education said it was impossible, but my eyes and ears knew better. Everything the church said made this evil and soul destroying but it was Louisa and I knew better. I could feel her love. By accepting those phenomena as real I embraced a spiritual path in which I could communicate across time and space. Since then many others have seen her work through her portrait in our ritual room.
6. *Look for messages from your own loved ones.* Not everyone will hear from their friends and relatives immediately after their crossing. They are busy meeting and greeting their own soul circle on the other side. Many souls have a lot of integration to do, especially if they did not believe in life after death,

reincarnation and the life energy that connects us all to All Being. My mother came through in three days to write my name in the clouds and the word 'Whee.' My father took six months or more. He then came through with my mother and the two dogs Flash and Tippy. He put a hymn in my head to sing to a glorious sunset. I did not realize it was him until I came to the third line. By then I was crying, partly because what he had done was so sweet and beautiful and partly because it was such a surprise. I had stopped looking for the message from him. Perhaps you know the hymn.

For the beauty of the earth
For the beauty of the skies
For the love which from our birth
Over and around us lies.
Lord of All to thee we raise
This our hymn of grateful praise.[113]

I knew it was my Dad because no one ever loved me as unconditionally as he did, even though I challenged him and fought against it and failed to appreciate him, as my nemesis story shows in Chapter 16. He loved me from the day I was born and has never stopped. Thanks Dad.

Developing our skills as mediums quiets our fear of death. The continuity of life is made evident as our loved ones cross the veil to speak with us. They teach us and give us guidance. They warn us when danger is around the next corner. John, an old friend and lover, announces himself with the fragrance of coffee and cigarettes. He has warned me about auto accidents, faithless friends and lies. He also reminds me sometimes when I have forgotten to pay a bill that will soon be overdue. Mediumship opens up the wisdom of death.

Maithuna, Merger and Near Death

The language we used previously in the section about sacred

sexuality merging consciousness with All Being and losing our sense of boundaries and individual identities is similar to the death experience. That is why orgasm is called the little death. Death and orgasm both join being and non-being in a joyful reunion of all the soul fragments, connections between souls, and connections beyond the soul. Since most people do not find it possible to truly die and then come back to the same body and use that information constructively within a spiritual circle, sexual experience will have to do!

Actually, those with out-of-body and near-death experiences have the ability to hold that perspective of being dead or nearly so, and experiencing the ecstasy of spirit while still living. If they are also sexually open to the spiritual merging of orgasm they can speak to the similarities. We can resolve some of our conflict with death by walking into the central abyss of consciousness through our sexual union.

The regional chapter of the International Association of Near Death Studies (IANDS) meets near my home. I have met with the group and told some of the stories I relate in my book. I was introduced to the group through the work of its area organizer, David Bennett. Dave's story of dying twice and a full merger of consciousness with the universe one other time is related in his book *Voyage of Purpose*. There is no question Dave died and returned. All the supposed neurological explanations of brain discharges creating white light illusions do not fit his experiences. He drowned. He died on the operating table. He remembers. His experiences are documented. He sums up the wisdom of those journeys when he says, 'Dying is hard, but returning to life is even more difficult. Once you have experienced the Light of God, the Peace, the Love...you long to go back...'[114] That is true whenever we glimpse the reality of what exists on the Otherside.

The Passage Between the Worlds

Many meditation practices and shamanic journeys prepare the initiate to enter the realm of the dead, to merge consciousness with

All Being, or to see for ourselves what is on the Otherside. I have found these journeys to be very different for various students, depending on people's preconceptions and religious training. It is all valid, and perhaps reflective of my favorite Baptist joke.

> A good Witch died and passed into the Summerland. She immediately connected with her family and friends, who were delighted to show her around. The Summerland was beautiful. Her favorite flowers bloomed everywhere. The light was warm but not hot, the land clean and fertile, the air pure. There was music and laughter. People were at peace and she felt free until they came to a funny building made of wood and painted white.
>
> 'Shh!' Her guide warned her. 'We have to be quiet here.' They crept passed the building without making a sound, ducking under the windows and staying out of sight. The good Witch thought this was odd, considering how free she had felt everywhere else. She knew there were people inside the building because she could hear them talking, and someone yelling at them in a loud angry voice which she also could not understand. How could anyone be angry in the Summerland?
>
> 'What was that all about?' the good Witch asked when they had moved far enough away to speak out loud.
>
> 'Oh them,' replied her guide, casually. 'That was just the Baptists in their church building. They think they are the only ones up here, and we don't want to spoil it for them!'

Having been a Baptist for many years, that joke always makes me laugh. As fundamentalists, we were all certain we knew the only truth there was. I suppose the denomination and even the religion is interchangeable in the joke. People who believe they access Heaven through faithfulness to an institution or a particular deity or to a book or a set of rules may find the afterlife reflects their beliefs for as long as their souls need those beliefs. Eventually they will be led to question and grow into a more complete experience of all the possibilities on the Otherside.

Similarly, those of us who think we understand the nature of going into the light at our deaths with our soul identity intact expect to meet our family members and friends who have preceded us. They may or may not be in recognizable forms. The identities they assume are also reflective of our soul's evolution and life review. We too grow into a more complete experience of all the possibilities as we integrate our life lessons and the other dimensional context of what we call the Summerland. The reality of merging with the light and becoming part of the One goes beyond the reunion of souls. Meeting our loved ones after death begins a process of becoming more and merging more completely. Our reconnection with our soul group is not the whole process, nor even the most important part of the afterlife.

To heal our fear of death, we can meditate on the tunnel of light between this world and the next. Others see a rainbow bridge instead of a tunnel. When we see this passageway in meditation we can proceed up to the threshold of the Otherside, as long as we mean to come back. If we have not used up our number of days, coming back will be automatic though the temptation to stay is real. For those who think this might be an easy way out, the passage will close or block them from crossing even to the threshold. Suicide is never an option. We have to solve our problems, not give up on them.

A Story Connecting the Worlds

During a class on sound vibrational healing, Satira was playing three of her large crystal singing bowls. First we cleared the chakras that were tuned to those bowls. Then we listened in a state of bliss to the music of the bowls, very like the music of the spheres[115] in my opinion. At some point I realized that a vortex had been created by the tones and existed above and through my crown chakra. I could reach through the vortex. I called on the presence who was communicating with me and asked him to 'pull me on up.' I put my hand up through the vortex, at least I did in my mind's eye. A male hand reached down and grasped mine as if to pull me through. I recognized him as my spirit lover, Manannan Mac Llyr. Just as my head was about to crest through the vortex into the light where I might see more of him than his hand, a voice from behind him said, 'No, it is not her time.' The bliss was so beautiful we were both disappointed. I settled back down in my chair, still holding hands through the vortex until Satira finished her music. When the vortex dissolved my hand returned to my lap with a sweet sense of loss. The gatekeepers will not let us pass through until it is time. When it is time to cross, I intend to call Manannan Mac Llyr and ask again that he pull me through. I have every confidence he will.

This experience was underscored by another odd synchronicity shortly after my experience with the singing bowls. I was waiting in the car for Merlin, listening to an independent radio station which plays obscure songs. At the time in 2010 I was bombarded by special messages hidden in the lyrics. There must have been a dozen that fall and winter quarter that were such obvious messages they took my breath away. That does not always happen. I do not automatically think electronic devices are giving me instructions. On this one occasion, *Haul Me Up* by Richard Thompson came on the radio. I had never heard the catchy tune before so I listened closely. It took me a moment to make the connection to my experience back when Satira was playing the singing bowls to open our crown chakras. When I recovered from the initial shock I decided Manannan Mac Llyr must have been unable to find a song called *Pull Me Through*. Admittedly the verses are a bit dark, but I had been in that kind of mood so it was not at all inappropriate. The music by Richard Thompson is found his album *Dream Attic*[116]. I take comfort in this experience, a lot of comfort!

Psychopomp and Hospice Experience

To understand the process of dying, we need to sit with someone who will bless us with the lessons of the passage. That may be an animal companion, a patient in hospice or hospital, or someone in our family. My parents would not leave while I was there, but Merlin and I learned these lessons from Patches and Bandit, two aged cats who asked us to sit with them as they prepared to leave their bodies and as they died. The process took as long as they needed. Their life force dimmed to the imperceptible, and their breathing seemed to stop. What happened next astonished us. I cry even remembering it.

In my first experience with this death crossing, I ventured a guess that Patches had left so quietly we did not see her go. At that point she raised up her head, focused her one good eye on me, irritably I thought, and thumped me with her hind leg which had rested near my hand. I apologized. Later, may be 30 minutes more, her four legs started to move back and forth as she lay on her side, as if she were walking. She was paralyzed from a series of strokes, but there was nothing hesitant in her movements. She walked and walked, until she passed through the tunnel and entered into the land of the dead where I could not follow. Her body died. She did not.

Months later, Bandit went through the same passage the same way, just in case we thought it was an anomaly. We saw her grow more separate from her body to the point she seemed absent. Then she looked at me keenly to say she was still with us so I would not make the same mistake I had with Patches. When Bandit was ready, we saw her walk, laying on her side, powerfully moving through the dimensions into the Summerland. The cats had no fear and no church-led expectations. They moved freely into spirit. Death was a transformative release, for them and for us.

When my father was ready to cross over, I was sitting with him in the nursing home, singing his favorite songs. It occurred to me that he likely did not know how to get out of his body. He was a good Christian with no practice in astral projection except in dream time. I began to explain how one can move out of one's crown and stand next to the bed. I explained there was a life cord attached between the physical body and the astral body, that it stretched as far as it needed for travel around the world. I explained that in dreamtime, the cord always brought him back to his body, that in all likelihood he had traveled out of his body frequently though he did not remember it. I explained that if it was time for him to cross to the light he could expect my mother, his parents and others he knew to come and get him. He was free to go. All he had to do was to cut that cord like the umbilicus is cut when a baby is born. Then he could go on to his reunion with the Elders. I said my goodbyes, and in the astral body so did he. His physical body was barely conscious. His astral body moved easily up and out of his physical body in the bed. Then he told me to go home. He wanted to walk around the nursing home and see his favorite nurses.

After a brief discussion I acquiesced. I had not intended to leave my vigil at the foot of his bed. I understood he wanted me to think of him up on two feet, moving around enjoying himself. He did not want the death throes of his disabled body to be an image seared in my mind. I left. Merlin and I were home maybe 20 minutes when the call came. My father had crossed.

When I work shamanically with Soft Moon Rising we often journey to assist souls who may be stuck in ordinary reality though their bodies have died. This is a specialized area of training as a psychopomp which people build on after journeying to death and back. I cite it here to say I have been privileged to stand in the passageway between this life and the next and watch the soul move into the reunion in the light. I cannot see far into the Otherworld because it is so bright, but I have repeatedly seen that first recognition and embrace when a soul is reunited on the Otherside with family members and friends.

My training as a psychopomp opened up after the spirits took me into death where I could experience maithuna. I was journeying to recorded music with my mentor Lydia. Suddenly I was catapulted out into the universe, disintegrated and spread about in a random pattern. That is the best way I can describe it. My consciousness became alert and self-aware while my molecules were distributed around the blackness of space, interspersed with those of everyone else. I had no confusion about which orange dots belonged to the identity that had been me. Yet I had no more attachment to them than to the others. We all hummed in harmony and bliss. Formless and conscious, aware of myself and of everyone else, I loved it! Then the drumming tape stopped. I knew I was supposed to return, but that seemed too much to ask. Then I thought about Lydia. I knew my body lay on Lydia's couch where the shamanic journey started and ended. I did not want her questioned by the police about how I had died. I returned to ordinary reality with a great sense of loss. That journey changed me. Once I was back, I found I had much greater tolerance for life's annoyances. I knew they were temporary and I knew what comes next.

Death and the Otherside bring us a variety of dimensional experiences. We see our friends and guides as physical light beings. We can converse and communicate with them. We gain more soul education with them there. As spirits ourselves, we can communicate with people who live on earth. Our success with that depends on their readiness as well as our developing skill as spirits. We appear to each other in dreams. In other dimensions we are lights and shapes. In one we merge fully with All Being and rest in that. Those ecstatic states of being co-exist with this one in ordinary reality—concurrent and co-existent. We access those concurrent states of being through trance.

The Dance Between the Worlds

Given this information about death, I enjoy leading students in *The Dance Between the Worlds*. This is a ritual dance I received from guides and people in my ancient lineage through the ancestral journeys taught by Crow Swimsaway and Bekki Shining BearHeart[117]. We begin in the light, dancing the dance of this life working in circles and spirals, holding hands and connecting with one another.

When moved by Spirit, two people break off from the group and form an arch at the left side of the central altar. The arch represents the passageway through death and into the Otherworld. When the arch is made, the dancers approach it while acting out their feelings about death and passages.

One by one, alone, and in any order we dance through the arch experiencing whatever difficulties seem appropriate to the gatekeepers. Sometimes they refuse a dancer entry. Sometimes they catch them between their arms and hold them. Sometimes they lower the gateway so the dancer turns back or crawls through. Sometimes they hold the gate open wide and welcome them home.

When all have passed over the dance continues, individually at first. We all dance until we understand our lives in the underworld. Slowly people connect with each other until the entire group has made another chain of dancers, this time in a different order. They spiral or circle, break off and rejoin the stream of dancers.

When two people in the line are moved by Spirit, they break off and form another arch, this time on the opposite side of the altar. This arch represents the passageway of rebirth and reincarnation into the physical world. When the arch is made, the dancers approach it while acting out their feelings about birth and rebirth.

One by one, alone, we dance through the arch experiencing whatever difficulties seem appropriate to the gatekeepers. They frequently make the passage a birth experience through a narrow gate, but the choice is theirs.

When all have been reborn the dance continues, quickly connecting with others into relationships. Eventually the group will unite and make another chain of dancers that will form a circle and then ground the energy as the music winds down.

After grounding and making notes, we explore our feelings and insights about passing between the worlds, being gatekeepers and being one left alone. When Avian danced around the life circle, she repeatedly avoided the gateway, as if she could live forever. While all the others had crossed and formed new relationships, she continued to skip about, refusing the invitation of Death. Eventually the gatekeepers went and captured her, wrapping their arms around her yelling, 'Car Crash!' They dragged her to the Otherside where her friends held her and comforted her. A simple dance can be a confrontation with our shadow.

We believe, because we are told it is true, that we cannot know anything about what happens when we die. We are held in ignorance and remain afraid of the unknown. Yet our experiences in the Web PATH Center reveal rich details about the dying process and the work we take on to integrate our mortal lives with our immortal souls once we leave this earth. People like Dave Bennett have gone there and come back. Psychopomps have seen through the entrance into the light when they escort souls home. We have repeated opportunities to merge our consciousness with the Divine. All it takes is the will to understand.

Journaling on Death and Destiny

What are your experiences with death? How do they relate to your destiny? In identifying why you are here and where you are going, people typically examine what they believe happens after death. To explore your own beliefs, set up a sacred circle, ground and ask your guides to describe life on the other side of death. Ask them to explain how this vision integrates with your life purpose so that you can encounter both death and destiny as Kate Whitaker did. Make it clear to yourself and everyone else you mean to return to ordinary reality to share this insight. Then take dictation as automatic writing, or enter a silent meditation which you record afterward. When you are finished, ground, open the circle and drink some fresh water.

Chapter 19

Identity and the Karmic Circle

Apart from the classes we teach, Merlin and I frequently work with past life healing when people request help with shadowy memories or stuck places in their lives that seem to make no sense in their current histories. We use hypnosis for regressions, shamanic journeys to explore other times and places, and guided meditations to find clues to past lives. Both of us find this practice fascinating. Learning about a past life can resolve some of the questions people have about their life choices, particularly when their actions seem inexplicable otherwise. I believe we are meant to make sense of patterns and connections between and among our soul group in our journey to learn who we are and why we are here. Certainly understanding something about our other incarnations explains where we came from and where we can go from here. On the other hand, past life identities are not excuses.

Three Propositions on Reincarnation

Here is how I understand the multiple life experience. *First, time and geography are illusions.* All the lives are concurrent, but they have a chronological overlay that matches our sense of history. Thus we will discover life stories set in this century and well as other centuries because this makes sense to our mortal self. I think of them as period pieces like historical films. They seem very real in their time and place, as does *Downton Abbey* or *Emma,* or *Oliver Twist* when I see those stories on the screen. What I discover about a past life may be equally produced and directed by my guides, Higher Self or the deities themselves. I cannot answer exactly how that works, but I know what I learn is only a film clip created from a vast amount of footage. There is a great deal more information attached to a memory than what I recall. What I learn may be heavily edited by either my own soul or another. The reasons for the editing may not be made clear to me. I am, after all, one of the actors not the screenwriter, not the director—except, of course, when I am the screenwriter and the director. It gets complicated.

Secondly, most of the people in my life drama have volunteered for their roles. Their participation is usually an act of love. They agreed to help me out in this Earth School drama so I can learn important soul lessons from them and with them. They are in school too and I volunteered in the same way they did. We planned this life and the others.

Frequently the same characters assume different roles in different lives and participate in the life drama together. The cast of characters is often referred to as our soul group. A soul group is like a tribe or family of souls who have deep connections together and share their path. They are committed to each other. They switch roles. Lovers, parent-child, best friends, worst enemies, boss and worker, teacher and student, grandparents and grandkids; the combinations are many. We experiences all of them at one time or another.

Sometimes our dearest soul friends are only strangers passing in the grocery store with no other connection. We feel the click of their presence as they walk away and wonder what that was all about. In this life, they had a bit part, a cameo performance. Other times we have a passionate connection and insist this one person is our soul mate, and no other is or can be. In truth there is an entire group of souls who fill that place in our hearts if they are allowed.

Third, when we reincarnate, we also explore various racial and ethnic lives. We try different genders and sexual orientations. We live in many different places around the globe. In addition, we live in different dimensions and universes. Little of that Otherworld information filters through because our minds have no context for it.

In channeling the spirit entity Seth, Jane Roberts wrote that we have concurrent selves and parallel lives as well as probable selves. Our soul exists in totally different bodies and lives during the current time period. These are usually not connected to one another.

Our soul also lives out the infinite choices we make, so one aspect of ourselves lives in this consciousness with this spouse or partner while another lives with the one that got away in a parallel or divergent universe. That life may not be complete but a type of soul fragment, experiencing the possibilities perhaps as a sort of dream. Our current consciousness may have no awareness of that. The data is collected by our Higher Self and used in the life review when our experience ends.

The complications of our soul's many manifestations need not be embraced or understood to benefit from past life encounters. However, understanding our multifaceted nature does help us remain flexible. Whatever we think we learn, there is more to it. Fragments from within the soul group may recombine to form an identity which is remembered by more than one person. Could we both be Alexander the Great? Maybe. Or perhaps we were part of his inner circle and have memories which we share. Perhaps we have experienced the life of a military conqueror and identify with Alexander the Great as an archetype of who we were. The study of reincarnational identities is useful, but not a field of study for either/or thinking. It is a bit like nailing jello to the wall. What we learn rarely stays where we put it.

Family, Relationships and Karma

Karma is the energetic memory of other experiences in the many bodies a soul may hold which we bring into our current bodies to help in our soul's evolution. Understanding our karma and releasing its energy and attachment to our body and soul is a path of enlightenment. Karma is one way souls evolve. Karma helps us balance the events in our history, both the positive and negative events. Karma brings us challenges as well as grace. We participate in making karmic links between lives.

I realize many people have written that karma has been transmuted, that we are no longer collecting karmic debt, that we can resolve our karma by various tapping exercises, that the Age of

Pisces released our karma and it is not a relevant concept in the Age of Aquarius. Perhaps I am not sufficiently evolved to see that happening any time soon, but I dispute the notable authorities who have proposed those ideas. As long as we involve ourselves as a human race in wars, in an economy based on scarcity, and in the wielding of power over others in our institutions and our personal lives, I believe we will continue to find the karmic balance useful for the education of our souls.

Those who reject the concept of karma tend to experience karma as a negative punishment. That is a misunderstanding of the principle. I think we have to ask ourselves why we have accepted punishment as such an important aspect of human life. Even in understanding the earth changes, many people seem to revel in the prospect of the bad guys finally getting their just desserts. Why are we so quick to point out what someone does that is 'wrong'? Why do we think we know that? When did we learn the 'rest of the story' and why do we think no one else did? Human beings fall into a dualistic fallacy of right and wrong—usually 'I am right and you are wrong.' In the words of transactional analysis, 'I'm okay and you are not.'[118]

If we truly believe that, we are perpetuating the judgment myths of the monotheistic religions. We would need absolution from sin, which Pagans claim not to accept. In approaching the resolution of karmic connections in our lives, we need to move into a belief system that allows for a more open view similar to 'I'm okay, you're okay.' If we can end the cycle of judging ourselves and others negatively, we move into the state of grace where we can experience universal love. There the possibilities are endless. Then karmic resolution is one of those possibilities.

Karma is not punishment for bad deeds done. It is a balancing act which helps us view the themes of many lives from every imaginable angle. Edgar Cayce, the 20th century American seer, explained that we choose to explore our karmic balance through four laws:[119]

The law of cause and effect;
The law of consequences;
The law of continuance; and
The law of contrast.

If we put these together with our study of our personal relationships they might look like this. Suppose we previously lived a life in a community of people who took very good care of their physical health. They were fit, able to select wholesome nutritious foods, and were dedicated to beauty and health. However, they did not understand the Navajo concept of beauty as spiritual balance and harmony, and tended to focus only on the surface appearance of relationships and connections.

By the *law of cause and effect,* we might begin our journey in our next life with a deep spiritual hunger that leaves us frustrated and empty. We find our efforts to satisfy that spiritual need hampered by our lack of experience coming from the past life. The effect of spiritual frustration in one life in this case is caused by the spiritual neglect from another. We may then elect to incarnate with a spiritual teacher in the role of parent, partner or child who can help us discover the way of spiritual practice. We do not, however, always appreciate or understand the teachings of that person who sometimes appears to be a thorn in the flesh. Moving beyond our appearances will be one possible theme of the new life, but it may feel uncomfortable to explore the unseen issues of faith.

On the other hand, as *a consequence* of our experience with such a focused physical life in the past we are reborn with a body which helps us develop our spiritual aspect. That could be a very physically fit body capable of advanced yoga practices, which helps us find enlightenment through the movement of energy through the body channels including an awakened kundalini. This is similar to the cause and effect but not exactly the same. This fit, attractive body may bring us into connection with a lover who shares the tantric path in a deep and satisfying way, and we find enlightenment through sacred sexuality. Or the physically fit body might become a marathon runner and find enlightenment through meditative long distance running.

Then, with the *law of continuance,* we keep experiencing our fitness from a previous life; we find that maintaining a healthy weight is a simple matter. Our bodies desire nutritious foods and we are not hooked on sugar or empty calories. Our family enjoys good health and an active lifestyle. We may feel very puzzled by people who make poor food choices and struggle with their weight because it is so easy to live healthily and be fit.

However, by the *law of contrast* we or someone close to us chooses to experience a dissimilar life by developing a chronic health problem like asthma, rheumatoid arthritis or by having severe disability from an auto accident, perhaps even the loss of a leg or paralysis. Our contrasting life experience becomes a point of friction with our past life, and by working through the friction and dis-ease we are able to learn deeper lessons both physically and spiritually about balance and acceptance. What seemed puzzling about other people's choices before makes better sense when we can look at both sides of the issue.

If we are able to assess our family relationships and primary connections with lovers, friends and foes, we will see that our emotional connections work in a circle of energy, ebbing and flowing within the structures of our lives. My relationship with my partner Merlin includes a life in a nomad tribe in the Middle East where he was my mother, sister to the woman who was my mother in this life. In the ancient world I was born with a club foot, firstborn of twins. Both of us should have been put to death—I as a deformed child and my twin as the second unlucky one. The midwife could not bring herself to do that. I still have a difficult relationship with that twin who was favored because she was whole and beautiful. It's a long story.

In another life, Merlin was my brother in 12th century England. I find the intricacies of those medieval times fascinating; I am writing a series of novels about that life. A wide circle of my current friends within the Web community have found themselves in the characters and stories of Fawsetwood. On one occasion I posted my black and white drawing of the cottage in the Fells based on a picture I had taken during a research trip in Cumbria, UK. Two of the Web members identified it as a place they had seen in meditation or dreams of past life experiences. Their narratives fit securely in the framework of the story which they had not heard before.

Another who had read my rough draft and knew from shamanic journeys how she fit it, looked at the sketch and identified it immediately. 'That's it!' she exclaimed. She was even more amazed when I showed her the photograph of the larger reconstructed mill that carries the same name. When Merlin and I physically stood in the dooryard of the old mill, he shook his head. The driveway and entrance were wrong. Then he saw the grassy, overgrown pathway headed in the other direction between the trees.

'We came in that way,' he announced in full confidence.

These shared lives have contributed richness to our current life through physical travel in England, multiple AHA! moments, and resolution of several mysteries about things gone awry in this life.

In yet another life, Merlin and I were thieves, vagabonds in medieval France picking pockets and stealing what we could in the marketplace with our band of brothers. He was strong and tall, the leader of the troupe. I was a short ill-favored man who was charged with defending his back, probably because I was not much use for any other role in a good fight. In our last foray, the gendarmes were called to catch the thieves. We were fighting for our lives, and it was going badly. I, in an act of personal preservation generally known as great cowardice, ran for my life. Looking back over my shoulder, I saw our leader go down with a spear in his shoulder, killed on the spot as far as I could tell.

I escaped. I ran all the way to a vineyard in southern France where I eventually married the vintner's daughter and lived happily ever after, except for the burden of guilt I carried from my friend's death. This time around, one of my karmic purposes is to watch Merlin's back more successfully than I did before. Although we have avoided pitched battles in the streets, our activist work has afforded many opportunities to defend him in more subtle ways.

Our relationship with our many selves and our family members uncovers our karmic cycle. The points of friction we experience with one another indicate our karmic purpose. One of the clues to this might be the placement of the planet Saturn in our astrological chart. As Father Time and the rule giver, Saturn reflects our main karmic mission. What happens in our late 20s and again in our late 50s coincides with the 29-year cycle of Saturn. (Twenty-nine years is an approximation of how long it takes Saturn to move through all 12 houses of our chart at 2.5 years per house.)

In my natal chart, Saturn is in my 7th house of relationships. That means my karmic mission (the main one at least) is to address relationship issues as they have replayed themselves in my history and in my family history, both immediate and generational. My watching Merlin's back fits in with that. So does my familial respiratory issues and uncovering their psychological source. This is an example of spiritual work to the 7th generation.

Here are the meanings of the 12 astrological houses in brief. Most of them look a lot like the topics addressed in these chapters on physical, mental, emotional and spiritual healing.

Aries 1st House: Physical appearance and identity
Taurus 2nd House: Material possessions and money
Gemini 3rd House: Communication
Cancer 4th House: Family, home
Leo 5th House: Friends, social life, entertainment
Virgo 6th House: Community and organizations
Libra 7th House: Relationships
Scorpio 8th House: Transformation, death, rebirth, and sexuality
Sagittarius 9th House: Beliefs, ethics, spirituality, education, long distance travel

Capricorn 10th House: Achievement in profession, career
Aquarius 11th House: Connection with groups, global perspective
Pisces 12th House: Inner being, dreams, consciousness

Journaling on Your Saturn Cycle

In your BOS attach a natal horoscope chart. Then start piecing together the role that Saturn plays in your chart. Look at your astrological chart and find Saturn. In which house (section of the circle) does it reside in your birth chart? What does that house rule? If Saturn is in your first house, you might find Saturn rules your appearance. The example above used in understanding contrast, consequence, continuance and cause and effect could apply to you in some way. Were you born a beautiful child? Was there a birth mark or other unusual appearance noticed at your birth? Are both your parents known to you? Are there secrets?

If Saturn is in your second house of material possessions and money, then your work in understanding personal economics, saving, spending and earning money may dominate your life one way or another. Did people buy you savings bonds when you were born? Was your birth a financial pinch for your family? Are you the heir who was long anticipated? Has your family cycled through generations of struggle in relative poverty?

If Saturn is in your third house of communication, information, writing, the internet, counseling, journalism, miscommunications may be your theme. Storytelling may be an activity that resonates strongly. Was your birth announced and celebrated? Are stories told about your arrival as an infant? Did a family member keep a baby journal about you? Is there a scrapbook of your significant events reported in news clippings, pictures or concert programs?

In the fourth house of family and home, nesting, children, and intergenerational connections, the appearance of Saturn may make these relationships fulfilling or problematic. When you were born, whom did your family live with? What was the house like? Who took care of you? These people or situations are apt to repeat and make patterns in your life. Did you know your grandparents or great grandparents? Is there a genealogist in the lineage that keeps track of the family? Should it be you?

With Saturn in the fifth house of friends and social connections, you find fulfillment and challenges with your peers outside the home. When you were born, were you placed in childcare while your parents worked? Did your parents make playdates with other children? Did a group of parents meet to socialize every weekend and set the children together to work out their friendships? Did the kids in your neighborhood play together or join scout groups and team sports together? Were you popular? Did you also have close friends?

In the sixth house of community and organizations Saturn indicates you may be involved in local or national organizations which aim to improve life. You could be either an organizer or a recipient. As a child you may have been helped by social programs. You could have been a poster child for a cause, or placed in your stroller and rolled down the street during demonstrations your parents attended. You may have been carted to meetings and played on the floor while people talked about ideas and reform. What organizations did your parents belong to when you were young? Have you followed their lead or gone in a different direction?

If Saturn is in the seventh house of relationships those trust issues and human connections play out on the stage of your life for joy or grief. Do you know if there were challenges early on in your life? Did people keep their promises or betray them? Did you feel safe?

Saturn in the eighth house of transformation leads you through many changes in the emotional dreamy world of sex, death and rebirth. The Tower card of the tarot may seem like your life's story. Did you have night terrors as a young child? Visits from the ancestors? Did someone significant die when you were so young you didn't know what that meant? Did you see adults engage sexually? Was there sexual abuse in the family? This placement of

Saturn can be very challenging.

Saturn in the ninth house of beliefs opens up your exploration of education, spirituality, or faraway places. You use these to build wisdom or go through such institutions as a naïve fool. From infancy, were you on the road with your family? Did you live in a home where ideas were discussed? Was education valued, even in your play time? Did people attend religious services or meditate at home? Did they talk about beliefs?

In the tenth house of career, you may find fulfillment or frustration in your chosen profession and shift what you do for a living as Saturn cycles the chart. At birth, were people around you engaged in drudgery or imaginative employment? Was your path set out for you by the family business? Did you spring from a long line of teachers or auto mechanics? What expectations did people have for you? Did you follow their career choices or strike out on your own?

In the eleventh house of groups and global perspective Saturn encourages you to relate to larger ideas and projects that shape the world either as a shaker and mover or part of the masses experiencing the shifts of fortune tied up with climate change or economic cycles. From your birth, was there talk about how people got along around the world? About global politics? Were you encouraged to gather pennies for UNICEF or other organizations? Did someone donate to an international charity to celebrate your birth?

In the twelfth house of dreams and consciousness, Saturn's presence increases or frustrates your ability to manifest your visions. You may be drawn into psychology as a patient or therapist. How were your needs met in that magical thinking stage of infancy? Were you fed when you were hungry or did you have to wait for the proper time? Were you kept dry and warm or neglected? From that early treatment we mold our expectations about whether or not we influence what happens to us.

Once we know the placement of Saturn in our natal chart and have a theory about its significance, we compare that theory to what our family can confirm about our first year of life. Lots of us have no idea how we were raised as infants and even less of how that started us out in making assumptions about life. Having a conversation with the people who raised us can reveal how our lives play out, especially when compared to the karmic theme presented by Saturn in the chart.

Once that theme is clear, we then compare the circumstances present in our birth and infancy to our experiences at age 29, assuming we have lived that long. How did that theme play out at the end of our young adulthood?

In my case Saturn is in the seventh house of relationships. Trust issues and human connections which were so solid in my younger years turned around and reversed in my 20s. My birth family was nurturing. I was a trusting soul, to the point of being naïve. Working in Washington DC as a teacher, living on my own, I found my trust betrayed, misused, and misinterpreted. I was so naïve I simply could not accept that people did not have my best interests at heart. I thought I was misunderstanding their actions. As a result, I had my heart broken at age 28 and returned home to lick my wounds at age 29. My family came through as did a new set of friends who were as wonderful and trustworthy as my family. I recreated the security experienced in my infancy.

If we have lived long enough, we look at the same issues at age 58. If we are younger than that, we look ahead and brace for round two. Sure enough, the same pattern was repeated when I was 56. I still naïvely thought I knew what people meant when in reality I was projecting my own values and expectations on them. Apparently I had not figured out that though we are all connected in the web of life, we carry a different set of expectations. We play by different rules. We have combined different life lessons into our personal philosophies.

Once again, I nearly crashed and burned. I found my trust betrayed, misused, and misinterpreted, though this time I knew those were personal interpretations of events which were not shared among all the players. Some of them actually thought I was at fault! I laugh at my outrage now, but at the time I was shocked. In reality, what all of us players from my soul group experienced was failed communication, projection, denial and naïvety. I crawled up out of the abyss by age 58, the return of Saturn in my chart. My original birth family had all crossed to the Summerland. Merlin, as bewildered and puzzled as I was, stood in their stead. We journeyed to England to look for our past, in this life and others. It was a deeply healing journey. I have a long way to go before I reach round three at age 87. Now I know better, I hope I do better.

In looking at the placement of Saturn in our charts, we can follow its 2.5 year progression from house to house and compare that to the past. Saturn's pattern occurs all the way around the chart, not only in the anniversary placement every 28-29 years. At age five Saturn is two houses past its location at birth. That position is repeated at 34 and 62.

For me that places Saturn in the ninth house of beliefs, education and long distance travel. At five I went to school. I hated it so much I became gravely ill. At 34 my landlord insulated my house with a chemical that made me so sick I had to move. Everyone denied that was the cause so I had to research environmental illnesses to support my actions. At 62 I reached the end of a series of illnesses which had initially been environmentally triggered and then emotionally magnified. I wasn't fully healed until I made a spiritual journey to England. Since in the third pass of Saturn I found healing, it would seem that cycle is completed. We have full power to influence how these themes play out. We can re-write these scripts. To do so is an act of the will, of magic and creativity.

In writing about our patterns, we have the opportunity to find our own truth. We can in meditation ask Saturn himself what the lessons are. We can study our biography. What happened when we were born? What was the story of our family at that time? What happened when we were 29? How did the pattern repeat at 58?

Saturn the planet in our chart and Saturn the Roman God of

agriculture (harvest) and justice (karma) can help us project what may be our karmic mission in this life even if we are not yet 29 or 58. We can study Saturn's placement in our current chart. Right now Saturn is in my tenth house of profession. I have taken on writing as a new career. It is a strong and wonderful phase of Saturn for which I am grateful.

If we are not yet far enough into the first Saturn cycle to figure out a pattern, we can study the tenth house (career/achievement) and eleventh house (connections with groups/global perspective) which are ruled by Saturn. Saturn is not necessarily in these houses in our natal charts. The planets which are in that house add to our understanding of our karmic mission.

If Venus, for example, were in the eleventh house, then perhaps our reason for being here is to express love to the world on a global scale. We might make magical rose quartz grids and beam positive thoughts of love and peace around the world. We might join a world hunger organization as a donor or employee. We might use our creativity in art or music to encourage others to get involved in defending Mother Earth against pollution.

Any choices we make should come from the totality of who we are and what we can do, not from a single planet in our birth chart. Nevertheless we are here to balance and celebrate our karma. If that balance involves love and compassion, so much the better. Finding wisdom from Saturn can help answer the soul question: *Why am I here?* Evidently I am here to write books after all!

Family Karma

I have learned in the course of this study in emotional healing, that my karmic mission of teaching people how to love and be in relationship is part of my family karma. My mother was so much better at this than I am, I am humbled. I suspect she agreed to play that role to me as a model of what one can do. I suggest that many of us will find our karmic thread resonates in our family's generational history. If so, we have a privileged opportunity to help heal longstanding wounds and assist our ancestors across time. Because time is both cyclical and an illusion, such things are possible.

My Family Story

Between the fall of 2001 and the spring of 2004 I developed a severe respiratory and sinus infection that was insufficiently diagnosed and treated by a series of medical professionals. Gradually, by peeling back layers and layers of family history and karmic connection through a variety of healers, I learned how the family karmic chickens had come home to roost. I was given the opportunity to heal seven generations of karmic grief and guilt in the lineage of my mother's grandmothers through our shared illness.

One of the first discoveries in this quest came during WinterFest 2002 when the drummer Mz Imani[120] demonstrated Alchemical Healing using me as a guinea pig. Through an active meditation, I learned that the inability to catch my breath was not only an allergy, but also a stopped up grief for not being present when my mother died. She had spent five months in the hospital after an automobile accident. When it was clear she was not going to recover, she and the rest of us agreed to remove her from the ventilator. She lived several days after that, and elected to cross over when I was not there. I am sure she did that to make the crossing easier for her and to spare me, but I foolishly took it to heart and accepted responsibility for something that was not my fault. I made a judgment about what I should have done.

Once I understood the mistake I had made, I released my pain and guilt, but the symptoms continued. Further exploration in meditation and dreams with my mother, my grandmother Pearl, and my great grandmother Louisa, the one whose photo hangs in my ritual room as my first spirit guide, revealed they had not been present when their mothers had died either. They shared my feelings and medical condition. As I worked with them in trance, we told each other the stories of our lives. My mother's story and grandmother's story were partly known to me in ordinary reality. Through trance and psychic investigation, I gradually discovered seven different ancestors with the same painful experiences. How unusual, I thought! None of us could be there for our mothers? The simple fact itself was a continuation of the karmic theme between generations and a consequence for the one making the crossing without her daughter's assistance.

Various efforts at releasing the karmic connections between us met with moderate success. Finally in a healing massage session at the direction of one of our healers, I brought the grandmothers all into the room together and had them turn around, embrace and forgive one another. Actually no one seemed angry at all. They were all too wrapped up in self-imposed guilt going all the way back to Ireland. After this was accomplished, the medical community suddenly figured out how to treat my infection and I was able to heal my body and presumably help my grandmothers. All of them had the same medical symptoms after their mothers had died. They carried the respiratory symptoms to their graves.

I was ecstatic! What a breakthrough! Then in a season or two I revisited the respiratory illnesses. I learned there were additional themes of grief held in common among the women of my lineage and which needed healing. When I worked through those, I still cycled through respiratory health and wellness. The story was not finished yet. I did not find complete freedom from our family plague until I visited England, walked the sacred stones and breathed her sea air. I cannot explain why that finally resolved my respiratory illnesses, but it did that and unlocked my creative block so I could spend the rest of my life writing and finishing books. In my life, this healing was deep magic. I believe it was also magical in theirs.

I do not think I am the only person given the opportunity to change the family karma and medical history. I suspect if we had enough information we could find similar themes in every family. However, this story is an illustration of two of the principles I keep stressing as I mentor and teach.

The spiritual, mental and emotional issues which are not addressed in our invisible bodies will make themselves known in the physical bodies if that is the only way we can be clear about what needs attention. Once present in the physical body there is a need for physical healing in addition to the other healings which work on the other bodies. Whether we start on the physical and work through the emotional, mental and spiritual bodies in order is immaterial. All of them are involved.

All time is now. The past, present and future are artificial constructs we as people on this planet have relied on to make three dimensional realities work. When we step outside this dimension in dream time, in ritual, in meditation or in healing, we can change the past and the future through work done here in what we perceive as the present. It is never too late to love. It is never too late to forgive. It is never too late to heal.

Meditation on Your Family Karma

Use a family photo to discover connections, secrets, surprises, blessing, talents or old wounds which have defined family relationships and assumptions.

Select a random photo from your collection which includes a group of related people. It may include generations of family members you do not know. Trust spirit to select the photo needed. Using a photograph of your birth family is not necessary if you were raised by an adoptive or foster family. If you lived in a group home or other similar collective, use a photo from that grouping. Our family is made up of the people we had relationships with, not those who shared DNA to make us. We may be able to identify themes and intergenerational karma with the psychic skill of psychometry. Here's how:

Set yourself in sacred space. Ground. Create an altar with candles and incense around your photo. Select an indigo candle for vision, a sky blue candle for communication, a green candle for healing and a white candle for spiritual connections. Cinnamon incense is particularly effective for this kind of work. I use a pinch of cinnamon spice sprinkled on a charcoal block once it has reached the white ash stage. Cinnamon will produce a lot of smoke, so be frugal with it. Alternatively you can use a cinnamon incense stick or cinnamon oil in an infuser. Consciously open your brow chakra. Clear its indigo color.

Gaze at the photograph with your third or inner eye. Do not be fooled by what you see in two dimensions on the page. You are not analyzing the photographic image. You are connecting with the astral emotional energy surrounding these people. You can discern this information with the help of your spirit guides. Look for dispassionate, neutral information coming from outside yourself, but which comfortably rests in your heart. Otherwise you will be projecting your own issues into the picture.

Take your time. When you have received a message, check it against your inner bell to see if it rings true. You should feel an energetic confirmation and rightness about the message. Nevertheless, if the information is difficult to receive because of related grief, abuse, or dishonesty ask the guides for assistance in understanding what you have heard or seen. Step away from judgments. Seek the wisdom of the experience. Your life and theirs may have uncomfortable parallels. You may have natural reflexes to distance yourself from them. Denial, projection and procrastination are very common reactions to this working. Wait and see. You do not know the rest of the story. There is always the possibility that your information is either symbolic or dead wrong.

When you are settled about what the spirits have to say about the photograph, come back to your ordinary consciousness. Ground. Sip some juice or water.

Journaling on Your Discoveries

When you have returned from your journey, describe the physical picture and people. Explain who they are and what your relationship is in ordinary reality. Include any connections and disconnections that you know about. How did they get along with each other?

Then describe the psychic information you received in your meditation. Include your own emotional reaction to that information. You may experience some automatic writing, as if you are taking dictation. The story continues beyond what you learned in the meditation. Allow it to unfold. When you are done, assess what you think is accurate or inaccurate in that information. Acknowledge any pattern that may exist in your life that is mirrored in theirs. Make some suggestions about the significance of those patterns. Let this insight ripen over time. Dreams, trances, rituals, even seemly random television shows and movies may broaden your insight into this investigation. Finding the rest of the story may take years. Talk to the ancestors or living relatives as openly as you can. See what healing people seek and learn to help them. That ability to create magic for them is one reason why you are here.

Our primary relationships continue the family karma with people outside our birth family or adoptive family. This karmic relationship may or may not include our spouse, partner or lovers. The souls involved in our thematic karma can be friends, parent-child relationships or colleagues. However, our personal issues of gender and sex will surface as we work on these relationships. The questions I ask now are not easy questions. Address them simply at this point and resolve to go back and work with them over time.

Questions in Your BOS

Continue the journaling exercise by writing some questions in your Book of Shadows. Include the answers when you know them. Leave space to add material as your self-knowledge increases.

What relationships do you have or have had which remind you of the issues identified in the Family Karma exercise? Describe the similarities and differences. Let your memories surface over a week or two. The shadow selves hide a lot of this information from our conscious self.

How do you think these issues have influenced your choices in making and breaking romantic relationships?
How do you think these issues have shaped your pleasure and satisfaction with your sex life?
How do you think these issues have influenced your choices in creating a sense of family in your life?
How have your choices about and the events related to childbearing in your life been influenced?
How do you think these issues have influenced your friendships and ability to be close to others outside your primary relationships?

I want to emphasize there are no right or wrong answers to these questions. We are not judged or punished for the answers. Opening our hearts to who we are and where we came from heals us. These patterns are tough life choices we made in order to explore levels of mad, sad, glad and scared in this life. We engage in these challenges for our own soul's growth and to assist the people close to us in that same growth. Underlying it all is love, even when it feels like something else.

Learning to Love Well

Love is not a concept that we understand deeply. I use *The Mastery of Love: A Practical Guide to the Art of Relationship* by Don Miguel Ruiz to challenge some of the assumptions my students have about love. We confuse love and possession in our relationships. Ruiz compares them as love and fear.

Love accepts the other without a check list of obligations or expectations. Possessiveness of the other keeps score on both counts.
Love respects the other. Possessiveness is distrustful and checks cell phone

and internet histories.
Love is compassionate. Possessiveness pities.
Love is responsible. Possessiveness ducks out of work and pushes the other to make up for them.
Love knows nice matters. Possessiveness is unkind, even mean.
Love trusts the other to do their best. Possessiveness is jealous and has a set of rules to make the other behave.

Sadly, many of us have learned fear and possessiveness at home. Those qualities masquerade as love in popular culture. I ask my students how much fear is present in their homes. Saying we are not afraid of our children, parents, spouses, partners and friends is easy. The truth is we often feel duty bound to meet their expectations because we fear disapproval. We often hold resentment inside because our expectations go unmet. We may even have a list of rules for our relationships. The best I can offer in those cases is the good news: there is a lot of room for people to grow in their families. That is why they came here to incarnate together. Learning real love is a soul lesson.

Ruiz writes: 'I love you the way you are and you are free to be the way you are. If I don't like [that] then I'd better be with someone who is the way I like her to be.'[121] We have a couple of healing choices when we find ourselves in fear-based relationships.

First, we need to understand how to be loving instead of fearful. We need to heal the fearful part of us and our histories. That is a personal responsibility. Whether or not our family members are willing to seek their own healing is irrelevant. When we change ourselves, the home changes. Our soul mission does not include changing anyone else, controlling people's relationships or forcing healing. Our job is to love. That is not the same thing as giving in or being untruthful. Loving our children means we say 'no' at appropriate times. Loving our partners means we allow them the respect and freedom necessary for their own soul growth. Loving ourselves means we repair our boundaries and make decisions which enhance our own evolution.

Second, we need to accept that all our relationships change. People come and go in our lives. Loving with an open hand removes some of the sting experienced in these passages when they move away from us. Their leaving is not about us as much as it is about them. Fear closes the hand around someone else's heart—a sure way to squeeze the life out of love. Sometimes we are the ones who must move on, despite our vows. Again and again we make choices based on our life script, which is our intention formed before we arrived in this life. Fulfillment comes from within, not from our relationships. We do each other injustice when we expect a lover or spouse to complete us. We have arrived in this life to work on our own completion.

That is not to say a fearful relationship is doomed. Individually we can end fear and move into a place of love and joy, including soul ecstasy. That change may be sufficient to shift relationships out of possessiveness and into love. That is the full soul success of being loving.

The karmic cycle of a soul is reflected in that soul's relationships in a single life and across time. Our past life histories reveal some of the circles made by our life choices. Lovers, children, and opponents all create telltale eddies around us. They give us clues to the mysteries of our lives. We find meaning in those patterns created by our connections between and among our soul group. Through them we deepen our understanding of who we are and why we are here. No matter what our history, that is a truth to be celebrated in gratitude.

Chapter 20

Celestial Circle Dances

There are three principle circle dances of Gaia the Earth Mother and one of Luna Mother Moon which shape our ritual celebrations and in turn our identity as Witches, Wiccans and Pagans. Three of them are familiar because they can easily be seen. All four of them contribute to a deeper understanding of our personal identity and that of the quartered circle. They serve as a metaphor for our lifecycle from birth to rebirth. They also reflect our emotional ebb and flow which integrates the people driving and riding our bus into a resilient identity. This integration is what is meant by being balanced.

The first of these circle dances is the rotation of the earth around her own axis, the spinning, twirling dance which takes 24 of our hours. The rotation of the earth gives us the rising and setting of the sun and the moon, i.e. Gaia's dance with Luna and Sol. This dance defines our day and night and reveals the phases of Luna in our sky. Earth's rotation also provides a daily experience with rising, routine, retreat, rest and return.

The second of these dances is the earth's revolution around Sol, the Sun God, which is the path or choreography of her dance over 365.25 of our days. The revolution of the earth gives us the seasonal variations of the Wheel of the Year, i.e. Gaia's dance with the Earth God and the pattern of the changing light of the sun from spring to summer to fall to winter and back again. The revolution provides a deeper experience of rising, retreat, resting, and returning since each season lasts long enough to make us wish for the next one.

The third is the earth's axial weaving among the four north stars in her history: Polaris, Alpha Cephai, Vega and Alpha Draconis. This is her ballet or story spread across 26,000 of our years in round figures. The weaving or wobble of the earth's axis, known as the precession of the equinoxes, gives us the shift in ages of the earth which occur about every 2,200 years. We have seen only four ages in our recorded history, though the precession passes through 12 of them before returning to the beginning of its circle. The pattern spans so much time, we easily ignore it. There is only one degree of change in a human lifetime. This history dance provides perspective and humility in human faith that there is a larger picture beyond our experience.

The fourth dance is the phasing of Luna from new moon through full moon and back to dark moon each lunar 'moonth' over 27.3 days. A full lunar cycle is 29.5 days, which allows for the distance the earth traveled in her revolution during the month, so some sources split the difference at 28 days and call it a lunar cycle. This turning of the moon mirrors the passage of day and night, the turning of the wheel of the year, and the journey of the ages of the earth through the zodiac. We feel the lunar shifts in our emotional bodies in very specific ways which can enhance our magical lives and psychic skills, or unbalance the body/mind connection when we are overwhelmed by moon power.

By understanding these natural cycles we learn about the ebb and flow of a single life and its recycling from one life to another. We better understand who we are when we see how the light grows, fades and reappears. We also can learn to include the energy of these shifts into our lives. The cyclic energy of the sun, earth, moon and stars is echoed by the quartered circle in all its forms—ritually cast, laid out in stone, excavated in the earth, or drawn in art or architecture. Our natural cycles are Ouroboros wrapped around the planet. The cycles show the rise and fall of Lamia. Understanding that wisdom is essential in our journey. We deepen our discovery of our identity as we enter the cycles. We become the moon, the sun and the stars.

The Rotation of the Earth

I encourage readers to spend several days watching the lights and shadows cast by the rising and setting sun. Seeing the passage of light even in a single season opens up an inner understanding of the earth's rotation as an energy cycle. For night owls, watching the dawn sky is an awakening of the consciousness as well as the body. Some people have never seen a sunrise!

Beginning before sunrise we see a promise of light in the predawn lightening of the sky from east to west. On a clear day the morning light spills over the horizon teasing us with the possibilities of a sunny day. The dawn sun colors the clouds with shades of blue, yellow and pink that can stop the heart with their beauty. Then the sun crests the edge of the earth to show himself bit by bit—an arc, a semicircle and finally in his fullness as the young Sun God. The rising seems rapid in the face of the long promise of dawn. At our home the sun rises over a drumlin. Its light is filtered by deciduous trees until it rises above their tops. This morning light seems more pristine than at any other time of day. The light seems cleaner, clearer and brighter. It has an edge to it.

The dawn is a new beginning or birth. We can try again, undo the mistakes of yesterday, and this time succeed. The dawn brings hope and optimism. The joy of endless possibilities radiates out with the light. We can do anything! Years ago my muses gave me a song to sing to the rising sun in the quartered circle. In the east, the words are:

All hail to the east, where each day is born.
Stretch out your arms and mend what is torn.

The ancients rose to greet the sun with ceremony. Traditional Northeast forest Indians in New York known as the Haudenosaunee or Iroquois dance seven turns in all four directions to greet the rising sun with the Dance of Life. They open the wing of eagle on the right arm and the owl on the left balancing the day and night, the active and passive, thought and intuition of human kind. They send the blessings of the dance to Father Sky and Mother Earth and they take them to heart. It is a beautiful dance that connects the day to the soul of the dancer. To walk in beauty and harmony within the circle, each of us needs a waking ceremony to express our gratitude for being alive.

As we become involved in our routines, most of us stop midday for lunch. At that point we can watch the sun rise to its highest point overhead. That zenith changes with the seasons. Since at my home we are at about 78º latitude, the sun never stands directly atop as it does at the equator. Wherever we are, high noon sun is a fulfillment of the new day's promise. This is the light at its most powerful. Over the next two hours we will experience its greatest intensity in light and heat. We take that opportunity to recharge our bodies with food, consumed thoughtfully with thankfulness. From that small ceremony, we assess our progress and direct our energies for the rest of the daylight hours. The noontime verse of my Sun Song is this:

All hail to the south, the sun heats her blood.
Embrace each other to understand love

The noonday sun interrupts our rushing around in daily routines. It is a time for passion, siesta, pause, meditation. Oddly in Christendom, the high sun was associated with the noonday demon of acedia. Not easily defined, acedia is understood as a loss of connection, the state of uncaring despair when nothing really matters. The loss of meaning in life stems in part from a disbelief in the self as well as rejection of any spiritual significance. Poet and essayist Kathleen Norris follows acedia in her own life and through its references in the church and in the world of letters. She finds medieval monks made reference to acedia as the noonday demon because it was when the sun was highest that they most questioned their vocation in a contemplative order.[122] Writers have attributed writers' block to acedia, the inability to accept anything one has to say as having value. Beyond depression or low self-esteem, acedia saps the very life out of the living, leaving them with a dry husk of existence. Creativity is dead. Norris understands the noonday demon to be a spiritual drought. Contemplation, prayer and reconnection with her traditional faith eventually draw her out of the lethargy of failure. In the quartered circle, the noonday demon arises in the south, a place of creativity and magic. These are acts of decision and will. Isolation from our self-determination is a paralysis of the will. It resides in one root of depression.

The best remedy I know for losing oneself in the shadow, filled with doubt and despair while standing in the light, starts with lunch: healthy nutrition, whole foods and pure water. The noonday demon retreats in the face of meaningful activity: yoga or tai chi get the blood flowing again and reconnect us with our source. By breathing through our bodies, transforming the energy cycle in us, we find a place of internal hope and peace from which we can emerge with confidence. We connect with our source which is All Being. Life is productive and fun. We make it so.

The noontime hours mirror our young adulthood. Filled with physical vitality, we can be pulled away from our goals by self-doubt. We can listen to the negative messages of others who quit before they achieve success. We can set aside our dreams for the needs of others. We can wallow in what appears to be failure because we did not finish school, or married too young, or have no key for advancement. Or we can reconnect with our divine mentors and try again. There are many ways to find success. Norris is right about one thing. The noonday demon of despair and failure is driven back when we reach out spiritually and find another hand connecting with ours.

The noonday sun gives us an option in assessing our progress. We can let our failures bring us down and continue to fail. On the other hand we can celebrate our courage and accomplishments. I heard the actress Elizabeth Olsen say her father asked his children every day what they tried and failed. Then he would applaud and celebrate the boldness of their lives. He encouraged them to try something else new, or go back and try again. Olsen felt rewarded for her courage and risks. She was confident that eventually life turns out okay. Her story struck me as a fine example of how one handles the noonday demon head on.

From midday through the afternoon hours, the light wanes toward dusk. The angle of the sun may be exactly what it was in the morning, but the light has a mellow sense to it. It holds the promise of an end to the day's work. The afternoon hours complete what we started during the day. We make what corrections we identified in our noonday assessment. We may push a little harder to finish a page or a project. In the end we choose what will be seed for tomorrow's work. There is a sense of relief in that, knowing there will be more days, more opportunities to shape our work. We retreat from the routine on the way home, shaking off the burdens of production to embrace family.

For some, the day's end ceremony of the young working professional has become entwined with alcohol and happy hour. The congregation at the local bar is more frenetic than happy. Although socializing over a pint has its charms, in a contemplative life a closing ceremony to end the day's work increases awareness of who we are and why we are here. A drink dulls our self-knowledge and mutes what we meant to know. Finding oneself in a noisy crowd is an unlikely epiphany. Finding a life partner there who can walk this path is equally improbable. Happy hour is not the joy the soul needs.

When the sun edges toward the western horizon, we stop and wait for the sunset which often displays another set of beautiful colors in the sky before the world descends into twilight. Our tired minds and bodies welcome the rest. With a healthy meal and companionship, we take time to share our day's experiences. We watch some television or read a book. The physical, mental and emotional bodies unwind.

For parents who are caught up in the frenzy of child rearing, softness in lighting, gentle sounds and conversation can prepare the children for the night. Too much of our evening activities stimulate all of us into a struggle with sleep. Clubs, evening meetings, video games, athletics, and household chores become adrenaline producing competitions. The workday never seems to end. Although some meetings are positive additions to a rich social life, others are exercises in spinning our wheels with activities. Frenzied activities and an over-full calendar are distancing techniques which keep us so busy we fail to notice who we are or where we go. The twilight hours are times of reflection. They provide a quite communion with self and loved ones, if we allow such intimacy. Creating a balance between staying in and going out is the gift of the evening hours. It is also reflective of maturity. The words of my Sun Song for the evening hours are:

All hail to the west, it's where we shall sleep.
Let go of longing, desires will keep.

Understanding that the joys and challenges which occurred during the day are temporary is a cornerstone of wisdom. My grandmother used to say of difficult times, 'This too shall pass.' I learned her words were equally true of the intense joys of life, not that love doesn't last. It does, but it changes. The rush of new relationship happiness is insufficient to build a lifetime of commitment, for example. There is a deep peaceful joy that comes from being centered in the circle, connected to all the phases of light and experience. That is what lasts in love and everything else. What my grandmother didn't say was that what passes returns. What we think is gone comes back again, in one form or another over time or outside it.

As night deepens, the lights come on in our houses. The dusk settles into night as the sun journeys on the opposite side of the world. Wise eyes seek out the radiance of the night. We can see in the dark with cat's eyes. Foolish eyes jump at shadows and are afraid of the dark. Feeling the shifting of light to dark and back again is part of our being at home on the earth. Starhawk warns us of groups that 'proclaim their devotion to the light without embracing, bowing to the dark; for when they idealize half the world they must devalue the rest.'[123] When we connect to the ebb and flow of the day, month, year and ages we honor the dark and allow for its passing. The words of my Sun Song for our midnight experience are these:

All hail to the north, a place of the night.
Respect her wisdom revealed in moon light.

The night wisdom comes to us in dreams and in astral travel. We receive dimly remembered teachings from our spirit guides as our bodies sleep. Keeping a dream journal or recounting our dreams first thing in the morning are helpful in our evolution as souls who pass seamlessly from light to dark and back again.

The passage from dawn to noon to sunset and dusk and then through the dark of night is the passage of a human life. We are born, we rise to our strength. We mature and mellow, losing the power we held as a young adult but holding the wisdom gained by aging. Our vitality wanes as our light dims. We fade with the sunset. We appear to sleep in death through the dark, but what we really do is rise again on the Otherside to live a different life. In a lifetime this is the passage between the worlds into the land of the dead.

In a mortal day of 24 hours, the night is the journey into dreamtime. We stay in dream time until the new dawn. We rise up from our beds and shake off our dreams under the influence of a new sun. From the deathbed, we rise up from the Otherworld and shake off our memories. Following the sun's path, we are reborn in the morning to spend a lifetime trying to remember. Like the quartered circle, the day is divided into morning, noon, sunset and evening. A life is divided into childhood, youth, maturity, and death. As we shall see so are the seasons of the year, the precession of the seasons and the phases of the moon.

The Revolution of a Year

Although the Witch's year begins with the darkening night of

Samhain, aka Halloween, I begin my examination of the cycle with spring so it follows the same path as the 24 hour day described above. Seeds in the earth sprout new life in the spring which we mark as the vernal equinox around March 21st in the northern hemisphere and September 21st in the southern hemisphere. At that point we are poised between the dark of midwinter and the light of midsummer. The awakening of dawn is mimicked by the trees budding to leaves. Spring bulbs poke through the soil and the grasses green up. Animals mate or give birth in their estrus cycles. Spring draws winter to an end and initiates the birth of the new growing season. We hold the same hopes for a new season with our gardens that we hold for the work of the new day. We believe we will avoid the mistakes of the past. Our seeds and plants will grow and be fruitful. There will be enough rain. Our marigolds and petunias will protect the tomatoes and beans from pests. The deer will have enough food in the wild and leave our tender plants alone.

The tropics have a different seasonal rhythm so although the calendar tells them it is spring or fall, the parallel to the ebb and flow of daylight is different. The changing tides, rainfall, fruit and tree cycles speak regionally of the growth, maturation, harvest and fallow energy flows. Wherever we live, we seek entrance into the earth's rhythms through those cycles. Imposing our expectations will do no good. We must discover what is already there. The elders who are still tied to the land know those rhythms. Witches living outside the temperate climates must discover those rhythms to work with Gaia as she dances in their land.

For us in the temperate zones, spring planting continues until close to summer solstice. Then the harvest of the early strawberries begins. The quick turning from planting beans to harvesting berries reminds me that although the longest day arrives around the 21st, (June in the north, December in the south), solstice marks the beginning of the end as does the noonday demon. After this point the light begins to wane into the afternoon of the year. Its strength dies back and the harvests begin first at summer solstice, then at

Lammas, and finally at Mabon's autumnal equinox. Gradually the Vegetation God gives up his strength for our sustenance in a constant sacrifice of grain, fruit, vegetables and animals. John Barleycorn, Mabon, Greenman, Adonis, and Osiris are some who are familiar to us. He has many names.

Finally with the autumn, the strength of the Harvest God dies and descends below the earth through the fall and early winter. We celebrate the hard work of harvest with feasting, thanksgiving and storytelling. The autumn rituals of Mabon and Samhain involve us in teaching ourselves and the children about the dark and death. We experience the sacrifice of the Corn God as we follow our own aging bodies into the earth. We reach across the thinning barrier between this and the Otherworld to speak with the dead. We express love and communion with them, ask advice and find healing. Our rituals help us understand none of us will get out of this alive, not forever. We will be harvested souls drawn back into the light just as the seasons are.

The harvest is complete at Samhain. What is left in the fields then remains there for the Death Crone. She has frightful names such as Hecate, Hel, the Morrigan, Kali-ma, or Tiamet. She holds the power of the night in her body. She washes the clothing of warriors in the ford of a stream to foretell their deaths. She is merciless in her terrible love that requires the last drop of courage from our hearts when we face Death. She demands fearlessness. She is the wise woman and the grandmother who is not fooled. In the end we become crones and sages. We descend to her underworld and learn the lessons necessary at the end of life. We rest.

The Crone descends into the dark until she gives birth to the light which is reborn at Yule as a vulnerable child. That infant light born of the longest night of winter solstice (December 21 or June 21) is celebrated as hope for the coming spring. Yet all of us in temperate climates know we will slog through weeks of cold, snow and intemperate weather as the infant light increases to warm the earth enough for plants to awaken. More than the night-time of a mortal day, winter can be the long dark night of the soul when shortages pinch the budget, wind seeps in around the windows and our spirits flag in the extended gray darkness of winter.

Seasonal Affective Disorder (SAD), the modern version of the noonday demon, lives not at the height of day but in the dark. It also saps our will to thrive. We hide in our houses; we mope about thinking there is nothing left for us. We spend the dull winter days contemplating our despair instead of reaching out to find merger with our source. A healing response to SAD is the same as to acedia and the noonday demon. Eat well, breathe deeply, move. Through nurturing the body and the soul we find ourselves and defeat our imaginations.

Oddly this human despondency comes at noon, at dusk and in the dark. It is a false face. Unmasked, we see it as an illusion about our powerlessness and irrelevance. We can address it directly to cut off its authority. We can also let it pass of its own accord, because it does. As the light changes during the day, as the sun changes during the seasons, so do our moods. Even in the good times, I like to remember there are days when I feel disconnected. I like to remind myself they are part of a cycle that ebbs and flows so I can play with the feelings of love and despair. These are shadows of who I really am. I let them drive the bus once in a while for the experience. The cycle of light in both rotation and revolution includes the dark without fear because we know dawn comes. In the dark night of the soul is a barren land. The barrenness can be transformed to a winter fantasy by snow and frost which sparkle in the sun. All is a matter of perspective. Expect beauty. The landscape will change to bloom with spring rain and sunshine. If I embrace the dark as a place of rest and beauty, I will be energized for rebirth.

The Precession of the Equinoxes

Never an easy concept to explain, the precession of the equinoxes describes ages of time. The usual explanation of the earth's wobble on its axis is simply too abstract to mean anything to most people, even if we spin a top to observe it wobble on its axis. The top leaves us with the impression that the earth will wobble out of control and spin out of orbit, which is not at all the point.

To illustrate precession in a hands-on fashion, I pick a student to be Gaia, the earth. She sits in an office chair holding a globe with a thin dowel run through the poles like the earth's axis. She holds the earth at a 23º angle, just like the real thing. I have four more volunteers standing at approximately equal intervals around an oval in the room. They are the four north stars: Polaris, Alpha Cephei, Vega and Alpha Draconis (Thuban). I give them posters with their star names on them to make the process clear. Gaia begins with the North Pole pointed at Polaris and turns her chair around deosil with the axis pointing at each north star in turn. This single turning of the pole among the four different pole stars takes approximately 26,000 years. This is not a perfect illustration since it demonstrates the change among the pole stars but not the rotation and revolution of the earth nor the proper movement of the stars themselves, which happen all through the process, but it makes a point that there is constant slow change in the orientation of the earth relative to the stars.

In this exercise, Gaia will see that not only did she draw an oval in the air toward the ceiling with the North Pole, she drew one in the air facing the floor which would show the changes in the orientation of the South Pole to the stars. Currently the South Pole has no bright star in its field to serve as a polar star. Eventually the Southern Cross will connect with this cycle. There is a cone extending up from the North Pole toward the four north stars and another one extending down from the South Pole toward the south stars.

Because the earth's axis is tilted at that 23º angle, the stars in the background give us the impression from earth that they move forward themselves, when it is really the earth's movement that creates that illusion. The stars and the zodiac constellations shift to rise one month later in about 2,200 years. That figure of 2,200 years is also an approximation since the length of an age varies with the placement of the constellations and stars around the ellipse. Two millennia plus two centuries represent a 30º shift or 1/12 of a circle from one zodiac sign to the next. Of course the shape is an ellipse, not a circle, so the length of each age varies. The next, the Age of Aquarius, begins between 2100 CE and 2800 CE depending on how the beginning is defined. Each shift from one age to another takes about 30 lifetimes. Currently we are moving from the Age of Pisces to the Age of Aquarius. Given the subtle slow nature of the shift, each age carries with it characteristics of the previous age and the anticipated one. We paint with a very broad brush in discussing the precession.

In recorded history we have noted the Age of Taurus, the Age of Aries, the Age of Pisces and the Age of Aquarius. The Age of Taurus represented by the bull corresponds to the age of the Mother Goddess frequently symbolized by the skull and horns of the bull which resemble the uterus and ovaries. The bull cult is strongly connected to the island of Crete, the myth of the Minotaur and labyrinths. Aries represented by the ram corresponds to the age of the patriarchs: Abraham, Moses and Zeus. The myths of Herakles, the *Illiad* and *Odyssey* resonate with the heroic Ares for which both the zodiac sign and age are named. Pisces, represented by the fish, corresponds to the age of faith rooted in Christianity, Buddhism and Islam. Aquarius represented by the Water Bearer ushers in, we hope, an age of compassion and increased humanity. The avatars of the age and the defining stories are ahead of us.

These ages and symbols have connections in mythology which can be quite surprising. In the Age of Taurus from around 4300 BCE, the North Star was Draco (Alpha Draconis) the Dragon, which fits the Goddess Tiamet described as a serpentine monster by those who defeated her. The Goddess was seen in the horns of the bull which resemble the womb and fallopian tubes, and the bull dancers of Crete were renowned for their celebration of the Goddess. Bull fighting and the running of the bulls is a degeneration of this ancient tradition.

I believe the rejection of the Divine Feminine rose during the subsequent centuries as the precession of the equinoxes wove its dark moon mystery in the retreat of the Goddess from this world. The stories about the supremacy of Zeus over Hera, and his appearance as a bull in raping Europa show the gradual shift to male dominance during the age of Aries around 2100 BCE. The patriarchs continued to exert their power over the world as Abraham and Moses with the God Jehovah overshadowed Sarah, Hagar, Keturah and Miriam with Goddesses Sophia and Shekinah. The loss of matriarchal authority reflects the shift in pre-eminence toward the patriarchal God. One of the symbols of Judaism is the ram or ram's horn. The ram was the animal often sacrificed by the Jewish tribes in their rituals. In Greek mythology, Zeus transformed himself into a ram to escape his pursuers when the Olympian Gods defeated the Titans.

The North Star was in the slow process of moving from Draco to Polaris which it reached around 1 CE and the Age of Pisces. The sign of the fish in the Age of Pisces has been adopted as the symbol of Jesus and Christianity. In history it has appeared in Islamic references and coins though after centuries of religious wars between Christians and Muslims one can understand it is unwelcome in Arab societies. The fish symbol is actually the *vesica piscis*, which is an almond shaped oval defined by two arcs and symbolizes the vagina. Nevertheless, the motif became associated with the age of faith within the male monotheistic religions. The sacrifices to the patriarchal Gods were replaced by faith. This is true in both Christianity and Islam. Faith in the principles of the religion became sufficient to save the soul without blood sacrifice. Similarly in Buddhism, sacrifice of the ego and of personal comfort evolved as support for the goal of enlightenment rather than blood sacrifice.

The introduction of love, forgiveness, healing and compassion in these religions foreshadows the return of the Goddess in the Aquarian Age. This foreshadowing is analogous to a new moon. It is the crescent stage of her rebirth. Obviously, the socio-political world reflected in 2,000 years of the Christian church and Islamic mosque still suppressed the Divine Feminine, but the cult of Mary and the increase of women's roles in society, in the family and in spiritual institutions prepare a path of return for the Shining Ones. Gaia's axis weaves a literal new age under the North Star of Polaris in the constellation of the Little Bear. The Divine Feminine re-emerges in the Age of Aquarius.

The Shining Ones' return is symbolized by the rose. Their consciousness unfolds in layers. There is always more to the story. I suggest, however, that this re-emergence combines the energies of male and female in the Aquarian Age. The zodiac symbol for the water bearer is two parallel zig zag lines, not one. Compare this to the sign for Gemini and Cancer, which also incorporate a balance of two energies. These energies preceded the Age of Taurus and stretch our Goddess memories back to prehistory. The Age of Gemini would have been 6400 to 4300 BCE. The Age of Cancer would have been 8600 to 6400 BCE. The lessons we knew before and lost, the lessons we must learn again, are in fact the lessons of the equinoxes, that of balance, polarity and change.

I recognize that the common wisdom in scholarship goes against evidence of a prehistoric Mother Goddess cult. I agree it is highly unlikely there was a unifying world religion that recognized a single Goddess. On the other hand, I believe there is ample evidence that the people who left amulets, art and icons represented the Divine Feminine in a variety of forms that reflected local geography, myth and culture. The local culture included different languages. Language shapes ideas and belief systems. The Mother Goddesses could not have been the same for people around the Mediterranean and people of the icy north. Perhaps their Goddess stories were similar because the stories traveled with our ancestors and their DNA out of Africa tens of thousands of years ago.

Nevertheless the Divine Feminine was perceived differently because of tribal differences and family differences. Yet the aspects of the Goddess were known in her many different guises. She is all the phases of the moon. She can be seen in all the hours of the day and in all the seasons of the year. The Divine Masculine who is represented as her brother, her consort and/or her son is also seen in these natural cycles, though differently. The Divine Feminine is seen as turning but not dying. The Divine Masculine is seen as sacrificed and reborn. In myth, Persephone, Inanna, and others descend to become Queen of the Underworld but return to the light. They do not die. Osiris, Odin, the Greenman, Mithras and Jesus are killed and their bodies sacrificed. They return through rebirth, often as their own sons. When a people find their Gods and Goddesses in nature, these are the cycles that they see.

In any case, the North Star is mutable. It changes. The change is slower than the constellations it selects as emblems of the ages, but it changes nevertheless. Before our eyes, one thing becomes another, in the mother, in the mother. Day to night, season to season, age to age, Gaia and Sol reflect our journey from birth to maturity to death and back again as we evolve our souls. Luna does the same.

The Phases of the Moon

The apparent growth of the moon from crescent to full and back to crescent, disappearing and returning is another mirror of our life cycle. We may think of the moon in her three phases of waxing new moon crescent (Maiden), full moon (Mother), and dark moon (Crone). These phases reflect the Triple Goddess and some tropical or sub-tropical divisions of the year based on climate and rainfall. Or we can consider four moon phases of Maiden, Mother, Matriarch and Crone if we want to continue our metaphor of the quartered circle with parallels to the temperate zone season. In either case, the phases of the moon connect with our psyche as revelations of the Lunar Goddess.

In each phase we see what is intended to be revealed but not all that the moon is. We see a waxing silver crescent as the growing maiden and identify with the youthful hopeful energy of spring and the dawn. The spherical moon co-exists with and in and around the crescent, but we see only the Maid.

The revelation of moonlight increases each night until we see the full flat white disc of the Mother Moon. She is more than that revelation because behind the flat disc is a sphere, an unrevealed occult side that never turns her face to us. The full moon holds the potential of birth and fruitful lives. Like the noonday sun she can drive us crazy with self-doubt and uncertainty as we face ourselves. She can light our way. She can give us joy in our accomplishments and hope for greater things to come. She is the power of summer and the longest day.

Further around the circle, we enter the waning half-moon, the Matriarch. Her power is found in embracing the growing dark as she releases the Mother and becomes the intuitive psychic Crone Goddess. Like the twilight and Mabon, her power is in the occult. It is hidden. Some of her strength is offered as a gift to her devotees. In maturity we become wise if we have worked for it. She loses nothing by giving her wisdom to us, because her greatest power is in the dark, but we gain by walking with her there. Like the autumn season, we enter harvest, thanksgiving and reach out to the ancestors.

Finally Grandmother Moon, the invisible dark, pulls at our senses and teases our intuitive powers. She manifests as nothing and all things at the same time, even in the same space. Dark moon rests as the earth rests in winter, as the earth's people rest at midnight. There in the dark our creativity begins to move in dreams. Our souls map new plans for the coming light. Our bodies are repaired or recreated. We sit in Grandmother's lap feasting on milk and cookies. We know we are safe.

The moon phases reflect the phases of a woman's life, which is part of the reason we most often associate Goddesses with the moon power. The waxing crescent of the maiden reflects menarche as a child passes through initiation into puberty; the full moon represents the fertility of a menstruating woman, the waning moon representing the menstruating woman who has borne and raised her children and is free to move into the full power of her own choices and creativity; and the dark moon the great power of the crone who has reached menopause and the ability to hold her blood as magic within. Then with her magic as her strength she walks into Death. These are women's blood mysteries in a nutshell.

Meditation on a Celestial Dance

Select one of these great cycles to sit and contemplate, entering your insights into your journal or BOS. The turning of day and night, the changing of the seasons or the phases of the moon are more observable so may be a better place to start. People who have spent years dancing with the light and dark in their natural cycles may wish to take on the precession of the equinoxes. For your meditation, first identify the current cyclic phase. Start where you are in time and space. If you contemplate the moon, start with the current phase and follow the cycle. If you contemplate the seasons, begin with today. If you contemplate the hours, start with this time.

Then once again, center yourself in your body, being aware of any tension you feel. Release that and let it go out of your consciousness. Send your grounding energy deep into the earth, anchoring on the bedrock. Draw the earth energy to you. Feel safe, rooted and connected to the earth. When you are ready send your energy shooting through you from the earth to seek the chosen celestial: earth, sun, moon, or north star in space. Seek out that celestial consciousness, remembering the earth is also a celestial if observed from outer space. Call to the consciousness by one of the names commonly used. Earth Mother or Gaia, Luna the Moon Goddess, Apollo the Sun God, Polaris the North Star are some of their names. Expect someone to answer. Remain conscious of your grounding and your connection to your earth body sitting in meditation, but let your soul soar.

When someone answers, be aware of any shifts or change in light. Pay attention to any physical scenery which is projected into your meditation. The details may be important. Then turn and look back to the earth. Realize your consciousness is really in another dimension communing with a celestial. Give honor to your celestial teacher in the four directions and listen. Being aware of the phase of the cycle represented by this teacher, send out your conscious energy and ask with humility to learn about the turning phases of his or her cycles. Listen. Ask questions. When you understand, give thanks and depart back to the bedrock, release your anchor, and return to your body. Sit with your hands on the ground while you review your vision. Record what you learned, and discuss it with trusted friends. Think about this in ordinary reality to integrate the magical with the mundane. This experience is one of the first you take in becoming the earth, sun, stars, or moon, which to one degree or another, describes the Wiccan path. Repeat this meditation as the cycle changes. Even the Precession of the Equinoxes shifts every year of a lifetime to change 1° in 71 years. In the longer cycles, if you are very brave and grounded, you can ask your teacher to show you the full cycle unfolding in your meditation.

The Spiral Dance

The spiral dance is more than a book title. Dancing in the line of Witches spiraling deosil into the center of the circle, and then turning to dance outward widdershins, and then spiraling in again is a profound and beautiful experience, as long as the leader understands that the spiral dance mirrors the natural cycles of the celestials that we have studied in this chapter. At the 2002 New York State Pagan gathering in Seneca Falls NY I was privileged to lead the dance as a slow, stately and meditative pattern. We spiraled in and out several times, coming closer together, until on the last pass I felt bold and empowered enough to kiss each person as they passed me. It was sweetness and love itself.

In the spiral dance one experiences the different energies in deosil and widdershins energy. This is also true of a double circle dance if the circles change direction or the dancers change circles. I participated in a dance like this at Starwood in a workshop led by Anodea Judith several years ago. We started as partners facing each other in two circles. The outer circle went widdershins and the inner circle went deosil, each circle holding hands and facing the other. We were to look into each other's eyes as we met and moved past each other in a simple step-slide pattern. We sang:

We are a circle, within a circle, with no beginning, and never ending.[124]

All the faces became holy as we sang and danced. I cried when I saw a woman who looked like my mother. I don't know what all those people thought to see tears streaming down my face. It didn't matter. I felt my mother reach across the veil and look at me out of a stranger's eyes. I stayed with that circle, held on tight to the people on my right and left and kept dancing. Just like life.

More recently during the interviews I conducted with students for this book, Peg told me what a profound difference her mother's death made in Peg's work with the elderly. I rely on Peg to teach students about death and its transitions. She said that being bereaved herself when her mother died unexpectedly made all of her education and experience deeper. A few weeks before our interview, she and her husband were out shopping in a large chain store. She looked up and saw a woman walking away from her that appeared to be her mother. The gait, the hair and clothes all seemed real. She never saw her face, but the experience was shattering. As we talked about that, I remembered a waitress who for no obvious reason, stopped at our table and told us she had lost her fiancé that summer when he was killed in an accident in his truck. She said she kept seeing him drive by the restaurant in broad daylight, looking through the window as if to say he was all right. I had assured her he was indeed all right.

Peg passed on words from another wise woman. At her mother's wake, Peg was told that sooner or later, she could expect to see someone that looked so much like her mother her heart would stop. Her shopping experience had a context so she recognized it when it happened. She interpreted that as a communication from the dead, a reassurance that the lifecycle continues and the soul does not die. I understood that clearly when it happened to me. The waitress accepted my reassurance she was not crazy for thinking the same thing. I have no idea how universal this nudge from spirit may be, but here are three examples unrelated to one another. *The Scientific American* published an article by Vaughn Bell that indicated 80 percent of us have experiences with the dead, which were termed grief hallucinations.[125] The term hallucination means something different to Bell than mental illness and brain deceptions, given his extensive research in neuroscience and altered states of consciousness. It does not carry a pejorative connotation but is part of the mind healing itself through grief.

Life surely continues into night and back to day. Whether we are in a circle dance or a meditation of the cycles of the universe, the message is exactly that. Life continues. The soul lives, the eras of history change, but we will meet again. This reality too shall pass, but it will also come back and be reborn.

Chapter 21

Unspoken Rituals in Circle Casting

Holding an awareness of the cycles of light and dark reflected to us by the celestials strengthens our ability to create secure and transcendent sacred space. Clearly for the facilitating ritualists, there is more going on behind the scenes than is apparent to the celebrants of a ritual. What happens that goes unsaid? How is sacred space created if all things are part of All Being? How can any space be profane if all spaces are woven into the web of All Being?

The easy answer that there is no difference between one space and another comes to mind, yet we know there is a palpable difference inside the cast circle. We can feel its boundaries. We know when it has been torn.

We also know there are physical places in the world which feel unsafe or profaned. In two counties adjacent to mine a commercial waste disposal corporation is creating mountains of garbage trucked in from major metropolitan areas including New York City 265 miles away. They are scars on the land, even though the corporate interests insist they will create recreational areas and ski slopes on them. The area smells bad. The potential for water contamination is a great concern to those who love the earth, since the Montezuma National Wildlife Refuge is a bare five miles away. These trash mountains feel profane.

How are both concepts true at the same time; that all space is here and sacred but some places have been set aside as dumps? Others are places of carnage and battle. Others are neighborhoods of neglect where crime and poverty color life in a cruel pattern. Our spiritual search for identity eventually leads us to seek a resolution to the paradox. When we know who we are, we become empowered to defend the sacredness of the earth. Ultimately a person's spiritual path leads to involvement in the sentient life of Gaia through her circling, rotating, revolution and evolution. There is not one truth here. We will not all be in agreement on how to address the sacredness of Gaia nor how to gain our livelihoods or secure our food. For each of us, these choices about where to live, how to live, what to eat, when to involve ourselves in collective actions, are shaped by our experience of the sacred. For many of us, that begins with the quartered circle.

When we cast a circle and perform ritual we say we are between the worlds. I understand that to be a transcendental experience. In other words, when we move between the worlds we go beyond ordinary reality into mysticism. Our journey between the worlds is individual and intuitive even when we are working in a group. Because it reaches beyond physical reality into the emotional, mental and spiritual bodies, descriptions fall apart. There is no scientific method or measurement readily at hand to test and define the knowledge of those in-between worlds. Advanced mathematics, sacred geometry and string theory physics approach the understanding, but are not in my view helpful to many practicing Witches.

The Mystical Experience

Walter T. Stace (1886-1967), professor of philosophy at Princeton University, examined the problem in *Mysticism and Philosophy*.[126] After careful analysis, Stace rejected common explanations which minimized mystical experience as a metaphor, as an emotional response to stimuli, and as too profound for words. His theory of mysticism concludes that the ancients described their mystical experiences in figurative and literal languages after the fact, but that during the rapture itself, were unable to do so. I would suggest they were unwilling to do so, given the blissful reality of transcendence. To draw oneself back to the facility of language from the depths of silence disrupts the spiritual merger which is hallmark to transcendence.

I have reworked the citation of Walter Stace's description of transcendental mystical experiences used by James Swan in *Sacred*

Places.[127] For me, moving between the worlds is a transcendental experience with these characteristics:

The experience of Unity with All Being at a soul level—an Aha! moment or epiphany;
Being outside time and space and unaware of or at least unconcerned about the limits of ordinary reality;
Being in touch with the ultimate realities of Spirit and of dimensional shifts—Jane Roberts and Seth refer to these as the psychic senses or inner senses;
Feeling joy and ecstasy, which includes a kundalini rush—the reason the Great Rite and sacred sex are a key part of Wiccan thealogy;
Sensing Divine Presence over the altar and within the people, often identified by name and signifying our personal correlation with the Lady and the Lord;
Experiencing a state of being that is beyond adequate description or explanation and is akin to our remembering who we are in our spirit bodies;
Awareness of and knowing the paradox of being human and spirit, male and female, light and dark, unified polarity—remembering who we are in our soul.

My Story: A Teaching from Kwan Yin

In a trance meditation experienced in ritual space, I found myself in a Buddhist shrine to Kwan Yin. You may know her as the Goddess of Compassion, a bodhisattva who has postponed her transition to nirvana until all humanity has evolved sufficiently to transition with her. There was a beautiful life-sized statue of her on a pedestal to one side of a floral altar. I felt her presence within me and around the altar. *(Sensing Divine Presence over the altar and within, often identified by name.)*

I was entranced with her presence. She is a Goddess I encountered in the Museum of Natural History in New York City, one who spoke to me through her statuary and whom I had loved and admired for a long time. As I acknowledged that inner connection in my trance, the statue came alive and called me by name. I was overjoyed. *(Feeling joy and ecstasy, which includes a kundalini rush.)* She was actually present standing before me. I fell on my knees in awe and worship with the intention of staying there.

Kwan Yin laughed and climbed down from the pedestal, good naturedly scolding me:

'No, no, no, not that. This!' she said as she led me over to the steps which wound around the pedestal.

She pointed up at the platform, indicating I should climb up there and stand. I was aghast. She could not be serious. She held my hand and insisted I mount the stairs, which were small and narrow. The edges had crumbled some over the ages. I did not like it at all, fearing I would fall down and embarrass myself or worse yet, break a leg. She laughed again, that wonderful musical sound that brought joy right up out of my center. She believed I could climb up there and not make a fool of myself. Moreover, she thought I belonged up there.

I finally stood up on the pedestal, holding my hands out for balance. The platform wasn't very large, maybe twice what my feet required, with no hand holds. I felt very frightened and out of place. When Kwan Yin took my seat before the altar and gazed at me adoringly, I felt even worse. Apparently none of the other worshippers noticed the change. They kept chanting and lighting incense. They made offerings and looked up at me with love shining in their eyes. I felt like the worst imposter, fit to be struck by lightning.

I understood what she was doing, intellectually at least. She was trying to demonstrate how we are both divine and mortal, spirit and body. (*Awareness of and knowing the paradox of being human and spirit, male and female, light and dark, unified polarity.*)

When I gained that awareness she nodded her approval. Then she came and guided me down from the pedestal. She returned me to my place of worship before she ran lightly up the steps and assumed the pose of the original statue. I thought that was the end of it, but she turned and looked deep in my eyes and winked. She was not finished yet, or I wasn't.

In a few moments she came back down the steps, took my hand and guided me back up on the platform. I felt a little more confident. The steps were easier, the platform not so scary. However, I still felt like an imposter. She smiled and lit incense at my feet and bowed. I groaned internally, thinking, 'This is not appropriate.'

I do not know how long it took for her to still my discomfort. Eventually, she signaled I should come back down, this time without assistance. She scurried back up and held my gaze. We exchanged places half a dozen times or more over an unspecified period of time. The worshippers continued to behave as if there were no difference between us. I lost my fear of falling and concern that people would punish me for this audacity. (*Being outside time and space, unaware of or at least unconcerned about the limits of ordinary reality.*)

Finally I was able to accept this exchange of energy and feel my divine nature extend out to those assembled before me including Kwan Yin herself. I sent them love and blessing and joy. The chants rose louder and more beautiful. The incense smelled sweeter. I understood I was being changed, going through shifts of consciousness that would remain when I returned to ordinary reality. I accepted this experience as a real event in my soul's life, a direct teaching from one of my patrons. My ego was stilled and opened to the changes. I also knew I could return to this place when the trance was over. I knew the way. (*Being in touch with the ultimate realities of Spirit and of dimensional shifts.*)

At that point, Shiva entered the shrine and greeted both of us as one. He danced before the altar first with Kwan Yin who seemed to shift into Parvati, his wife. When I descended to the altar, he danced with me. Kwan Yin morphed from one form to another. So did I. Then I realized I had been changing my form all along. It happened as I ascended the pedestal and when I engaged in the dance with Shiva. I could not describe how the shapeshifting occurred; only that it did. (*Experiencing a state of being beyond adequate description or explanation.*)

Finally, as I danced with Shiva, Kwan Yin descended from the pedestal the three of us danced together as one. As that realization entered my consciousness, another friend joined us. The process began again, this time between Shiva and my friend. She was taught to exchange places on the pedestal while Kwan Yin and I observed the process and adored them. Then I realized that all the people in the shrine who adored the Gods were themselves the Gods. They were also humans. (*The experience of Unity with All Being at a soul level.*) I had a moment of self-recrimination for being so dense. Of course that was the truth of this vision. Of course they were all different people and all the same. Of course I was in them and they in me. When I heard Kwan Yin's laugh, I landed abruptly back in ordinary reality.

This trance vision happened well over 20 years ago; maybe more than 25 years ago. I write about it as if it were yesterday. The magic of it still lingers in my soul. My identity is still connected to it. The power of the ecstatic circle remains as a transcendental mystical experience. The flowers on Kwan Yin's altar were pink and fragrant. The Goddess was dressed in green and gold; the God in blue and gemstones. There were toned gongs striking softly as we changed places. The chanting lulled us all into deeper and deeper places within the soul. There were white and red pillar candles burning around the room with white votives placed in shells. There were benches to sit on, though many people stood. There was an elaborate mandala painted on the wall behind the altar. There were red, silver and gold tapestries in alcoves with golden arches. I know. I was there.

Enabling Transcendence in a Wiccan Circle

In his book *Sacred Places,* Swan sides with William James in writing about the psychology of the sacred, indicating a transcendent vision lasts only about half an hour,[128] but of course if one is outside of time and space that limit is meaningless. The usual order of a Web Wiccan ritual builds peaks and concludes according to their description of a transcendent vision. I have added the ritual practices we commonly use in parenthesis with their stages in transcendence to demonstrate the parallel to our usual ritual practice.

Swan and James indicate the experience begins with an emotional arousal and connection with a higher power (*call to circle, the challenge*).

It continues with a trigger that shifts consciousness (*smudging, grounding, casting the circle*). Their claim is that this trigger destabilizes the ego. I submit it is the one occasion when the ego is stable—albeit not in control.

Then this is followed by a peak experience (*calling the quarters and encountering the deities*).

This in turn sets the stage for the manifestation of power, prophecy, visions, etc. (*meditation, cone of power or other magical working*).

The episode concludes with a return to ordinary reality (*grounding, releasing the deities and quarters, opening the circle*).

If we are truly open and engaged in the process, the transcendent connection with Spirit between the worlds is inevitable. Thus, there is a conscious decision on the part of the priests and priestesses in making powerful ritual happen within the circle and moving that circle between the worlds. This is the essence of the unspoken ritual of the circle casting.

How do the priest and priestess open the way for this transcendence to occur? The location of the ritual—its geography, the design and setting of the room, its cleansing and décor set the stage for an ecstatic experience. The personal partnership with the deities brought by the priest and priestess to the circle magnify any human intention by adding direct participation by divine energies. As in my trance story with Kwan Yin, the spirits co-create the mystical encounter with the mortals. The invisible mental, emotional and spiritual processes of the priest and priestess during the ritual work throughout the visible rites weave energy beyond ordinary reality into the circle and the quarters. The celebrants are affected by this energy and able to use it as they wish for their greater good. Their personal divine patrons work that magic individually in the manner in which each soul is able to receive it. Thus a first timer is not unduly overwhelmed and a seasoned Witch is transformed and challenged. A skeptic watches and leaves convinced nothing happened.

Location

Geography and geomancy can support us in moving between the worlds when the circle is conducted in dedicated interior space or outdoors in the wilds near sites of active chi (running water, living trees and gardens, mountains or other places where energy has collected over the centuries). *Geography* literally means the *description or graphing of the earth,* but the academic discipline has extended to include our human and cultural footprint on the land. *Geomancy* is defined by the ancient Greek philosopher Pliny as *the art of earth divination,* which is reading the energies present in an earthly geographic area to understand what the area is meant to be, or to determine the activities best suited for the place. How much stronger ritual and magic are when one can use a dedicated sacred place in the wild, like a stone circle or medicine wheel!

Originally we held Web rituals at our home in a dedicated ritual room. The area itself holds the ritual chi generated by 15 years of sabbats and moon rituals, classes, initiations and rites of passage. Two four-foot pocket doors which slide open between the sunroom and the ritual room are constructed according to the ratio of the Golden Mean as are all the doors and paneling in the house. The

Golden Mean is actually a spiral pattern within an enclosing rectangle approximated by the Fibonacci series, a math formula which says *'What is, plus what was, is what will be.'* We know the power of the spiral as a symbol of connection, growth, evolution, or enlightenment. The spiral dance embraces us in the energy of the spiral. The nautilus shell is a physical spiral of this nature. During group meditation, we may have felt ourselves swaying with the energy of the spiral, weaving in a circular motion because the Golden Mean was present in our bodies in a way that is different from ordinary reality.

What the Golden Mean brings to us and to architecture is a sense of connection with the past and the future. It takes what we know, adds what we learn and produces a new concept. Then it takes the new concept, adds what we know again and reaches up to a new level, always building on the known. This is an infinitely repeating concept, although the mathematical diagrams do have a starting point. Esoterically there is no beginning or end to the spiral though in this dimension of reality such a concept is difficult to imagine let alone depict visually. In math the Fibonacci progression goes like this:

$1 + 1 = 2$
$2 + 1 = 3$
$3 + 2 = 5$
$5 + 3 = 8$
$8 + 5 = 13$
$13 + 8 = 21$

It continues infinitely. This ratio, *phi,* is numerically 1.618:1, and is made by measurements set so that in a triangle the lesser length A is to the greater length B as the greater length B is to the total length C. It is the ratio of the pentagram as well.

One of the reasons that locations which reflect the Golden Mean feel so right to us is their resonance with our bodies which are built on the same ratio. Think of the Da Vinci's Vitruvian Man who stretches out his arms and legs in a perfect circle. He embodies the *phi* proportions from fingers to hand, hand to arm, arm to torso and so on. In addition, the Golden Mean is reflected in the shapes of crystals, their auric energy fields and, I suspect, in our own auras which would be evident if we had the sight or technology to accurately view the human auric fields.

In popular culture there was a 2012 television drama in the US created by Tim Kring entitled *Touch*. The premise focused on a single father raising a presumably autistic son who was a child mathematical and intuitive genius. The child used the Golden Mean and Fibonacci progression to communicate since he did not speak. His number sequences connected unlikely events into a demonstration of cause and effect that baffled the adults. Instead of supporting the chaos theory in Edward Lorenz' butterfly effect (a butterfly flaps its wings in Brazil which leads to a tornado in Texas), *Touch* seems to support order and intention behind the chaos. In either case, chaos or cause and effect, the morphing of connections between seemingly disconnected events, remind us of Jung's synchronicities. Events appear to merge as, 'One thing becomes another, in the Mother, in the Mother.' In our effort to create transcendent mystic events, this morphing from one to another level of consciousness is at the core of the quartered circle.

The spiral associated with the Golden Mean mirrors the spiral of energy raised with the cone of power. At the high point of a magical working the priestess leads the circle of celebrants in gathering their energy into a collective circle and sending it out into the universe or down into a talisman to create the change they have envisioned together. Rather than a random spray of scattered energy sent out like bird shot, the cone of power is best woven from the energy offered by each participant into a spiral which winds inward from the edge of the circle toward the center in the same way the spiral dance winds inward. The cone of power then ascends in a spiral upward, often sent out with a group gesture of raised hands to be caught by the deities and directed to the recipient of the magical working. Led with intention and skill, the celebrants can feel the cone build, grow and launch.

In addition to the geometry of a place, its *location* enhances the transcendent experience. In our basement is a giant rock which was unearthed when Merlin had the dirt floor dug out before a new concrete floor was poured. It obviously has resided there longer than the house has been built. Unable to remove the rock because of its size, the workers dug a deeper hole, flipped it over so it would be beneath the new floor and then covered it with concrete. In so doing they found a broken piece of crockery under the stone, the foot of a tureen's pedestal marked as *Iron Stone China*. However, this was a magical encounter. There was a flaw in the firing of the piece. The mark actually says *Iron Stone Chi*. I laughed when I saw it.

The piece also carries the royal motto *Hon y soit qui mal y pense*. Legends about that motto connect with Witchcraft and the Order of the Garter. Those stories may be fanciful but I was delighted nonetheless that the rock in the basement brought me such a treasure. The rock is a powerful participant in creating our sacred space. It resonates with the stones in the Avebury Stone Circle to bring that energy partway around the world to shape our rituals into transcendence.

We can view place and location through three different lenses to study how sacred places collect and reflect powerful chi. First, there are homes, shrines and buildings like ours made from human hands. Second, we find notable places of enhanced formations and buildings located on powerful nodes around the world. Third, majestic surroundings with natural power in the history, hills, valleys, waters and peaks distribute chi across the earth's surface and through it.

Constructed Sacred Sites

Near my home in the US is Willard Chapel, a beautiful stone building originally part of a seminary. The Tiffany interior is one of the few surviving locations which combine that opalescent stained glass, furniture and architecture typical of Art Nouveau. Though it is now a rented hall for weddings, concerts and similar gatherings, the presence of the sacred continues within. Churches, retreat centers, and spas all are building projects that create a sense of the sacred within their walls. The construction materials, the floor plan, the decor, the interplay of light and shadow, the energy and chi of the interior and grounds, all contribute to the sense of a place being set apart for something special. Although it is near a ley line, there is nothing there to suggest it was itself a collection of powerful energies prior to its construction.

Enhanced Power Spots

Sacred places which are constructed to enhance powerful geographic locations include the Cathedral at Chartres, which displays the most famous labyrinth in the floor of its sanctuary. It is this labyrinth which was the inspiration for Lauren Artress' research and book *Walking the Sacred Path: Rediscovering the Labyrinth as a Spiritual Tool.*[129] The Cathedral at Chartres combines the constructed sanctuary with the power of the former Pagan shrine it covered over. Ely Cathedral in Cambridgeshire, UK, has a different labyrinth inlaid in the tiles at the entrance. These adaptations of a Pagan power spot for a Christian church or cathedral are common. The Cathedral at Wells in Somerset, UK, is sited where there were seven natural springs. The grounds hold a holy presence. Religious politics seems not to alter the power of the land.

Another example is found at The Springs at Clifton in New York State, USA. The sulfur springs is a natural spa which the First Nations of people recognized. A hospital was set there in the 1800s to take advantage of the healing waters and the healing reputation of the location. More recently a holistic healing center has been set up within the hospital campus which includes hot spa treatments with the sulfur spring water, salt water or with clear water; a nine course labyrinth and garden; and art as a healing modality along with acupuncture, chakra healing and Reiki. There is also a Chinese herbal medicine apothecary and certified staff onsite. In Clifton Springs, the building and construction enhances the natural sacred healing springs.

The oracle and temple at Delphi in Greece is another example of an enhanced setting for a natural sacred geography. The Temple of Apollo was built over an earlier shrine to Gaia. The oracle sat over a fissure where she was exposed to entrancing fumes from the deep earth. Stone circles and henges are also sacred construction projects, sited in locations of power where ley lines intersect. Castlerigg in Cumbria, near Keswick, UK, is surrounded by powerful fells. The stones in the circle mirror them, a presence which is felt when one stands inside the circle. The circle is tied into the land. Avebury Stone Circle in Wiltshire, UK, was set to mark the stars and constellations of the ancient world, according to Nicholas Mann in *Avebury Cosmos*.[131]

Natural Power Spots

The third type of sacred place is the totally natural location of power and majesty which needs no enhancement. Mount Baker, Mount Rainier (Grandfather Mountain) and Mount St. Helens (Grandmother Mountain) in Washington on the West Coast are such locations. The Four Corners area of the Navaho and Hopi Tribes in North America see each of the four directions defined by one or more mountains which the Diné call *Sis Naajini* in the east, *Tsoodzil* in the south, *Dook'o'ooshiid* in the west, *Dibe Nitsaa* in the north, *Dzil Na'oodihii* in the center and *Ch'ool'i'i* east of center. The Black Hills are similarly sacred to the Lakota, who remain less than impressed by the white man's sculpture of American presidents on the face of Mount Rushmore. What an affront to the people who lived in harmony with that land! The New Forest in the UK is similar. The land itself holds magic, but it has been abused by the military in war time. The forest has been cut over large portions of the land. Yet the land retains its power. The people are fenced in and the animals roam free.

Lakes, rivers, waterfalls, valleys, gorges, caves all are locations of great spiritual power for the people who live in tune with the land. Old growth forests, deserts, sandstone mesas, ocean inlets and bays gather and hold chi in the land and the waters. Near our well in the field behind the house is a single tree that speaks to me of the sacred. The face of the Greenman appears in its foliage each spring, different from year to year. Lake Ontario near where I live and Skaneateles Lake where I was born both speak to me of the Goddess, especially as the setting sun or the risen moon reflect on their waters. The Seneca River carries an ancestral message for me because my great-great-great grandfather Isaac and his father Henry Abrahams conducted a ferry across it before Bonta Bridge was built and before they shortened their name. When I cross the Seneca at any bridge I call it My Grandfathers' River. I know it is named for the First Nation people we call the Seneca, but I also know Abrams is a Seneca Nation surname. I do not know how our ancestors met, but I do know it is our river to protect and love together.

As priest and priestess we enhance the magic of the quartered circle when we understand spatial significance and earth energies. We also understand more of our own identity when we connect with Gaia in an intimate manner through circle casting and grounding, sacred formations and geometric proportions.

Partnership with the Divine

The second process which creates the opportunity for transcendence is in the partnership held between the priest, priestess and the God and Goddess called for the ritual. Our personal history determines how this happens. In my case, I have the experience with Kwan Yin which opens my heart to the Divine presence any time I think of it. There are other trance experiences which increased the identity connections with the Divine and my various bodies (physical, emotional, mental and spiritual). Having a spirit lover in Manannan Mac Llyr is one of them. Having a shamanic guide walk into my body and remain with me for several weeks of dual consciousness is another. In Merlin's case, a lifetime acquaintance and partnership with Queen Mab and the forest where he walks as the Greenman carries the Divine presence. He need not conjure this awareness. It is there without thought.

In ritual it is up to us to remember our experiences with the Divine and work within their coaching. Our working, although scripted, turns into channeling at various points in the ritual. We have done that so often the transition is seamless. I am often teased because what the program script says and what I say or do are often two different things. Taking the teasing in good humor, I explain a good ritual is full of surprises. In fact the written program is only an outline to keep the ritual on track. It is open to improvisation and revision without notice, because the Gods and Goddesses are in the house. I remember during a drawing down the moon ceremony where the Goddess selected several women to join me around the cauldron to speak the moon wisdom. The moon was drawn into each one. We spontaneously started to circle the cauldron and then put our hands over it, one on top of the other to create the Witches' mill. No one planned that. Some of the women did not even know what it was. Someone else's hand went out first and the others joined it without a word because someone inside of them remembered and understood.

Merlin uses the power of the transformative circle to weave protection around the group as the Man in Black. He monitors the physical casting of the circle to maintain its integrity. He watches the celebrants to make sure they are working within their own abilities. He oversees the grounding at several points within the workings. He speaks for or by the God. He is the measurer of ethical workings, knowing when a thing should not be done, when a spell is manipulative, when raising a power is ill-timed. Spiritual ecstasy is tethered to the earth through the priest. He holds us to our commitment to do no harm. Although he holds these abilities in ordinary consciousness and uses them all the time, his insight is enhanced in ritual space by the Divine connection and invocation.

Inner Senses at Work in the Priest and Priestess

The third process which makes ecstatic transport in ritual space possible is the use of our inner senses. The priestess and priest who enhance transcendence in ritual have opened their inner senses in ordinary consciousness. These senses are part of their thinking all the time, or nearly so. The Inner Senses are described in Chapter 19 of Jane Roberts' book *The Seth Material*.[131] When I teach, I frequently describe them differently within my own experience.

The first of these is an *empathetic connection* with the physical world around us, both human and non-human. Seth calls this *Inner Vibrational Touch*. In our heart center, we contact, touch and have empathy for trees, rocks, flowers, animals, reptiles, birds and yes, even humans. We feel the warmth of the rock in the sun as the rock feels it, as the snake lying on the rock feels it, as the child leaning on the rock staring at the snake feels it. We know what the tree is feeling, what the axe or chain saw is feeling, and the logger as well; all without judgment or fear because we know and see all facets of the diamond. I challenge students to apply this inner sense of deep empathetic connection to one of the current wars or places of violence and unrest in the world. I ask them how many different viewpoints can they feel? How many can they feel without judgment? What does that do to their politics? Claiming to love nature and all humanity is one thing. Doing it is another.

The second inner sense is *Pagan Standard Time* or what Seth calls *Psychological Time*. Neither he nor I name this as chronic lateness. Rather, we understand that time is flexible, that it stretches to accommodate the event and contracts in order to leap ahead when it needs to. Psychological Time is journey time, time as we experience it in a regression, a meditation or a journey to other worlds under the drum. If we are comfortable in this dream time, and learn to use it in ordinary reality, we begin to experience the illusion as illusion, first hand. I ask my students to explain how they experience time. When have they been aware of changing or bending time? When have they stepped out of time? How do those experiences impact on our concept of age? Those are questions worth journaling about.

Another inner sense is that of a *shapeshifting vision of our identity,* which combines several of Seth's listed inner senses. Shapeshifting our identity relates to my Kwan Yin vision. The experience of shapeshifting and contact with the Gods along our soul lineage of incarnations, ancestors and spirit guides creates in the priest and priestess a concept identity. A concept identity is an ideal essential being beyond our human limits. We freely perceive the physical experience of the microscopic self or macrocosmic self, i.e. those concepts outside our illusion of time and space which we can experience in our awareness but usually avoid because they are too confusing. Shamanic shapeshifting is one aspect of this, but there is more than animal/human/plant shifting. There are spirits too. I ask my students when do they become the Other? What enhances their abilities to do that? What interferes? Does this experience extend to friends and family and foes, that the student is the Other and the Other is the student?

The next inner sense, *full empathetic merger with the Other,* combines empathy, fluid time and shapeshifting. Because we know we are all of the same essence, we dare extend our consciousness to merge with the essence of others. We see through their eyes and hear through their ears. This merger is not a head trip where we imagine such a thing. It is full being in each other akin to astral sex. Seth explains: 'All entities in one way or another are enclosed within themselves, yet also connected to others. Using this sense you penetrate through the capsule that encloses the self.'[132] To test their ability I ask students to look deeply into the eyes of their classmates and exchange that selfless/self-affirming connection. Then we ask what helps and what hinders the connection? On the mad-sad-glad-scared feelings scale, which is predominant?

Another inner sense leads us to a *transcendent reality check,* which is a great help in holding the energy for a transcendent circle. The unenlightened world thinks making a reality check is a limiting experience that brings flighty or unstable people down to earth. I challenge anyone interested in transcendent spirituality to know that from earth we can move out of our conventional limitations. Our reality is bigger than this world and this dimension. I mean something entirely different than the common wisdom when I say 'get real.' When we allow our innate knowledge of spiritual non-ordinary reality (universal reality outside of our earth-illusion) to surface in our consciousness we can easily grasp why the universe is a safe place. We know how to open the soul to all experience in an expansive breath. We live through love in cosmic ecstasy. When we become aware of universal reality, those are not just pretty words. They are shared experience among us all in ritual space and possibly outside it. We all have that innate knowledge. Without it we could not construct our illusion which Seth calls a *camouflage system*. I ask my students to explain how ordinary reality might be considered camouflage? What is the secret behind the camouflage? What are they hiding from?

In her spiritual evolution, Jane Roberts experienced the microcosm and macrocosm in a surprising and, for her, frightening trance experience. I have whimsically named this inner sense *The Incredible Shrinking Woman and Man*. This inner sense involves being able to expand or contract our bodies to enter other realities. Not all dimensions are of this size and shape. Crossing dimensional realities may mean becoming very small or gigantic. Shamanic journeys can give us experience in these kinds of dimensional shifts. The less we are married to our bodies and their current appearance, the easier this skill is.

When I was a child eating peanut butter and jelly on my toast, I used to pretend that eating on one side made me very tiny and eating on the other side made me very large, like Alice in Wonderland. The lumps of jelly and crunchy peanut butter bits were like unknown power spots that would send me in either direction, but I would not know which was which until I bit them. The challenge of course was to balance them and come out the right size when I was done. I encourage students to try that with toast or rocky road ice cream or some other food with varied texture. Over time it became more than a fantasy. The exercise enhanced my ability to work in trance and journey between the worlds.

Having the ability to move between large and small while eating our morning toast helps with the next inner sense: *Disentanglement from the Camouflage System*. We step out of the illusion. Even though we know there is a basic reality that differs from the earth plane we still may not easily separate our experience here from the common reality of the universe. We need to know what is illusion and what is infinite without losing the ability to function in the physical universe. Grounding and balance are crucial to keep our heads on straight. There are folks who circle with us who are afraid to enter into deep meditation because of a fear of becoming delusional. Seth would say working only in ordinary reality is delusional, but even Jane Roberts questioned her sanity and held back from the full entrance into what could have been a healing that saved her life. I ask my students how they know how far to go in disconnecting from the camouflage. What is real in their lives on each auric level (physical, emotional, mental and spiritual)?

As a priest or priestess creating a circle in which transcendence is possible we need to consciously change the cellular vibrations of body and soul, which is the next inner sense. I enter the ritual space to call the Guardians of the Watchtowers before the ritual begins. I then sit there and sing until the cellular shift occurs. Drumming, rattling, playing the Tibetan bowls, didgeridoo or rainstick are other options.

When we enter dreams, shamanic worlds or meditative dimensions we do so by changing our vibrational rate with our personal song, the song that holds the body in shape. Seth refers to this as *becoming conscious air.*[133] Whether that is illustrative or literal I do not know. Chanting and toning, or singing will shift the vibrational field of the body. Reiki symbols also do that. In one of our classes Ravija, prior to receiving her first Reiki attunement, felt physically irritated by Tibetan singing bowls. After the attunement, she could resonate with them and enjoy the peaceful sense and sound they promote. Drumming, either the repetitive sound of the shamanic drum or the dance rhythms of a drum circle, also alter our vibrations. We sometimes call that shifting our consciousness but it is the same thing. We open our physical reality to other realities.

I ask students what other realities they regularly inhabit. Where would they like to journey and explore? Then we construct a means to take them there using sound. This process is easier if they have already found their personal power song, as we discussed in Chapter 9. That process is typical of core shamanism, but not well known in Wiccan practice. People who have trouble shifting their physical entity into ritual mind and body are sent out into nature to sing until the personal power song comes to them. Then they are ready to move into other realities.

The final inner sense which I think might be helpful for us when we seek transcendent mystic experiences is that of *conscious incarnation*. Our energy personalities or *source selves* must learn how to become human and physical in order to give birth to one of our human personalities. The entrance is through the womb just as the return to the source self is through death. Our inner senses know we chose this incarnation, and the reasons for it. Bringing that to consciousness increases our sense of peace, identity, and merger with All That Is. Dr. Michael Newton's work in *Life Between Life Therapy*[134] is instructive in this remembering. For the priest and priestess interested in leading deep transformative ritual, entrance into this awareness makes the difference between intellectual knowledge and deep knowing. They truly remember who they really are if they have found the instructions for this conscious incarnation. Then they can open the circle to the spirits who lead other people to the same place. They intentionally create an environment for that karmic awareness.

Patrons and Guides of the Celebrants

The fourth process which creates the opportunity for transcendence resides in the ritual celebrants and their relationships with Spirit. Each of us has spirit guides, ancestors and deities who work with us as our patrons. In Wicca, I understand them to be Gods and Goddesses who have selected us as Kwan Yin selected me. I was minding my own business walking through a museum and there she was. We have different patrons at different times in our lives. Some of them are regional. When I visited Hawaii, Pele conducted intense lessons in my dreams which worked on my unconscious. Other than the interaction with the earth in her islands, I have no memory of what she did, other than her comment, 'It's about time you got here. We have work to do.' Our patrons are like that.

In opening the door for a transcendent experience in ritual, Merlin and I depend on the host of Gods, Goddesses, guides and spirits to create magic within the hearts and bodies of those who assemble. New people may not know this process is at work within them. The patrons work sending love, hard lessons, weaving magic around us, unknown and unrecognized until we are able to see them. We are not alone, but we think we are.

In ritual, everybody brings somebody with them. We light a candle to greet the ancestors who say they attend because ritual is like a bright light drawing them in. The Guardians recognize them and let them pass through the gates. We light candles for the God and Goddess called for that ritual, but we also know others attend to shape the experience for the mortals they shepherd through life. The spirits who serve as advisors in Earth School are present also. A ritual circle can get crowded! Those in the Web who have the ability to sense this often comment that the circle was full of spirits.

Although we do not need to ask our patrons to attend ritual, we enhance our alliance when we do. The divine patrons are not so interested in worship, although everyone enjoys adoration, as they are in bringing us into a deep relationship with them. This relationship includes roles we expect: mentor-student, parent-child.

It also includes roles that are uncomfortable: lover, friend, confident, co-creator, ally. We live amid cultures that preach the Divine is the other. To suggest intimacy and partnership smacks of blasphemy or presumption. In Paganism, such is not the case. Yes, our physical bodies are mortal, our inner senses dulled, our vision limited by our humanness. We have no proscription against growing beyond our limitations. We take nothing away from the Gods by approaching them as partners. How could we? We are only human. Except, of course, when we are divine.

I suspect some people are more comfortable with the Gods safely removed to the altar. Yet if we accept the parent-child model of our relationship, how much more intimate could we be? A child curled on a parent's lap listening to stories is a tender loving image. A youth changing oil or tires on the car under parental supervision has both edges and softness to it. The youth may not know it is time to learn car maintenance so he/she resists. The parent persists. So it is with the Gods. They are involved in our Earth School timetable. They know the curriculum. For the honor student, there is time to become the teachers and stand with the faculty. Personally I would rather hang out in the teachers' lounge than sulk in the hallways, grousing about too much homework.

Individually Designed Maithuna

What has this to do with the unspoken ritual of circle casting? The Gods and Goddesses are involved in creating the mystical experiences at levels each celebrant can embrace. These inner senses are at work and play behind the scenes. They are operative in all the experienced ritualists gathered in the circle. We cast a circle to give ourselves a psychic canvass on which to draw our creative rituals. We set wards and channel energy toward or away from our personal space. We construct buildings, sanctuaries, shelters, fire circles, groves, shrines, and nemetons to do the same. By working in ritual and peace, we change the atmosphere of our circles in a way that is tangible even when the circle has been opened. The humming remains after ritual is complete. It becomes stronger and more focused if a ritual space is used repeatedly for sacred work. A great deal of energy is raised and directed in preparation for a ritual and also during the ritual that functions behind the scenes to support transcendence and magic.

Sacred Geometry and Magic

Ronald Holt, in his article *Experiencing Sacred Geometry Without Intellectually Understanding It*[135] connects the dots of the Golden Mean Spiral to ritual transcendence by calling the Golden Mean Spiral the Door of Love. The spiral dance validates that claim for Witches. How open our hearts can be when we join hands and move in the sacred spiral, turn and look in each other's eyes as we pass one another! The spiral dance is a deep moving meditation. If we are to understand that we are beings of love, and that actions outside love distort and cut us off from who we really are, then we would do well to enter into our seasonal rituals as deep comprehensive meditative experiences. We can amplify their transformative work with daily meditation. There is so much more in heaven and earth, than is dreamt of in our culture's philosophy.

Holt is poetic in his description, which I find helpful when we study the transcendent. He writes: 'Simply put, the Golden Mean Spiral is a doorway that weaves the ethereal and material dimensions together. In another context I would say that *God left us one door of eternal mystery and exploration: the Golden Mean Spiral or the door of love…* [T]he Golden Mean Spiral is an expression of the basic energy of creation that we call love.'[136]

I believe Holt refers to the Golden Mean Spiral as a doorway because he sees it as an infinitely repeating form which crosses the dimensions from the physical into the spiritual. I understand that to be analogous to moving from ordinary reality into the upper and lower world dimensions. It is probably not always clear to those attending ritual or shamanic circles, but what we are creating (when we are successful) is a true dimensional shift, so that the answer to the question, 'What do we mean when we say we are between the worlds,' is, in part, that we moved into another dimension of reality and consciousness. The keener our experience with alternative realities, the more complete the dimensional shift.

Another aspect of sacred geometry is its mutability, that is its fluid nature of constant change. The *Kore Chant* by Z Budapest, '*She changes everything She touches, and everything She touches changes,*' is an example of intuitive understanding of how things really work. In sacred geometry, the pyramid becomes the cube, becomes the octahedron, becomes the dodecahedron... The morphing or shapeshifting from one form to another is continuous. Holt connects this constant change with the natural mandalas he says surround us at all points with invisible or auric lines of power. These natural mandalas hold strong implications for setting up crystal grids around a charged sacred object or within a sacred circle for ritual or magical purposes. We may envision a five-point crystal grid, and it begins in that shape, but the strength of the circle is such that energy echoes in multiples of five. Out of the flat pentacle star, an energetic 10-point star grid in two dimensions develops on its own, and then morphs into a solid or three dimensional dodecahedron (12-sided figure with each flat surface made of a five-sided pentagon with the pentacle inside).

If this all makes your head spin, it is supposed to. Holt states that in activating a sacred geometric form we are tuning ourselves to the harmonics of that form. These forms resonate more strongly in crystals I might add. Holt charges us to imagine 'that at every point in the body where energy is transmitted or received, living, changing, three- or four-dimensional geometric mandalas are continuously created.'[137] The forms are fluid. They evolve. This is true of the Platonic solids (pyramids, cubes etc.) and of the circle, quartered circle, pentacle, sphere and the spiral.

We can open ourselves to these energies which expand the heart and likely the other chakras with meditation on the form because of that form's dynamic nature. Crystal platonic shapes are commercially available by the set. Our classes have had some surprising insights holding those forms, moving into them and attuning to them. We have also found other energy connections through art both in meditating on and creating mandalas.

Mandalas

Holt made reference to the natural mandalas which surround us at all points. What are they? Humans and their spirit partners or star partners have marked the land and air with our sacred symbols. Petroglyphs, stone circles, earth mounds, temples, cathedrals, pyramids all seek to tie earth and sky together in sacred space. The mandalas of Buddhism are repeated over several cultures as medicine wheels, Celtic knots, pentacles, dream catchers and even in scientific diagrams of the solar system, of atoms, or the chlorophyll molecule.

The word *mandala* is a Sanskrit word meaning the best part or the *cream of the crop*. There are formal examples of intricately detailed mandalas from the east which were used as educational tools for the Buddhist monks traveling throughout Asia teaching the life and values of Buddha. These original works are referred to as *palace architecture*. They are usually two-dimensional drawing, paintings, or tapestry wall hangings. Sometimes they are models and sculptures in three dimensions, and in some cases the mandala is an entire complex of actual buildings and courtyards. The sand paintings made on the ground in such beautiful detail and then erased showing the fleeting nature of physical reality, are mandalas. The construction of a traditional mandala includes these characteristics:

The Void is represented at the center. It may be blank; it may contain the sky, a star, a Goddess or other sacred image.

The inner court surrounds the Void. This is often populated by deities who figure in the story lesson or theme of the mandala.

The outer court surrounds the inner court. This is populated by saints, mortals, demons and spirits.

There are four gates into the outer court set in the cardinal directions. Each gate is guarded by appropriate image.

Outside the palace is a cemetery. This is so that the departed souls can join in the sacred energy of the palace and of the story.

The artwork is elaborate. Spirit beings and mortals sit in ornate niches, holding symbols of their power or role. The background is minutely detailed with representatives of the myths associated with the beings, animals, plants, buildings, tools and instruments of their vocations, which help identify the place and people and tell the story. If one does not know the story, then it can be confusing without a teacher.

I think of the mandala as a story board. Each one is different, organized around a theme or a narrative. Monks carried them to tell the story of Buddha, of the bodhisattvas, of the seven Principles or the four Truths or other wisdom. The Blue Beryl is one of these.

The Blue Beryl was prepared in the 1600s at the direction of the 5th Dalai Lamma to Sangye Gyamtso who spent 20 years documenting the art of Tibetan medicine's understanding of physiology, pathology, diagnosis, and treatment in these drawings. They are complete records of anatomy, herbalism, formulas, and protocol. Each monastery which had a medical school received a full set for its students and practitioners. These doctors clearly had a fuller understanding of the body than their 17th century counterparts in Europe. They even had a depiction of the circulatory system of the fetus in utero. Teachers and healers using the mandala could educate student and patient alike.[138]

Stupas, a three dimensional model or building, were originally mandalas developed as grave markers for enlightened masters but quickly became temples or homes for the deity or patron. A Japanese pagoda is a familiar form of a stupa. Again, symbolism is chosen to represent the truths and activities associated with that divinity. Making a stupa to celebrate a personal encounter with the Gods and patrons would be a sacred journey of its own. Gothic cathedrals built around the cross-shape actually can be viewed as stupas if the grounds and landscaping complete the circle motif, or if the circle is represented in some other fashion. Several of the tapestry mandalas appear on rectangles of cloth. The circle will be within the design or around the Gods.

Journaling on Transcendence

In an effort to embrace the abstract concepts of enlightenment as a priest or priestess, design a mandala to illustrate the spirits of the quartered circle. I suggest making it practical as a storyboard to teach your children or a class of beginners. Stick figures, photos, pictures cut from magazines can replace original drawings for those who still insist they are not creative and cannot draw. The preliminary sketches for a mandala are instructive. They help the mind hold onto the truths we discussed in this book. My Wicca IV students create a final project, the mandala being one option.

A mandala could illustrate the correspondences of the four elements in the quartered circle showing colors, animals, psychic skills, human auric connections and the Elemental beings. All these might be assembled in each of the four directions, displayed in the outer court around an appropriate deity placed in the inner court. The center may be void or contain a representation of Spirit in a circle. The appropriate Guardians are placed at each entrance. They may have the form of our teachers. Members of the class or circle appear along the borders with a cemetery outside the palace to honor the ancestors. When completed our family and friends and the truth of the quartered circle appear all in one drawing. It is a profound experience to figure out how to put it all on paper, let alone to discuss it with a class.

Mandalas are understood in terms of a circle created for sacred ritual work through which we move forward toward full enlightenment. This circle is in fact the four levels of Wiccan study currently offered by the Web PATH Center. This book works with all four levels of study limited to the topics of personal identity and the quartered circle. We could draw a mandala of that too, with Wicca I in the east, Wicca II in the south, Wicca III in the west and Wicca IV in the north. Our initiations, course work, memories or meditations from each level of our investigation of self and the circle would be illustrated in the details of each direction with the Elementals or the Guardians in the center.

A related term to the mandala is yantra. Like a mandala, a yantra is a work of art with deep spiritual significance, often organized around the circle. Some teachers and many current books use the terms interchangeably, but there is a significant difference. Yantras do not usually have human or divine figures. They rely on the sacred geometry of the design itself to bring deep spiritual truths into the viewer's consciousness. Carl Jung referred to mandalas and yantras as archetypes and universal symbols. We are familiar with the archetype as the Jungian approach to understanding the Gods and Goddesses. The deities are psychological symbols for love, courage, growth, emergence or rebirth represented in human bodies.

Yantras approach the same concepts using symbols instead of spirit beings. A quartered circle represents the four directions. The Medicine Wheel represents the journey of the soul through many levels of the four directions. The pentagram represents the elements and spirit, the stages of life (birth, growth, maturity, aging and death) or any number of other progressions. The Celtic knot and the intricate drawings of the Celts are also yantras representing the wisdom animals, the wheel of the year, the renewal of life and infinity.

In Wiccan ritual we inscribe the sacred space—indoors or outdoors—with a circle. Then we set up our ritual yantras (unpopulated mandalas) as energy forms: the quartered circle as we call the Elementals, and the pentagram as we draw the five-pointed star in the cardinal directions. If we use a crystal grid we include that as a third yantra. These icons become so familiar that we lose track of their power and meaning. Consider them closely for a moment.

The Quartered Circle

The quartered circle represents the endless nature of infinity. We move around and around without interruption, experiencing the ebb and flow of light and dark, the four seasons or the phases of the moon. As one cycle ends and a new one begins. We have looked at each of these passages in detail and understood that like Ouroboros they are complete in themselves with no beginning and no ending. They represent All Being. Web Wiccan Consciousness celebrates this spiraling endless circle. We observe the sabbats and esbats both to remind ourselves of the ebb and flow and to extend our conscious merger with it. Endings and beginnings are markers on a much larger journey. This continuous flow of life explodes the story of Lamia into another truth. Her fall from beauty and goodness, her shapeshifiting to serpent and her restoration by Thoth reflect a larger truth to us. Wait. We, like the old man and his horse, recognize we do not know the whole story. There is always more to any truth. Dividing the circle in half and quarters provides us with benchmarks on the way around the perimeter. The radii draw us into the center where we confront ourselves. Then we go out again and circle the edges of consciousness anew.

Journaling on the Quartered Circle as a Yantra

In your BOS, draw the quartered circle in any way you wish as long as it is uniquely yours. Use color, symbols, images, pictures to re-create your circle. Sit in stillness with your drawing until you know something new. Be at rest and focus on the image. Still the mind. We are not reasoning our way around the circle. We are waiting for revelation. Questioning your choices or criticizing your drawing will get you nowhere. Wait in stillness. When revelation arrives, sit with it until it leaves of its own accord. Then make notes in you BOS.

Meditation: Making a Stone Circle

Now take those revelations and re-create them in physical space with the stones you gathered in Chapter 4. Bring your basket of rocks to your altar, either indoors or out. Ground, center and create sacred space. Renew your connection with each rock. Tell the rock spirits you wish to create a quartered circle with them to strengthen your partnership. You hope to better understand who you are, where you came from and where you are going. Then lay out the rocks in a circle with one in the center. If you have enough stones, add rays from the center to the four directions. Be aware of why the east stone is in the east, west stone in the west all the way around the circle. Each has joined your consciousness to help choose their placement. Read the stones. What are their symbols and messages? Sit with this information as you ask them: *Who am I? Why am I here? Where did I come from? Where am I going?*

When you are finished, thank the rocks. Decide together if the rocks can stay where they are or go where they should be. Then return to ordinary consciousness. Ground. Give thanks again. Honor the process by remembering it.

The Pentagram

When we cast a circle and call the directions, we draw a five-pointed star in a circle in each quarter which is, as we said, a yantra. This pentagram represents an even more complex set of inter relationships than the quartered circle. As before, the circle retains its connotation of endless unified energy of beginnings and endings merging into new beginnings. The five-pointed star has layers of meaning. A survey of the writings by Starhawk, Vivienne Crowley, or the Farrars quickly supports how varied the designations can be. For the Web there is only the process of discovery, the journey into silence as one becomes the pentagram and learns the designations one's own mind/body/spirit connection understands. This experience is the embodiment of the pentagram and it is individual.

Journaling on the Pentagram as a Yantra

In your BOS, draw the five-pointed star in a circle in any way you wish as long as it is uniquely yours. Use color, symbols, images, pictures to re-create your pentagram. Sit in stillness with your drawing until you know something new. Be at rest and focus on the image. Still the mind. We are not reasoning our way around the pentagram or its five points. We are waiting for revelation. Questioning your choices or criticizing your drawing will get you nowhere. Wait in stillness. When revelation arrives, sit with it until it leaves of its own accord. Then make notes in you BOS.

Meditation: Become the Pentagram

An alternative exploration of the pentagram gives you an opportunity to merge with the yantra.

Instead of focusing on your drawing, find a quiet place to lie down and become the pentagram. Stretch your arms and legs out like the Vitruvian Man so that you look like a five-pointed star. Imagine a circle of light drawn deosil around the points of the star represented by your head, hands and feet. Trace the outline of the star with your mind, starting with your right foot moving up to your left hand (the most common) or from your head down to your left foot. There are other variations used in drawing an invoking pentacle. People have generated more heat than light in debating them.

Retrace the pentacle over your body multiple times until its beginning and ending are unclear to you. The energy flows seamlessly from point to point over and through your body. Then rest in the symbol as your awareness understands you are the pentagram.

When you are ready, focus on each point of your pentagram (head, hands and feet) and let them name themselves. This is not an intellectual exercise. Your brain does not need to supply names. They will rise up out of you whole and complete. As you lie there in this altered state, learn the names and their meanings. This meditation is about you and your identity. Remember it. When the revelation ends, return to ordinary reality slowly.

> Release the pentagram by tracing it over your body backward from the way you drew it. Retrace it as many times as needed until the energy wanes and fades. Open the circle inscribed around the outside by spiraling it widdershins several times. When the circle and the pentagram have left, sit up carefully and ground. Then make notes. Drink water. Keep this revelation to yourself. It is part of who you really are.

In setting up ritual space, we embody the changing light and dark of transcendence as the facilitating ritualists. We understand that wounds and healing, dumps and majestic mountains all reflect the power of being. There is no sacred place without the profane. Neither are rejected by All That Is. That is true of our souls. They are sacred and profane. That is true of our Gods. They are loving; they are frightening. We all embody good and evil and are sacred. The light and the dark create us. We create them. We can do so in peace. We can do so in love. We can do so and harm none. When we understand this truth and extend it to those gathered in ritual space we create the unspoken ritual of the quartered circle.

Chapter 22

The Web Sigil: A Yantra of Identity

The sigil of the Web PATH Center and of my spiritual work as Anemone Webweaver is an eight-armed spider web with three rounds of webbing looped about the arms and a void in the middle. The significance of this double quartered circle in triplicate teaches us all the lessons about Web Wiccan Consciousness contained in this book. It also answers the big four questions:

Who am I?
Why am I here?
Where did I come from?
Where am I going?

What is a Sigil?

In chaos magic, a sigil is usually understood to be crafted by the magician and used in calling up spirits related to the sigil. It is a tool used in holding power over a spiritual entity one fears, or is at least a little nervous about. By now you know I have a different understanding of wielding power and working with spirits.

I understand a sigil to be a sacred symbol—perhaps one which combines runes, letters or other glyphs—to blend the energy and meaning of those symbols into a powerful intuitive yantra. The power works on the observer. It transforms those who make commitments to practice ritual and magic under its aegis. It represents the spirits who share common goals with those people. We see the sigil; we think of the spirits. They think of us.

The eight-armed spider web divides a circle into the four quarters as any ritual circle might. The second division into eight segments corresponds to the eight sabbats: four solar holidays made of the equinoxes and solstices and four cross quarter days. It also corresponds to eight moon phases with the ninth phase of the dark moon residing in the center void. All the correspondences of day and night, seasons of the year and phases of the moon fit within its sacred space. In the three levels of webbing around the arms of the circle are the maiden-mother-crone designations, the past-present-future blending of time and the above-below-center dimensions of the world tree. These world tree correspondences can also be understood as the shamanic realms of lower world, middle world and upper world. We teach Pagan ethics using three of the axioms commonly shared among Pagans:

An it harm none do what you will.
The Rule of Three: What we send out comes back multiplied.
The Thelemic Law: Love is the whole of the law; love under will.

The triple webbing also represents the light, and the dark and the shadow. The triune blending of opposites finds representation in this web: two opposing forces and the wisdom that unites them. Our Web community is dedicated to finding that reunion between supposed opposites. We are an open teaching circle that includes men and women in partnership to support an inclusive sharing of power and process. We include adults and children, which supports a consciousness of storytelling as education. We seek common ground and power in our differences so that a third thing emerges, one which is balanced and at peace.

In entering the Web sigil as a yantra we enter Web Wiccan Consciousness. We discover wisdom about our identity; we find a snapshot of who we are and what we weave into our realities. Each time we play with the Web sigil we find the picture has changed and we have grown. In your journal, draw an eight-armed web with three rings of webbing and a void in the center. The outer ring of webbing connects the eight arms of the web at their points. The other two levels are evenly spaced inside the web. The third is the innermost and defines that empty space in the middle.

Drawing the Web Sigil

Most likely you will have to erase the crossing point of the eight arms inside that center. Most of us draw the web and forget to leave the middle blank. Make your web large enough to write on each line and segment of webbing. You may have to sketch several versions until you have enough space to write on and an empty spot in the center. The process of self-discovery is messy. Be prepared to scratch out ideas and re-write them. Let the first and second versions of your web be worksheets. When you get to the end of the process you can create a neat self-study and put it in your BOS. Date that entry. Five years from now your web will look very different. That is as it should be. You are perfect where you are now and you will be perfect then too.

Once you have an eight-armed spider web connected by three rings of webbing with a void in the middle, place an N at the top point for north. On the other three parts of those cardinal quarters place E, S and W. The main equal-armed cross will represent the four directions.

On the line that runs from the north point to the center, write BODY. On the line that runs from the east to the center, write INTELLECT. On the line that runs from the south point to the center write WILL. On the line that runs from the west to the center write EMOTION. This is not new material. We have learned to look at ourselves in connection with the four directions as beings with a physical body, an intellectual brain, a will which combines our intelligence and feelings, and a heart full of emotions. Our spirit is in the center void. This sigil represents who we are.

Now consider the cross quarter arms of the web, the other four rays that extend from the outside of the web to the center. These are spaced evenly in between the first four. Starting in what would be the northeast section, write RECREATION on one side of the arm and HEALTH on the other side of the same arm. Our recreation and health are two of the ways we combine our body-mind, the physical and intellectual aspects of ourselves. This is the combination of north and east and of earth and air on our sigil. People who perform heavy physical labor like construction, carpentry, ditch digging and gardening might also place WORK next to RECREATION.

Moving to the southeast arm located between INTELLECT and WILL, write EDUCATION on one side and PRODUCTIVITY on the other side. Our education, formal or not, and what we produce with our work and attention are ways we combine our minds and will. This is the combination of east and south and of air and fire on our sigil. People who earn their living with their minds might also place CAREER or WORK next to PRODUCTIVITY.

Moving to the southwest arm located between WILL and EMOTIONS write CREATION on one side and MAGIC or SPIRITUALITY on the other. I specifically avoid using the word RELIGION because it lacks the dynamic and independent nature of a person's spiritual path. Obviously anyone working with this sigil on personal identity is free to change it as it suits them. Otherwise it would not be personal identity. I find our creativity, magic and spirituality are the avenues of connection between our will and emotions. This is the combination of south and west and of fire and water.

Moving to the northwest arm located between EMOTIONS and BODY write the words PROCREATION and FAMILY on one side and LOVE on the other. This is the combination of west and north and of water and earth. Friends may also belong on this line, or if the emotional-physical connection is too intimate to describe our key friendships, we may place them where they best fit. Some friends connect with us over our recreational activities. Others are school chums. Others are partners in ritual and magic. You may include them on these arms or on the connectors weaving between the arms as described below.

When you are satisfied you have set up a framework for your own activities and characteristics sit with it as a sigil and observe it. Be grounded as you engage in this observation. What does the sigil teach you? Jot down any ideas that arise. If you are usually afraid of spiders and find the spider web uncomfortable, write about that.

How do the opposite sides of the web mirror you? Is there an insight in considering the body and the will on the same continuum in your life? Is there wisdom in seeing intellect and emotions on the same continuum? Does your physical labor reflect something interesting about your spirituality or magic? Is it creative? Make notes. Then simply sit with the sigil as a yantra when you have finished thinking about it. Let it absorb into your unconscious and make suggestions to your awareness as the quartered circle and pentagram did in the previous chapter.

Making the Sigil about You

When you are ready to proceed, make a long list of things you do in a day or roles you fill. Keep it simple. Say you are a writer instead of describing what you write. Fewer words are better. Make a list of characteristics you have, particularly in relationship to your activities. Include the lights and shadows.

For example, if you attend classes at the local university then you are a student. You describe yourself as committed because you are going to finish that degree no matter what. You might also admit you are smart because you are doing well in academics. Praising your abilities and accomplishments is an important part of this process. However, you might also recognize you miss a lot of social events because you have to study and write papers so you would also describe yourself as isolated or perhaps lonely.

Identifying characteristics and feelings which are true but might become stumbling blocks is also important. Do this for every regular activity you have and every role you fill on a regular basis. Each activity should have one or more positive characteristics of yours which helps you in that activity. It should also have challenges which on any given day could throw you off track. In the example above, being isolated and lonely might undermine a student's resolve to get an A on the next test. Instead of studying, the student hangs out at the corner bar the night before, enjoying friends and companionship.

Once we have completed those lists we are ready to figure out where they go on the web. In making decisions, use index cards to sort your list into the proper segments before you write anything on the web. Put one descriptive word on each card and then match them up. In class we lay out a huge web on the floor with yoga straps and yarn. Then we set cards with labels on the appropriate rings and in a segment that makes sense.

As you work through this self-study, your insight will get clearer and change. Originally I assumed yoga was a recreation-intellect connection. After looking more closely I realized my daily yoga stretches connect productivity and the will. I understand productivity to be allied to self-discipline and goal achievement. There are many days when I do not want to bother with yoga stretches, and some days when I skip them. Even though one might think yoga connects the mind and body, for me the exercise of the will and self-discipline is even more important. My productivity and will connection is yoga. My supporting characteristic is commitment. My stumbling block is procrastination. On days I skip my stretches, I always tell myself I will do them later in the day and I never do.

Think carefully about how you connect health and work with the body and mind; productivity and career with the mind and will; creativity, the arts and ritual with the will and heart; and love, family and relationships with the heart and body. Find those activities on your list. Add to your list if you forgot something. If the cross quarter arms need different labels to make sense of your own activities and beliefs, change them. Here are suggestions if you feel stuck but they are not true for everyone.

North: Body/Earth
Physical health
Body image
Appearance

Northeast: Body and Mind connection
Labor: Housework
Recreation: Workouts in the gym
Medical healing: Reiki

East: Mind/Air
Intellect/Mental work
Intuition/Vision
Philosophy

Southeast: Mind and Will connection
Education: Reading/Study
Career: Teaching, Counseling etc.
Self-discipline: Tai Chi, List making

South: Will/Fire
Decisiveness
Focus/Magic
Spirituality

Southwest: Will and Emotion connection
Creation: Community organization, Politics
The Arts: Writing, Music performance
Ritual: Full moon celebrations

West: Emotions/Water
Feelings
Balance
Crisis resolution

Northwest: Emotion and Body connection
Relationships: Friends and dating
Sexuality: Partnership or marriage, Family
Procreation: Parenting, Nurturing

When you think you have collected your activities and characteristics into the groups which reflect your personality around the circle, begin to fill in the loops that connect the web's arms with the names of things you do, qualities you have and helps or hindrances to your transformation in each area. Notice the three levels. Here is how they work:

Outer Ring: List the things you do/are, i.e. teacher, magician, singer, lover, each in the segment which makes the most sense to you. Physical education teachers may place 'teacher' on the line connecting recreation and intellect in the northeast segment. Philosophy teachers may place 'teacher' on the line connecting career and will in the southeast section or on the line connecting will and spirituality in the southwest segment. Music teachers who are passionate about their career may place it on the southwest segment. Occupational therapists who teach daily living skills to people they hold in deep compassion may place it in the northwest between emotion and body. The 'right' answer is the one which fits you.

Middle Ring: Underneath each of the words you placed on the outer ring, list descriptive words for qualities you have, i.e. empathetic, wise, dedicated. These qualities support you in your activity. A physical education teacher might list healthy and strong in the middle ring under teacher. A philosophy teacher might list logical and insightful. Our music teacher might list talented and passionate. The occupational therapist might list compassionate and patient.

Inner Ring: Underneath each of the descriptive words you used to explain your strengths, list the other words which revealed challenges. You may be in the process of transforming those qualities. You may experience them as blocks. You may feel stuck with those qualities. A physical education teacher might find chronic fatigue and asthma are stumbling blocks. A philosophy teacher may find impatience with disinterested students is a challenge. The music teacher may find arthritic fingers a challenge. The occupational therapist may find report writing and documentation difficult.

The challenge can be physical, mental, emotional or in a lack of will or decisiveness. What the challenge is reveals something about where the activity is located on the web. That location reveals what this challenge means in your soul's education. We learn far more from things which are challenging than from those which come easy. If you feel stuck in identifying one area or another, ask yourself what keeps you from seeing into the first and second levels of your self? That should uncover your personal road block on the third level, i.e. a teacher who is dedicated may also be disorganized. Many times we simply do not want to know our shadow selves. One option is to leave those areas blank until they reveal themselves. Areas which are not filled in are as important as those which are.

Looking for Connections

When you have worked all around the web you will be able to look at the arms of the web and see where being disorganized connects both to the right and left, and across the circle. Sometimes that placement gives you a clue about why you are disorganized. The dedicated teacher on the east side of the web may be balancing the overwhelmed parent described across in the west side of family emotions and procreation. The disorganization comes from the tension between home and job. Dig deeper in the relationship area. The overwhelmed parent may be masking a dysfunctional family—past or present. To transform the disorganization, the sense of being overwhelmed can be resolved by healing the pain stemming from the wounded family relationship. Healed wounds free up energy. The teacher may have exactly the same responsibilities as before, but has more energy at play to meet the responsibilities. I make that sound easy. Of course it is not. It is, however, possible.

Students often need to do this exercise many times to get through the third ring in a revealing way. Many people have difficulty simply identifying what to put on the arms of the web, let alone on the webbing. Typically some aspect of the self around the circle will be difficult to connect to the others. The body-mind connection is obscure for many who live in their heads instead of their bodies. The emotional-physical connection may be difficult for people who deny their feelings. Have fun with these possibilities. Laugh at yourself. Remember, learning about who you are moves you closer to the center. In the web sigil, that is the void where the total YOU sits.

After a few days, return to the web you completed. Study it for connections. Talk to people you can trust about what you think it means. Meditate on the areas that are blank or unclear. Humans are complex. We are humans doing, humans thinking, humans deciding, and humans feeling. We rarely graduate to humans being. Friends, family, jobs, schools all reward successful action and outcomes. They may fail to honor our skill in sitting. Being present with our selves and our souls at the center of things is undervalued. Presence is difficult to maintain. For that reason alone, being present with one another and the self should be applauded.

In the silence of our inquiry about *Who am I?* one student took the name *I Am*! That is exactly the point. We are. You are. I am.

Our webs may reveal specific parts of us that need healing. Blank areas connected to the mind and emotions may be filled with shadows that can benefit from counseling. The inability to identify our feelings even when we meditate on them may indicate pain or crisis we have put away for another time. This is that other time. Figure it out and find help.

Empty areas in the physical section may hide physical and medical issues we have denied. Chronic conditions deserve healing. Pain is the body's request for treatment. Healing combines all the pieces of our selves as much or more than surgery and pharmaceuticals. Physical healing is an opportunity to understand our connections across the web to find the causes of symptoms and dis-ease.

Recurring negative thoughts, obsessions, bias, prejudice, memory loss, and confusion can be related to brain chemistry. They can be symptomatic of physical ills related to blood sugar, blood pressure and some dis-eases. They also can be rooted in self-recrimination and guilt or childhood abuse and tattered boundaries. People who use drugs and alcohol to self-medicate because of personal pain and addiction cannot complete this exercise without showing those tatters. People who have mental or emotional side effects from prescription drugs given for their medical conditions may see the side effects clarified by this process. If the picture that emerges on someone's web is alarming in any way, I encourage students to take those concerns to the appropriate professional. Being wounded is okay. It is part of our perfection now. Being healed is okay too. It is part of our perfection for tomorrow.

However, western medicine is an art as much as it is a science. Our illnesses and disabilities are imperfectly understood as bio-mechanical conditions. They are that. They are also dysfunctions of the emotional body, mental body, the magical body and spiritual body. Combining alternative healing with western medicine can clear up stubborn conditions. In chronic illnesses, the soul gains great wisdom about how it has expressed itself in this and other incarnations when it understands its medical condition. We can never afford to arrive at the medical doctor's office expecting to be fixed. We are participants in our healing.

Soul Fragmentation and Retrieval

Sometimes our quest for identity leads us to the conclusion that our souls have been fragmented. In shamanic practice we understand souls shatter in grief. Pieces chip off in crisis, anger or fear. Those soul fragments live truncated lives in the lower world where they escaped to survive. They often live out a timeless existence at the age of their departure. Our blind spots or blanks around the web may reveal pieces of ourselves that are missing because of this fragmentation.

Whether or not we consider this description a metaphor for

distancing ourselves from the past when we lost control of our lives or a literal description of our multiple probable selves is immaterial. The challenge is to reunite our selves as healthy, complete souls living in harmony in our many bodies. A first step in this healing can be to invite the soul fragments to come home.

To create a homecoming, we set up a ritual or meditation with grounding, sacred space, music, the Elementals and Guardians. We invite the ancestors and guides to help. Then we open our chakras and call our names starting with the name we had at birth, our nicknames, middle names, surnames, names associated with teasing and ridicule, magical names, professional names, married names, pet names, and secret names. Some names we will have forgotten but they come back to mind. We imagine each of those names attached to a part of us. They come to the circle through one of the four gates, admitted by the Guardians. We talk to them to learn where they have been and why. We invite them back inside of us. Soul fragments will return if they are ready. The memories connected to their departure will surface. Those recollections can be difficult. This is an exercise in remembering and re-membering.

In this ritual we are putting ourselves back together. When we are as complete as we can be in one session, we ground again. We release any parts of our soul who desire freedom or refuse to reunite. We can try again when we are in a place they can embrace. Then we release the ancestors and guides as we thank them for their help. We open the sacred space and return to ordinary reality.

As we review our work we journal about the process. We include the consciousness of the reunited parts of ourselves in that record. We make plans to integrate those memories and pieces of ourselves by taking them through our daily routine, looking at our activities from their point of view. If a teenage fragment has rejoined us, driving to work may be a new thrill. Our joy in driving a car has come back. We play the radio loud and sing along with the music. We beat time on the steering wheel. We also set cruise control within the speed limit with our adult selves and watch the mirrors carefully.

This is a new partnership of the self. It needs to be grounded and wise.

For soul fragments resisting our contact and who have hidden themselves away in the lower world, shamanic soul retrieval by a trained professional remains an option. The shamanic worker can teach us about the process, explain why a soul fragment might resist contact, and negotiate with that fragment for its return. The shamanic worker will also connect us with specific animal allies to assist with the reunion. Not everyone who practices shamanic journeys is trained or skilled in soul retrieval. There is no licensing, nor should there be, but one must choose carefully. The shamanic worker should first journey to his or her own guides for permission to do this work in connection with our animals. Their cooperation should not be taken for granted. These allies take the shamanic worker on the journey and perform most of the hard work associated with a soul retrieval. The shamanic worker will credit them and keep his or her own ego in check.

The soul fragments who refuse to return may require us to make changes in our lives. We should look at this dispassionately and decide what can be done. A fragment who split off because we were in a violent relationship will not agree to return to battering. A fragment who left because of substance abuse will not return to live in the midst of addictions. A fragment who left because of a dangerous work environment which exposes workers to unventilated chemicals or poorly maintained equipment is unlikely to return to risk life and limb. When we become aware that our soul fragments may have more clearly drawn boundaries than we do, the challenge to make changes in our lives is clear. We are souls connected to infinite love and wisdom. What are we doing in situations like that? Yet some of us are stuck there. When this realization arrives in our consciousness it is time to act. The shamanic worker may be able to help sort through the complications of changing our lives. If not, we need allies who can.

A word to the wise—I am wary of people who are not from tribal communities yet use the word 'shaman' to describe themselves. I use the words shamanic worker or shamanic practitioner rather than claiming to be a shaman, which I am not. I shy away from people who charge excessively and have no sliding scale for people of limited financial means. Soul retrieval is what I understand to be a spiritual gift. Celebrating a shamanic healing is service. Churches take offerings but they do not charge fees. Some people look at soul retrieval as a shamanic healing more akin to medical treatment. Doctors charge fees though many of them work on a secret sliding scale. I also rely on my inner bell to tell me if I am dealing with the right person for my healing. Someone may be an ethical, skilled and trained shamanic worker, but not the right person to journey for me.

We always need to be smart in our choices.

The Circle is Completed

The web sigil, the quartered circle and the pentagram all explore our connections with the self, the Elementals, the Guardians, the ancestors and the deities. Their interplay is constantly changing. Change is the truth found at the conclusion of our journey to discover our identity within the quartered circle. Or is it the beginning of our journey? Both the beginning and the conclusion are the same in Web Wiccan Consciousness. This is Ouroboros. We are souls attending Earth School to continue our personal evolution as magical spirit beings. We are not the same as we were when we first set our consciousness in this direction. We are not the same as we will be if we return to our notes and meditations to read through them again.

I remind students they are perfect where they are at that moment and they will be perfect later when they finally draw a completed web. Perfection is a process. Rather than criticize ourselves for our failings, we need to recognize we learn from the tough stuff. That challenge is part of the process. Instead of hiding our weaknesses, we need to reveal them. We can heal from our pain. We can change our skewed beliefs. We can re-value ourselves. Our wisdom about our self and our soul is constantly changing. We are on a dynamic, exciting path. Life is an adventure. You come too.

Endnotes

1 Erik Erikson, *Identity and the Life Cycle,* New York: W.W. Norton & Company, Inc., 1980.

2 Carl Gustav Jung, *Man and His Symbols,* New York; Doubleday and Company, Inc., 1964.

3 Abraham Maslow, 'A Theory of Human Motivation' *Psychological Review* (1943) reprinted in *Twentieth Century Psychology* ed. P. Harriman, New York: Philosophical Library, 1946; and *Toward a Psychology of Being,* Princeton, NJ: Van Nostrand Co., 2nd edition 1968.

4 Starhawk, *Truth or Dare: Encounters with Power, Authority, and Mystery,* New York: HarperOne, 1989.

5 Starhawk, *The Spiral Dance,* Harper Collins Publishers, 1979 re-printed with new end notes at 10-year anniversaries.

6 'When DNA Is Not Destiny', Sharon Begley, *Newsweek,* December 1, 2008, vol. CLII No. 22, p. 14.

7 David Keirsey and Marilyn Bates, *Please Understand Me* and *Please Understand Me II,* Prometheus Nemesis Book Company 1984 and 1998.

8 John G. Neihardt , *Black Elk Speaks: Being the Life Story of a Holy Man of the Oglala Sioux,* University of Nebraska Press, Lincoln and London, 1979, p. 155.

9 Jeremy Narby, *The Cosmic Serpent: DNA and the Origins of Knowledge,* New York NY: Jeremy P. Tarcher/Putnam, 1999.

10 Andrew Collins, *The Gods of Eden—Egypt's Lost Legacy and the Genesis of Civilization,* Rochester, VT: Bear and Co., 1999 and *From the Ashes of Angels—The Forbidden Legacy of a Fallen Race,* Rochester, VT: Bear and Co., 1998.

11 Ken Carey, *Return of the Bird Tribes,* NY NY: HarperOne. 1991.

12 Judy Chicago, *The Dinner Party,* NY: Penguin, rev. 1996.

13 Patricia Monaghan, *The Goddess Path: Myths, Invocations and Rituals,* Woodbury: MN: Llewellyn, 1999.

14 John William Waterhouse (1849-1917), Pre-Raphaelite artist,

painted two versions of the subject: *Lamia and the Soldier* 1905 and *Lamia* 1909. Both are of the same model in a pink dress with scale-like designs in the fabric. Both have a long snake skin draped around or across the model's lap. The first depicts a medieval knight in armor. The second shows Lamia alone. Waterhouse is interesting in the Pagan world because of his mythic subjects including *The Magic Circle* (1886) showing a dark headed woman before a cauldron with a sword raising power.

15 Starhawk, *The Spiral Dance*, NY NY: HarperOne, p. 62

16 Starhawk, *The Spiral Dance*, NY NY: HarperOne, p. 115

17 Genesis 3:22-24 KJV.

18 Theosophists are most commonly identified with Madam Blavatsky (1831-1891) and the beliefs of the Theosophical Society she co-founded with HS Olcott and WQ Judge. There is also a Theosophist tradition dating back through the Renaissance and Middle Ages. Prior to that theosophy was a synonym for theology. In the esoteric sense, Theosophists connect deity, nature and humanity in an interlocked triangle of being. This triangle reflects the spirit world as it interfaces with ordinary reality. Direct communication with both the Divine and Nature are desired human goals. Blavatsky indicated there was an ultimate reality behind our myths and beliefs. She taught that reality could be understood through occult science which she described as a preserved and ancient knowledge passed to selected individuals through the ages. She has been criticized for her racial and ethnic biases about those individuals, anti-Semitism and failure to cite her sources from her wide reading of history and philosophy.

19 Gnostics refer to the early Christian sects which were decidedly dualistic, pitting the positive and negative aspects of God against one another in an eternal dual for the world. The dark is evil and material. The light is good and immaterial or spiritual. Thus this world is rejected in favor of the spirit. They

tend to be ascetic, leading lives of fasting, celibacy and poverty. However, their critics claimed they were wildly sensual, recognizing no superior church authority and thus prone to sin and error, including sexual practices in their religious services. Aeon, Archon and Abraxas take on divine or semi-divine status under Gnosticism, as do many other spirit beings emanating from the One Source. Our understanding of Gnosticism was extended by the discovery of the Nag Hammadi scrolls in 1945. For additional information consult *The Gnostic Bible: Revised and Expended Edition*, Willis Barnstone and Marvin Meyer, eds., Boston: Shambhala Publications, 2009.

20 Audrey Yoishiki Seo, *Enso: Dark Circles of Enlightenment*, Boston: Weatherhill, an imprint of Shambhala Publications, 2007.

21 A *gatha* is a short poem usually four lines but no less that is chanted for meals or for other meditative times. One I found that I thought fit us is:

When I panic at losing my bearings
I vow with all beings
to acknowledge the error is panic,
not losing familiar ground.

22 Marija Gimbutas, *The Goddesses and Gods of Old Europe: Myths and Cult Images*, Berkley CA: University of California Press, 1974 and 1982.

23 Starhawk, *The Spiral Dance*, NY NY: Harper Collins Publishers, 1999 p. 169.

24 Kathy Jones, *Spinning the Wheel of Ana: A Spiritual Quest to find the British Primal Ancestors*, Glastonbury: Ariadne Publications, 1994, p. 193.

25 Louise Felding, 'A View Beyond Bornholm–New Perspectives on Danish Rock Carvings,' Copenhagen: Scandinavian Society for Pre-historic Art, 2009.

26 Madonna Gauding, *The Signs and Symbols Bible*, London: Octopus Publishing, 2009, p. 377.

27 Nicholas R. Mann, *Avebury Cosmos: The Neolithic World of*

Avebury Henge, Silbury Hill, West Kennet long barrow, the Sanctuary and the Longstones Cove, Washington: O Books, an imprint of John Hunt Publishing, Ltd., 2011, p. 236.

28 Marija Gimbutas, *The Language of the Goddess,* New York: HarperCollins, 1991, p. 296.

29 Marija Gimbutas, *The Goddesses and Gods of Old Europe 6500-3500 BC Myths and Cultures,* Berkley: University of California Press, 1992, p. 89.

30 Barbara Donley, *Arianrhod: A Welsh Myth Retold,* Oakland CA: Stone Circle Press, 1987.

31 William Shakespeare, *A Midsummer's Night Dream,* Act 3, scene 2, line 115.

32 Nevill Drury, *The Watkins Dictionary of Magic,* London: Watkins Publishing, 2005, p. 113.

33 Barbara Walker, *The Woman's Encyclopedia of Myths and Secrets,* San Francisco: HarperCollins, 1983, p. 339.

34 Retold from William R. Mistele, *Undines: Lessons from the Realm of the Water Spirits,* Berkley, California: North Atlantic Books, 2010.

35 Peter Berresford Ellis, *The Druids,* Grand Rapids: Eerdmans Publishing Company, 1995, p. 133.

36 The Acts of the Apostles 19:31-16

37 Eliphas Lev translated by Arthur Edwar Waite, *Transcendental Magic: Its Doctrine and Ritual,* York Beach, ME: Samuel Weisner, Inc., 1992, p. 27-28.

38 Peter Berresford Ellis, *The Druids,* Grand Rapids: Eerdmans Publishing Company, 1995.

39 Deepak Chopra, *Quantum Healing: Exploring the Frontiers of Body/Mind Medicine,* New York: Bantam, 1990.

40 Thomas Moore, the psychologist and former Roman Catholic monk, teaches about the soul, the self and responding to crisis through several books including *Care of the Soul: A Guide for Cultivating Depth and Sacredness in Everyday Life,* New York: Harper Collins, 1994.

41 James Hillman 1926-2011, was associated with the C.G. Jung Institute in Switzerland. He later developed archetypal psychology and went into private practice focusing on the soul and archetypes in his writings including *The Soul's Code: In Search of Character and Calling,* New York: Grand Central Publishing, 1997.

42 Deepak Chopra, *The Third Jesus: The Christ We Cannot Ignore,* New York: Harmony Books, 2008, p. 182.

43 Jane Roberts, *Seth Speaks: The Eternal Validity of the Soul,* Englewood Cliffs, NJ: Prentice Hall, 1972, p. 84.

44 Jane Roberts, *Seth Speaks: The Eternal Validity of the Soul,* Englewood Cliffs, NJ: Prentice Hall, 1972, p. 89.

45 Jane Roberts, *Seth Speaks: The Eternal Validity of the Soul,* Englewood Cliffs, NJ: Prentice Hall, 1972, p. 129.

46 Jane Roberts, *Seth Speaks: The Eternal Validity of the Soul,* Englewood Cliffs, NJ: Prentice Hall, 1972, p. 86.

47 Robert Graves, *The White Goddess,* 2nd ed., London: Faber and Faber, 1999, p. 7.

48 Andreas Corbin, 'Air I Am', *Circle of Song: Songs, Chants, and Dances for Ritual and Celebration,* Kate Marks, ed., Lennox, MA: Full Circle Press, 1993, p.54.

49 Philip Carr-Gomm and Richard Heygate, *The Book of English Magic,* London: John Murray Publishers, 2009, p. 263

50 Raven Grimassi, *Encyclopedia of Wicca and Witchcraft,* St. Paul MN: Llewellyn Publications, 2000, p. 386.

51 Raven Grimassi, *Hereditary Witchcraft: Secrets of the Old Religion,* St. Paul MN: Llewellyn Publications, 1999, p. 227.

52 Raven Grimassi. *Encyclopedia of Wicca and Witchcraft,* St. Paul MN: Llewellyn Publications, 2000, p. 384.

53 *Michael,* dir. Nora Ephron, writer Jim Quinlan et. al., Turner Pictures, 1996.

54 Thomas Aquinas, *Summa Theologica,* Second and Revised Edition, 1920, literally translated by Fathers of the English Dominican Province. Kevin Knight. New Advent (2008).

http://www.newadvent.org/summa.

55 Ken Carey, *Return of the Bird Tribes*, New York: HarperOne, 1991.

56 E. M. Berens, *The Myths and Legends of Ancient Greece and Rome: Being a Popular Account of Greek and Roman Mythology*, University of Michigan Library, 1892, p. 215.

57 James Redfield, *The Secrets of Shambhala*, New York: Warner Books, 1991, p. 133.

58 James Redfield, *The Secrets of Shambhala*, New York: Warner Books, 1991, p. 133.

59 'Padmasambhava,' translated by Erik Hein Schmidt, *Dakini Teachings: A Collection of Padmasambhava's Advice to the Dalini Yeshe Tsogyal* , Shambhala Publications, 1999.

60 Kay Whitaker, *The Reluctant Shaman: A Woman's First Encounters with the Unseen Spirits of the Earth*, New York: HarperOne, 1991, p. 35.

62 Kay Whitaker, *The Reluctant Shaman: A Woman's First Encounters with the Unseen Spirits of the Earth*, New York: HarperOne, 1991, p. 39.

63 Ted Andrews, *Animal-Speak: The Spiritual and Magical Powers of Creatures Great and Small*, St. Paul, MN: Llewelyn, 2002, p. 144.

64 Hank Wessleman, *Spiritwalker: Messages from the Future*, New York: Bantam, 1996, p. 330 ff.

65 Hank Wessleman, *Spiritwalker: Messages from the Future*, New York: Bantam, 1996, p. 339-340.

66 Kay Whitaker , *The Reluctant Shaman* p. 198.

67 Whitaker, p. 199.

68 Whitaker, p. 203.

69 Whitaker, p. 161.

70 Whitaker, p. 211.

71 Diane Stein, *All Women are Psychic*, Freedom, California: Crossing Press, 1988. The psychic skills I relate to the chakras are: 1 root chakra, past life recall; 2 belly chakra, clairsentience; 3 solar plexus, manifestation and connection to the Higher Self;

4 heart chakra, empathy and divine love; 5 throat chakra, clairaudience; 6 brow chakra, telepathy, and clairvoyance; 7 crown, channeling and astral projection.

72 Tayannah Lee McQuillar, *Rootwork: Using the Folk Magick of Black America for Love Money and Success,* New York NY: Touchstone Publishers, an imprint of Simon and Schuster, 2003, p. 8.

73 Judy Hall, *The Crystal Bible: A Definitive Guide to Crystals,* Cincinnati OH: Walking Stick Press, 2004, p. 244.

74 Judy Hall, *The Crystal Bible: A Definitive Guide to Crystals,* Cincinnati OH: Walking Stick Press, 2004, p. 67-68.

75 Richard M. Fleming, M.D. and Tom Monte, *Stop Inflammation Now!* New York: G. P. Putnam's Sons, 2004, p. 36.

76 J.V. Cerney, D.C., *Acupuncture Without Needles,* New York: Prentice Hall Press, 1999, p. 116-119. These points are: GB14 (on the forehead slightly above the center of the eye and eyebrow, bilateral), ST1 (below each eye on the center of the boney orbital rim that runs around the eye), ST 6 & ST7 (at the jaw hinge and in the hollow in front of it, bilateral), K22 (in the chest on the right side of the tip of the breast bone), GB 20 (on the back of the head behind the lower ear on the boney ridge; look for an indentation about halfway to the center, bilateral), GV13 (on the spine, upper back about the furthest point you can reach yourself, the 2nd and 3rd thoracic vertebrae; alternatively lean against the edge of a door frame to press); LI 4, (web of the finger and thumb of each hand; skip this one if pregnant), SI 3 (base of little finger on the top side of both hands).

77 John E. Upledger, D.O., O.M.M., *SomatoEmotional Release: Deciphering the Language of Life,* Berkley CA: North Atlantic Books, 2002, p. 144-146. These pain points are: LI 4 (web of the finger and thumb of each hand; skip this one if pregnant), ST36 (1-2 inches below the knee cap and laterally to the outside); GB 36 (on legs 1/3 distance down from knee toward ankle outside fibula (bilateral), P 4 (underside of arm centerline, halfway

between wrists and elbow, bilateral) and GV16 (base of the skull in the hollow where the head attaches to spine).

78 Katy Dreyfuss, *The Reflexology Deck: 50 Healing Techniques*, San Francisco: Chronicle Books, 2004, cards 30 and 40.

79 John Thie, D.C., *Touch for Health*, Marina DelRay, CA: DeVorss Publications, 1966.

80 Donna Eden and David Feinstein, *Energy Medicine*, New York: Tarcher Press, an imprint of Penguin, 1999.

81 William Safire, The Herald Journal, 'On Language', August 30, 1989, p. A10.

82 Timothy Wyllie, *DETA*, Santa Fe NM: Bear, 1992.

83 John E. Upledger, D.O., O.M.M., *Your Inner Physician and You: CranioSacral Therapy and SomatoEmotional Release*, Berkley CA: North Atlantic Books, 1997, p. 181.

84 Carl Jung and Stanley Dell, *The Integration of the Personality*, New York: Farrar & Rinehart, Inc., 1939, p. 93.

85 Hank Wessleman is previously cited as the author of *Spiritwalker: Messages from the Future.* The other books of that trilogy are *Medicine Maker: Mystic Encounters on the Shaman's Path* and *Visionseeker: Shared Wisdom from the Place of Refuge*, both of which extend our understanding of the spirit beings called the Dorajuadiok. All three volumes are published by Hay House.

86 Marklyn Champagne and Leslie Walker-Hirsh, *The Circles Curriculum*, Santa Barbara: James Stanfield Publishing Co., 2002.

87 Earnie Larson and Jeanette Goodstein, *Who's Driving Your Bus?* Hoboken, NJ: John Wiley & Sons, 1993.

88 Debbie Ford, *The Dark Side of the Light Chasers*, New York: Riverhead Books, 1999.

89 Debbie Ford, *The Dark Side of the Light Chasers*, New York: Riverhead Books, 1999, p. 9.

90 Sunbear *et.al*, *Walk in Balance: The Path to Healthy, Happy, Harmonious Living*, New York: Simon & Schuster, 1989, p. 119.

91 SARK, *Glad No Matter What: Transforming Loss and Change into Gift and Opportunity*, Novato CA: New World Library, 2010, p. 172.

92 Sonia Johnson, *From Housewife to Heretic* New York: Doubleday, 1981; *Going Out of Our Minds: The Metaphysics of Liberation*, Freedom CA: Crossing Press, 1987; *Wildfire: Igniting the She/Volution*, Albuquerque: Wildfire Books, 1990.

93 Tom Cowan, *Shamanism as a Spiritual Practice for Daily Life*, Freedom CA: Crossing Press, 1996.

94 Kate Marks, *Circle of Song: Songs, Chants, and Dances for Ritual and Celebration*, Lenox MA: Full Circle Press, 1993, p. 201.

95 Deepak Chopra, *Quantum Healing: Exploring the Frontiers of Mind/Body Medicine*, New York: Bantam Press, 1990.

96 This routine for emotional release was compiled by my partner Merlin over a period of years using the following references: J.V. Cerney, *Acupuncture without Needles*; John Thie, D.C. *Touch for Health*; John D. Upledger, D.O., *Your Inner Physician and You: CranioSacral Therapy* and *SomatoEmotional Release*.

97 John D. Upledger, D.O., M.M.O, *Somatoemtional Release*, Berkley CA: North Atlantic Books, p. 13.

98 Elpeth Odbert, Haven Community, Keyser WV, http://www.elspethofhaven.com/index.html

99 Frank Shapiro, *The Yale Book of Quotations*, New Haven CT: Yale University Press, 2006, p. 415.

100 Sarah Ban Breathnach, *Simple Abundance: A Daybook of Comfort and Joy*, Boston, MA: Grand Central Publishing, 1995.

101 Sarah Ban Breathnach, *Simple Abundance: A Daybook of Comfort and Joy*, Boston, MA: Grand Central Publishing, 1995, p. ii.

102 Sarah Ban Breathnach, *Peace and Plenty: Finding Your Path to Financial Security*, Boston, MA: Grand Central Publishing, 2010.

103 Sarah Ban Breathnach, *Simple Abundance: A Daybook of Comfort and Joy*, Boston, MA: Grand Central Publishing, 1995, p. 12.

104 Deepak Chopra, M.D., *The Path to Love: Spiritual Strategies for Healing*, New York: Three Rivers Press, 1997, p. 13.

105 Rinda Blom, *The Handbook of Gestalt Play Therapy: Practical Guidelines for Child Therapists*, Philadelphia: Jessica Kingsley Publishers, 2006, p. 145. Although this reference is for child therapists, the technique created by Fritz Perls and others works equally well with adults.

106 Laura Davis, *I Thought We'd Never Speak Again: The Road from Estrangement to Reconciliation*, New York: HarperCollins, 2002.

107 Laura Davis, *I Thought We'd Never Speak Again: The Road from Estrangement to Reconciliation*, New York: HarperCollins, 2002. P. 133

108 Laura Davis, *I Thought We'd Never Speak Again: The Road from Estrangement to Reconciliation*, New York: HarperCollins, 2002. P. 212.

109 William Shakespeare, *Othello*, Act I, scene 1, line 118.

110 Robert Schwartz, *Courageous Souls: Do We Plan Our Life Challenges Before Birth?*, Chesterland, OH: Whispering Winds Press, 2007.

111 Michael Newton, *Life Between Lives: Hypnotherapy for Spiritual Regression*, Woodbury, MN: Llewellyn Worldwide, 2004.

112 Claude M. Steiner M.D., *Scripts People Live: Transactional Analysis of Life Scripts*, New York: Grove Press, 1994.

113 Folliot S. Pierpont, 'For The Beauty of the Earth', 1864, http://www.hymnsite.com/lyrics/umh092.sht

114 David Bennett and Cindy Griffith-Bennett, *Voyage of Purpose: Spiritual Wisdom from Near-Death back to Life*, Scotland: Findhorn Press, 2011, p. 38.

115 Music, sacred mathematics and philosophy converge in the esoteric belief that the planets, sun and moon have sound and relationship in a celestial harmony known as the music of the spheres. These ideas were developed by Plato in *The Republic*, Pythagoras as described by Pliny, by Boethius in *De Musica* describing medieval music and in Rosicrucian writings by Max Heindel. John Milton the English poet combined his ideas with those philosophers. http://innersonickey.org/?page_id=147

http://humanityhealing.net/2010/09/what-is-the-music-of-the-spheres/

116 Richard Thompson, 'Haul Me Up' from *Dream Attic,* Los Angeles: Shout! Factory 2010.

117 *Crow SwimsAway* and *Bekki Shining BearHeart,* Church of Earth Healing and Seventh Direction Publishers, New Marshfield OH.

118 Thomas Harris, *I'm Okay—You're Okay,* New York: Avon, 1976, p. 66

119 Nancy Pohle and Edgar Cayce, *How to Discover Your Past Lives,* ARE publications, Virginia Beach VA, 1984.

120 Mz Imani, *Shamanic Journeys Staff & Alchemical Healing Teachers,* http://www.shamanicjourneys.com/staff.php.

121 Don Miguel Ruiz, *The Mastery of Love,* San Rafael CA: Amber-Allen Publishing, 1999, p. 63.

122 Kathleen Norris, *Acedia and Me: A Marriage, Monks and a Writer's Life,* New York: Riverhead Books, Penguin Group, 2008.

123 Starhawk, *Dreaming the Dark,* Boston: Beacon Press, 1982, p. 21.

124 Kate Marks, *Circle of Song: Songs, Chants, and Dances for Ritual and Celebration,* Lenox MA: Full Circle Press, 1993, p. 201.

125 Vaughn Bell, 'Ghost Stories: Visits from the Deceased', *The Scientific American,* December 2, 2008.

126 William T. Stace, *Mysticism and Philosophy,* New York: The New American Library, 1960.

127 James Swan, *Sacred Places: How The Living Earth Seeks Our Friendship,* Rochester, VT: Bear & Company, 1990, p. 77.

128 William James, *Varieties of Religious Experiences,* New York: Modern Library, 1902.

129 Lauren Artress, *Walking the Sacred Path: Rediscovering the Labyrinth as a Spiritual Tool,* New York: Riverhead Trade, Penguin Group, 1996.

130 Nicholas R. Mann, *Avebury Cosmos: The Neolithic World of Avebury Henge, Silbury Hill, West Kennet Long Barrow, the Sanctuary and the Longstones Cove,* Winchester, UK: O-Books,

John Hunt Publishing, 2011.
131 Jane Roberts, *The Seth Material*, New York: Bantam Books, 1981.
132 Jane Roberts, *The Seth Material*, New York: Bantam Books, 1981, p. 282.
133 Jane Roberts, *The Seth Material*, New York: Bantam Books, 1981, p. 286.
134 Michael Newton, *Life Between Lives: Hypnotherapy for Spiritual Regression*, Woodbury MN: Llewellyn Publications, 2004.
135 Ronald L. Holt, 'Experiencing Sacred Geometry Without Intellectually Understanding It', *The Golden Mean Spiral and the Merkaba*, Flower of Life Research LLC, 1999. http://www.floweroflife.org.
136 Ronald L. Holt, 'Experiencing Sacred Geometry Without Intellectually Understanding It', *The Golden Mean Spiral and the Merkaba*, Flower of Life Research LLC, 1999, p. 1
137 Ronald L. Holt, 'A little philosophy on Sacred Geometry', *The Golden Mean Spiral and the Merkaba*, Flower of Life Research LLC, 1999, p. 2.
138 *Serinda Gallery*, 'Atlas of Tibetan Medicine: Catalogue of 77 Tibetan Medical Paintings from the Illustrations of the Blue Beryl Treatise of Sangye Gyamtsi 1635-1705', (2009) available from http://www.serindiagallery.com/artists-and-collections/the-atlas-of-tibetan-medicine / (accessed April 21, 2012). See also the *New Age Journal*, September/October 1998, p. 74.

Bibliography

'I will be gentle with myself', *Circle of Song: Songs, Chants, and Dances for Ritual and Celebration*, compiled by Kate Marks. Lenox MA: Full Circle Press, 1993.

'Padmasambhava,' translated by Erik Hein Schmidt. *Dakini Teachings: A Collection of Padmasambhava's Advice to the Dalini Yeshe Tsogyal*. Shambala Publications, 1999.

Andrews, Ted. *Animal-Speak: The Spiritual & Magical Powers of Creatures Great & Small*. St. Paul, MN: Llewelyn, 2002.

Aquinas, Thomas. *Summa Theologica*. Second and Revised Edition, 1920, literally translated by Fathers of the English Dominican Province. Kevin Knight. *New Advent* (2008). http://www.newadvent.org/summa.

Artress, Lauren. *Walking the Sacred Path: Rediscovering the Labyrinth as a Spiritual Tool*. New York: Riverhead Trade, Penguin Group, 1996.

Ban Breathnach, Sarah. *Peace and Plenty: Finding Your Path to Financial Security*. Boston, MA: Grand Central Publishing, 2010.

Ban Breathnach, Sarah. *Simple Abundance: A Daybook of Comfort and Joy*. Boston, MA: Grand Central Publishing, 1995.

Begley, Sharon. 'When DNA Is Not Destiny', *Newsweek*. December 1, 2008, vol. 152 No. 22.

Bell, Vaughn. 'Ghost Stories: Visits from the Deceased', *The Scientific American*. December 2, 2008.

Bennett, David and Cindy Griffith-Bennett. *Voyage of Purpose: Spiritual Wisdom from Near-Death Back to Life*. Scotland: Findhorn Press, 2011.

Berens, E. M. *The Myths and Legends of Ancient Greece and Rome: Being a Popular Account of Greek and Roman Mythology*. Ann Arbor: University of Michigan Press, 1892.

Blom, Rinda. *The Handbook of Gestalt Play Therapy: Practical Guidelines for Child Therapists*. Philadelphia: Jessica Kingsley Publishers, 2006.

Carey, Ken. *Return of the Bird Tribes.* New York: HarperOne, 1991.

Carr-Gomm, Philip and Richard Heygate. *The Book of English Magic.* London: John Murray Publishers, 2009.

Cerney, D.C., J.V. *Acupuncture Without Needles.* New York: Prentice Hall Press, 1999.

Champagne, Marklyn and Leslie Walker-Hirsh. *The Circles Curriculum.* Santa Barbara: James Stanfield Publishing Co., 2002.

Chicago, Judy. *The Dinner Party.* NY: Penguin, rev. 1996.

Chopra, Deepak. *Quantum Healing: Exploring the Frontiers of Body/Mind Medicine.* New York: Bantam, 1990.

Chopra, M.D., Deepak. *The Third Jesus: The Christ We Cannot Ignore.* New York: Harmony Books, 2008.

Chopra, M.D., Deepak. *The Path to Love: Spiritual Strategies for Healing.* New York: Three Rivers Press, 1997.

Collins, Andrew. *From the Ashes of Angels: The Forbidden Legacy of a Fallen Race.* Rochester, VT: Bear and Co., 1998.

Collins, Andrew. *Gods of Eden: Egypt's Lost Legacy and the Genesis of Civilization.* Rochester, VT: Bear and Co., 1999.

Corbin, Andreas. 'Air I Am', *Circle of Song: Songs, Chants, and Dances for Ritual and Celebration.* Kate Marks, ed. Lennox, MA: Full Circle Press, 1993.

Cowan, Tom. *Shamanism as a Spiritual Practice for Daily Life.* Freedom CA: Crossing Press, 1996.

Davis, Laura. *I Thought We'd Never Speak Again: The Road from Estrangement to Reconciliation.* New York: HarperCollins, 2002.

Donley, Barbara. *Arianrhod: A Welsh Myth Retold.* Oakland CA: Stone Circle Press, 1987.

Dreyfuss, Katy. *The Reflexology Deck: 50 Healing Techniques.* San Francisco: Chronicle Books, 2004.

Drury, Nevill. *The Watkins Dictionary of Magic.* London: Watkins Publishing, 2005.

Eden, Donna and David Feinstein. *Energy Medicine,* New York: Tarcher Press, an imprint of Penguin, 1999.

Ellis, Peter Berresford. *The Druids.* Grand Rapids: Eerdmans

Publishing Company, 1995.

Ericson, Erik. *Identity and the Life Cycle*. New York: W.W. Norton & Company, Inc., 1980.

Felding, Louise. 'A View Beyond Bornholm-New Perspectives on Danish Rock Carvings.' Copenhagen: Scandinavian Society for Pre-historic Art (2009). http://www.ssfpa.se/pdf/2010/FeldingA10.pdf. Accessed January 12, 2012.

Fleming, M.D. Richard M. and Tom Monte. *Stop Inflammation Now!* New York: G. P. Putnam's Sons, 2004.

Ford, Debbie. *The Dark Side of the Light Chasers*. New York: Riverhead Books, 1999.

Gauding, Madonna. *The Signs and Symbols Bible*. London: Octopus Publishing, 2009.

Genesis 3:22-24 KJV.

Gimbutas, Marija. *The Goddesses and Gods of Old Europe 6500-3500 BC: Myths and Cultures*. Berkley: University of California Press, 1992.

Gimbutas, Marija. *The Language of the Goddess*. New York: HarperCollins, 1991.

Graves, Robert. *The White Goddess.* 2nd ed., London: Faber and Faber, 1999.

Grimassi, Raven. *Encyclopedia of Wicca and Witchcraft*. St. Paul MN: Llewellyn Publications, 2000.

Grimassi, Raven. *Hereditary Witchcraft: Secrets of the Old Religion*. St. Paul MN: Llewellyn Publications, 1999.

Hall, Judy. *The Crystal Bible: A Definitive Guide to Crystals*. Cincinnati OH: Walking Stick Press, 2004.

Harris, Thomas. *I'm Okay, You're Okay*, New York: Avon, 1976.

Hillman, James. *The Soul's Code: In Search of Character and Calling*. New York: Grand Central Publishing, 1997.

Holt, Ronald L. 'Experiencing Sacred Geometry Without Intellectually Understanding It', *The Golden Mean Spiral and the Merkaba*. Flower of Life Research LLC (1999) http://www.floweroflife.org. Accessed November 10, 2011.

James, William. *Varieties of Religious Experiences*. New York: Modern

Library, 1902.

Johnson, Sonia. *From Housewife to Heretic.* New York: Doubleday, 1981.

Johnson, Sonia. *Going Out of Our Minds: The Metaphysics of Liberation.* Freedom CA: Crossing Press, 1987.

Johnson, Sonia. *Wildfire: Igniting the She/Volution.* Albuquerque: Wildfire Books, 1990.

Jones, Kathy. *Spinning The Wheel of Ana: A Spiritual Quest to find the British Primal Ancestors.* Glastonbury: Ariadne Publications, 1994.

Jung, Carl Gustav and Stanley Dell. *The Integration of the Personality.* New York: Farrar & Rinehart, Inc., 1939.

Jung, Carl Gustav. *Man and His Symbols.* New York: Doubleday and Company, Inc., 1964.

Keirsey, David and Marilyn Bates. *Please Understand Me.* Del Mar, CA: Prometheus Nemesis Book Company 1984.

Keirsey, David and Marilyn Bates. *Please Understand Me II.* Del Mar, CA: Prometheus Nemesis Book Company 1998.

Larson, Earnie and Jeanette Goodstein. *Whose Driving Your Bus?* Hoboken, NJ: John Wiley & Sons, 1993.

Lev, Eliphas, translated by Arthur Edwar Waite. *Transcendental Magic: Its Doctrine and Ritual.* York Beach, ME: Samuel Weisner, Inc., 1992.

M. Steiner M.D., Claude. *Scripts People Live: Transactional Analysis of Life Scripts.* New York: Grove Press, 1994.

Mann, Nicholas R. *Avebury Cosmos: The Neolithic World of Avebury Henge, Silbury Hill, West Kennet long barrow, the Sanctuary & the Longstones Cove.* Washington: O Books, an imprint of John Hunt Publishing, Ltd., 2011.

Maslow, Abraham. 'A Theory of Human Motivation' *Psychological Review.* (1943) reprinted in *Twentieth Century Psychology.* ed. P. Harriman, New York: Philosophical Library, 1946.

Maslow, Abraham. 'A Theory of Human Motivation' Psychological Review. (1943) reprinted in *Toward a Psychology of Being.* Princeton, NJ: Van Nostrand Co., 2nd edition 1968.

McQuillar, Tayannah Lee. *Rootwork: Using the Folk Magick of Black America for Love Money and Success.* New York NY: Touchstone Publishers, an imprint of Simon and Schuster, 2003.

Michael. dir. Nora Ephron. Writer Jim Quinlan et. al., Turner Pictures 1996.

Mistele, William R. *Undines: Lessons from the Realm of the Water Spirits.* Berkley: North Atlantic Books, 2010.

Monaghan, Patricia. *The Goddess Path: Myths, Invocations and Rituals.* Woodbury: MN: Llewellyn Publishers, 1999.

Moore, Thomas. *Care of the Soul: A Guide for Cultivating Depth and Sacredness in Everyday Life.* New York: Harper Collins, 1994.

Mz Imani. *Shamanic Journeys* (2011). 'Staff & Alchemical Healing Teachers', http://www.shamanicjourneys.com/staff.php. Accessed August 23, 2012.

Narby, Jeremy. *The Cosmic Serpent: DNA and the Origins of Knowledge.* New York NY: Jeremy P. Tarcher/Putnam, 1999.

Neihardt, John G. *Black Elk Speaks: Being the Life Story of a Holy Man of the Oglala Sioux.* Lincoln NE: University of Nebraska Press, 1979.

New Age Journal, September/October 1998, p. 74.

Newton, Michael. *Life Between Lives: Hypnotherapy for Spiritual Regression.* Woodbury, MN: Llewellyn Worldwide, 2004.

Norris, Kathleen. *Acedia & Me: A Marriage, Monks and a Writer's Life.* New York: Riverhead Books, Penguin Group, 2008.

Odbert, Elpeth. Haven Community, Keyser WV, 'Healing Your relationship with Money and Right Livlihood'. *Grandmother Elspeth* (2011) http://www.elspethofhaven.com/index.html. Accessed august 23, 2012.

Pierpont, Folliot S. 'For the Beauty of the Earth', 1864, *HymnSite* C.A. Radke. http://www.hymnsite.com/lyrics/umh092.sht. Accessed August 23, 2012.

Pohle, Nancy and Edgar Cayce. *How to Discover Your Past Lives,* ARE publications, Virginia Beach VA, 1984.

Redfield, James. *The Secrets of Shambhala.* New York: Warner Books,

1991.

Roberts, Jane. *Seth Speaks: The Eternal Validity of the Soul*, Englewood Cliffs, NJ: Prentice Hall, 1972.

Roberts, Jane. *The Seth Material.* New York: Bantam Books, 1981.

Ruiz, Don Miguel. *The Mastery of Love.* San Rafael CA: Amber-Allen Publishing, 1999.

Safire, William. *The Herald Journal*, 'On Language', August 30, 1989, Syracuse NY.

SARK. *Glad No Matter What: Transforming Loss and Change into Gift and Opportunity.* Novato CA: New World Library, 2010.

Schwartz, Robert. *Courageous Souls: Do We Plan Our Life Challenges Before Birth?* Chesterland, OH: Whispering Winds Press, 2007.

Serinda Gallery, 'Atlas of Tibetan Medicine: Catalogue of 77 Tibetan Medical Paintings from the Illustrations of the Blue Beryl Treatise of Sangye Gyamtsi 1635-1705', (2009). http://www.serindia-gallery.com/artists-and-collections/the-atlas-of-tibetan-medicine/ (accessed April 21, 2012).

Shakespeare, William. *A Midsummer's Night Dream.*

Shakespeare, William. *Othello.*

Shapiro, Frank. *The Yale Book of Quotations.* New Haven CT: Yale University Press, 2006.

Stace, William T. *Mysticism and Philosophy.* New York: The New American Library, 1960.

Starhawk. *Dreaming the Dark.* Boston: Beacon Press, 1982.

Starhawk. *The Spiral Dance: Anniversary Edition.* NY NY: Harper Collins Publishers, 1999.

Starhawk. *Truth or Dare: Encounters with* Power, Authority, and Mystery. New York: HarperOne, 1989.

Stein, Diane. *All Women are Psychic.* Freedom, California: Crossing Press, 1988.

Sunbear et.al. *Walk in Balance: The Path to Healthy, Happy, Harmonious Living.* New York: Simon & Schuster, 1989.

Swan, James. *Sacred Places: How The Living Earth Seeks Our Friendship.* Rochester, VT: Bear & Company, 1990.

SwimsAway, Crow and Bekki ShiningBearHeart. *The Church of Earth Healing* http://www.church-of-earth-healing.org/. New Marshfield OH.

The Acts of the Apostles 19:31-16 KJV.

The Gnostic Bible: Revised and Expended Edition, Willis Barnstone and Marvin Meyer, eds., Boston: Shambhala Publications, 2009.

Thie, D.C., John. *Touch for Health.* Marina DelRay CA: DeVorss Publications, 1966.

Thompson, Richard. 'Haul Me Up' from *Dream Attic*. Los Angeles: Shout! Factory, 2010.

Upledger, D.O., O.M.M., John E. *SomatoEmotional Release: Deciphering the Language of Life,* Berkley CA: North Atlantic Books, 2002.

Upledger, D.O., O.M.M., John E. *Your Inner Physician and You: CranioSacral Therapy.* Berkley CA: North Atlantic Books, 1997.

Walker, Barbara. *The Woman's Encyclopedia of Myths and Secrets*. San Francisco: HarperCollins, 1983.

Wessleman, Hank. *Visionseeker: Shared Wisdom from the Place of Refuge.* New York: Hay House, 2001.

Wessleman, Hank. *Medicinemaker: Mystic Encounters on the Shaman's Path.* New York: Bantam, 1999.

Wessleman, Hank. *Spiritwalker: Messages from the Future,* New York: Bantam. 1996.

Whitaker, Kay. *The Reluctant Shaman: A Woman's First Encounters with the Unseen Spirits of the Earth*. New York: HarperOne, 1991.

Wyllie, Timothy. *DETA,* Santa Fe NM: Bear, 1992.

Yoishiki Seo, Audrey. *Enso: Dark Circles of Enlightenment,* Boston: Weatherhill, an imprint of Shambhala Publications , 2007.